THE CREATION OF
A COMMUNITY

*The City of Wells
in the Middle Ages*

DAVID GARY SHAW

CLARENDON PRESS · OXFORD
1993

Oxford University Press, Walton Street, Oxford OX2 6DP
Oxford New York Toronto
Delhi Bombay Calcutta Madras Karachi
Kuala Lumpur Singapore Hong Kong Tokyo
Nairobi Dar es Salaam Cape Town
Melbourne Auckland Madrid
and associated companies in
Berlin Ibadan

Oxford is a trade mark of Oxford University Press

Published in the United States
by Oxford University Press Inc., New York

© David Gary Shaw 1993

British Library Cataloguing in Publication Data
Data available

Library of Congress Cataloging in Publication Data
Shaw, David Gary.
The creation of a community : the city of Wells in the Middle Ages
/ David Gary Shaw.
p. cm. — (Oxford historical monographs)
Includes bibliographical references and index.
ISBN 0–19–820401–9
1. Wells (England)—History. 2. Cities and towns, Medieval—
England—Wells. I. Title. II. Series.
DA690.W46S48 1993
942.3'83—dc20 92–42694

Typeset by Pentacor PLC, High Wycombe, Bucks.
Printed in Great Britain
on acid-free paper by
Biddles Ltd., Guildford and King's Lynn

Acknowledgements

The publication of a first work properly calls for richer and fuller thanks than it is ever possible for an author to make. The line of helpers runs all the way back, and many people who helped make the writer and the thinker, in small ways and large, are sadly forgotten. And, of course, there is not the space or the time to list even the most significant influences. Some will recognize their roles. All I can do here is to thank those who have helped to turn me towards medieval history and made this particular project possible.

That I am a medieval historian I owe to Nancy Partner, and it *is* something for which I give thanks; that I found Wells as a suitable subject I owe to Gervase Rosser; that I found Wells and its archives welcoming and accommodating I owe to Jean Imray, formerly of the Town Hall Archives, and Linzee Colchester, formerly of Wells Cathedral Library; that I was able to pass successfully through the, for a North American, disorienting experience of Oxford 'bureaucracy' I thank Maurice Keen, and for his subsequent help.

I thank David A. T. Peterson and Patricia St. Clair for assistance with graphs and tables.

I am also grateful to the owners and keepers of the records of the Wells Town Archives, Wells Cathedral Library, Lambeth Palace Library, the Somerset Records Office (Taunton), and the Public Records Office (Chancery Lane, London), as well as to the staffs of the several libraries on which I have relied: the Bodleian, the History Faculty (Oxford), Balliol College, McLennan (McGill University), and Olin (Wesleyan University).

The time and money to write this work, which has taken some six years, were made available by the Commonwealth Scholarship Commission, which allowed me to spend three years in Oxford, the Social Sciences and Humanities Research Council of Canada, and Wesleyan University. I am truly grateful.

The suggestions of R. B. Dobson and of Gervase Rosser greatly improved this work by clarifying my concerns and raising problems, not all of which I have met as decisively as I would have liked. Most of all I thank the constant, friendly help of Barbara Harvey, whose sensitivity and encyclopaedic knowledge of the history and scholarship of later medieval England saved me from many shallow statements and many plain blunders. She allowed this work to display whatever complexity or depth it does finally have, less encumbered by the weight of my errors.

D. G. S.

June 1992
Middletown, Connecticut

Contents

List of Figures

List of Maps

List of Tables

Abbreviations

AH	Wells Almshouse Document
CA	Communar's Accounts
Carus-Wilson	E. M. Carus-Wilson, *Medieval Merchant Venturers* (London, 1954)
CBI	Convocation Book I
CBII	Convocation Book II
CBIII	Convocation Book III
CChR	*Calendar of Charter Rolls* (London, 1903–)
CCR	*Calendar of Close Rolls* (London, 1892–)
CFR	*Calendar of Fine Rolls* (London, 1911–63)
Class Conflict	Rodney Hilton, *Class Conflict and the Crisis of Feudalism* (London, 1985)
Colchester	R. H. Britnell, *Growth and Decline in Colchester, 1300–1525* (Cambridge, 1986)
Coventry	Charles Phythian-Adams, *Desolation of a City: Coventry and the Urban Crisis of the Late Middle Ages* (Cambridge, 1979)
CPR	*Calendar of Patent Rolls* (London 1901–)
CS	Camden Society
DB	*Domesday Book*, 2 volumes (London, 1783)
EA	Escheator's Accounts
ECHR	*Economic History Review*
EETS	Early English Text Society
FA	Fabric Account
Gottfried	Robert Gottfried, *Bury St Edmunds and the Urban Crisis of the Later Middle Ages: 1290–1530* (Princeton, NJ, 1982)
JEH	*Journal of Ecclesiastical History*
London	Sylvia Thrupp, *The Merchant Class of Medieval London* (Ann Arbor, Mich., 1948)
LPL ED	Lambeth Palace Library, Estate Document
P & P	*Past and Present*
PRO	Public Record Office

RI	Wells Cathedral Register I (*Liber Albus* I)
RII	Wells Cathedral Register II (*Liber Ruber*)
RIII	Wells Cathedral Register III (*Liber Albus* II)
RS	Rolls Series
SANHS	*Proceedings of the Somersetshire Archaeological and Natural History Society*
Sawyer	P. H. Sawyer, *Anglo-Saxon Charters* (London, 1968)
SDNQ	*Somerset and Dorset Notes and Queries*
Serel	Thomas Serel, *Historical Notes on the Church of St Cuthbert, in Wells* (Wells, 1875)
SMWI	*Somerset Medieval Wills, 1383–1500*, ed. F. W. Weaver, SRS 16 (1901)
SMWII	*Somerset Medieval Wills, 1501–30*, ed. F. W. Weaver, SRS 19 (1903)
SRO	Somerset Record Office
SRS	Somerset Record Society
Swanson	Heather Swanson, *Medieval Artisans* (Oxford, 1989)
TRHS	*Transactions of the Royal Historical Society*
UHY	*Urban History Yearbook*
VCH	Victoria History of the Counties of England
Vicars-Choral	Wells Vicars-Choral Charters
WCC	Wells City Charter
WCAC	Wells Cathedral Charter
Westminster	Gervase Rosser, *Medieval Westminster, 1200–1540* (Oxford, 1989)
Winchester	Derek Keene, *A Survey of Medieval Winchester*, 2 volumes (Oxford, 1985)
WTA	Wells Town Archive Document
WTD	Wells Borough Title Deed

Introduction

THE APPEAL OF THE SMALL TOWN

The medieval town's appeal is complex. More than any other field within medieval history, the study of towns provokes historians to view things as complete, sometimes sealed units. They have something of the microcosm to them. For while it is well known and well reiterated that most people lived rural lives and worked the land directly, it is in the study of the town that the features of social, cultural, and economic life present themselves in all their diversity—and diversity appeals. Money was everywhere, attracting people and encouraging record-keeping. Thus the towns drew the world towards them, and a great variety of the ideas and actions of townspeople were recorded.

Studying such a world, it is possible to strengthen our appreciation of the crucial connections between mentality and economy, social structure and political life. The display of such cross-currents is one of the aims of this book. To this extent, this study of Wells is concerned with the particular dynamics and development of one English town, especially in the later Middle Ages. But the conclusions drawn inevitably raise another and broader issue. Wells was in many ways quite an ordinary town, and so it can stand for the hundreds of significant smaller towns which were, I believe, so essential to the economic, social, and cultural life of medieval Europe. Throughout I have tried to address current issues in medieval urban historiography, so that the example of Wells as a small town can be added to the stock of knowledge and the various debates.

Part of what makes towns so approachable is their particular political and juridical development. Towns were more aggressive communities than villages. Many of them had received special privileges which allowed them to act as semi-independent localities in a sometimes wide range of jurisdictions. The issue of urban independence has long been at the centre of town studies, but very often it has been pursued only through its dry legal form, as a form of corporation history. This study of Wells works hard towards adding details to the history of town feeling as manifested by the body of citizens, looking at the political and constitutional ferment in the context of collective ambition and group self-esteem.

COMMUNITY AND THE BOROUGH COMMUNITY

An important group of themes centres on this body of citizens, known then and in this book as the 'Borough Community' (*communitas burgi*). The word 'community' is extremely popular and emotive today. It occurs in the title of a great many of the historical monographs on medieval English social history, even when the works themselves seem only slightly involved with the issue. Precisely what is meant by the term in historical literature is vague and various, and I would like at least to place my understanding of it in context and on the page.

Historiography carries in its style and traditions a resistance and scepticism towards universal claims. Despite the power of generalizations, every historical structure or event is incorruptibly unique. Therefore, I assume that the multitude of historical communities bear only a family resemblance to each other. There are no fast and sure characteristics or criteria, such as the sociologists who have forged some of our most expressive language of community and society have sometimes made it seem.

'Community' implies that there are people who are understood in the public domain to be part of a group. It does not seem to be enough, in other words, that historians or others can unite people into analytical categories which reflect the interests, needs, or actions of the group. Unlike socio-economic groups such as the poor or the rich, a community must have some sort of articulation: traditions, a particular group mentality, or institutions. Failing this, there is no community. To this extent, then, many modern uses of the term which unite individuals along sexual or racial or national lines are inappropriate, or at least run ahead of their evidence. There is, as yet, no community of redheads.

It is almost a consequence of the public nature of communities that they must act. It is by their banding together and engaging in protest or convivial pleasure that we would come to know that the redheads had taken it upon themselves to become a community.

The requirement to act is even more clearly essential in historical circumstances, for without such action there is very little compelling evidence that the community even existed. For the Middle Ages there would very probably be no evidence at all.

The question must immediately arise, however, of whether a community persists and exists when it is not in fact engaging in such activities. Michael Taylor, and those influenced by him, have put forward what I shall call the concept of 'occasional community'. He notes that community exists alongside the other bonds and allegiances, such as family and self.[1] As Gervase Rosser has argued, community 'is not a continuous state, but is realized momentarily at particular conjunctures'.[2] In this light, community is somewhat peculiar, something which comes and goes. What gives it the ability to retain its effectiveness after a long hiatus is the social unity fostered by a 'dominant élite' too weak to be truly coercive.[3] On certain issues the individuals feel that they share the same concerns, and it is in aid of that business, whether parish church construction or provision for the poor, that community becomes relevant.

This calls to mind the theory of *Gesellschaft* in Tönnies. For him, a community whose joint actions were really just a conjunction of its individual members' own desires was no community at all, but a' society (*Gesellschaft*), which he plainly took to be a morally inferior form of social life.[4] In the theory of occasional community, the meaning of the collective is exhausted by its actions. Opposed to this, Tönnies posited the *Gemeinschaft*, following Gierke to a great extent.[5] This was a true and natural bond which existed between people by virtue of ties of family, neighbourhood, and friendship. In its romantic essence it contained a touch of selflessness, as opposed to the interested, joint-stock nature of the *Gesellschaft*. Tönnies' notion of *Gemeinschaft*, even if theoretically acceptable, would be virtually impossible to prove for any aspect of the Middle Ages, and difficult enough for any time. But he seems

[1] Michael Taylor, *Community, Anarchy and Liberty* (Cambridge, 1982).
[2] *Westminster*, 248.
[3] Ibid. 225.
[4] Ferdinand Tönnies, *Community and Society*, trans. Charles P. Loomis, 2nd edn. (New Brunswick, 1988), 64–7.
[5] Ibid., *passim*; Otto von Gierke, *Community in Historical Perspective*, trans. Antony Black (Cambridge, 1990), whose principal concept of affective community is *Genossenschaft*, which he took to be a real collective person, with a unified will.

right to have thought that there is plainly another meaningful side to a group's character. It is insufficient to describe community solely in terms of interested actions. What is it, after all, that makes isolated collective actions possible, especially when one considers how many collective actions are *not* particularly in the interest of some or all of its individual members?

A community must rely on background assumptions, sometimes unarticulated understandings, which allow collective actions to make immediate sense, and, indeed, to be considered as a definite good *just because they are for the group*. Where collective action consists solely in occasional and useful projects beneficial to all, most typically a business partnership, no notion of community is required. Indeed, community most obviously exists where people are often put upon to give their efforts, their time, and their money to projects and responsibilities which would be thought onerous, irritating, or unnecessary without the existence of such background assumptions.[6] Community requires that there be certain sorts of cultural assumptions, features of mentality, which dispose the individuals towards the group and its demands and needs.

Community thrives whenever there is a mentality which values the collective, and carries forward activities which are premised upon its particular way of thinking. But a community's endurance and vitality require more than this. A historical community will be more effective and long-lived if it has a permanent organization and standing officers or leaders whose main role it is to foster the mentality, the rituals, and the works of the group. The community's special forms of authority—its language, reputation, rituals, and wealth—are bolstered by appointed officers who are charged with preserving the group's power by keeping the relationships among its members lively and peaceful and by overseeing its wealth. The leadership takes the executive role in enhancing the effectiveness of the community.

The nature of community is such that there is a high degree of willing participation. Thus the members feel compelled by their beliefs and history to participate, rather than because of the threat of coercion. People may in fact shirk their responsibilities. Force may be threatened or used, but usually only as part of the accepted

---

[6] See C. J. Calhoun, 'Community: Toward a Variable Conceptualization for Comparative Research', *Social History*, 5 (1982), 105–29, and cf. his 'diffuse obligations'.

regime of the community, and especially against those who had accepted or even sought admission to the membership of the group. It is essential only that the membership recognizes the call of responsibility, and that coercion or fear is not the *basis* for involvement. It follows, moreover, that collective action can involve paid labour without it being community action.

This sketch of some of the features of community immediately raises some of the usual problems with the concept. In the nineteenth century, when many of these issues were first forcefully stated, they were often tied up with a romantic sense that the community was more primitive than modern society, and therefore was more natural and better. The turn towards mentality also seems to recall the appeal to the extraordinary harmony and unity of will discussed in nineteenth-century theory and in many modern sociological and anthropological studies of primitive communities. Lastly, there is the claim that the community is metaphysically different, and so transforms the individual into a mere member, an unimportant and dependent element in the people.

There is now an impressive body of work on communities and collective action which does not speak to any presentist concerns about the superiority of medieval community. Certainly, I do not support any such views. My claim is rather that there was a large and effective amount of collective activity in the Middle Ages, activity which was frequently infused by a 'fraternal' mentality which served to transform collectivity into community. This mentality assigned to the collective and its actions a high ethical value, a claim on the individual. Furthermore, it provided the ideas by which the individual saw his or her identity as constituted in part by the community and its claims.[7] Susan Reynolds has magisterially surveyed the vitality of medieval collective action, leaving no doubt as to its ubiquity and importance, but in no way romanticizing or recommending it.[8]

Nevertheless, there is the second, related, concern—namely, that those who study past communities tend to see in them harmony. The Middle Ages, critics seem to complain, come out looking too good, all their darkness shrouded in a halo of harmony. Part of this critique is animated from one or another view of historical

[7] See below, Ch. 6.
[8] Susan Reynolds, *Kingdoms and Communities in Western Europe, 900–1300* (Oxford, 1984).

development. Some desire a higher level of class conflict, while others want things to get better after the Middle Ages. What I would suggest, however, is that the prevalent mentality of medieval Europe, and pre-eminently its associations and communities, was in fact one which did lay great stress on a tradition of harmony. People thought and were taught that unity, harmony, love, and peace were positive goods. This was bound to affect actions so long as these notions were taken seriously or as uncontroversial common sense. It was, however, a question of how people saw and idealized their world. It does not mean that there were no differences of opinion, vicious conflicts, and long-term enmities. It does mean, however, that within a community such events and feelings were generally characterized as bad in themselves. The important point for the medieval period is not that there was more harmony and love than in the modern world, but that the culture made so much of these qualities, and considered them as incomparably higher values. It can and should be stressed that systematic abuse or advantage will very possibly be built into the mentality of such a community, so that it bears with it some of the signs of ideology in its Marxist usage. As I shall show below, harmony did tend to buttress authority in its support of stability and order. But where community existed, harmony was indeed a great glue.

Solidarity always seems to undermine individuality. The sort of nationalist romanticism with which Gierke glossed the facts of medieval fellowship especially helped to portray the medieval world as one in which collective personality was more important than it has become since then. Indeed, although Gierke's particular and rather metaphysical formulation has receded from view, social scientists have developed a deep-seated belief in the fact that individuality is modern and can be sharply opposed to the traditional and collective world of the pre-modern. This theme has often been repeated in studies of primitive cultures around the world and of the European past.[9] Part of the difficulty is not with the Middle Ages, but with the attempts of others to explain a change in which medievalists no longer believe with anything like unanimity. The issue has come to the fore of late with the

[9] An excellent discussion of the theory and empirical study of such material is found in Richard M. Smith, ' "Modernization" and the Corporate Medieval Village Community in England: Some Sceptical Reflections', in Alan R. H. Baker and Derek Gregory (eds.), *Explorations in Historical Geography* (Cambridge, 1984), 141–79.

appearance of Alan Macfarlane's *The Origins of English In-dividualism*.[10] The weakness of this book, it seems to me, has less to do with its late medieval assumptions, than with the fact that it continues to give credence to the existence of the closed, individual-stifling community anywhere, and especially in pre–1300 England. Individualism, understood as a cultural movement, is certainly not medieval, or really early modern. But the factual value of individuality, of selfishness, of the stress in law and private decision-making on the needs and desires of the individual, is in no way inconsistent with the existence of collective activity or, indeed, with the community.[11] The philosopher Charles Taylor has recently stressed the fact that there exists 'a diversity of goods' for people, and I would suggest that community and individual needs would, in many medieval circumstances (and modern ones), both be recognized as such goods.[12] Sometimes they were in conflict, forcing people to make difficult, reluctant choices, but, neverthe-less, both were present and powerful. What has changed in the ensuing centuries is the degree to which the mentality and ideologies have stressed community or individuality. So, in em-phasizing something real and important in English social history by outlining the development and nature of Wells as a community, I do not believe I am saying anything to challenge the importance of the individual in that same world. In village and town the Middle Ages is able to sustain a great deal of complexity, and a great deal of contradiction.

The added ambiguity of community in medieval Wells and other towns comes from the fact that the term most often used for the organization of the town's citizens was the 'Borough Community' (*communitas Burgi*). I believe the ambiguity is fruitful and appropriate. As I hope to show, the Borough Community was indeed a community, the most active part of the lay town community, the maker and keeper of Wells's mentality and institutions. But, to avoid any confusion, I shall use capitals when I refer to the civic institution, and lower case when I mean the town

[10] Alan Macfarlane, *The Origins of English Individualism* (Oxford, 1978).

[11] Caroline Walker Bynum, 'Did the Twelfth Century Discover the Individual?', in *Jesus as Mother: Studies in the Spirituality of the High Middle Ages* (Berkeley, Calif., 1982), 82–109, is very interesting on self, individual, and group in the Middle Ages.

[12] Charles Taylor, 'The Diversity of Goods', in *Philosophy and the Human Sciences* (Cambridge, 1985), 230–47.

as a whole or the concept generally. Degrees of community feeling will inevitably vary both in intensity and in extent. Without question, communities wax and wane. There will have been people who lived in the town and felt little for it, good or bad; but, at other times, even those without any interest or admiration for the Borough Community and its élite will have felt an association with Wells itself. It is of the nature of community that not everyone who is conscious of its appeal feels or thinks exactly the same thing. Thus burgesses, foreigners, and cathedral vicars had overlapping but different conceptions and responsibilities.

The constant element was locality, and community built itself up from this bedrock. In 900 there was no Wells, only some springs near a monastery, and by 1500 there was a town with a history, idiosyncratic institutions, and inhabitants who would be sure to identify themselves as coming from that place. One of those, Thomas Chandler, a churchman and scholar, wrote of the town's beauty in the mid-fifteenth century with a considerable renaissance enthusiasm. In dialogue form, he describes how two travellers, descending after a long, hard walk through the Mendip Hills, see Wells below and admire its churches and ecclesiastical buildings, but also the town itself. They praise 'The order and unity of the citizens, the just laws, the best policies, the delightful situation of the town, the elegance of the streets, the intrinsic brilliance of the houses, the prudent inhabitants, the beauty, artfulness, and suavity of it all.' A chancellor of Oxford University, Chandler had developed that attachment and respect for locality and one's home that is part of the colour of community.[13] How this came to be possible is part of the story that I want to tell. In the final analysis, the concept of community is needed because it allows us to give a more coherent account of the Middle Ages, and certainly of medieval Wells.

SOURCES

Any story is best told from as many sources as possible, and many sorts of documents have been employed in this study. The town of

---

[13] In 'A Dialogue in Praise of William of Wykeham', in *Memorials of the Reign of King Henry VI: Official Correspondence of Thomas Bekynton, Secretary to King Henry VI and Bishop of Bath and Wells*, ii, RS 56 (London, 1872), 321–2.

Wells has not received any large-scale historical treatment. Attention has generally been paid to the cathedral, both in its ecclesiastical and architectural guises. Partly for this reason, I have focused on the lay town rather than the ecclesiastical city when I have faced the problems related to social history. Furthermore, because so much of my aim has been to suggest issues of local lay mentality, I have steered away from the better-educated and atypical cathedral staff. Their sense of community would have been easier to establish, but would have proven less than I felt was needed, and would have proven it for the special case of a great and wealthy church.

One source requires particular comment because of its importance to almost every chapter. Called 'the great paper book' in Wells records, the Convocation Books are now bound in two volumes for the main period under discussion. They are extant from 1377, and cover some 600 pages up to 1500. They were the main records of the Wells Borough Community, of the citizens. As such, their great weakness is that they do not deal directly with those who were not burgesses: the clergy and the non-citizens. Their great strength is their combination of succinctness and comprehensiveness. They are at one and the same time a record of elections to all the civic offices and Parliament, a registry of leases of Community properties, a list of the admissions to the citizenship of the town, the minutes of the master's court (the main forum for business and trespass cases between burgesses), and a record of civic ordinances and constitutional amendments. The Convocation Books are, however, rather laconic, in relatively few of the law cases can one tell in detail what was at issue, and only infrequently is the conclusion of a given case made clear. Ordinances are recorded, but not the discussions that preceded them. Furthermore, in certain periods, notably before 1410, the scribes were a little more consistently generous in the amount of detail that they provided. Often my desire to know and say more has been thwarted by this soft-spoken document.

Other sources of importance are lucky survivals, which hint at the great losses. There is no solid series of manorial court records. Only a handful of years are extant. Most unfortunate is the loss of almost all of the bishop's bailiff's court records, which would have told us more about the relationships between citizens and outsiders. Rentals of community property are limited to one from each of the fourteenth, fifteenth, and sixteenth centuries. Parish documents are limited to occasional references in the Convocation Books and to accounts and inventories copied in the eighteenth and nineteenth centuries.

One of the more interesting and important sources is no longer available in the original. The '1437 constitution', as I shall refer to it, was copied out in the nineteenth century by Thomas Serel, a local antiquarian, who published it and other civic and parochial documents.[14] But this and some other papers have since disappeared. The document is obviously authentic and mainly accurate. The Convocation Books in fact refer on 11 July 1437 to constitutional ordinances written in 'another roll', which plainly meant the 1437 constitution.[15] Lists of citizens included in the roll are properly contemporary with 1437, and Serel even misread John Crappe for John Trappe.

The range of sources is interesting proof of the complexity of town life in the Middle Ages. There are the lord of the town's records, deposited now in Lambeth Palace, and the ecclesiastical records found among the bishop's registers and the cathedral records. Many economic facts are culled from central government records of tax assessments, legal mishaps, and those historiographically fortunate hiatuses between the death of one bishop and the appointment of another, when the king administered the estate and recorded the business. Poverty is reflected primarily by pious gifts to the poor in wills, the cathedral accounts, and the records of the almshouse. What we lack most are narrative sources, apart from several short ecclesiastical documents. This problem points back to my earlier discussion of community and individuality, because there is nothing like narrative for allowing the individual to emerge from the typical impersonality of administrative records. There may be paths to the types of individuals and informal groups of friends and families who shaped the social patterns of smaller towns such as Wells, but discovering them must, for the time being, be deferred while we try to depict the larger social groupings, their economic context, and their mentalities.[16]

[14] Serel, 36–41.
[15] CBI: 294. Serel, 36, did not transcribe the date, but only the year.
[16] I am currently attempting to establish some of the social networks of the town and any vestiges of individuality. Rather than provide an appendix of undigested facts relating to prominent individuals at the present time, I hope to produce something more amenable to interpretation and argument.

I

Origins

Wells was not one of those towns whose urban roots stretch back to Roman or Anglo-Saxon times. It had to wait until the first century of Norman rule to become a borough, and aside from this fact—the date of which is not known—little else is sure about its earliest history, the time before 1150. But 'borough' is primarily a legal term in a twelfth-century context, and it is the town, both much more and something less, that is at issue here. To answer the important question of the town's origins, this darker age must be probed, and any salient geographical, rural, and institutional features examined, so that the town may be placed in its broad historical circumstances. Many of the forces in play well before 1200 continued to shape, stimulate, and restrain the town throughout the later Middle Ages.

The advantages given to Wells by geography were always conditional. Before the foundation of the town, before the Conquest, even before the first church in the seventh or eighth century, people had long settled in the sub-Mendip region. The rough terrain to the north of Wells is littered with the barrows, hill-forts, and cairns of the upland Celts. To the south, around Glastonbury, are the remains of the lowland lake villages. For people anxious to have defensible homes, these sites made good sense, but they could hardly support a substantial population, uncongenial to agriculture as they were. Nevertheless, these habitation sites represent the two great topographical limits to the sub-Mendip region, two important constraints on Wells's future: the sixteen-mile-deep chain of rocky, often steep hills which rise to over 900 feet within two miles of the town; and the Somerset Levels, miles of moorland, once part of the Bristol Channel, and just as close to Wells.[1]

Much of the Mendips was covered by a royal forest which continued to creep southward with its forest law until a fourteenth-

[1] *VCH Somerset*, 2 vols., ed. William Page (London, 1906–11), i. 164–216.

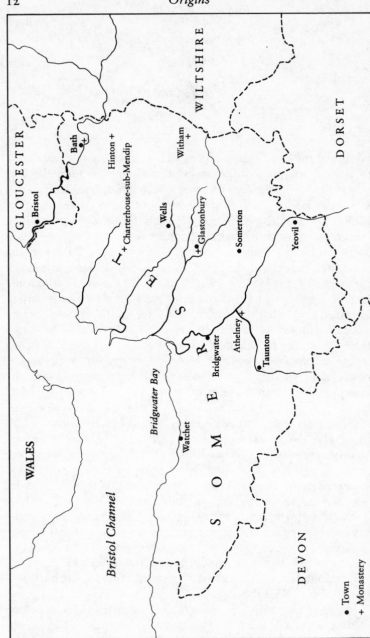

MAP 1. The county of Somerset

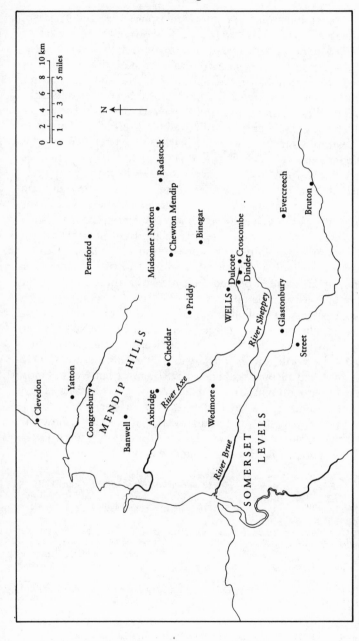

MAP 2. The Mendip region

century perambulation,[2] and the whole mass was cut by steep, inhospitable valleys. The Levels near Wells were to a great extent submerged and otherwise marshy before the Conquest. Even in the sixteenth century, when natural drainage and the industry of Glastonbury Abbey had reclaimed much of the alluvial plain for grazing, agriculture, or the collection of fuel, Meare Pool was a lake of several miles circumference, and shoddy workmanship on a dyke could lead to considerable loss of crops and livestock.[3] There were strict restraints on the amount of high-quality land available for settlement, and this determined that human activity would be limited. But it would also be concentrated. Aside from the sparsely populated 'islands' of Wedmore, Andersey, Panborough, and Meare to the south, the eleventh-century population lived in the sub-Mendip area in a chain of settlements that stretched from Wells on the east to Banwell on the west.[4] The hamlets and farmsteads of Wells Manor had collectively become the most populated link, and the city of Wells would be located at the end of the more level ground, at an altitude of 100 feet, nicely balanced between the heights and the worst damp.

The possibility of profitable farming—and thereby supporting a greater population—was the special advantage of the sub-Mendip region, and it was soon recognized. A Roman road passes three miles to the north, on its way to the Charterhouse-sub-Mendip lead-mines, and a Roman villa may have been sited in Wells Manor. A hoard of late Roman silver and copper coins as well as lead pigs have been found at Wookey Hole within the manor.[5] Archaeological remains have demonstrated that there was continuous lowland occupation from no later than the fifth century.[6] Writing in the sixteenth century, the traveller Leland was struck by the stoniness

---

[2] See 'Historia Major', in *Collectanea I*, ed. T. F. Palmer, SRS 39 (1924), 65; *VCH Somerset*, i. 32; *Mendip Laws and Forest Bounds*, ed. J. W. Gough, SRS 45 (1930), 64–92. The 'Historia Major' is one of three very short medieval historical writings about Wells Cathedral. It was compiled and completed by *c*.1410, and was copied into RIII: 296[d].–302.

[3] *Leland's Itinerary*, ed. L. Toulmin Smith (London, 1907), i. 149; for examples of broken dykes and damage, see *CPR 1313–17*: 411, and *CPR 1324–7*: 349.

[4] *DB* 89[b]; see R. Welldon Finn and P. Wheatley, 'Somerset', in H. C. Darby and R. Welldon Finn (eds.), *A Domesday Geography of South West England* (Cambridge, 1967), 145–6.

[5] H. D. W. Ellington, 'The Mendip Lead Industry', in Keith Branigan and P. J. Fowler (ed.), *The Roman West Country* (Newton Abbot, 1976), 183; and *VCH Somerset*, i. 355–70.

[6] Warwick Rodwell, 'The Anglo-Saxon and Norman Churches at Wells', in L. S. Colchester (ed.), *Wells Cathedral: A History* (West Compton, Somerset, 1982), 3.

of the soil under the city,[7] but even within the borough limits it was worth while growing grain. Every foot won from Meare Pool was a foot of rich but difficult to work alluvial clay, so the profitability of agricultural as opposed to pastoral farming must often have been questionable. Mixed farming in varying proportions has always been the rule in the area. Thus the soil was no less a limitation than topography on the region's development.

Comparing Wells to an estate of approximately the same tenant population gives a good idea of its early economy.[8] According to Domesday Book, there were fifty hides in Wells Manor—taking a hide to be a measure of tax assessment—and fifty-five ploughs, whereas the Worcestershire royal manor of Bromsgrove's thirty hides supported seventy-seven ploughs.[9] Wells was assessed at a higher level of tax and yet had many fewer ploughs, suggesting that its value was less dependent on its arable farming. Even allowing for variations in the amount of land represented by a hide, Wells was less committed to tilling the land that it had. Wells had an annual value of £61, or more than twice that of Bromsgrove. This excess of wealth must be attributed in great part to the pastoral economy. The Worcestershire entry records some woodland but no pasture, whereas Wells was exploiting three square leagues, more than any other place in Somerset.[10] The Exon Domesday, which unfortunately covered only the south-west and not Bromsgrove, records that Wells Manor had at least 34 head of cattle, 250 sheep grazing on the manor, and some pigs and goats foraging. Some woodland, furze, and gorse gave Wells a ready fuel supply, and help to emphasize that the manor's varied landscape and natural life were already contributing to its relative prosperity.[11] Next to agriculture, however, the sheep are the most conspicuous and promising feature, foreshadowing the later significance of the wool

[7] *Leland's Itinerary*, i. 144.

[8] Bromsgrove had 114 free tenants and 10 serfs (*DB* 172[b]), whereas Wells had 105 tenants and 27 slaves (*DB* 89[b-c].)

[9] On the question of the meaning and artificiality of the hide, see H. C. Darby, *Domesday England* (Cambridge, 1977), 9–10, who argues that in the West Country they were units imposed from above; see also Sally P. J. Harvey, 'Taxation and the Ploughland in Domesday Book', in P. H. Sawyer (ed.), *Domesday Book: A Reassessment* (London, 1985), 86–103; and David Hall, 'The Late Saxon Countryside: Villages and their Fields', in Della Hooke (ed.), *Anglo-Saxon Settlements* (Oxford, 1988), 116–20.

[10] *DB* 89[b] and 172[b]; Finn and Wheatley, 'Somerset', 183, fig. 43.

[11] *DB* 89[b] and 172[b]. I have used figures for Bromsgrove proper, excluding the two entries for appendages.

and cloth industries and their related trades for the region and the
city.[12]

The presence of pastoral activity partly determined the structure
of the early locality, making Wells—or allowing it to become—a
large manor settled in a distinctive way. The Anglo-Saxon manor of
Wells, whose origins are unknown,[13] covered about twelve square
miles, reaching from the outskirts of Glastonbury (Hartlake Bridge)
far up into the lightly inhabited Mendips. There the homestead and
later village of Binegar was already established, and no doubt sheep
were grazing then as now.[14] The slopes of the Mendips along the
north of the sub-Mendip region were suitable for sheep and goats,
if not for more permanent or numerous human settlements.

But hamlets needed to be near the various grazing areas as well as
the dispersed pockets of good agricultural land. An eleventh-
century charter and even a modern Ordnance Survey map illustrate
the complexities that the name 'Wells Manor' hides. Certainly
Wells was a form of multiple estate, even though nothing in
Domesday records the fact, possibly because each of the parts was
so small.[15] The Domesday returns for Somerset are full of entries
for tiny places, which today are often only farms, houses, or hills.[16]
The population of about 500 people must be imagined as dispersed
in small, isolated hamlets and homesteads rather than in one or two
sizeable villages.[17] Paradoxically, although geography made Wells
Manor the largest and one of the most densely populated parts of
Somerset, the microgeography of Wells produced a well-spaced
population. There were no fewer than twenty-seven of these
hamlets (*viculis*), possessing an average population of less than
nineteen.[18] Little sense of village community can have existed for
Wells Manor as a whole in the Anglo-Saxon period.

[12] On the future of wool and cloth, see below, Ch. 3.
[13] The time of its origin cannot be established, but see below, sect. 2.
[14] For Binegar, see Sawyer, 1042.
[15] On multiple estates, see G. R. J. Jones, 'Multiple Estates and Early Settlement',
in P. H. Sawyer (ed.), *Medieval Settlement* (London, 1976), 15–40; Hall, 'Late
Saxon Countryside', 104–7; Finn and Wheatley, 'Somerset', 137; Darby, *Domesday
England*, 15–17.
[16] Finn and Wheatley, 'Somerset', 143, counted such places as a third of the entire
return.
[17] I estimated the population by multiplying the tenants (105) by 4.5, which gives
a rounded figure of 473, and adding the slaves (27). The canons would be additional,
but 500 is the nearest round number: *DB* 89[b-c].
[18] This document (Sawyer, 1042) is spurious. I accept, however, that it gives a
correct late 11th-cent. picture of the manor. It displays a convincing and detailed
knowledge of the place.

The widespread availability of fresh running water helped to make it easier for both men and animals to thrive without having to congregate. Many of the hamlets had direct access to the watercourses—the River Sheppey, Keward Brook, St Andrew's Stream, and the River Axe—or were near the many springs. Although none of these watercourses was especially large, they were more than adequate. Nine mills stood over these streams in 1086, giving Wells Manor a very low inhabitant–mill ratio.[19] The mills were spread out to serve the similarly patterned population, further encouraging the decentralized activity. In many respects Wells Manor was not strongly disposed to the spontaneous development of urban life. But before the thirteenth century the ready availability of water was to counter this pattern of dispersal by providing a focus, the source of Wells's renown, and much of its prosperity: a church.

I. THE EARLY CHURCH

The main attraction that the Wells site possessed over other parts of the manor or the sub-Mendip region was that several springs rose there to feed the stream that now runs through the town. One of the springs is a holy well dedicated to St Andrew. Holy wells were not rare in Somerset—nearby Dulcote had one—yet at Wells it made all the difference. Situated close to the cathedral that it spawned, its religious history extends back beyond the coming of Christianity.

Recent archaeological work has uncovered a fifth- or sixth-century 'proto-Roman' mausoleum just west of the springs (and just south of the present cathedral). It was succeeded by a Christian mortuary chapel, which was surrounded by a lay cemetery.[20] By the eighth century a monastery had been established there, an advance squadron of the victorious Christian mission.[21] One of the skulls found in the tombs of the Anglo-Saxon bishops of Wells, perhaps not a bishop's, had been cracked by a sword-blow—a relic of some cultless, nameless martyr.[22] Notwithstanding this harsh evidence,

---

[19] DB 89[b].
[20] Rodwell, 'Churches at Wells', 3–5.
[21] RIII: 404.
[22] Rodwell, 'Churches at Wells', 21.

the foundation of the monastery on a pre-Christian site should remind us of Pope Gregory's sensible advice on conversions: the holy sites of the pagans were to be purged with holy water, but then the Christian rites and relics were established in the very same buildings, the places that the natives already held as sacred and to which they customarily came to worship.[23] At Wells the sacrament of baptism—the central event in a time of conversions—can only have gained appeal and lost some of its strangeness by the use of the water from the holy pagan well. Religious revolution succeeded, but it did so with the aid of cultural continuity.

The earliest reference to Wells makes it plain that in 766 the church was located in no town or *burh* but simply 'next to the great spring, which they call Wielea'.[24] The spring gave its name to the church, manor, hundred, and eventually the town. There is no early indication that there was a substantial settlement nearby. There need not have been; as at other places like St Margaret's church at Binsey, Oxfordshire, the holiness of the well was attraction and justification enough.

The modesty of the nearby settlements was matched by the church. For 200 years it was a small monastery, endowed with sufficient land for only a handful. Very possibly it functioned as a minster for the area before it became a bishop's seat.[25] Even after 905, when the large diocese of Sherborne was split into three sees—Sherborne, Ramsbury (Wiltshire), and Wells—to serve the expanding population of Christian Wessex, there was little change in the size of the monastic community.[26] In the early days the

[23] *Bede's Ecclesiastical History of the English People*, ed. Bertram Colgrave and R. A. B. Mynors (Oxford, 1969), 106–7.

[24] Sawyer, 262, and RIII: 404ᵛ: 'situm est iuxta fontem magnum quem vocitant Wielea'.

[25] Both St Cuthbert's parish church and the future cathedral church possess some characteristics of a minster. St Cuthbert's is referred to later as a mother church for certain chapels in Wells Manor, but its history probably began only in the early 12th cent., during Bishop Godfrey's episcopate (1123–35): see RI: 85 and 31; RII: 13 and 40. As for St Andrew's, the signs are dim but encouraging; it did receive some early Anglo-Saxon royal patronage from Cynewulf; it certainly served a large area and was called a 'monasterium' (R. III: 404): see John Blair, 'Minster Churches in the Landscape', in Hooke (ed.), *Anglo-Saxon Settlements*, 35–58; and M. J. Franklin, 'The Identification of Minsters in the Midlands', in R. A. Brown (eds.), *Anglo-Norman Studies*, vii. (Woodbridge, 1985), 69–88; G. W. O. Addleshaw, *The Beginnings of the Parochial System*, 2nd edn. (York, 1959), 12–15.

[26] See H. P. R. Finberg, 'Sherborne, Glastonbury and the Expansion of Wessex', in id., *Lucerna. Studies in Some Problems in the Early History of England* (London, 1964), 109–10.

bishop of Wells was sometimes abbot of Glastonbury, and the effective centre of Christianity in Somerset was probably at that nearby, most ancient, relic-rich place.[27] But the growth of the faith and perhaps of the population generally produced an increase in the traffic towards the church of Wells for the celebration of feast-days and rites of passage; and sometime between 905 and 1060 a new, still fairly humble cathedral church was built to accommodate the congregants and to increase the dignity of the see.[28]

Wells's origins are obscure, and considered speculation must play its part in producing even a slender outline. The principal question is whether the town was always what it might appear to be today: a small market town, greatly dependent on the cathedral for its existence and much of its growth. Wells's story would then be told after the pattern of Bury St Edmunds or St Albans. In these cases, a town developed outside the gates of a religious house, and grew in response to the escalating needs of the developing monastery. Indeed, Dr Rodwell has argued that the topography and street plan of Wells suggests that it was a town deliberately planned in the eleventh century, planned with the fact of the monastery at its centre.[29] Certainly the old church has an important place in the street plan, the High Street ending abruptly in the market-place outside the church's gate. But there are flaws in the analogy with the monastic towns, and an unwarranted assumption in the topographical argument.

A list of monastic houses would by no means be a list of towns. Nearby Glastonbury, the most telling example, had no fewer than seventy-two monks, not to reckon servants, in the twelfth century, but it generated no town until the end of the Middle Ages, and no borough even then.[30] Furthermore, unlike Glastonbury and other

[27] e.g. the abbots Althelm and Brihtwig: see the 'Historia Major', 59; Finberg, 'Expansion of Wessex'.

[28] Rodwell, 'Churches at Wells', 6; the previous structure was a two-celled building which Rodwell suggests might have doubled as a parish church.

[29] Ibid. 10–14, and 'Wells: the Cathedral and the City', *Current Archaeology*, 7 (1980), 38–44; see also Michael Aston, 'The Towns of Somerset', in J. Haslam (ed.), *Anglo-Saxon Towns in Southern England* (Chichester, 1984), 193–9. On the development of Anglo-Saxon and early Norman towns, see also James Tait, *The Medieval English Borough* (Manchester, 1936); Susan Reynolds, *An Introduction to the History of English Medieval Towns* (Oxford, 1977), 16–45; David Hill, 'Towns as Structures and Functioning Communities through Time: The Development of Central Places from 600–1066', in Hooke (ed.), *Anglo-Saxon Settlements*, 197–212; and Tim Tatton-Brown, 'The Anglo-Saxon Towns of Kent', ibid. 213–32.

[30] David Knowles and R. N. Hadcock, *Medieval Religious Houses* (London, 1971), 86; and discussions with Miss Lynn Marston of Leicester University, who is preparing a thesis on later medieval Glastonbury.

monastic towns, Wells was not a property of the convent, but of the bishops. The chapter of Wells had neither interest nor authority in any possible borough. It might have welcomed a town, but it could not have encouraged one as a matter of policy, because it was not. the principle landlord in Wells. Dr Rodwell's suggestion, while plausible, uses the fact that the High Street runs to the church as proof that it was a commercial high street in the eleventh century rather than a simple road, barred by the episcopal estates and the holy springs from running directly through the precincts to meet the Bath road. Furthermore, once the town had started to develop, it is natural enough that the market-place and high street would have been positioned to catch the festival traffic on its way to church. The question is to determine when the market and the urban streets were developed, not when a road to the church was constructed. Bearing this in mind, I propose to juxtapose the growth of town (manor) and church to establish chronologies of development which may indicate their relationship. First I shall consider the church.

A central source for the church's early history is the *Historiola de Primordiis Episcopatus Somersetensis*.[31] Internal evidence suggests that it was written during the episcopate of Reginald de Bohun (1174–91), that is, fifty years or so before Wells once again became a cathedral.[32] Its great value for the question that we are facing derives mainly from Bishop Giso's (1061–88) own account of his church and its development during his episcopate, which is quoted at length by the *Historiola*'s author.[33]

The story can be told from the eleventh century, and it is not a tale of success. Giso's years were hopeful, if at first tumultuous, caught up in a battle with the great lord, Earl Harold of Wessex. The bishopric had slowly accumulated wealth, often as the penance of kings, but many of its lands were disputed, and Earl Harold was the most powerful and, therefore, the most successful claimant, forcibly confiscating a number of manors.[34] Lesser men did the same. One Alsie was in possession of the manor of Winesham.[35]

---

[31] Printed in *Ecclesiastical Documents*, ed. Joseph Hunter, CS 3 (London, 1840); the original is in an early 14th-cent. hand-bound register of Bath Priory, now in the possession of Lincoln's Inn.

[32] *Historiola*, 28.

[33] Ibid. 15–20.

[34] Ibid. 16–18.

[35] Ibid. 17, and *DB* 89[c].

Giso considered excommunicating Harold, but the battle of Hastings ended their strife, and Giso, a Lorrainian, received Winesham and most of the other disputed properties from the Norman king, to whom he complained. Even before the Conquest Giso had tried vigorously to enrich his church, acquiring Wedmore from Edward the Confessor, Merk and Modesley from Queen Edith, and Combe, Worminster, and Litton by purchase.[36]

There were many pressing ways for Giso to spend his new income. When he arrived at Wells, he had found no impressive complex of buildings nor numerous ministers, but a 'mediocre church', staffed by 'four or five clerks', and none of the communal buildings—cloister, dormitory, or refectory—which Giso felt that an honest and a cathedral church required.[37] He built these buildings, recruited new men, and established a community of canons under some sort of fairly disciplined regime supervised by a provost, probably the rule of St Chrodegang of Metz.[38] The *Historiola* says Giso 'had lead [the canons] to live together regularly and religiously'.[39] By the end of his life there were probably ten canons living communally.[40]

Giso was also responsible for introducing a distinction between the bishop's property and that of his chapter, thereby laying the foundation for the sharp division between the two that characterized the later Middle Ages.[41] In effect, it would give Wells two ecclesiastical establishments of the first order rather than one. But

[36] *Historiola*, 18; DB 89[b] and [c] indicates possession of Combe, Wedmore and Litton; other grants are in Sawyer, 1042, 1115, 1116; *Codex Diplomaticus Aevi Saxonici*, ed. J. M. Kemble (London, 1846), 816, 834–7, and 839; H. P. R. Finberg, *Early Charters of Wessex* (Leicester, 1964), 542; see also RI: 17[d]–18, and RIII: 241.

[37] *Historiola*, 16–17.

[38] See Kathleen Edwards, *The English Secular Cathedrals in the Middle Ages* (Manchester, 1949), 3–5; Diana Greenway, 'The False *Institutio* of St Osmund', in Diana Greenway, Christopher Holdsworth, and Jane Sayers (eds.), *Tradition and Change: Essays in Honour of Marjorie Chibnall* (Cambridge, 1985), 81, for the revival of this rule for canons in 11th-cent. English cathedrals like Wells, Exeter, York, and Hereford. The rule came with the 4 'Lotharingians' who received bishoprics from Edward the Confessor: see Frank Barlow, *The English Church, 1000–1066* (London, 1963), 81–4.

[39] *Historiola*, 22; cf. William of Malmesbury, *Gesta Pontificum Anglorum*, ed. N. E. S. A. Hamilton, RS 82 (London, 1870), 201, for a description of Leofric's establishment of a very similar system, in the 'manner of Lorraine', for Exeter.

[40] *Historiola*, 22, says that the provost seized 'xxx libras et ultra'; in *Historiola*, 24, and RI: 31, the canons were each receiving 60s. p.a.

[41] *Historiola*, 20 and DB 89[b]–[c], show the canons of Wells, as distinct from the bishop, owning part of Wells Manor, Litton, and Wanstrow.

in 1086 the canons of Wells (perhaps excluding the provost) held
property worth only £20 a year, a small fraction of the bishop's
income.[42]

In 1088 Giso was succeeded by John of Tours, who quickly
acquired the old city of Bath and transferred his see there. Wells
was no longer a cathedral, and would not be for the next 150 years.
The damage was severe. It was not just that future prospects
seemed to have been blighted, but that recent efforts were so easily
negated. John was a man of firm, even harsh action. At Bath he
replaced the monks wholesale after finding them to be 'barbarians',
presumably meaning English and/or illiterate.[43] At Wells he tore
down the monastic-style establishment that Giso had created:
houses, dining-hall, dormitory, and cloister.[44] The canons were
turned out to live 'in common with the people', resecularized.[45]
This was bad; but perhaps worse was the fact that John gave £30 or
more of the church's rents to his steward Heldebert, whom he made
provost over the canons.[46] This must have represented the lion's
share of the revenues, but it is impossible to know whether
Heldebert was in control of all the cathedral's property. Giso had
described the provost's duties in his time as the care of the church's
'temporal concerns without, and of the brethren within', which
suggests that the provost held the chapter's properties as ad-
ministrator.[47] Heldebert did no less, paying the canons 60s. each
per annum.[48] The canons' oppression cannot have been relieved
until the provost's lands were returned to the chapter's control. The
monastic reform movement in eleventh- and twelfth-century
England has been connected by some historians to the growth of
the towns.[49] The effect of the reform on Bath is unclear, but on
Wells it was distinctly negative.

[42] The bishop's Somerset holdings were worth over £200 p.a. (*DB* 86[b], 87[a], and 89[b-d]).

[43] William of Malmesbury, *Gesta Regum Anglorum*, ed. W. Stubbs, RS 90, ii. (London, 1889), 387–8; *Historiola*, 21–2; on the transfer of sees, see Frank Barlow, *The English Church, 1066–1154* (London, 1979), 208–31.

[44] *Historiola*, 22.

[45] Ibid.; 'Historia Major', 61, adds the improbable suggestion that the site of the common buildings was used for a palace for the bishop.

[46] *Historiola*, 22.

[47] Ibid. 19.

[48] Ibid. 22; and *VCH Somerset*, ii. 162.

[49] e.g. James Campbell, *Essays in Anglo-Saxon History* (London, 1986), 143, posits a 'second order connection' between them.

Wells's recovery did not occur until the end of Bishop Robert of Lewes's episcopate (1135–66), although some improvement in the canons' circumstances came earlier. Bishop Godfrey's (1122–35) efforts to reacquire the estates were thwarted by a political alliance that won the favour of King Henry I, but a similar sort of manœuvre allowed Bishop Robert to win King Stephen's support and to make a deal with Heldebert's second heir, Reginald.[50] In exchange for the precentorship of Wells church and the use of the manor of Combe, he gave the bishop a property later sufficient to support several canonal prebends.[51] Later in the twelfth century, when the provost's estates had returned to the chapter's control, there were twenty-two prebends, making it likely that there were a dozen canons at Wells in 1150.[52] Reginald's kin were paid to withdraw their claims in the 1160s, and Reginald himself must have died shortly after.[53]

Bishop Robert was responsible for the turn-around at Wells, and it was plainly a matter of policy to strengthen a church situated towards the heart of the diocese, one which was under his direct control in a way that a monastery was not. The arrangement concluded with the precentor allowing Bishop Robert to raise the stipend of the canons from £3 to £5 each per annum.[54] Robert found new endowments, spruced up the dilapidated church fabric, and gave the church a new constitution modelled on Salisbury Cathedral's, despite the fact that Wells was not a cathedral at that time.[55] Regardless of this pretension, Wells church was a fairly humble institution for most of the twelfth century, a college of

[50] *Historiola*, 23–4. Heldebert passed the property and the office to his son John, who in turn passed them to his kinsman Reginald.

[51] RI:131. See Antonia Gransden, 'The History of Wells Cathedral, c.1090–1547', in Colchester (ed.), *Wells Cathedral*, 24–5.

[52] *VCH Somerset*, ii. 162.

[53] *Historiola*, 24; for arguments about when all the properties were returned to the convent's control, see Gransden, 'Wells Cathedral', 24.

[54] RI: 31.

[55] *Historiola*, 24–5 RI: 31; RII: 13 and 40; RIII: 9; and see the 'Statuta Antiqua', in Herbert Edward Reynolds (ed.), *Wells Cathedral: Its Foundation, Constitutional History and Statutes* (Leeds, 1881), 1–52. Greenway, 'False *Institutio*', shows that parts of the Salisbury regime did not exist in the 11th-cent., but were later interpolations based on evolved practice; but she agrees that Wells's arrangement in the 12-cent. included the complete list of officers outlined in the *Institutio* (p. 81); furthermore, *Dean Cosyn Manuscripts and Wells Cathedral Miscellany*, ed. A. Watkin, SRS 56 (1941) 87–8, prints letters exchanged between the chapters of Wells and Salisbury from the middle of the 14th cent. century asking for clarification of constitutional issues.

secular canons unable to control all of its property, of no great size, and holding services in a suitably modest Anglo-Saxon building.

The impact of this church on Wells Manor was, by any standard, minimal. Giso's clerks, slowly growing in numbers, and their servants were surrounded by a population of about 500, spread thinly over the manor. It is very unlikely that at this stage the church's development can have greatly altered the local status quo. There was possibly a hamlet or a small village closer to the wells and the church. A name has come down to us in several versions—Tidington, Cideston, possibly Tidesbury or Tideston.[56] Two documents declare one or the other of these place-names to be Wells's original name. But this putative settlement's nature and location are unsure; its history obscure.[57] It presumably lost its name as the church made itself the significant and memorable fact of the area.

2. THE DEVELOPMENT OF THE TOWN

It is impossible to assess what Wells was like before the church became dominant. We cannot therefore gauge the earliest impact of the fluctuations of the church's fortunes on the area. It is necessary to derive the eleventh-century situation from speculating on what is known of the church and from what Domesday Book suggests. A monastic cathedral, however small, must have altered the economic life of the region by presenting new options. These were limited by the frailness in size and property of the monastery itself. But it did give 'Wells' or any nearby hamlet a small customer for any agricultural surpluses—quite small because, in 1086 the canons' share of Wells Manor was worth £12 per annum, or roughly 20 per cent of the whole. They may have been able to supply many of their needs without recourse to any market. Six of their fourteen hides of land in the manor were held in demesne.[58] All that was required for certain was a baker, and a baker does not a borough make.

---

[56] Sawyer, 1042; *Historiola*, 14; WTD 115; WCC 3; and AH 55.

[57] Sawyer, 1042; *Historiola*, 14. For speculation as to its location, see Aston, 'Towns of Somerset', 193–4; and Michael Havinden, *The Somerset Landscape* (London, 1981), 210–14.

[58] *DB* 89[b].

But the church must also have given some individuals the option—and presented others with the requirement—of living near the church as servants of the canons. This attraction must have been strengthened by the dissolution of the monastic structure in 1090, when the canons were forced to live outside the church. Each of the canons would have established a household of his own, no doubt with more servants than the more efficient monastic formula would have required. Therefore the numbers of agriculturally non-productive people in the area would have increased. The church had a centripetal force of a clear but low order, attracting population and food towards itself, with a somewhat increased power once the canons were resecularized. But this very strength was short-lived, offset by the removal of the bishop's interest and patronage, and by the sequestration of the church's property.

Domesday Book's description of Wells makes no mention of attributes associated with an eleventh-century borough or town—neither mint, nor market, nor burgesses, nor third penny.[59] Furthermore, there is no distinction made between a core village—a potential town—and the other parts of the large manor. This leaves little reason to doubt that contributing motivations for the bishopric's removal to Bath were the Councils of London of 1075 and 1078, or like-minded deliberations. The policy stated at these councils was that bishops should move their cathedrals from country villages to significant and populous places.[60] In 1075 the bishops of Sherborne, Lichfield, and Selsey became bishops of Salisbury, Chester, and Chichester respectively, while the 1078 council stated that sees would be placed in Exeter, Lincoln, and Bath instead of Crediton, Thetford, and Wells. William of Malmesbury wrote that Bishop John of Tours, fearing himself less glorious if he lived in an 'inglorious vill', moved to Bath, 'urbs tam insignis', a city so famous.[61] As late as 1125, when William wrote this, there was no way one could confuse rustic Wells with an *urbs*, a city.[62] Bath had more burgesses within the city than spacious

---

[59] Ibid.

[60] *Concilia Magnae Brittaniae et Hiberniae*, ed. David Wilkins (London, 1737), i. 363 and 367; see Barlow, *English Church 1066–1154*, 208–31; Campbell, *Anglo-Saxon History*, 141. Rodwell, 'Churches at Wells', 10, calls Wells a 'planned town' in opposing this view.

[61] *Gesta Pontificum Anglorum*, 193–4, and *Gesta Regum Anglorum*, 387.

[62] On the possibility that the terminology of towns had more precise technical meanings than might first appear to be the case, see Campbell, *Anglo-Saxon History*, 99–108, where it is argued that *urbs* would only have been used by Bede for an important town with Roman origins; by the same token, William of Malmesbury

Wells Manor had tenants.[63] Notwithstanding its suffering in the war of 1088, Bath was populous, potentially rich, and—as important—ancient and privileged. All these considerations further favoured it over Wells. The fact that Bishop Giso had resisted the plans for an earlier transfer of the see should be put down to the work and commitment that he had given the church, and to Wells's more central position in Somerset. Bath was on the northern edge of the diocese, less able to serve the faith than Wells, especially at a time when there were still few parish churches. The eleventh-century Geld Inquest found in the Exon Domesday notes only six parish priests spread out through the nineteen manors of the bishops of Wells.[64] In short, the church of Wells must have fostered some growth in nearby communities, perhaps enough to make a village out of a hamlet, but by the end of the eleventh century the church itself was stagnant. There was still no town at Wells in 1100.

Wells the town took its first vital step at the time when the church of Wells was just starting to recover its direction and yet was still small and sluggish. One document vividly and inadvertently captures both aspects. In one of Bishop Robert's charters written between 1135 and 1166 Wells's existing fairs were extended from one to three days, a clear proof of their success and of the bishop's appreciation of the profit and activity. One of the witnesses, however, was Reginald the precentor, heir of the provosts, whose life, and the property that he held for its duration, symbolized the restraining of the church's ambitions.[65]

The town and church must each have contributed to the remarkable twelfth-century growth of the other. The same Bishop Robert who rescued the church created the town.[66] Wells was a town planted in the twelfth century. It bears some of the signs of its

calls Wells a vill, which Bede and, presumably, William did not use to indicate an urban place (ibid. 108). For the date of William's first recension of his histories, see Rodney M. Thomson, *William of Malmesbury* (Woodbridge, 1987), 3–4.

[63] *DB* 87[b]; Finn estimated Bath's Domesday population at 1,000 in Finn and Wheatley, 'Somerset', 197–8.

[64] *VCH Somerset*, i. 531; Addleshaw, *Beginnings of the Parochial System*; John Blair, 'Local churches in Domesday Book and Before', in J. C. Holt (ed.), *Domesday Studies* (London, 1987), 265–78.

[65] WCC 2.

[66] Bishop Reginald's charter refers to a previous charter of Bishop Robert, the tenor of which it says it follows (CBII: 86); and 'Historia Major', 62, says Robert gave the town a charter.

origins in its topography. It has been noted that towns whose territory was carved out of existing manors frequently possessed little in the way of common land.[67] Wells had none. Unfortunately, the exact date of its foundation is lost. Signs of considerable vitality in the 1170s and 1180s point to an early date for the borough's beginnings, probably in the 1130s and 1140s. This would also account for William of Malmesbury's characterization of Wells as insignificant compared to Bath, as not even a town, which would be false well before 1200. Wells was a Norman town, the creation of a Norman bishop of Bath during the great period of English medieval town foundations.[68]

Nothing in place at the start of the century suggested that there would be a thriving market and industrial town there by the end. These activities can flourish without a borough charter, but, with the church quite unable to provide the critical impetus, the success of Wells can only be adequately accounted for by the creation of the borough and the successful stimulation of a region's potential buyers and sellers. By establishing a borough, the lord was aiming to create a permanent market-place, a centre of population and production. A new charter of burghal privileges could have critical demographic consequences, attracting people, and thereby creating the centre of population that Wells Manor had always lacked. A twelfth-century town was either ancient and established (possibly decayed) or, as in Wells's case, new and, hopefully, necessarily growing. Like any seedling, stagnation augured death.

The establishment of a borough represented an act of mutual convenience whenever it was a success, a business deal in effect. The difference between a successful town and a disappointing chartered village (or worse) was whether the lord found clients to satisfy. In Wells's case, Bishop Robert made a general invitation, renewed and reinforced by Bishops Reginald and Savaric, for people to come to Wells, take up a trade or deal in the market being

---

[67] Tait, *English Borough*, 49, 71, 77, and 96.

[68] For the extent of 12th-cent. and early 13th-cent. urban development, see *British Borough Charters, 1042–1216*, ed. Adolphus Ballard (Cambridge, 1913), 1–37; M. W. Beresford, *New Towns of the Middle Ages* (London, 1967), esp. 327–38, which understates the situation, since he is mainly concerned with planted towns, not towns which have developed organically from villages or otherwise; Wells is not included among his foundations. This is not to deny the importance of the earlier, mainly royal foundations of the 9th–11th cents., about which, see Hill, 'Towns as Structures and Communities', 197–212; Haslam (ed.), *Anglo-Saxon Towns*.

established, and start life on new and intriguing terms.[69] It was
accepted from the first. The previously mentioned charter of Bishop
Robert shows the growth of the early fairs; Bishop Reginald's
second charter outlines new boundaries for the borough, to allow,
he said, for more building;[70] and Savaric's charter expands the
boundaries further.[71]

The terms of the offer were radical, although Wells's version was
in no way unique or especially enticing when viewed next to its
contemporaries.[72] The first and critical feature of any twelfth-
century borough foundation was a new attitude, legally enforced,
towards that small part of the manor's land which was removed
from the usual terms of tenure by labour services, customary dues,
and tenuous family rights over the land's future.[73] This was now to
be the borough.

Each immigrant who succeeded in gaining tenure of a messuage
within the borough found himself transformed in legal terms.[74]
Now his time was his own, as he owed no labour services.[75] The
property, too, was his own, for he could leave it by will, as a villein
never could, mortgage it, or sell it as he desired.[76] But as expressive
of the rite of passage that the new burgess had undergone in coming
to Wells was the right to live, work, or travel elsewhere, returning

[69] WCC 1, 2, and 3; CBII: 86; 'Historia Major', 63, says that the bishop 'released
[them] perpetually from servile works, by which they had been greatly oppressed
hitherto'; see also Beresford, *New Towns*, 191–225; Reynolds, *English Medieval
Towns*, 98–102. M. de W. Hemmeon, *Burgage Tenure in Medieval England*
(Cambridge, Mass., 1914), and Tait, *English Borough*, provide some of the detailed
arguments involved in the debate over the meaning of becoming a burgess, as well as
further references.

[70] CBII: 86.

[71] WCC 3.

[72] e.g. cf. Ipswich's royal charter, printed in Charles Gross, *The Gild Merchant*
(Oxford, 1890), ii. 114–23; *British Borough Charters*, 112–254, details the major
mercantile, jurisdictional, and financial elements of full charters, most of which were
not in Wells's; James Tait, *Medieval Manchester and the Beginnings of Lancashire*
(Manchester, 1904), 62, shows that Wells was not alone in its inferior situation.

[73] See *British Borough Charters*, p. xliv; on the question of where, *vis-à-vis* the
manor, a town might be placed, see Beresford, *New Towns*, 98–141; and E. M.
Carus-Wilson, 'The First Half-Century of the Borough of Stratford-upon-Avon',
ECHR, 2nd ser., 18 (1965), 49.

[74] See Hemmeon, *Burgage Tenure*; Reynolds, *English Medieval Towns*, 98–102;
Tait, *English Borough*, 96–108.

[75] 'Historia Major', 63.

[76] WCC 1. For discussion of the nature of the properties, which may not have
been roughly uniform in size, see A. J. Scrase, 'Development and Change in Burgage
Plots: The Example of Wells', *Journal of Historical Geography*, 15 (1989), 363.

only at his pleasure and without penalty or the obligation ever to return. He possessed the land, but it no longer possessed him.[77] Of no less significance, he could pass these privileges and the land to his heirs.

In the earliest days little village feeling or solidarity was sacrificed by coming to the town. There was a parish church in the town which dated from before 1135 and served the entire manor.[78] Considering the decentralized social world of Wells Manor, the town arguably offered a more intense community life in addition to a very modest amount of collective authority and influence over the town's affairs. Bishop Reginald's second charter expanded the fairs, and waived tolls, which he might have imposed during the fairs, 'at the request of our burgesses'.[79] Like all rites, becoming a burgess was an event that committed the individual and his family to a group. The borough was not entirely unlike the Church, in so far as membership altered the terms in which an individual understood his place and role in the world.[80]

For their part, the bishops of Bath made explicit some of their reasons for creating and encouraging the borough. They wanted 'to increase their honour, dignity, and rents', as Bishop Savaric's charter honestly and unashamedly put it.[81] To achieve the first two aims, they needed to succeed on the economic front, expanding their rental income and the overall activity of the town. Landlords had little to lose in the creation of a borough, especially in much of the West Country, where the land was of relatively low value and yielded correspondingly low rents.[82] Instead of yielding, say, 4*d.* an acre per annum, arable converted to borough use would yield 48*d.* per annum, twelve times as much.[83] And if, as is probable, arable in

---

[77] WCC 1.

[78] RI: 31. In Wells the parish church (St Cuthbert's) was within the borough boundaries, so the townsmen did not have to travel far or use a subordinate chapel. The country people continued to come to St Cuthbert's, only it was now in the town. Tait, *English Borough*, 55, noted that the subordinate urban chapel was unknown in the south west; but elsewhere the planted towns had trouble over the parish question: see Beresford, *New Towns*, 169–75.

[79] WCC 3.

[80] See below, Chs. 4 and 5.

[81] WCC 3; cf. Beresford, *New Towns*, 55–97.

[82] See Beresford, *New Towns*, 65–71, esp. table 3.

[83] The size of an original site was about a quarter-acre in Wells, owing the bishop 12*d.* ground-rent: e.g. WTD 49, a rare example of an undivided messuage; but see Scrase, 'Development and Change', 363; cf. Carus-Wilson, 'Stratford-upon-Avon', 49–50.

the area yielded less than 4*d*. an acre per annum in the twelfth
century, the landlord would have been even more satisfied with the
growth of his income from even a small borough. On the other.
hand, if the borough failed to acquire the attributes of a town, it
would fade away, tenants of all types scorning it because of high
rents.[84]

Markets and fairs were another new source of income for the
bishops. Indirectly, the activity and interest that these stimulated
could entice immigrants to move to the town. But the direct reward
for the bishops were the tolls that they levied on goods brought in
for sale at Wells's market, as well as the rents that they charged for
a place to sell one's goods or for a market stall.[85] Fairs were free of
tolls, but rents for stallage and the like might have been charged. It
is possible that a fair was held shortly before the borough came into
being, but at any rate there were three a year before 1166, and five
by 1201. Fairs filled three days a year around 1150, six by 1174,
nine by 1192, twelve by about 1200, and nineteen by 1201.[86] This
is one rough but clear indicator of the successful progress of the
bishops' creation and its profits.

The last principal economic advantage to the bishops were the
profits of justice in the form of new courts. There was the bailiff's
court, which oversaw the greater part of the day-to-day business of
the town such as market infractions and broken contracts;[87] and a
perquisite of the fairs was the piepowder court, which distributed
speedy merchant-law justice. Fines and amercements were drawn
from each of these sources, but the bishop retained his other
jurisdictions as owner of the hundred and frankpledge courts to
which the burgesses continued to owe suit.[88] The more burgesses
and other people were attracted to Wells permanently, the larger
would be the bishop's court receipts.[89]

The prosperity of the town also contributed to the bishop's
prestige by marking him as a more substantial—because a

[84] There were, of course, many possible reasons for a town's failure: see
Beresford, *New Towns*, 290–315.

[85] Cf. ibid. 63–4.

[86] WCC 2, 3, and 4.

[87] WCC 1 and 3.

[88] The profits of justice were a significant, but not the main, source of revenue
from a planted town (Beresford, *New Towns*, 66, table 3.1).

[89] *Rotuli Hundredorum*, ed. W. Illingworth and J. Caley, ii. (London, 1818),
134; and *Placita de Quo Warranto Edward I–Edward III*, ed. W. Illingworth, ii.
(London, 1818), 703; WCC 7; and RI: 107–8.

wealthier—lord, and by making Wells a better place for one of his churches. Urbanity and the focus of the diocese were related issues. Wells ceased to be an episcopal seat in the eleventh century because it was not a town. But in the thirteenth century it recovered the honour in great part because it had become a thriving borough. By 1200 Wells had become a viable alternative to Bath as the diocesan administrative centre, a place that could offer suitable amenities to the more sophisticated canons and clerks increasingly needed by the bishops for official business. By 1210 a bishop was once again resident in Wells, and his staff was never to leave the newly built palace, tangible confirmation that the bishops had achieved their goal and had made a city.[90]

King John granted a charter to Wells in 1201, elevating the community's status by making its members the king's burgesses and safeguarding their position from any episcopal changes of heart.[91] A legal and social entity was confirmed, and some of its inhabitants were privileged and acknowledged as a distinctive and permanent social group. A royal charter did foster the recognition and construction of a viable urban community. To a great extent, Wells was constitutionally complete not long after its foundation. There would be no legally enforceable alteration in the structure of power in the city until the sixteenth century.

Indeed, later medieval Wells was almost complete in terms of its general character, institutions, and economic structure before 1300. The precise nature of each component—its nuances, the quality of relations between the different communities of the town, economic growth and decline—can only be made out later, but we would do well to fill in the other chief facts of the city now, and see what these suggest.

Wells became a cathedral city once more by a bull of Pope Innocent III which required the bishops to take the title of bishop of Bath *and* Wells.[92] It had symbolic and social significance for Wells—and still does. Group identity is made more meaningful by such special acknowledgements. The immediate practical difference to the church or town was not marked, but there were long-term implications. They would now benefit consistently from the many

[90] Robert. W. Dunning, 'The Bishop's Palace', in Colchester (ed.), *Wells Cathedral*, 229.
[91] WCC 4.
[92] RI: 80[d]; *Calendar of Entries in the Papal Registers Relating to Great Britain: Papal Letters, 1198–1304*, ed. W. H. Bliss (London, 1893), 245, 246, and 247.

endowments from the faithful of the diocese, including the large gifts of the bishops, and the smaller ones found in lay wills and the donations of the fraternity of St Andrew. Ecclesiastical buildings were expanded. The work of the fraternity helped to perfect the great church which was begun towards the end of the twelfth century, but which was dedicated only in 1239, when the nave and west front were joined.[93] Of greatest relevance to the town, and most indicative of the thirteenth-century growth of St Andrew's Cathedral, was the increase in the number of prebends—and this meant the number of substantial clergymen at Wells—from twenty-three in the twelfth century to fifty in 1263, when Dinder was added.[94] There would, however, be no further expansion.

There were few other churches in Wells. The parish church of St Cuthbert and the hospital of St John the Baptist were the only others with staff. The hospital was a humble affair, established in the first decade of the thirteenth century by Bishop Jocelyn and his brother Bishop Hugh of Lincoln, both natives of Wells Manor.[95] A chapel was erected in the Southover area in the twelfth century, fashionably dedicated to Thomas Becket. But it never developed into a parish or staffed church, presumably reflecting the limited suburban growth after the twelfth century. Whatever expansion the later Middle Ages would bring, religious life would take place within these already established institutions, with the single exception of the fifteenth-century almshouse.[96]

Evidence of the town's development in the thirteenth century is relatively sparse, but what there is suggests that it, too, was approaching maturity. It thrived, but in that atmosphere of fierce competition which produced the lengthy 'procession of failure' which Professor Beresford has chronicled.[97] Bishop Jocelyn fought a successful campaign to stop a market from being erected five miles away in Shepton Mallet in 1235, but two years later he was unable to prevent the same vill from initiating an annual fair of three days' duration.[98] The widespread creation of boroughs,

[93] On the development of the cathedral complex, see John Harvey, 'The Building of Wells Cathedral, I: 1175–1307', in Colchester (ed.), *Wells Cathedral*, 52–75.

[94] C. M. Church, *Chapters in the Early History of the Church of Wells, 1136–1323*, (London, 1894), 340; *VCH Somerset*, ii. 163.

[95] *VCH Somerset*, ii. 158–9; and below, Ch. 8, sect. 4.

[96] See below, Ch. 7, sect. 4.

[97] Beresford, *New Towns*, 290–315.

[98] *CCR 1234–7*: 152 and 252.

markets, and fairs in the twelfth and thirteenth centuries ultimately set limits on the growth of all but a few towns. The bishop of Bath had established a borough at Radeclive, in the Mendips west of Cheddar, as early as 1179. It received a royal charter in 1189, but it was a failure, only heard of once again.[99] At a time of intense urban competition Wells benefited from the extra activity stimulated by the church and Wells's own early success. As the bishop's capital, Wells was the centre for a large group of clerks, a stable market for consumables of all sorts.

But the cathedral and administration were only a part of Wells's strikingly diverse economy. Wells was an industrial town from its early beginnings. Bishop Reginald's first charter (1174–80) indicates that Wells was involved in the processing of hides into leather.[100] It is tempting to see this earliest industrial activity as the basis of Wells's more robust future compared to the numerous simple market towns or villages adjacent to monasteries. The development of the leather trade and glove-making was another important bond between the town and its countryside. Wells drew surplus food to its market from the fields nearby, and the hides from the pastures. The glove industry was probably at the heart of the early borough economy. All admissions to the freedom of the city in the late medieval Convocation Books are illustrated with a drawn glove and paid for in part by a dozen pairs, although by that date glovers were not especially conspicuous in the city.

Leather gloves gave way in the thirteenth century to wool and then cloth, and it was these industries and the numerous trades involved in them that were to dominate later economic life. At the time of the Hundred Roll inquests Wells was already involved in the wool trade, and must have been for decades.[101] The cloth trade was strongly enough established by 1260 for Tucker (fuller) Street to have received its name.[102] In 1232 there was already at least one fulling mill at work in the town.[103] The cloth industry would yield plenty in wealth and work in the coming centuries. It was another excellent adaptation of the town to its environment, combining the wool of the manor and the Mendips with the waters of Wells.[104]

[99] Beresford, *New Towns*, 484–5.
[100] WCC 1.
[101] *Rotuli Hundredorum*, ii. 134 (1281).
[102] WTD 4.
[103] *Two Cartularies of Bath Abbey*, ed. William Hunt, SRS 7 (1893), ii. 53.
[104] See below, Ch. 3, sect. 2.

It was an act of policy of a twelfth-century bishop that made Wells, but it was a single feature of a larger plan. The same bishops who established markets, fairs, and borough were simultaneously resurrecting, refurbishing, and supporting the church of Wells. In both cases geographical considerations were decisive. There were no towns within twenty miles of Wells in 1130, and the bishop had no church of importance for his administration of Somerset that was closer to the centre of the county than Bath, excluding the hostile Glastonbury, and one was badly needed.[105] Wells was an obvious choice; it had old claims to importance. Thus town and church flourished together, assisting each other, but the development of one was not simply the result of the prosperity of the other. Wells was always more than market support for the church. From the borough's first days this was a relatively minor, if fortunate, aspect of the economy.

Wells's prosperity was also due to the general population growth throughout England.[106] When the bishops asked for burgesses, people came from all over Great Britain, although, as elsewhere,[107] most came from within the manor.[108] The manor itself shows signs of growth, since it became necessary to subdivide it sometime before the thirteenth century.[109] Wells's timing was perfect. It was established early enough to attract sufficient immigration from the resources of this population boom, and ·grew quickly enough to

---

[105] The independence of Glastonbury was always a problem for the bishops. Savaric succeeded for a time in forcing himself upon the abbey as abbot and bishop of Bath and Glastonbury (1206–19): see *The Chronicle of Glastonbury Abbey*, ed. James P. Curley and trans. David Townsend (London, 1985), 186–97; 'Historia Major', 64; *Papal Letters, 1198–1304*, 22 and 97; *VCH Somerset*, ii. 16–18.

[106] See M. M. Postan, *The Medieval Economy and Society* (Harmondsworth, 1975), 35–8, and *Medieval Trade and Finance* (London, 1973), 130–1; J. D. Chambers, *Population, Economy and Society in Preindustrial England* (Oxford, 1972), 20; T. H. Hollingworth, *Historical Demography* (London, 1969), 387; J. C. Russell, *British Medieval Population* (Albuquerque, NM, 1948); and J. Z. Titow, 'Some Evidence of the Thirteenth-Century Population Increase', *ECHR*, 2nd ser., 14 (1961), 218–23.

[107] Carus-Wilson, 'Stratford-upon-Avon', 50; see below, Ch. 2, sect. 6, for later immigrants.

[108] These origins, among others, are indicated by the last names of pre–1300 inhabitants mentioned in the surviving charters.

[109] Phyllis Hembry, *The Bishops of Bath and Wells, 1540–1640: Social and Economic Problems* (London, 1967), 30, discusses changes in the extent and boundaries of the manor. The change can be seen by comparing the hamlets listed in *Codex Diplomaticus*, 816, with the manorial court records of the 14th cent. (LPL ED 1176, 1177, 1178). The difference is that, by the later period, Wookey was a manor and parish of its own, omitted from Wells Manor.

fight off the challenges of the later markets and boroughs: the earlier into the English medieval town sweepstakes the better.[110]

Potential growth, however, was limited by the rough terrain of the sub-Mendip region, which in turn limited the total population and, therefore, basic market demand. The very shape of the region—more like a string of points than a centre (Wells) with its hinterland—mitigated against growth beyond a certain extent. Wells, furthermore, was no port; it had no commercially useful waterway to the sea twenty miles away, and was only a day's ride from Bristol and Salisbury, great towns that would at times stimulate Wells, but which would never let her rival them.

Wells's size and its role as a regional centre allow it to represent a great many aspects of the smaller English town—the most numerous, perhaps in aggregate the most populous, variety of urban community, and certainly the most characteristic and important in the fabric of medieval country life.[111] Such towns were the hearts of the countryside. Furthermore, their internal nature can be examined more completely than many larger towns simply because the evidence can be encompassed more easily. Here the various forms of social life, the elements of the community, the sources of its identity, the struggles, can be examined and placed in telling relationships to each other. Every county had six to twelve of these smaller centres. Wells only loses its typicality because it was, from the mid-thirteenth century, a cathedral city with a strikingly diverse economy. In appreciating it by these two lights—regional capital and cathedral city—more of the medieval town in England comes into view.

[110] Beresford, *New Towns*, 302–6 and 331, fig. 57, makes this point vividly. Only 6% of towns planted at the same time as Wells (in the 12th cent.) failed, but 23% of those established between 1200 and 1250 did so. The pattern in Wales and Gascony was quite different.

[111] On the subject of small towns and for references, see below Ch. 2, sect. 2.

2

The Size of a Small Town

I. THE PHYSICAL CITY

Much of Wells's particular interest derives from its relatively small size. The populated, well-developed areas of the town ran from Southover on the west, through the centre of the town and the liberty, to the end of the eastern suburb. All in all, the distance was about one and a half miles. Following the roads, from Tucker Street, the other western arm, to the same eastern point is roughly two miles. A two-mile stretch of more or less uninterrupted buildings on both sides of the streets gives the misleading impression of a large town. Towns like Hereford, Gloucester, Nottingham, or even Salisbury or Winchester did not possess such a stretch of urban façade.[1] The sixteenth-century traveller Leland put it simply: 'The town of Wells is large.'[2] But Leland was wrong, misled by the size of the churches and the lengthy development of the main thoroughfare. For the breadth of the developed town was only a third of a mile at its greatest point, and more typically a quarter of a mile. The total area within the greatest extent was only about seven-tenths of a square mile. Except for short stretches, Wells was nowhere three streets deep. Physically, Wells was only of moderate size by the standards of medieval England, and much of its grandeur came from the large and various cathedral complex.

Throughout the later Middle Ages Wells presented itself vigorously and impressively to the onlooker. The imposing cathedral and the tall and elegant parish church gave it—and still give it—its basic shape. They lie at opposite ends of the city, and can be read as symbolically presenting the ecclesiastical and the lay populations and powers of the town. This is because St Cuthbert's was the sole parish church, built and maintained by the town's governing body, which in fact used the church for its own deliberations. The cathedral and the adjacent palace were the seats

[1] See *The Atlas of Historic Towns*, i. ed., M. D. Lobel (London, 1969), relevant maps; *Winchester*, enclosed maps.
[2] *Leland's Itinerary*, ed. L. Toulnun Smith, 5 vols. (London, 1907), i. 144.

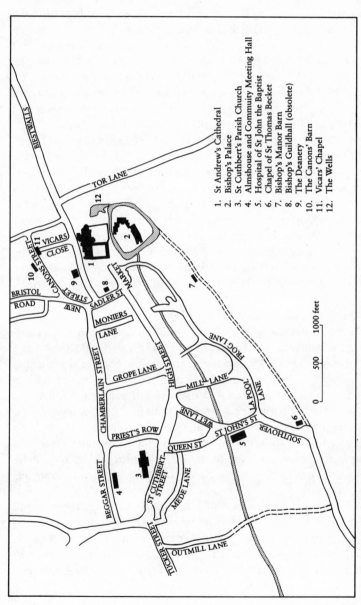

1. St Andrew's Cathedral
2. Bishop's Palace
3. St Cuthbert's Parish Church
4. Almshouse and Commuity Meeting Hall
5. Hospital of St John the Baptist
6. Chapel of St Thomas Becket
7. Bishop's Manor Barn
8. Bishop's Guildhall (obsolete)
9. The Deanery
10. The Canons' Barn
11. Vicars' Chapel
12. The Wells

MAP 3. The City of Wells in the later Middle Ages

of the lord of the town, the bishop, and the ecclesiastical administrators on which he relied. There were no walls around the city, although the burgesses had had dreams of erecting a wall as a sign of their integrity in the 1340s. This absence was not uncommon among English towns, especially the smaller ones. The physical constraints on expansion were provided mainly by geography and the ecclesiastical liberties. Thus, on the north and east of the town the land begins to rise quite steeply in places, and this served to delay development. There was a stream and a flood-prone plain to the south, just behind the High Street (La Pool Lane), which also reduced southward expansion. But more important were the permanent ecclesiastical establishments. The cathedral church and its liberty, which enclosed the houses of its ministrants and servants, blocked most eastern development, and marked the end of the borough. To the south was Wells Manor, the bishop's manor from which the borough had once been removed. To the west was the hospital of St John the Baptist and its lands. Its position determined that twelfth- and thirteenth-century suburban development would take place on Southover and Tucker Streets, two thin arms, which stretch out from the core of the city to surround the substantial holdings of the hospital.

As we shall see, for most of the period under discussion there was no great demand for new developments. Those in place by 1300 represented the extent of the town, and they were divided according to function between a commercial core and a suburban periphery. The core was distinguished by a high level of property subdivision, which, together with the high rents found in this area, indicate the importance of access to the High Street, Sadler Street, and the adjacent market for economic success in the retail trades. It was in these areas, too, that most of the inns were located to attract the travellers, presumably on their way to the market or the cathedral for business.[3]

At the same time, there was a considerable degree of social diversity in the core, reflected in the housing. Often there would be a successful burgess's large and impressive house, usually built in local stone, but the same lot would also have a cottage or two which were appropriate for labourers to rent.[4] Other large holdings

---

[3] CBII: 114, 132, 168; CA, 1497–8; and A. J. Scrase, 'Wells Inns', *SDNQ* 31 (1984), 378–95.

[4] e.g. RIII: 114; CBII: 165 and 172.

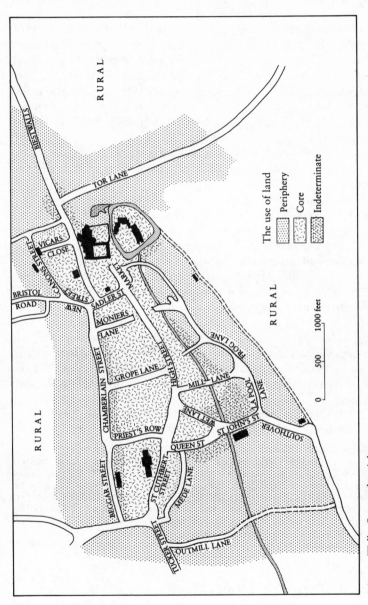

MAP 4. Wells: Core and periphery

had garden space—at the centre of town a perquisite of moderate wealth, although very common in the periphery.

Many central properties were somewhat specialized: ovens were installed by bakers, and woad furnaces by dyers.[5] There were numerous shops and stalls for retailers all over the High Street. Street specialization is difficult to establish in Wells, but tuckers (fullers) continued to be attracted to Tucker Street throughout the Middle Ages, presumably because of its access to some running water, and brothels or prostitutes were usually found in Grope Lane and in some of the suburban areas.[6] But on the whole the town was too small, and its trades too diverse, to require much professional topographical subdivision, which was not all that common in England anyway.[7]

Surrounding the core was an area of more spacious holdings. Again, it appears that both the rich and the poor lived here, although their houses were possibly more segregated by street than in the core. Evidence from the early sixteenth century supports the impression of the property deeds of earlier decades in suggesting that Chamberlain Street was popular with wealthier people, whereas Southover contained people of more modest means.[8]

The periphery was distinguished, however, by the fact that its lands had a different function from those in the core. The predominance of industrial and agricultural use is striking, and can be opposed to the core's concentration on retailing. There was, it must be stressed, a great deal of industry in the core and shops in the suburbs, but the proportions were very different. Mills, for instance, would be over water, whether in the core or the periphery, and whether they were grinding grain or fulling cloth.[9] But it is in the suburbs that we find the many rack-yards for stretching and

---

[5] These were mentioned in leases as valuable fixtures of the properties.

[6] M. D. Lobel (ed.), *Historic Towns*, i. (London, 1969), map 3, for brothels on similarly named streets. In some early deeds the original name, Gropecuntelane, is used. It is possible that after the town developed, the brothel(s) moved into the suburbs. See also *Calendar of Inquisitions Miscellaneous*, (London, 1968), 161, vi. for the 'inn in a suspect place', apparently in the suburbs. See Ruth M. Karras, 'The Regulation of Brothels in Later Medieval England', in Judith M. Bennett, *et al.* (eds.), *Sisters and Workers in the Middle Ages* (Chicago, 1989), 100–34.

[7] *Westminster*, 124–5, fig. 8. Margaret Bonney, *Lordship and the Urban Community* (Cambridge, 1990), 161–8; *Winchester*, i. 335.

[8] See Table 10, below.

[9] For mills, see e.g. WCAC 238, 472; RIII: 351; *CPR 1354–8*: 138–9; *CPR 1348–50*: 307; SRO DD/B, Reg. 2: 401; CBI: 15, 37, 44, 48, and 210; A. J. Scrase, 'The Mills at Wells', *SDNQ* 31 (1982), 238–43. Also Richard Holt, *The Mills of Medieval England* (Oxford, 1988), and below, Ch. 3, sect. 3.

drying fulled cloths,[10] and that the aforementioned Tucker Street was located. There was also a considerable amount of pasture in the periphery, as well as curtilages of arable land adjacent to the houses. Closes of land were often traded separately from any houses, which underlines the fact that they had a value of their own when used to grow grain or vegetables,[11] to build barns to store grain,[12] to dry cloths,[13] to erect dovecotes,[14] or to keep animals on pasture prior to butchering.[15] The topography and use of land are a good indication of the variety of economic life and the use of space that even a small town could sustain.

This picture is complicated further by the impression made by the cathedral and the bishop's household. One large area of the town, outside the jurisdiction of the borough, was the site of many of the private and communal houses of the vicars-choral and the canons. Here were some of the monumental buildings of the town, many of which are still standing. Aside from the cathedral itself and the adjacent walled and moat-surrounded bishop's palace, there is Vicars Close, a small, handsome street of small houses, completed by the 1360s.[16] There are also impressive dining-halls and chapels attached to this little college. On the cathedral green itself were the houses of some of the principal dignitaries of the church: the dean, the chancellor, and the archdeacon of Wells. All impressive stone buildings, many covered, like the cathedral, in artistry, the cathedral buildings point to the significance that the cathedral had in the town's economy, and the way in which it gave, and gives, a patina of grandeur and stability to a modestly sized town.[17]

2. THE SMALLER TOWN IN MEDIEVAL EUROPE

The small town has emerged lately as an analytical type in English medieval history. By European standards, most—if not all—

[10] e.g. CBI: 9, 311; CBII: 74; WTD 71, 77, 88, and 158.
[11] e.g. AH 7.
[12] e.g. WTD 119; CBI: 167, 169, 227, and 271.
[13] See above, n. 10, and CBI: 51, 119; CBII: 74, 132; and AH 62.
[14] e.g. CBI: 97, 271, 311; CBII: 41 and 211.
[15] CBI: 291 and CBII: 84.
[16] See Warwick Rodwell, 'The Buildings of the Vicars Close', in L. S. Colchester (ed.), *Wells Cathedral: A History* (West Compton, 1982), 212–26.
[17] See Nikolaus Pevsner, *North Somerset and Bristol* (Harmondsworth, 1958), 318–23; and Colchester (ed.), *Wells Cathedral*, 159–80.

English towns except the capital were on the small side. There were twenty towns in France in 1300 with populations over 10,000, and most of these were much larger.[18] Italy had forty towns of this size in the early fourteenth century.[19] At the end of the Middle Ages Italian travellers noted how few were the large English towns.[20] But it would seem that too rich a selection of large cities has hidden much of the picture, because the small town flourished everywhere. In Germany towns of fewer than 1,000 people were common;[21] across northern Europe half the urban population lived in towns with fewer than 2,000 people, and 90 per cent of urban communities were within this category.[22] Further study of the southern part of the Continent will almost certainly reveal that there, too, very small towns were numerous and important.[23]

Rodney Hilton has been especially active in making this point for England.[24] He has estimated that in the last quarter of the fourteenth century at least half the urban population lived in boroughs with populations of less than 2,000. He selected a figure of 500 inhabitants as a non-doctrinaire threshold for urban life.[25] His case-studies of the small Midland towns of Evesham, Eynsham, Halesowen, and Thornbury have gone a long way towards proving that such small places were distinctly urban in function.

[18] Jacques Le Goff, 'L'apogée de la France urbaine médiévale', in Jacques Le Goff (ed.), *Histoire de la France Urbaine*, ii. (Paris, 1980), 190–1.

[19] R. H. Britnell, 'The Towns of England and Northern Italy in the Early Fourteenth Century', *ECHR* 2nd ser., 44 (1991), 21–35.

[20] See e.g. *A Relation, or rather, a True Account of the Island of England*, ed. C. A. Sneyd, CS 37 (1847), 31 and 41; on town size in Europe, see J. C. Russell, 'Population in Europe, 500–1500', in *The Fontana Economic History of the Middle Ages*, Carlo M. Cipolla (ed.) (London, 1972), 31–5.

[21] H. Bechtel, *Wirtschaftstil des deutschen Spätmittelalters, 1350–1500* (Munich, 1930), 34 ff.

[22] N. J. G. Pounds, *An Historical Geography of Europe, 450 BC–1330 AD* (Cambridge, 1973), 358.

[23] Fernand Braudel, *Les Structures du Quotidien: Le Possible et l'impossible* (Paris, 1979), 423–5 shows that the small town flourished later, and offers an excellent discussion of this type of society; cf. F. W. Maitland, *Township and Borough* (Cambridge, 1898), 24; and *Coventry*, 7–15.

[24] See R. H. Hilton, *The English Peasantry in the Later Middle Ages* (Oxford, 1975), 76–94; id., *A Medieval Society: The West Midlands* (London, 1966), 167–216; id., 'Towns in English Feudal Society', in *Class Conflict and the Crisis of Feudalism* (London, 1985), 175–86; id., 'The Small Town and Urbanisation: Evesham in the Middle Ages', ibid. 187–93; 'Lords, Burgesses and Hucksters', *P & P* 97 (1982), 3–15; ; 'Towns in Societies: Medieval England', *UHY* (1982), 7–13.

[25] Hilton, 'Towns in Societies', 8–9; cf. Russell, 'Population in Europe', 32 ; and Sylvia L. Thrupp, 'Medieval Industry, 1000–1500', in *Fontana Economic History*, 236.

Other models have been suggested. Professor Raftis has argued that the vill of Godmanchester, neither large nor a borough, provides a prototype for the small town.[26] It may have displayed a few of the features of a town, it may have been another kind of community intermediate between town and village, but we should resist calling it a town. We can preserve a certain technical crispness for the term if we deny it to places like Godmanchester, where most of the people made most of their living directly from agriculture. Yet the place was about as populous as a town like Wells. The same criticism can be made about some of the places described and discussed as towns elsewhere.[27] A town and its people are always involved in some farming and gardening, but in the true town these activities will always be distinctly auxiliary.

On the other hand, in an English context there has been a distinct and continuing tendency to describe some of the country's largest towns as small. Bury St Edmunds and Colchester are two recent examples of places whose historians have stressed their moderate scale.[28] It will be especially worth while to distinguish towns by size and economic function to see whether the difference between the medium-sized and smaller centres was simply one of quantity, or whether there were essential differences. In the mean time, Professor Hilton's town categorization seems the simplest and most judicious. According to his scale, towns like Bury and Colchester were among the middling to larger English towns.[29]

3. THE SIZE OF THE POPULATION

The poll tax of 1377 is the earliest and best source from which to estimate the medieval population of Wells. The list of taxpayers for the city is lost, but we know the total amount that they paid, and we know that everyone paid the same amount. Dividing the sum,

[26] J. A. Raftis, *A Small Town in Late Medieval England: Godmanchester, 1278–1400* (Toronto, 1982).

[27] e.g. J. C. K. Cornwall, 'English Country Towns in the 1520s', *ECHR*, 2nd ser., 15 (1962), 67.

[28] Gottfried, 107, and *Colchester*, 15–16, who goes so far as to entitle the first part of his book 'Rusticity'.

[29] Hilton, 'Feudal Society', 175–7; id., *A Medieval Society*, ch. 5. has argued for two categories of small town; the diversified market centre, and the industrial town which concentrated on one or two specialized industries.

we learn that 901 men and women over the age of 14 paid the tax.[30] To account for children, the indigent, and those who evaded the tax, we shall use a factor of 2.0 rather than Professor Russell's factor of 1.5, which seems to underestimate those who evaded the tax and perhaps the number of children and indigent.[31] Applying the factor produces a total lay population of 1,802.

Too often, urban estimates of population omit an adequate provision for the town's resident clergy.[32] In a village the numbers would have been small, maybe a vicar and a clerk or two, nothing to alter significantly the total population. But in a town, and especially a smaller town like Wells, where there was a large ecclesiastical institution, the clergy could represent a sizeable proportion of the inhabitants, able to have a considerable influence over the economy. From the clerical poll tax of 1377 a figure of 155 clerics has been extracted.[33] This number includes not only the cathedral's staff of 77, but the canons' personal assistants (10), scholars at the cathedral school (34), the brothers of the hospital of St John (10), the parish church staff (14), and unattached clerks (10). There is no reason to suspect any underassessment here, so the population of the entire city in 1377 was about 1,957, just under Hilton's upper threshold for small towns, but well within this category once the clergy, whom Hilton did not assess, are excluded.

Remarkably, 8.2 per cent of the population were in religious orders. Whereas the clergy to lay ratio was 1 : 51.8 for the county as a whole, in Wells it was 1 : 8.7 using Russell's multiplier (1 : 11.6 using ours).[34] The existence of such a high proportion of unproductive people had considerable ramifications for the local economy, especially when that group was as wealthy as the clergy were.

[30] PRO E179/169/36; and J. C. Russell, *British Medieval Population* (Albuquerque, NM, 1948), 142–3. Cf. J. Topham, 'A Subsidy Roll of 51 Edward III', *Archaeologia* 7 (1785), 342. On the urban poll taxes, see P. J. P. Goldberg, 'Urban Identity and the Poll Taxes of 1377, 1379, and 1381', *ECHR*, 2nd ser., 43 (1990), 194–216.

[31] For discussion of the appropriate multipliers, see M. M. Postan, 'Medieval Agrarian Society in its Prime: England', in *Cambridge Economic History of Europe*, i, ed. M. M. Postan, 2nd edn., (Cambridge, 1966), 562; Russell, *Medieval Population*, 124–30; John Hatcher, *Plague, Population and the English Economy* (London, 1977), 13–14; *London*, 49–50.

[32] J. C. Russell, 'The Clerical Population of Medieval England', *Traditio* 2 (1944), 177–212.

[33] PRO E179/4/1.

[34] Russell, *Medieval Population*, 140.

It is difficult to estimate the population of the city before 1377. The visitations of the plague after 1348 had a tremendous impact on the town. The pestilence's first and deepest cut through Somerset claimed perhaps 40 per cent of the population.[35] The subsequent thirty years saw continuing high mortality. In Wells and other towns which were involved ever more deeply and prosperously in the cloth trade the post-plague period was a time of unusually high immigration.[36] This influx makes it all the more difficult to guess at the 1345 population. Nevertheless, since the town had only advanced modestly from its tax ranking of 1334 to its ranking in 1377, there is no reason to think that this immigration made up for the plague mortality and restored pre-plague population levels.[37] Before the Black Death the city's population was perhaps as high as 2,500. In 1300 it was at least this size.[38] After the plague it had fallen to about 1,500, but grew to nearly 2,000 by 1377.

Topographical evidence indicates that, although the town experienced a period of considerable growth in the thirteenth century, the damage of the fourteenth century was to some extent permanent. Peripheral streets such as Tucker, Beggar, and New, which had been established in the thirteenth century, were failures

[35] E. H. Bates Harbin, 'The "Black Death" in Somerset, 1348–49', *SANHS* 68 (1917), 89–112; J. F. Chanter, 'The Court Rolls of the Manor of Curry Rivel in the Years of the Black Death, 1348–9', *SANHS* 56 (1910), 85–98; see also Russell, *Medieval Population*, 214–34, esp. 222–3; Hatcher, *Plague, Population*, 22–9; J. F. D. Shrewsbury, *A History of Bubonic Plague in the British Isles* (Cambridge, 1971), 63–8; J. M. W. Bean, 'Plague, Population and Economic Decline in the Later Middle Ages', *ECHR*, 2nd ser., 15 (1963), 423–4.

[36] e.g. *Colchester*, 86–97; Hatcher, *Plague, Population*, 34, notes growth of York, Newcastle, Norwich, Boston, Lynn, Coventry, Southampton, and Bristol; see Russell, *Medieval Population*, 260–70, on general growth.

[37] R. E. Glasscock, *The Lay Subsidy of 1334* (London, 1975), 263, 272, and 273.

[38] On the important question that we are not taking up—when did population begin to decline—see Barbara Harvey, 'The Population Trend in England, 1300–48', *TRHS*, 5th ser., 16 (1966), 23–42; ead., 'Introduction: the "Crisis" of the Early Fourteenth Century', in Bruce M. S. Campbell (ed.), *Before the Black Death* (Manchester, 1991), 1–24; and Richard M. Smith, 'Demographic Developments in Rural England, 1300–48: A Survey', ibid. 25–77; M. M. Postan, 'Some Economic Evidence of Decline in Population in the Later Middle Ages', *ECHR*, 2nd ser., 2 (1950), 221–46; id., *The Medieval Economy and Society* (Harmondsworth, 1975), 39–41; J. Z. Titow, *English Rural Society, 1200–1350* (London, 1969), 66–78; Bruce M. S. Campbell, 'Population Pressure, Inheritance and the Land Market in a Fourteenth-Century Community', in Richard M. Smith (ed.), *Land, Kinship and Life-Cycle* (Cambridge, 1984), 87–134; Jack Ravensdale, 'Population Changes and the Transfer of Customary Land on a Cambridgeshire Manor in the Fourteenth Century', ibid. 197–225.

by the later fourteenth century.[39] The subdividing of urban properties had already peaked by 1325, and was virtually non-existent for the remainder of the fourteenth century.[40] Furthermore, it was clear that the ambitious boundaries of the city (most notably, New Street and Beggar Street on the north-west side) would never be filled or fully developed.[41]

Population after 1377 can be assessed from several sources which together can produce a fairly well-developed picture. A terminal count can be derived from sixteenth-century evidence, the best of which is the Henrican lay subsidy. The returns, for this, while much smaller as a sample than the poll tax, were much fuller than the Edwardian lay subsidies. Furthermore, they have been studied in detail by historians, who have evaluated their accuracy and suggested multipliers.[42] Wells's return includes 221 names,[43] of whom 167 were assessed on their goods, and 54 on their wages, the latter representing some of the humbler men of the town who probably did not have families, and so were taxed notwithstanding their small income.[44] There were only a few women on the list, and they were mainly widows of substance. Generally, those taxed were heads of households.

It has been estimated that evasion and exemptions amounted to between 33 and 37 per cent of the total.[45] Applied to Wells, the 209 probable heads of households represent only two-thirds of the city's households. Thus there were approximately 314 households. Charles Phythian-Adams has argued persuasively that an average household in contemporary Coventry had 3.8 individuals.[46] Since

[39] New Street is mentioned first in 2 later 13th-cent. deeds, and we cannot say exactly when it was developed: RI: 85^d and 87.

[40] A. J. Scrase, 'Development and Change in Burgage Plots: The Example of Wells', *Journal of Historical Geography* 15 (1989), 353 and fig. 3.

[41] These streets were especially rich in cottages, gardens, and empty plots (tofts). Beggar Street was virtually uninhabited, an industrial street.

[42] Cornwall, 'Country Towns' 57–60, seems to me convincing on this point, but the possibility of considerably higher evasion is made clear by *Coventry*, 12–13; see also Colin Platt, *Medieval Southampton* (London, 1973), 263; and *Winchester*, 368–70.

[43] PRO E179/169/156.

[44] Twelve of the wage-earners were called *serviens* and were attached in the return to a particular master. They probably lived with their masters and did not have households of their own. For this reason, they are excluded from the household calculations that follow. On the problem of the servants in the return, see *Winchester*, 368; and Cornwall, 'Country Towns', 66–7.

[45] Cornwall, 'Country Towns,' 59–60; *Winchester*, 368, calculates evasion at between 10 and 33%; *Coventry*, 12, puts it as high as 50%.

[46] *Coventry*, 238–48.

Coventry was entering a population crisis characterized by 'a penury of people' which cannot be assumed at Wells, we have preferred a slightly higher factor of 4.0. This yields a total lay population in 1524 of 1,256 people.[47] The clerical population probably did not fall significantly, and certainly not substantially, after 1377. Fewer canons lived in the city,[48] but most of the cathedral positions involved actually tending the church and were endowed. Furthermore, there had been some new chantry endowments requiring more chaplains.[49] There were still about 150 clergy at Wells, representing more than 10 per cent of the total population of 1,406 people. The size of the lay city fell from 1,802 in 1377 to 1,256 a little less than 150 years later, a fall of nearly a third.[50]

To put this population decline into perspective: Wells could have realized this significant transformation by an average net loss of only 3.2 people net per annum during the intervening years. The social and economic impact of decline can only be discussed fully when the trend and rates of change are known.

4. POPULATION CHANGE: DILAPIDATION AND DECAYED RENTS

The population of medieval towns could be startlingly volatile, owing to high mortality rates and a migration pattern closely tied to the prevailing economic conditions, often short-term fluctuations in the demand for labour. Coventry saw its population fall by almost 14 per cent in the three years from 1520 to 1523.[51] There is no

---

[47] Ibid. 244. A factor of 3.8 would yield a population of 1,193; Russell's lower estimate of 3.5 would yield only 1,099 people (*Medieval Population*, 22–38); while *Winchester*, 368, uses a higher family multiplier of 4.5. This has been a disputed subject, but mainly in the context of the rural family; see e.g. J. Krause, 'The Medieval Household: Large or Small', *ECHR*, 2nd ser., 9 (1957), 420–32; Titow, *English Rural Society*, 83–91.

[48] In 1394–5 there were 20 canons in residence in the city (CA, 1394–5), but in 1490–1 there were only 12 (ibid. 1490–1).

[49] e.g. the chantries of Bishop Bubwith (ibid. 1430–1) added four new chaplains; John Storthwayt also endowed a chaplain (RIII: 306–10).

[50] Absolute decline of the urban population in the later Middle Ages is not a contentious issue: see e.g. A. R. Bridbury, 'English Provincial Towns in the Later Middle Ages', *ECHR*, 2nd ser., 34 (1981), 3–4; *Colchester*, 202; D. M. Palliser, *Tudor York* (Oxford, 1979), 124; S. H. Rigby, 'Urban Decline in the Later Middle Ages: The Reliability of the Non-Statistical Evidence', *UHY* (1984), 49; Gottfried, 70.

[51] e.g. *Coventry*, 289–98; cf. Jacques Rossiaud, 'Crises et consolidations, 1330–1530', in Le Goff (ed.), *Histoire urbaine*, ii. 473–6.

reason to suppose that any such upheaval took place at Wells, but it reminds us of the fragility of our snapshot estimates, even when they are accurate for the year in question. By examining the extent of property dilapidation and declining rents, we can suggest some conclusions about the pattern of population change between 1377 and 1524.

The evidence of urban dilapidation is striking, if sometimes difficult to date.[52] Perhaps the most notable instance of dilapidation in Wells is the history of Moniers Lane. This street was developed in the 1340s, first through piecemeal acquisition, by the merchant Peter Moniers. He acquired enough properties in the block between Sadler Street and Grope Lane to create the new lane in about 1343. He left it to his wife when he died in the early 1350s.[53] Strikingly, it continued to thrive in the 1350s, and was sold for £133 6s. 8d. in 1369, coming into the cathedral's hands.[54] At that time it was covered by houses, a bakery and its appurtenances, and a cottage. But in 1425 part of the lane was let as a toft, an empty plot, to which there had been no earlier reference, and nearly 100 feet, or one-third of the lane, were let to Thomas Frome in the same year as a garden, worth only a shilling.[55] By the 1460s and 1470s the lane had only two houses upon it and was mainly tofts and gardens.[56] Subsequently, the street entirely disappeared. Moniers Lane prospered even in the wake of the plague crisis, presumably riding a wave of post-plague immigration. It succumbed to some other malaise at the beginning of the fifteenth century.[57] It is clear, then, that much of the topographical contraction was not due to the plague, from which there must have been at least partial recovery.

By the first quarter of the fifteenth century tofts—decayed, unused building sites—were numerous in all parts of the town. In

---

[52] See R. B. Dobson, 'Urban Decline in Late Medieval England', *TRHS*, 5th ser., 27 (1977), 4–8; cf. *Coventry*, 35, and *Westminster*, 74–7.

[53] WCAC 336 (1355) calls Margery a widow. For a complete discussion of Peter Moniers and his properties' history, see Anthony Scrase, 'Peter le Monier and his Lane', forthcoming.

[54] WCAC 391.

[55] WCAC 582; and Vicars-Choral, 4.

[56] Vicars-Choral, 10.

[57] See *Westminster*, 65–74, and *Winchester*, 243–6, which note the recovery of rents and property development after the plague visitations, especially from the 1360s and 1370s. For similar early 15th-cent. developments, see *Westminster*, 74–81.

Wells and most urban usages the term 'toft' or 'toftum' meant a building site, the site of a house.[58] The *Oxford English Dictionary*'s examples also indicate that it referred to the piece of land, not the physical house. In *rural* circumstances it could mean an entire homestead, but in a town it usually meant a piece of land where a house or building had once stood. A 1592 example is decisive for us: 'A toft is the place wherein a messuage hath stand.'[59] The toft implies extreme decay, an empty site. Many of our examples below will unequivocally bear out this definition. But for the present there is the Southover toft which was yielding 16*d*. to the town in 1427–8, but which property had once returned 9*s* per annum.[60] No streets were spared the existence of empty, unproductive space. In 1423 the town let a Grope Lane toft to Richard Dyer, and it sat between a privately owned toft and a tenement.[61] In 1433 Thomas Sholer rented a High Street toft, as did William Beaufitz in 1438.[62] The empty spaces were universal, no street was without them, and the High Street was particularly affected.

Many of the toft conveyances or leases stipulated that the property was to be rebuilt. Often the borough made it a condition of taking up a toft that the tenant build a tenement within a specified amount of time. Thus, when John Chew took possession of a Priest Row toft in 1444, he promised to build within the year.[63] John Leve the dyer rented a Wet Lane property in 1411, and was to build a house within two years or face a 100*s*. fine.[64] In other words, the owners, in this case the borough, were looking to have their properties restored to value, but, as often as not, they were unsuccessful.

A cathedral property on Mill Lane, described as ruinous in 1372, worth only 3*s*. per annum, was let sometime between 1381 and 1392, when it was described as a toft. The tenant agreed to build a house there, but by 1396 it was let anew, still with no house, being worth only 1*d*. per annum.[65] In 1426 the town let a Beggar Street

[58] *The Revised Medieval Latin Wordlist*, ed. R. E. Latham (London, 1965), 486, gives the meanings as 'toft, building site'.
[59] *The Compact Edition of the Oxford English Dictionary*, ii. (Oxford, 1971), 3340.
[60] SRO DD/CC 111736.
[61] CBI: 237.
[62] CBI: 276 and 297.
[63] CBI: 314.
[64] CBI: 189.
[65] Sherwin Bailey, *Wells Manor of Canon Grange* (London, 1985), 138.

toft to the chaplain Thomas Willy at a rent of 4s. per annum under condition that he build a house, but he had given up the property within two years, when the town passed it on to Henry Selwood under the same stipulation, but with a rent reduced to 3s. 4d. per annum.[66] Indeed, the rapid turnover of tenants was not rare, suggesting that they could find a better deal.

Very often we can see properties on their way to becoming tofts through the failure of the tenants to fulfil the maintenance contracts to which they had agreed. In 1409 the town called William Laurence and John Bikhull into court to warn them to repair their tenements.[67] In 1411 John Port was warned to make amends to his Wet Lane tenement,[68] and in a concerted effort in 1466 five different tenants were similarly warned.[69] No doubt this pressure was often successful, but it also happened that a tenant who had taken a property under condition to build on it did nothing, and that necessary repairs were not executed. The main reason for this record of poor maintenance was the existence of a tenants' market. The standard lease, requiring the tenant to take care of repairs and to leave the property in as good a condition as he found it, became almost a formality, not taken very seriously by the tenant. Indeed, in 1466, at the very time that the town was trying to enforce the maintenance clauses, some of their new leases stipulated that the Borough Community would do the repairs itself.[70] It did try to raise the rents to compensate for the new costs, but little success can have followed this stratagem, as the burgesses soon reverted to the old form of lease. Tenants were scarce and held the upper hand in their relations with the landlord. The town received the rent, dilapidated or not, but, once the tenant was gone, there was often little chance of renting a declining tenement anew without great financial outlay.[71]

If physical dilapidation was the most obvious proof of the fact that the tenements and other properties of fifteenth-century Wells

---

[66] CBI: 253 and 262; SRO DD/CC 111736 describes Selwood's holding as a parcel of land.

[67] CBI: 177.

[68] CBI: 195.

[69] CBII: 59.

[70] e.g. ibid. 56 and 114; *Winchester*, 237, notes that property repaired by the owner usually carried a rent one-third higher.

[71] e.g. CBII: 144. Scrase, 'Development and Change', fig. 3, indicates the fact that some development and investment was always taking place.

were in reduced demand, there is also more direct and precise evidence. The Borough Community of Wells was one of the city's largest landlords in the later Middle Ages. The rent collector's account for 1427–8 has survived, and, fortunately, it indicates when rents were 'decayed' and by how much they had been reduced. The accounts refer to some 130 properties, which probably represented a quarter of all properties in Wells.[72] An account for 1550–1 is also extant, and provides for some long-range 'snapshot' comparisons. We know, by comparing some of the entries with information from the leases recorded in the Convocation Books, that the list of decays is only partial. The situation was worse, therefore, than the statistics reflect.

We cannot assign a precise chronology of decline, because we do not have a series of accounts. We can, however, dismiss the possibility that the decayed rents of 1427–8 are obsolete survivals of those caused by the fall in population between 1340 and 1370. The Borough Community only really began to accumulate a lot of property after the plague. A fragmentary account of *c.*1370 (only the left half survives) indicates that the Community then possessed fewer than ninety properties.[73] Furthermore, we can trace many of the decayed properties, and see that they were conveyed towards the end of the fourteenth and in the early fifteenth centuries.[74] The 1427–8 account probably reflects recent changes in rental values; certainly it will include those depreciations which took place since 1400, very probably since 1420, and possibly within the last year.

The rental losses recorded were substantial. About 24 per cent of the tenancies were paying less than they had done. Revenue was down by £10 7*s*; total income was £60 7*s*. 8*d*. Every area of the town was affected, but most striking was the High Street, the centre of activity, where most of the valuable properties were located. Only 13 per cent of the properties elsewhere showed declining rents, but the figure was 53 per cent on the main thoroughfare, 20 out of 38 holdings. Overall, the income from rents across the Community's estate was down 14.6 per cent.[75] In a period

[72] According to A. J. Scrase's survey, deposited and mapped in Wells Town Archives.

[73] WTA 86.

[74] See below, Ch. 4, sect. 3, for a discussion of the accumulation and total value of Community property.

[75] SRO DD/CC 111736.

generally associated with inflation, the decline in the value of urban property is all the more meaningful, pointing strongly to a fall in the demand for accommodation and in the number of people in the city. The timing of Wells's difficulties corresponds to the evidence of dilapidation and contraction which has been discovered in other English towns.[76]

The intensity of the difficulties can be observed by seeing the lengths to which landlords such as the borough were willing to go to satisfy their individual tenants and to have repairs carried out. The timing of these troubles confirms our chronology of decline. In 1408, instead of paying for repairs as he was bound to do, the enterprising Ralph Averey induced the borough to waive half of his two-mark rent.[77] In 1422 Robert Polglas repaired his High Street tenement only when the town remitted his rent for a year.[78] And in the same year Averey managed to receive yet another 40s. to reroof his tenement.[79] The town was also willing to help out by providing materials, as in 1429, when they gave the freestone for a chimney that John Pecher was to add to his house.[80] Similarly, in 1437 they gave John Cornish a keystone and door-jamb for refurbishments.[81] The same Pecher rented a Southover messuage in 1433, and the town promised two wagon-loads of stone if he would build a house within two years.[82] The able negotiator Ralph Averey rented a site in La Pool in 1428 on condition that he build a well-made house within two years. The rent was to be 4s. per annum, but if he failed to build, he would be charged 13s. 4d. per annum for five years.[83] Thomas Sholer rented a High Street toft in 1431 at a rent of 12d. per annum, at which low rent it remained for sixty-one years, even though he was to rebuild the tenement.[84] In 1423 the town effectively relaxed a rent for five years if the tenants would rebuild their dilapidated house.[85] Alice Pope was offered the remission of a year's rent if she would undertake repairs to her tenement in 1425.[86] Again, the examples reflect the fact that the 1420s and

---

[76] *Westminster*, 80, summarizes the findings.
[77] CBI: 175.   [78] CBI: 234.
[79] CBI: 234; see also Alice Pope's remission of 1425 (CBI: 248).
[80] CBI: 270.   [81] CBI: 294.
[82] CBI: 283.   [83] CBI: 263.
[84] CBI: 276.   [85] CBI: 236.
[86] CBI: 248.

1430s were years of deepening crisis. Unable on the basis of rents to entice people to come to the city, the favourable terms mainly benefited those who had work and interests in the town already.

From the 1420s until mid-century the borough exerted itself to attract or to keep tenants, and to stop the erosion of its inheritance.[87] But it was competing against other landlords, individual and corporate. The cathedral escheator noted in 1438–9 that many of the houses under his supervision were let at reduced rents, others were without tenants, still others ruinous.[88]

It is possible that there never was much of a recovery from the difficulties of the first decades of the fifteenth century, and that, at best, a slower slide prevailed. In the last two decades of the fifteenth century and the beginning of the sixteenth the town had great difficulty in finding anyone willing to accept the position of civic rent collector. Several of those who did take it on were unable to make their accounts balance.[89] As early as 1467, around the time that the town was again pressing for properties to be properly maintained, a general fine of 50s. was threatened (in a non-property case) for 'the repair of the common rents of the town', where previously the recipient of the fine would have been the St Cuthbert's fabric fund.[90] And the financial retrenchment apparent at the beginning of the sixteenth century is indisputable. The town council was forced

to sette a sadde rewle in tyme comynge for the meteynynge of the churche of Seynte Cuthberte and also for the byldynge and Reparacion of the comon lyflode [livlihood, i.e. rental properties] the whiche lyflode is now full ruynense and gretely in Decay. And can not be competently a mended and repayred with oute grete summes of money.[91]

Communal entertainments and stipends were withdrawn. And in 1511 the council took the extraordinary step of requiring incoming councillors to make a contribution towards the rebuilding of a decayed High Street property.[92] The decline took place at varying speeds, aggravating some pre-plague waste and the perhaps limited

[87] For example, there were 10 relevant entries in 1447–8 (CBI: 322).
[88] EA, 1438–9.
[89] e.g. CBII: 134, 138, 174, 192, and 267.
[90] CBII: 62.
[91] CBII: 239.
[92] CBII: 264.

plague damage, but it would seem that the fifteenth century was indeed a time of great and persistent contraction and consequent dilapidation. By the beginning of the sixteenth century there is no reason to be surprised at the town's complaint. The Community's accounts for 1550–1 show income from urban properties as only £57 7s. per annum, less than the income of 125 years earlier, and in the face of some general inflation.[93] This poor financial showing gives further support to our earlier population estimates, pointing to the weakness of the demand for housing throughout the period from 1420 to 1550. The fifteenth-century Borough Community and the town itself were in a constant low-level crisis, but they had no weapons with which to defend themselves. The city shrank.

5. POPULATION CHANGE: THE ADMISSIONS LIST

The argument for decline receives further and more detailed support from an examination of the city's freedom lists, which are conveniently extant from 1377.[94] The difficulties of using these lists to speculate about a town's overall population have been noted by historians.[95] The burgesses represent varying proportions of the populations in different towns, but always a minority. The poor, the more humble trades, labourers, and women are heavily underrepresented.[96] Children, as always, do not appear. Worse, however, is the possibility that the proportion of people who received the freedom of the city was controlled by the authorities

---

[93] WTA, 1550–1 Borough Community Account.

[94] CBI and CBII.

[95] R. B. Dobson, 'Admissions to the Freedom of the City of York in the Later Middle Ages', *ECHR*, 2nd ser., 26 (1973), 16; *Exeter Freemen 1266–1967*, eds., M. M. Rowe and Andrew Jackson, Devon and Cornwall Record Society, ES 51 (Exeter, 1973), pp. xii–xiii; E. M. Veale, 'Craftsmen and the Economy of London in the Fourteenth Century', in E. J. Holleander and W. Kellaway (eds.), *Studies in London History*, (London, 1969); and D. J. Keene's review, 'Sources for Medieval Urban History', in *Archives* 11 (1974), 221–2; D. M. Woodward, 'Sources for Urban History: The Freemen's Rolls', *Local Historian* 9 (1970), 89–95. In addition to Veale, they are used in, *inter alia*, *Colchester*, 95–6 and 202–5, and A. R. Bridbury, *Economic Growth: England in the Later Middle Ages* (London, 1962), 4–6, 19–30, and 61–2.

[96] For further discussion of burgess membership, including the place of women, see below, Ch. 5, sect. 1. For an idea of the level of participation from trade to trade, see J. F. Pound, 'The Validity of the Freemen's Lists: Some Norwich Evidence', *ECHR*, 2nd ser., 34 (1981), 53, table 2.

for political and economic reasons, and fluctuated because of non-demographic factors.[97]

In Wells's case, there was no alteration in the price of admission throughout the period. Nor is there other evidence of a significant change in admissions policy.[98] The composition of the burgesses also strongly suggests that there was no radical change in the kind of man admitted. The fairly humble tradesmen, tilers for instance, continue to be represented alongside the great merchants at least into the sixteenth century.[99] Also, a rather large proportion of the adult men joined the guild. Both in 1377 and 1524 we can estimate this proportion, and it was relatively stable. In the early period burgesses accounted for roughly 11 per cent of the total population, and in the 1520s about 9 per cent. There is therefore a sound basis for considering the trend and size of the freedom admissions as a rough indication of population, although the decline of the freemen probably slightly exaggerates the decline of the whole population.

The rates of admission between 1380 and 1530 are displayed in Figure 1 on a decade-by-decade basis. There were no sharp drops in the rate of admission apart from the 1480s, and this contraction was from the surprisingly high enrolment of the 1460s and 1470s. After five decades of relatively stable admissions (1380–1429), averaging 82 per decade, the next thirty years averaged only just over 66, a fall of about one-fifth. Furthermore, decline in the decennial rate is evident from 1410. This indicates a steady contraction from that date for forty years, but no sudden onset of crisis.[100]

The effect of declining admissions on the total burgess population was sharper than Figure 1 suggests, however, and its pattern may reflect the population trend of the city. Table 1 takes into account an estimated rate of decease as well as admission to the ranks of the burgesses. This necessarily makes the evidence speculative to the extent that the tabulated data have assumed that new burgesses will disappear from the rolls exactly twenty years after entering them. Twenty years has been found elsewhere to be the life expectancy of a burgess from the time of his admission to the Community.[101] The Wells evidence suggests that this figure is

[97] Dobson, 'Admissions to the Freedom', 18; and Maryanne Kowaleski, 'The Commercial Dominance of a Medieval Provincial Oligarchy: Exeter in the Late Fourteenth Century', *Mediaeval Studies* 46 (1984), 356–8.
[98] See below, Ch. 5, sect. 1.
[99] See below, Ch. 5, sect. 2.
[100] For very similar conclusions, see *Westminster*, 171.
[101] Palliser, *Tudor York*, 148 n. 7.

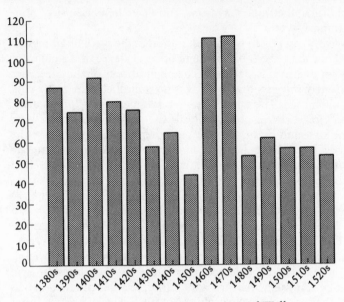

FIG. 1. Decennial admission to the freedom of Wells
Source: CBI and CBII.

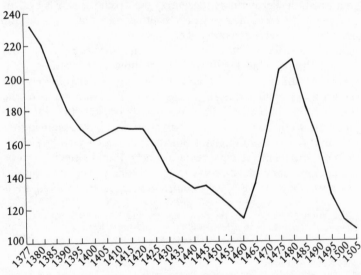

FIG. 2. Estimated burgess population (five-year averages)

TABLE 1. *Estimated Burgess Population*
(five-year averages)

Years	Burgesses	Years	Burgesses
1377	232	1445–9	134
1380–4	220	1450–4	128
1385–9	199	1455–9	121
1390–4	180	1460–4	114
1395–9	169	1465–9	136
1400–4	162	1470–4	169
1405–9	166	1475–9	204
1410–14	170	1480–4	210
1415–19	169	1485–9	182
1420–4	169	1490–4	161
1425–9	158	1495–9	128
1430–4	142	1500–4	113
1435–9	138	1505–9	107
1440–4	132		

Source: Admissions lists in CBI and CBII

plausible. Burgesses continued to be mentioned in the court records for about twelve or thirteen years after admission, but plainly survived for several years after this. Masters of the Community, for instance, had considerably longer official lives, but they were only recorded more thoroughly because of their continued political activity.[102] At any rate, a different assumption of longevity would only alter the detail of the table, not the general pattern.

The decline at the very beginning of Table 1 reflects the high immigration and burgess membership which was stimulated by the first decades of the cloth industry's boom, and perhaps by somewhat greater enthusiasm for the Community's political work against the bishop in the mid-fourteenth century.[103] The fall in the early sixteenth century—and, indeed, part of the decline throughout—must be moderated by the fact that, at the end of the period in question, the participation rate in the Community had fallen by about one-fifth. Figure 2 graphically displays the numbers of Table 1.

Bearing these factors in mind, the low point of fifteenth-century

[102] There is no reason to think that the differences in wealth among the burgesses were sufficient to affect their mortality. Most of them would have been quite secure by contemporary standards.

[103] On the cloth industry, see below, Ch. 3, sect. 2; and see below, Ch. 4, sect. 2, for the political circumstances of the 14th cent.

population can be confirmed to have been in the late 1450s and early 1460s. It was at this point that new admissions and the death of old members combined to reduce both the Community and, I am arguing, the overall population. The number of inhabitants may have been almost half the 1370s total; certainly, the decline was substantial. Fortunes were restored almost to their highest post-plague levels in the period from 1475 to 1484, to judge from the high admission and probable immigration levels of the 1460s and 1470s. Just such a surge in population had taken place after the first plague, with new streets suddenly being planned once again, and the immigration wave that set up the 1377 population apex under-way. In the 1470s some of the vacant houses and streets were reoccupied.

From 1480 the town was ageing and shrinking once again, as immigration and births failed to keep pace with deaths and departures. The overall trend from the late fifteenth century supports the plausibility of 1,260 as a figure for the town's approximate size from 1500.

6. MIGRATION

We have been claiming that population growth was determined by surges in immigration rather than by falls in the mortality rate or by increased fertility. A number of historians have made it clear that mortality was very high in late medieval towns, and remained so, perhaps becoming worse in the latter part of the fifteenth century. Most strikingly, John Hatcher has demonstrated that the 'exceed-ingly well fed, clothed and sheltered' monks of Christ Church, Canterbury, faced deteriorating expectations of life from the 1430s.[104] Urban congestion and sanitation were probably to blame. They allowed disease to develop quickly and to spread all too effectively. Even after the worst ravages of the plague were past, conditions deteriorated.

Other studies have confirmed that townsmen were quite unable to reproduce themselves. Robert Gottfried has noted how few wills

---

[104] John Hatcher, 'Mortality in the Fifteenth Century: Some New Evidence', *ECHR*, 2nd ser., 39 (1986), 19–38, esp. 33; see also Bean, 'Plague, Population', 430; and Robert Gottfried, *Epidemic Disease in Fifteenth-Century England* (Leicester, 1978), 138–9.

show evidence of surviving sons.[105] For a number of reasons, his results almost certainly overstate the generative failure and the sharpness of the mortality, but there is no question of the nature of the difficulty.[106] Wells provides proof of its own.

Although the burgesses generally attracted 25–30 per cent of the eligible population (resident adult men) into their ranks, the proportion admitted by virtue of patrimonial rights, their fathers' membership, was always small. From 1380 to 1529 such admissions to the freedom constituted only 14.8 per cent of the total.[107] Virtually all other burgesses were drawn from the ranks of the 'foreigners', the completely unenfranchised. Some of them were probably the sons of inhabitants of the town who had never been able or willing to join the burgesses, but the majority must have come to Wells as immigrants, either as apprentices or young journeymen.[108] Renewal from outside was essential for community maintenance and growth. Furthermore, the admissions by patrimony grew throughout the fifteenth century, suggesting that immigration may have been declining.

The origins of the burgesses of Wells are not recorded in the list of admissions, as at Romney and other towns.[109] But, on the evidence of place-name surnames, most came from fairly nearby.[110] This was also the case at Romney, Winchester, Leicester, Nottingham, Norwich, and York—everywhere, it would appear, except London.[111] Most common were those from Wells Manor's hamlets and a group of Mendip and Somerset vills within about a twelve-mile radius of the city. The bulk of those whose names indicate that their origins were further afield came from the West Country,

[105] Gottfried, *Epidemic Disease*, 194–5.

[106] First among these is his failure to account for pre-testamentary disposal of property to principal heirs. Very often, property enfeoffment took place during the father's lifetime. There is also the possibility that providing his son with an apprenticeship was sometimes considered gift enough, for a father, especially for second sons.

[107] Comparable proportions have been found elsewhere: e.g. Kowaleski, 'Commercial Dominance', 357; Dobson, 'Admissions to the Freedom', 10.

[108] For more on the foreigners, see below, Ch. 7, sect. 1.

[109] A. F. Butcher, 'The Origins of Romney Freemen, 1433–1523', *ECHR*, 2nd ser., 27 (1974), 16–27; and *Colchester*, 96–7.

[110] See Peter McLure, 'Patterns of Migration in the Late Middle Ages: The Evidence of English Place-Name Surnames', *ECHR*, 2nd ser., 32 (1975), 67–82; and *Winchester*, 371–9.

[111] Butcher, 'Romney Freemen', 20–2; *Winchester*, 371–9; McLure, 'Patterns of Migration', 178, table 4.

especially the south of Somerset. Cornwall and Devon were well represented, but overall representation from the north and east, from nearby Gloucestershire for instance, was distinctly lower. There was an eastward drift of population.

Men also settled in Wells from further away. Names like London, Romsey, Wycombe, Yarmouth, Winchester, Galeway, Scot, and Leicester occur, indicating origins all over Britain, even though we cannot be sure that they came directly to Wells, rather than after years or even lifetimes at a nearer town or village. But people certainly immigrated over long distances. French and Burgundian merchants were in lot and scot in Wells, living with their families, before the Black Death.[112] In 1439 John Power paid a fine for leave to stay in Wells rather than return to his native Ireland.[113] John Viltere, a 'ducheman', became a burgess in 1408,[114] while in 1436 men from Delft, Leiden, and Schiedam—all in Holland—were living in Wells alongside a Danziger.[115] In 1523–4 the lay subsidy return also noted four aliens as present and taxable in Wells, about 2 per cent of the total.[116] The trade routes and paths of the English armies took the native inhabitants away, but often brought back merchants and skilled craftsmen to enrich even one of England's smaller cities. Small and 'provincial' in the later Middle Ages, Wells was nevertheless open to, and settled by, people from all over the country and beyond.

7. RELATIVE SIZE

For most of the later Middle Ages Wells was a small town. It had a population of less than 2,000 for the entire period after the Black Death, although it may have been as large as 2,500 in 1300. At no point, however, was it ranked higher than fortieth among the towns

[112] CPR 1324–7: 23 and 311; CPR 1327–30: 373; CPR 1334–48: 427. On resident aliens, see Sylvia L. Thrupp, 'The Alien Population of England in 1440', *Speculum* 32 (1957), 262–73; and *Winchester*, 380–4.

[113] CPR 1391–6: 460.

[114] CBI: 175.

[115] CPR 1429–36: 543, 549 (2), and 582; cf. an alien subsidy return such as PRO E179/235/60 (1452–3), which lists aliens, but does not specify where in Somerset and Dorset they lived.

[116] PRO E179/169/156. Thrupp, 'Alien Population', 266, thought aliens across the country constituted no more than 1% of the population; in a town such as Winchester the figure was 3%, see *Winchester*, 363.

of England. In 1334 its collective tax assessment was forty-eighth in the nation.[117] According to the first poll tax, it was England's forty-first town. Towns then of a comparable size included Lichfield, Newbury, Bridgnorth, Cirencester, and Westminster. Derby, Reading, and Southampton were only slightly larger.[118] By 1524 Wells was probably no longer one of the top fifty towns, but nor had it suffered as many had. When John Leland made his tour through the city in the middle of the century, he described the town as 'large', and made no discouraging remarks about decay.[119]

In relative terms, Wells held its own for most of the period. Founded in the middle of the twelfth century, Wells experienced its most unrestrained growth before 1300.[120] By that date it had already successfully staked its claim as a town of some regional significance, relevant beyond its own immediate market area. The growth of the cathedral church from 1240 contributed to the town's growth and prestige. In the fourteenth century the rise of the cloth industry boosted Wells somewhat, but by 1325 or so it had already settled into its place. Not until the early modern period would the city begin to plunge in relative size, increasingly bypassed by trade and new industry as well as by the sort of large-scale tourism that Bath and other spa towns were generating in the eighteenth century.

Wells in the Middle Ages was never what it is today, a town of almost the lowest rank. It was always larger and more important in industry and administration than most of the very small west Midland towns which Professor Hilton has discussed. Thornbury, for instance, had only about 500 pre-plague inhabitants.[121] In discussing other aspects of Wells's economy, social organization, and culture, we should bear in mind this question of comparative size, so that we determine whether, in functional, anatomical terms, Wells and other towns of its size ought to be classified with the truly small town. It is possible that the upper threshold of the smallest kind of town should be set even lower, perhaps as low as a

[117] Calculated from Glasscock, *Lay Subsidy*.
[118] W. G. Hoskins, *Local History in England*, 2nd edn. (London, 1972), 278, app. 1; Russell, *Medieval Population*, 140–3; *Westminster*, 168 is a *c*.1400 figure.
[119] *Leland's Itinerary*, i. 144; in part, Leland was misled by the long expanse of main thoroughfare, but every town of 1,000 people and more was 'large' when compared to the thousands of other villages and hamlets.
[120] See above, Ch. 1, sect. 2.
[121] Hilton, 'Lords, Burgesses and Hucksters', 13.

population of 1,000. By the same token, we have seen that Wells flirted with this population figure in the fifteenth and sixteenth centuries.

Within the region, Bristol was ever the dominant urban centre, the great entrepôt that connected the western Midlands, the border counties, and Somerset to the world outside England, and even with the other side of the nation. Wells was only twenty miles away from the dominating port, through which its trade and traders moved. A sizeable city by any pre-modern criterion, Bristol was six times as populous as Wells in 1377, and had five times the taxpayers in 1524.[122] Wells was in its shadow.

Compared to the other Somerset towns, however, Wells was usually the largest of a group noteworthy for their moderate size.[123] Only in one evaluation, the 1334 lay subsidy, did any Somerset town (Bridgwater) exceed Wells.[124] Only seven years earlier, in a previous subsidy, Wells had been slightly larger than its rival.[125] In 1377 Wells and Bridgwater were the county's largest centres (lay populations of 1,802 and 1,716 respectively), followed by the distinctly smaller towns of Taunton and Bath.

By the sixteenth century, as Leland attested, Bridgwater was much depressed and shrunken.[126] Taunton had continued to grow. By 1545 the chantry surveyors estimated—very roughly—that Taunton had 3,000 communicants, while Wells parish (considerably larger than the town and borough) had only 2,000, and Bridgwater had sunk to 1,100 adults.[127] On a very local level, Glastonbury, which was not even a town in 1300, had become a thriving market centre by the fifteenth century. It may have had a population of 1,000 in the early sixteenth century, and its growth can only have hurt Wells, eliminating its exclusive market position in the area, and stopping it from developing into a middle-rank

[122] PRO E179/169/156; Russell, *Medieval Population*, 142–3; Hoskins, *Local History*, 278.

[123] See R. W. Dunning, 'Somerset Towns in the Fourteenth Century', *SDNQ* 29 187 (Mar. 1986), 10–12, who considers Wells to have been larger at all times.

[124] Glasscock, *Lay Subsidy*, 272.

[125] *Kirkby's Quest for Somerset*, ed. F. H. Dickinson, SRS 3 (1889), 272 and 278–9. Bridgwater paid more tax, but Wells had more taxpayers.

[126] *Leland's Itinerary*, i. 161–3: 'there hath faullen yn ruine and sore decay above 200 houses yn the toun of Bridgwater in tyme of remembraunce'.

[127] *The Survey and Rental of the Chantries, Colleges, etc.*, ed. Emanuel Green, SRS 2 (1888), 25, 57, and 155. The total for Wells included the rural parish, and cannot be taken to suggest that the population had grown substantially after 1524.

town.[128] Two market towns within six miles of each other could only hold down each other's potential growth.

Somerset grew wealthy between 1334 and 1515. In the early period, before the cloth boom, it was the twenty-third richest county, one of the poorer ones in fact. By the sixteenth century it had risen to the second wealthiest.[129] But it would appear that the growth was well distributed, tightly connected to rural success. The new growth was generated in the old villages. The growth of one town came at the expense of a neighbouring town, not the countryside. Thus a county of small towns remained so.

[128] See PRO E179/169/156; and *Survey and Rental*, 68. The implications of Glastonbury's size, namely, that it included a thriving market town—if not a borough—were confirmed to me by Miss Lynn Marston of Leicester University, who is preparing a thesis on medieval Glastonbury.

[129] R. S. Schofield, 'The Geographical Distribution of Wealth in England, 1334–1649', *ECHR*, 2nd ser., 18 (1965), 504.

3

Economy

An exhaustive economic history of medieval Wells is not an appropriate undertaking for a social and cultural history. But an outline of the economy—the work that the people did, the wares that they produced and traded, the industrial organization and conditions of labour, the vicissitudes that these elements suffered—is a necessity. Towns are distinguished more by their economic function than by their size. More than anything else, it is their role in the economy which separates them from—and, in another sense, joins them to—the countryside. Manufacturing and commerce are dominant in the town, rather than tilling the soil or raising animals. But the town's success is closely tied to the use of rural supplies of basic commodities.

Economy presses itself upon us because it is impossible to deny that economic structures, and the growth and decline of business, affected social and cultural change. Churches rose on a foundation of money as much as faith. Ideologies and simple ideas were influenced by the experiences and interests of people reacting to economic pressures as well as moral and religious conditions. An urban community's unity was achieved, if at all, only by absorbing the great diversity of urban economic life.

I. OCCUPATIONAL STRUCTURE

The variety of occupations in a given town provides one clue to its function. Here one can see whether the town is more than a simple market centre, and how much industrial activity and different handicrafts it could support. In this respect, Wells can be immediately separated from the very small towns. Midland towns like Halesowen and Thornbury supported about thirty-five occupations in the later Middle Ages.[1] There was considerably

[1] R. Hilton, 'Lords, Burgesses, and Hucksters', *P & P* 97 (1982), 11.

more diversity in Wells. About sixty different occupations—excluding the gentry and the clergy—can be positively identified. There were certainly more. The last names of Capper, Fletcher, Bowyer, Wright, Spicer, Roper, and Cardmaker all appear at Wells, but they are the only indications that such trades might have been followed there, even though these include some of the more basic and universal crafts. Taking these 'evasions' into account, we can estimate that Wells housed sixty-five distinct occupations. It was closer to the larger English cities in this respect than the little towns. Much larger centres such as Coventry and Bury St Edmunds had eighty-five and eighty-seven occupations respectively in the later medieval period, but they and Wells were dwarfed by London, which had no fewer than 180.[2] Wells's diversity underlines the fact that the city had an importance which extended beyond its own small market area, although we must not underrate the influence of the cathedral in stimulating varied demand, for Westminster, a similarly small sized town, also contained an impressive variety of trades, stimulated by the demand of a large monastery and the royal household.[3]

The simplest way to gain an overview of the economy is to examine the weight given to the various occupations in the city. The sources for this information are varied, but most of the assignations of craft or profession come from the burgesses' records.[4] Unskilled labourers and some of the more humble, less lucrative crafts do not feature greatly in these sources. Furthermore, merchants are also underrepresented, because of the idiosyncratic tendency at Wells not to identify merchants as such. Most of the merchant attributions have come from other sources.

The burgesses were not a very exclusive organization, and they can be taken as fairly representative of the skilled population of the

[2] Gottfried, 110–13; and *Coventry*, 311–17, apps. 3c and 3d; see also J. F. Pound, 'The Social and Trade Structure of Norwich, 1525–75', *P & P* 34 (1966), 49–69; E. M. Veale, 'Craftsmen and the Economy of London in the Fourteenth Century', in E. J. Hollanender and W. Kellaway (eds.), *Studies in London History*, (London, 1969), 139. For figures for the cloth trade, cf. A. R. Bridbury, *Economic Growth: England in the Later Middle Ages*, (London, 1962), 49.

[3] R. B. Dobson, 'Cathedral Chapters and Cathedral Cities: York, Durham and Carlisle in the Fifteenth Century', *Northern History* 29 (1983), 15–44; *Westminster*, 120.

[4] CBI and CBII are augmented by a variety of other royal, cathedral, and episcopal sources, including such things as witness lists in deeds, letters patent, letters close, and cathedral accounts.

city.[5] Collected by sector, the results appear in Table 2. The trades of 574 individuals have been identified. For comparison, figures for Bury St Edmunds and Coventry have also been included. Derived from wills and extending to 1530, Bury's figures are probably as accurate as Wells's, also erring on the side of the skilled worker as opposed to the labourer and the poor. The Coventry figures are more precise, but come entirely from the 1520s.[6]

The predominant position of the cloth industry is arresting. Over one-quarter of the craftsmen were primarily engaged in making cloth. Wells's share in this central export industry was more than double Coventry's, and 37 per cent greater than Bury's. Its magnitude suggests that Wells was first and foremost an industrial city. We shall return to examine cloth-making in more detail.

The place of basic marketing was also unusually well developed. The proportion of victuallers was nearly 20 per cent, which seems incredibly high, considering that in Bury it was half that, and only 12.5 per cent in Coventry. Certainly, the total for the brewers may be inflated by the inadvertent inclusion of part-time brewers. The proportion of bakers and butchers was just as high relative to the other towns, while the numbers of fishmongers and vintners was comparable. It is possible that, individually, Wells victuallers did a smaller amount of business than their contemporaries elsewhere. The trade of the surrounding countryside may have been more significant for a small town such as Wells than for the larger centres.

Furthermore, there was the presence of the cathedral. Unlike those following the usual regime at a monastery, most of the canons, vicars, and other employees of the church did not dine communally. They employed no bakers. They converted agricultural resources into cash, which was distributed to the ministering priests and canons. Throughout the fourteenth and fifteenth centuries the resident cathedral staff received an income from the church of between £500–600 per annum.[7] The resident canons,

---

[5] But see J. F. Pound, 'The Validity of the Freemen's Lists: Some Norwich Evidence', *ECHR*, 2nd ser., 34 (1981), 53; and Swanson, 5.

[6] *Coventry*, 311–17, tables 38–9; Gottfried, 111–13. Useful comparisons can be made to the many towns displayed in P. J. P. Goldberg, 'Urban Identity and the Poll Taxes of 1377, 1379, and 1381', *ECHR*, 2nd Ser., 43 (1990), table 8, 209–12; and Swanson, *passim*.

[7] CA, 1343–1500, *passim*. This does not include their prebendal income or the dean's large estate income.

TABLE 2. *Occupations by sector (%)*

Sector	Wells, 1350–1500	Bury, 1354–1530	Coventry, 1522
Building	8.7	7.9	2.5
Cloth-making	26.4	16.7	10.4
Garment	9.2	7.4	15.3
Labourers	0.3	1.4	4.0
Leather-workers	7.6	9.4	8.1
Leather-makers	4.4	5.8	2.5
Merchants	6.7	13.2	10.6
Metalworkers	7.2	6.4	9.7
Services	6.4	9.0	8.1
Misc. manufacturers	3.1	12.2	5.1
Victuallers	19.9	9.6	12.5
Miscellaneous	0.0	1.1	n/a

Note: n/a = not available

who numbered between ten and twenty in any given year, each ran
their own sizeable household, using much of their income to
entertain. They and the vicars-choral, even those who lived in the
close, all employed personal servants, so there must have been
around 200 people attached to the church and the diocesan
administration in the city; like a modern government in its capital,
they were wholly unproductive mouths to be fed. They drew
income from the diocese, from across Somerset, and fed it into
Wells's economy. The victuallers were first to profit from this
diversion.

In the middle of the fourteenth century the vicars-choral were
established in part as a college, with a common dining-hall, but
they continued to rely on the town's shops.[8] Not all the vicars were
accommodated in the close. They bought all they needed: bread,
meat, wine, and ale; and sometimes they bought faster than they
paid. In 1442 victuallers of the city complained to the principal of
Vicars Close about the late payment of bills.[9]

Furthermore, a cathedral was both a centre of administration
and of worship. While Wells was not an important pilgrimage site,
it received its share of visitors who, like the famous traveller
William of Worcester, marvelled at the cathedral before buying
accommodation and food for man and horse in the town.[10]

The relatively high showing of the garment-making crafts was
also partly a consequence of cathedral and church demand. Once
cappers and hat-makers are eliminated from Coventry's total—for
in that city this was an industry for the export market, sending caps
across the country and beyond—garment-workers made up only
4.2 per cent, compared to 9.2 per cent in Wells.[11] Demand for
tailoring was always high from the clergy. From schoolboys to
ministering canons and the bishop himself, there was a need for
ceremonial gowns and uniforms in the finest fabrics. Prayer and
position were both partly sustained by the finest of cloths, which
were kept in good repair.[12] The liturgy required a variety of
vestments for the vicars: white at Christmas, red for the feast of St

[8] Vicars-Choral, 1 and 2; and *CPR 1348–50*: 215.
[9] Register of the Vicars-Choral of Wells, 1442: 8.
[10] William of Worcester, *Itineraries*, ed. John Harvey (Oxford, 1969), 42–3 and
78–80.
[11] *Coventry*, 44–5.
[12] e.g. CA, 1392–3, 1394–5, 1400–1, 1407–8, 1416–17, and 1418–19.

Stephen, blue and white for St John the Evangelist's day, green and yellow for St Silvester's, and so on.[13] The tailors were kept busy on official as well as private clerical business. It was the overall smallness of Wells that allowed the cathedral, which had a large staff by any standard, to make such an economic difference: it meant that, in certain economic sectors, the town was like a place of much greater population.

Indeed, the influence of the cathedral might be seen in Wells's other areas of relative superiority over Bury: metalworking and building. The essential but simple art of the blacksmith was equally common in Wells and Bury. The difference between the towns was in the number of goldsmiths and pewterers in fifteenth-century Wells. The former frequently occur in the cathedral accounts,[14] and six pewterers were recorded from 1435, compared to none in Bury. Wells was a small centre for this young but growing luxury industry.[15] As for building, the work on the cathedral fabric and the surrounding liberty was continuous. The masons' yards were, and remain, a permanent and active part of the church precincts.[16]

Occupational tables, with their clear and distinct categories, can be misleading, especially with respect to the medieval urban experience. The separation of labour and ownership was less important then than it has become. Many small craftsmen were self-employed, but they often preferred to invest their small profits outside their own business. One of the most popular options for this was brewing.[17] Here the demand was fairly steady and the investment small. The wife often actually ran the operation. Among those amerced for brewing against the assize in 1421 were a limner, a wax-maker, a tailor, a baker, a weaver, a tiler, and a plumber. Only one man who was fined was a more or less full-time brewer; another was an innkeeper.[18] This reminds us that we can never produce more than a rough picture of the city's economy. Although

---

[13] See 'Ordinale et Statuta Ecclesie Sancti Andree Wellensis', in H. E. Reynolds (ed.), *Wells Cathedral: Its Foundation, Constitutional History and Statutes* (Leeds, 1881),: 95–6.

[14] CA, 1400–1, 1407–8, and 1446–7.

[15] For the pewter industry, see J. Hatcher and T. C. Barker, *A History of British Pewter* (London, 1977).

[16] L. S. Colchester, *Wells Cathedral* (London, 1987), 77: the masons' yard stands on the east side of the cloister, between the cathedral and the bishop's cameries.

[17] See below, p. 250; cf. *Colchester*, 269–71, app., table 1.

[18] LPL ED 1186/10.

central government tried to limit everyone to one trade, people in
Wells and elsewhere were always looking for small investments
with which to supplement their insecure incomes.[19]

2. CLOTH-MAKING

(i) Participation

The tendency to dabble in other businesses had much to do with the
buoyancy of cloth production in the city. In this respect, cloth-
making's impressive share of the known occupations (26.4 per
cent) actually underrates the importance of the industry. The
involvement of many people whose main business was elsewhere
allowed the industry to expand by drawing on the small savings of
many individuals. It was as if savings which the town's non-textile
craftsmen and chapmen had placed into a bank were then loaned
out to finance the industry's growth. In this case, however, the
savers were personally involved.

The detailed aulnage account of 1395–6 (for thirteen months)
reveals the breadth of participation in clothmaking and selling. The
later fourteenth-century accounts are the most reliable, free of the
streamlining found in many fifteenth-century accounts.[20] No fewer
than 112 people sold cloth in Wells during that year.[21] Several men
were dominant figures, obviously well-financed and organized
producers. But there can be no doubt that spare capital, probably
amounting sometimes to less than £1, found its way into the trade
from the hands of small-time, humble 'entrepreneurs'. We find, for
instance, that the baker John Stoke arranged for the production and
sale of 9½ cloths of assize; John Broke, a saddler, sold just one

---

[19] Swanson, 4–5, 9; John Hatcher, *Rural Economy and Society in the Duchy of
Cornwall, 1300–1500* (Cambridge, 1970), 220, 222–5; and Donald Woodward,
'Wage Rates and Living Standards in Pre-industrial England', *P & P* 91 (1981),
39–41; Simon A. C. Penn and C. Dyer, 'Wages and Earnings in Later Medieval
England: Evidence from the Enforcement of the Labour Laws', *ECHR* 2nd ser., 43
(1990), 361.

[20] Carus-Wilson, 279–93, the source for doubts about the aulnage accounts,
casts none upon this most extensive series. The burden of her argument is that the
accounts became standardized, and even fictitious, because the taxes were farmed
out. Later Somerset accounts, although earlier than some of those that Carus-Wilson
used, bear this out: e.g. PRO E101/344/7 shows that individuals of every aulnage
centre were farming the subsidy based on a rounded sum of cloths of assize.

[21] PRO E101/343/28.

cloth of assize (two *duodene*), and the butcher William Brackley brought four cloths to market. Only a quarter of the sellers' trades have been identified, but the presence of merchants—almost certainly a prominent force—and cloth craftsmen (weavers, dyers, and fullers) did not drive out the small and occasional producer. Cloth was perceived as profitable.

TABLE 3. *Cloth sales (13 Nov. 1395–18 Oct. 1396)*

Category	No. of sellers	% of total sellers	Duodene	% of sales
100 +	3	2.7	522	20.4
90–9	3	2.7	283	11.0
80–9	2	1.8	169	6.6
70–9	3	2.7	223	8.7
60–9	3	2.7	195	7.6
50–9	3	2.7	150	5.9
40–9	2	1.8	87	3.4
30–9	6	5.5	201	7.8
20–9	12	10.9	280	10.9
10–19	16	14.5	210	8.2
1–9	58	51.8	242	9.4
TOTAL	111	100.0	2562	100.0

Source: PRO E101/343/28.

Many of those who produced fewer than thirty *duodene* (the local half-cloth of assize) were weavers, fullers, and dyers who split their time between working up their own cloth, arranging for its complete production, and taking in piecework from the many other cloth-makers, large and small. Table 3 shows that eleven men controlled almost half the production, but their dominance is no more impressive than the fact that eighty-five people produced too little cloth to live off the proceeds, and yet they provided 30 per cent of the city's production, 732 *duodene*. This pattern of production was not unique to Wells. It was a feature of urban industry, which alone could draw on the pool of money generated by a town's marketing activities, its ready supplies of cash. The contemporary industries of Colchester and Winchester were organized in a similarly diffused fashion.[22]

[22] *Colchester*, 77–8; and *Winchester*, 309–10.

Women played a small role in controlling some of the production and sale of cloth.[23] Beyond their participation in the essential work of spinning, combing, and the more advanced cloth crafts, we find some of them acting as entrepreneurs.[24] Six women appeared in the aulnage list. Three sold fewer than ten *duodene* each, one sixteen; while two, Agnes Schecher and Joanna Shorthose, were in higher categories. Shorthose was recently widowed, and we can presume that she was carrying on her husband's business, perhaps preparing to wind it up. She processed an impressive sixty-eight *duodene*.[25] Schecher had for many years since her husband died been involved in various business activities.[26] Her thirty-three *duodene* are proof of the existence of independent women clothiers, albeit on a modest scale.

(ii) Organization of the Industry

The fifteenth century saw changes in the way in which cloth was made at Wells, which mirror to some extent the reorganization of the industry in other parts of England. The second half of the century witnessed the emergence of the self-styled 'cloth-maker'. It has been argued that, in contrast to the thirteenth- and fourteenth-century situation, great individual producers now developed integrated cloth-making businesses which dominated production. R. H. Britnell, in chronicling the history of industry in Colchester, noted how the number of cloth-sellers recorded in the aulnage accounts dwindled even as the amounts of cloth processed grew.[27]

The reality of the cloth-maker in Wells was embodied by a man like John Mawdleyn, whose business was large enough to earn a reputation which outlived him. The famous traveller Leland mentioned that Mawdleyn had been a Wells man.[28] In 1523–4 he was taxed on £200 of moveable goods.[29] A ten-time master of the

[23] Cf. Eileen Power, *Medieval Women*, ed. M. M. Postan (Cambridge, 1975), 56–67; *Coventry*, 88–91.

[24] *Winchester*, 299–300, discusses some rare details of combing and spinning production.

[25] Walter Shorthose's last appearance in the records was in 1392 (CBI: 103).

[26] CBI: 96 and 97.

[27] *Colchester*, 182–6; see also Gottfried, 106; E. Lipson, *The History of the Woollens and Worsted Industries* (London, 1921), 44–51. Cf. E. Coornaert, 'Draperies rurales, draperies urbaines: L'Évolution de l'industrie flamande au Moyen Âge et au XVIᵉ siècle', *Revue belge de philologie et d'histoire* 28 (1950), 60–98.

[28] *Leland's Itinerary*, ed. L. Toulmin Smith, 5 vols. (London, 1907), i. 145.

[29] PRO E179/169/156.

city, John Atwater, was another who was described as a cloth-maker and merchant in the later decades of the fifteenth century. He possessed stocks of dye, and owned a dyeing-house with the requisite furnaces.[30] John Tyler's will of 1512 makes the cloth-maker's organization clearer, since he made bequests to 'his weavers and tuckers'.[31] Unquestionably, then, many, if not all, of the stages of wool-processing and cloth-finishing that led to the final product were done under one man's auspices, under his own roof. The cloth-maker employed craftsmen on a permanent factory-style basis. The political ascendancy of all those who were described as cloth-makers underlines their economic success and the superiority of this form of industrial organization.[32] The profits were larger when all aspects of the business, often extending to the mercantile side, were kept under one man's control.

It is important, however, not to exaggerate the change that had taken place, both in terms of its scope and its newness. It must be recalled that, notwithstanding the utility of Colchester's fifteenth-century aulnage figures, the later aulnage accounts can be very misleading. The 1466 Bristol returns list 224 sellers, a year later this became a ludicrous 21; but a local record of 1483 contained forty pages of sellers.[33] Even where the quantities of cloths involved were right, the tendency was for the number of sellers to be reduced for administrative convenience. Furthermore, even by the fourteenth century a few people had garnered a large share of production; six men accounted for 30 per cent of Wells's in 1395–6.[34]

The change was one in emphasis, in direction. Even in the later fifteenth century the small cloth-maker had by no means disap-peared. It is almost as common to find a small-time fuller such as John Hembury renting a rack-yard and taking cloth in to be fulled in the 1450s as it was earlier in the century.[35] William Prior was but one later fifteenth-century weaver who can be confirmed as an

[30] *SMWII*: 389–91.

[31] *SMWII*: 159–60.

[32] John Atwater was the first of those who were designated as 'cloth-maker'. His magistracies were between 1453 and 1485 (CBII: 9, 12, 26, 33, 65, 94, 102, 121, 143, and 148); Mawdleyn was master in 1508, 1514, 1519, and 1520 (CBII: 252, 279, 296, and 301); Tyler was master 7 times between 1487 and 1506 (CBII: 154, 183, 189, 197, 209, 213, and 242).

[33] Carus-Wilson, 284–5.

[34] *Winchester*, 309, found that the top 6 producers accounted for only 20% of production.

[35] CBII: 15.

independent man who took in yarn to weave in the old fashion.[36] These men would still have committed their extra money to working up cloth, to small entrepreneurial activity. Nor had the dabblers disappeared. Brewers and pewterers were still engaged in the cloth industry in the later decades of the fifteenth century.[37]

Change in industrial organization came slowly and had nothing revolutionary about it. It is not surprising that there was no unrest among the craftsmen over the changes. The great men reorganized for greater profit and control. They probably did garner more of the production, but the small producer and the household system of production remained and continued to foster the personal independence of a large proportion of the city's textile craftsmen and of the many men and women who made a better living from a little cloth.

(iii) Magnitude of the Industry

Cloth-making's stature in later medieval Wells was immense, but in the thirteenth- and early fourteenth-century city wool was king. It brought considerable advantages to the town. It helped some of the burgesses to broaden their horizons and ambitions as they won a share of the wool trade. This was especially so from the early fourteenth century, when it became easier for the independent English merchant to gain access to wool supplies.[38] The townsmen were industrious enough to ensure that, when King Edward called an assembly in 1327, a parliament of the nation's leading wool-marketing towns, he expected two merchants of Wells to attend.[39] The Markaunts of the period—William about 1300, and the two Johns later on—were probably involved in this lucrative trade of sending Mendip wool overseas.[40] In 1339 the king ordered that all his wool that was being stored in Wells was to be sent to Bristol.[41]

---

[36] CBII: 22.

[37] e.g. John Grype in 1469 (CBII: 79) and William Abury in the 1480s and later (*SMWI*: 354, and CBII: 132.)

[38] See Eileen Power, *The Medieval English Wool Trade* (London, 1941), 46–50, 59–62. In addition, on the wool trade generally, see M. M. Postan, 'The Medieval English Wool Trade', in id., *Medieval Trade and Finance* (London, 1973), 342–52; Eileen Power, 'The Wool Trade in the Fifteenth Century', in M. M. Postan and Eileen Power (eds.), *Studies in English Trade in the Fifteenth Century* (London, 1933), 39–90; E. M. Carus-Wilson and O. Coleman, *England's Export Trade, 1275–1547* (Oxford, 1963); T. H. Lloyd, *The English Wool Trade in the Middle Ages* (Cambridge, 1977), 122–43 and 299–310.

[39] CCR 1327–30: 237.

[40] WTD 19, 22, and 23.

[41] CCR 1327–30: 81.

Wells was then, as a hundred years earlier and later, at the centre of the wool trade.

But much of the business was controlled by Italians and other great merchants from outside of the city, including the king's agents.[42] The participation of Wells's own merchants was to this extent limited. Furthermore, it is an economic truism that the handling of unprocessed raw material produces fewer benefits for the local economy than the addition of the manufacturing process. Thirteenth-century Wells prospered because the region's pastoral farming prospered, and the need to market the wool stimulated local commerce. Furthermore, population growth across the county led to increased demand for the goods and workmanship of the master craftsmen and shopkeepers of Wells.[43] A growing cathedral added its needs to those of the countryside and the expanding town.[44] Wells's market and fairs must have thrived, and the victualling, handicraft, and service sectors of the economy expanded. But most of this growth would have been secondary. Wool enriched Somerset, thereby indirectly stimulating Wells's market functions. In addition, local merchants grew richer and spent at least some of their profits in the city—on their houses, extra servants, a few luxuries.

But it was only when more of the profits found their way into cloth that a basic transformation of the city's economy took place. Cloth was being made for the market in Wells from at least the thirteenth century. It was a natural consequence of the ready and cheap supplies of good wool and running water which graced Wells and the entire sub-Mendip region. Nothing precise can be said about thirteenth-century production. There were weavers and dyers recorded in the first substantial series of documents extant, that is, from the later thirteenth century.[45] The industry was sufficiently well developed in the thirteenth century to dominate a street, and to occupy at least one mill in the town for fulling.[46] North Somerset industry was already of national importance, giving the name of 'mendeps' to a type of cloth by 1315.[47] We cannot say whether the

[42] CCR *1346–9*: 324; and Power, *Wool Trade*, 51–7; Carus-Wilson and Coleman, *Export Trade*, 40–1, 43; Lloyd, *English Wool Trade*, 123, table 12.
[43] See above, Ch. 1, sect. 2, and n. 106, below.
[44] See above, Ch. 1, sect. 1.
[45] e.g. AH 4, 5, and 12.
[46] WTD 4; and RI: 87.
[47] CPR *1313–17*: 344.

industry was depressed at the end of the thirteenth century, as has been argued for the country generally.[48] There is no reason to think so. Since much of the evidence for a general decline is doubtful, and there is no such evidence specifically for West Country industrial doldrums, it is best to assume that there was at least stability.[49] The smaller, newer cities like Wells probably turned to cloth in the thirteenth century and never turned away; possibly it was only the older established centres like Lincoln, Oxford, and Winchester which suffered.[50]

But Wells's great industrial explosion was part of the general reorganization of European cloth production which took place in the fourteenth century and witnessed the rise of England as a cloth-making and exporting nation.[51] Small centres, both towns such as Wells and villages, boomed from the 1330s, when the wartime embargo and subsequent heavy taxation on wool exports made cloth-making a natural investment.[52] It is to this period that the capture of the English cloth market has been assigned.[53] Certainly, there were more cloth craftsmen than ever in Wells.[54] The tenter-yards were becoming a valuable and frequently encountered use of city land.[55] By the 1340s the Wells merchant Peter Moniers can be found loading 100 woollen cloths on to ships outward bound from Bristol.[56] Soon after this, Moniers invested some of the proceeds of his successful trading into an ambitious land development scheme,[57] but, more importantly, for this marked a change, he

[48] Edward Miller, 'The Fortunes of the English Textile Trade during the Thirteenth Century', *ECHR*, 2nd ser., 18 (1965), 64–82.

[49] Carus-Wilson, 183–210; and, differently, A. R. Bridbury, *Medieval English Clothmaking: An Economic Survey* (London, 1982), 30–40. Most high- and medium-quality cloths were imported at this time.

[50] J. W. F. Hill, *Medieval Lincoln* (Cambridge, 1948), 326; Miller, 'Textile Trade', 70–6; and *Winchester*, 297.

[51] Carus-Wilson, 241–59; H. L. Gray, 'The Production and Exportation of English Woollens in the Fourteenth Century', *EHR* 29 (1924), 20–4; Carus-Wilson and Coleman, *Export Trade*, 138–9; cf. Coornaert, 'Draperies rurales', 72–9; and David Nicholas, *Town and Countryside: Social, Economic and Political Tensions in Fourteenth-Century Flanders* (Bruges, 1971), 76–116 and 203–21. For an alternative view, see Bridbury, *Clothmaking*, 12, 30–48.

[52] Lloyd, *English Wool Trade*, 144–92.

[53] Carus-Wilson, 242.

[54] e.g. WCAC 246; RI: 240–3; WTD 90, 97, and 99, provide names which indicate a substantial proportion of cloth craftsmen, or last names which indicate a cloth trade.

[55] e.g. WTD 71, 77, 88, and 125.

[56] CCR 1346–9: 561.

[57] See below, p. 252; it was worth over £100 in the 1360s.

acquired a fulling-mill.[58] The cost of building a mill in Somerset at this time was about £11, a substantial investment, expressive of confidence.[59] By 1345 the profitability of cloth-making was irresistible, and the industry was garnering a growing share of investment.

After the plague there is no mistaking the importance of Wells in the West Country's large share of national production. In 1353 the town was designated—along with Bristol, Bridgwater, and Bath—a county aulnage centre, proof that it had already attained a position of industrial and commercial importance in the cloth industry.[60] The early aulnage accounts reflect the liveliness of the industry, but they also remind us how small it still was. In the mid- and late 1350s Wells was the eighth largest production centre in the country, but it produced only 366 cloths of assize (732 *duodene*) between 1 December 1353 and Michaelmas 1354. Nevertheless, only Salisbury, Bristol, London, Winchester, Lincoln, Canterbury, and York could claim higher cloth sales.[61] This is impressive company for a town no larger than the fortieth in the nation.

The industry followed the broad pattern of the nation's export trade for the rest of the century. Both grew at an astonishing rate. The very full 1395–6 aulnage account captures a picture of the industry at its fourteenth-century zenith, before the export slump of the early 1400s.[62] Wells's production (converted to cloths of assize equivalent) was 1,281 cloths.[63] In forty years, times darkened by recurrent general demographic weakness, cloth production had almost tripled. Indeed, it had done better than this, since in the 1390s nearby towns and villages such as productive Croscombe were recorded separately from Wells. As it was, Wells was

[58] SRO DD/B, Reg. 2: 401.

[59] Richard Holt, 'Whose Were the Profits of Corn Milling? An Aspect of the Changing Relationship between the Abbots of Glastonbury and their Servants 1086–1350', *P & P* 116 (1987), 15–16.

[60] *CFR 1346–1417*: 385–6. For West Country industry, see Gray, 'English Woollens', 21–22 and App. 2; Bridbury, *Clothmaking*, 49–53.

[61] PRO E356/7: only 15 cloths were sold in Bridgwater and 54 in Exeter, but 289 in Bath; see Gray, 'English Woollens', 21–2. These figures are not commensurable with the later and more detailed returns of the 1390s. Here it is obvious that there were fewer aulnage centres and that each served a cloth-making region, for which urban production was only a part, albeit the greater part.

[62] See Carus-Wilson, 253–4, and the data in Carus-Wilson and Coleman, *Export Trade*, 138.

[63] PRO E101/343/28.

accounting for about 2½ per cent of the nation's entire cloth exports, despite its having a population of less than 2,000 people.[64] The industry's value to the town can be gauged roughly by its gross product. A medium-quality cloth, the predominating local variety, cost about 43s.[65] If we assume a constant price, cloth production was worth £944 5s. per annum in 1353–4, but as much as £2,542 in 1395–6.[66] Population had grown also, in part because of the cloth industry, but it had not tripled. While the figures are crude, they are very suggestive as to the industry's growth. The cloth industry's success helped to make the town and its individual inhabitants richer.

The vicissitudes of the industry after its early successes can in part be seen in the increasing share and number of cloth-workers recorded among the city's burgesses. This source is especially useful, since it will tend to represent the number of new businesses in the city which were mainly engaged in cloth production. Since only a proportion of burgesses' occupations are known, we have

TABLE 4. *Cloth craftsmen in Wells*

Decade	No. admitted to freedom	% of total known trades	Total new burgesses	Projected craftsmen
1380s	12	22.6	87	20
1390s	7	18.9	75	14
1400s	11	22.0	92	20
1410s	11	25.0	80	20
1420s	10	18.9	78	15
1430s	13	29.5	58	17
1440s	15	32.6	69	22
1450s	4	20.0	46	9
1460s	17	29.8	111	33
1470s	13	28.3	113	32
1480s	5	20.0	53	11
1490s	9	33.3	63	21

Source: CBI and CBII. Some occupational identifications were derived from other documents.

[64] This percentage is based on the national totals in Gray, 'English Woollens', 34, App. 2, and must be considered speculative.

[65] CBI: 83 (1386) values a *duodena* at 21s. 6d. Other local records confirm this as a reliable probable mean market price. Further support is to be found in H. L. Gray, 'English Foreign Trade from 1446 to 1482', in Postan and Power (eds.), *Studies in English Trade*, 7–10; and *Colchester*, 57–62.

[66] Based on an annual rate of 439 cloths.

calculated both the number of confirmed cloth craftsmen, as well as the projected number of craftsmen among all the new burgesses. This second figure (the last in Table 4) extrapolates from the positively identified craftsmen to those without any designated trade. Thus, if 22.6 per cent of new burgesses with identified crafts in the 1380s were cloth craftsmen, this percentage was multiplied with the entire pool of new burgesses (87) to yield a total rounded figure of 20 cloth craftsmen.

The cloth industry's share of the known occupations of all burgesses for the entire period was 26.4 per cent.[67] From 1380 until 1430 the industry's share of new burgesses was below this average, but rising towards it. But as the number of new burgesses fell in the 1420s and especially in the 1430s, the textile trades' representation rose, attaining 26.1 per cent in the 1420s and 1430s, and 31.0 per cent in the doldrums of the 1440s and 1450s. Moreover, our projections of the total number of new admissions of cloth-making craftsmen (the last column of Table 4) hardly reflect any hard times except for the 1450s. The industry, while failing to maintain its earlier size, employed about as many people between 1440 and 1460 as it had done in the last two decades of the fourteenth century. Thirty-four textile craftsmen were probably admitted in the two earlier decades, and thirty-one in the 1440s and 1450s.

At the same time, the number of victuallers in the city was dwindling, and this helps to underline the role of cloth-making in the fifteenth-century economy. The first twenty years of records show that there were in fact more new victuallers admitted than cloth-making craftsmen. But by the 1440s and 1450s the figures for the victuallers had fallen from their pre–1400 high of 25.8 per cent of all burgesses to 15.8 per cent. We have no reason to see this as reflecting anything but a decline in their business, a fall in population. The compelling conclusion is that the city's economy was in a state of considerable decline notwithstanding the relative strength of the cloth industry. From about 1430 to 1462 the overall economy shrank. That it did not fall desperately was due to the buoyancy of cloth production and its export market. The service sector, which included the taverners, hostellers, barbers, and cooks, slumped, along with the metal- and leather-working trades and the other small manufacturers such as the chandlers and blanket-makers. Without question, Wells the marketing centre, the focus of

[67] See above, Table 1.

sub-Mendip trade, declined sharply in the first sixty years of the fifteenth century. The success of cloth masked and mitigated the extent of the damage.[68]

The fluctuations in the number of cloth craftsmen in the city were to some extent a function of the export market for cloth. The sluggish export market of the 1410s is evident in the low number of apprentices and immigrants who went on to become masters and burgesses in the 1420s.[69] Exports in the 1450s and 1460s were also depressed. Bristol's cloth exports are probably the best indication of Wells's situation, although cloth from Wells certainly found its way out through London, Southampton, and possibly Exeter. Cloth shipments from Bristol never exceeded the level of the 1380s and the 1390s.[70]

Nevertheless, the general trade situation cannot explain the fall of the industry and the town in the 1480s, the depression which afflicted the city into the sixteenth century. National cloth exports remained strong, even if less of the trade went through the West Country's ports. Production across England continued to grow. Indeed, earlier in the century the export market for cloth had rallied, while Wells had idled or shrunk. After a mild decline in the mid-1420s, exports rose sharply from 1435 to 1448, when Wells was fairly depressed, certainly not growing. At that time 60,000 cloths were exported from England, 5,000–6,000 of these from Bristol. By 1500, when the difficulties attendant on the closing of the Hundred Years War were long past, the export trade was almost 80,000 cloths per year.[71] Again, Wells had no great part in this. The inevitable conclusion is that, for a great part of the fifteenth century, Wells's share of cloth production fell because it was unable to compete successfully for the important overseas market. It may have done better on the dark page of the domestic market, but there is no reason to think so, and internal trade has unfortunately left few records.

[68] The cloth industry's role as partial economic saviour has been discussed by M. M. Postan, *Essays on Medieval Agriculture and General Problems of the Medieval Economy* (Cambridge, 1973), 196–9. For more on urban decline, see above, Ch. 2, sects. 3–5, and below, Ch. 3, sect. 6.

[69] *Colchester*, 163, noted that the 1410s and 1420s were difficult times for Colchester's industry; *Winchester*, 301–2, found the same.

[70] Carus-Wilson, 29–95; Carus-Wilson and Coleman, *Export Trade*, 138–9 and 142–3.

[71] Carus-Wilson and Coleman, *Export Trade*, 138–9 and 142–3.

3. WELLS AND ITS COUNTRYSIDE

Wells's cloth industry was tied to the surrounding countryside in a relationship fraught with economic ambivalence. The wool that went into Wells cloth was raised on the nearby pastures on the sides of Mendip valleys. But the countryside played a role even at a later stage of production, enticing some work away from the city, especially the fulling of cloth in the mills on the many streams that run over this part of England. Wells merchants, among others, owned fulling-mills in Wells Manor and Wookey Manor and beyond.[72] In a letter of 1357 the king expressed concern that cloth was leaving the city prior to fulling, and therefore eluding tax.[73] Much of E. M. Carus-Wilson's evidence for the advance of the fulling-mill in the villages of England came from Somerset.[74] Mendip cloths were rarely so fine that fulling was considered inappropriate, so when the towns could no longer provide adequate fulling capacity, rural river-courses were turned to.[75] Wells was fortunate to possess a watercourse of its own, otherwise its decline might have been aggravated.

As it is, the industrial success of Somerset's villages was probably what denied Wells in the north of the county and Bridgwater in the south the industrial concentration which might have boosted their growth and size and made them the equals of towns like Salisbury, Worcester, or Colchester. The parish and village adjacent to Wells on the east, Croscombe, was a smaller version of famous Lavenham, the industrial village which produced more cloth than many a large town.[76] In the mid-1390s Croscombe was turning out

---

[72] See SRO DD/B, Reg. 2: 401; AH 143, 162, and 184ᵃ.

[73] *CCR 1354–60*: 431.

[74] Carus-Wilson, 190–7.

[75] Indeed, Miller, 'Textile Trade', 82, saw the fulling-mill as important to the 14th cent. expansion of the Mendip cloth industry. For the quality of Mendip wool, see T. Rymer, *Foedera, Conventiones, Litterae*, ed. J. Caley and Fred Holbrooke, iii (London, 1818), 369: Somerset wool sold for 10–11 marks a sack in the mid 14th cent.; Power, *Wool Trade*, 23; J. H. Munro, 'Wool Price Schedules and the Qualities of English Wools in the Later Middle Ages, *c.*1270–1469', *Textile History* 9 (1978), 118–69; T. H. Lloyd, *The Movement of Wool Prices in Medieval England* (Economic History Review Supplement 6; Cambridge, 1973), 10.

[76] On Lavenham and its impact on nearby towns, see *VCH Suffolk*, ii, ed. William Page (London, 1907), 256; and Gottfried, 14–23.

nearly as many cloths as Wells; fifty-six different producers in the vill collectively made 2,390 *duodene* per annum.[77]

Production in the countryside was more concentrated and perhaps more effectively organized than urban industry, as is suggested by the aulnage accounts of the 1390s. The average seller in Croscombe offered 42.7 *duodene* per annum for purchase, compared to 22.9 among their counterparts in Wells. Bridgwater and Bath producers averaged similar amounts of cloth as those in Wells. But the other great cloth villages in the area—pre-eminently Pensford and Frome—kept their astoundingly high production of 5,141 and 4,845 *duodene* per annum respectively in proportionately fewer hands even than Croscombe. Pensford sellers sold an average of 84.3 cloths per annum, and Frome producers 118.2. In Frome twenty-one men sold over 100 *duodene* each per annum, compared to only three producers of this calibre in Wells. Four Pensford men accounted for almost as much production as the entire city of Wells. Croscombe had eight sellers who produced more than 100 *duodene* per annum.[78] Unfortunately, the fifteenth-century aulnage accounts are unable to confirm unequivocally that the Wells industry failed to grow because of the continued and growing success of the countryside and its large, well-organized producers, who operated on a scale in the fourteenth century that few Wells cloth-makers attained at any time.

Despite the countryside's success over the city in cloth production, the burgesses of Wells often reached deep into their hinterland to control primary economic supplies through direct cultivation. First and foremost, the countryside was a location for agriculture, horticulture, and pasture, not industry. Much of the borough itself was devoted to such 'country' pursuits. Where there was not a tenter-yard for cloth, there was often a pasture, a garden, or a small arable field. On the furthest extremity of the town, only a shift in jurisdiction—leaving the city for the suburbs—not a change in land use, differentiated the 'urban' land from that of Wells Manor.

Much of the attraction of the manor was the low level of investment required. A small house and a tenth of an acre of land in town cost on average 8–10s. per annum to rent. But arable or pasture in the manor usually cost—at least after the plague—about

[77] PRO E101/343/28; see also E101/344/4.
[78] PRO E101/343/28; cf. E101/344/4.

4*d.* per acre per annum. At all times, both before and after the population reduction caused by the pandemic, the burgesses considered land to be a good investment. The epidemic of 1348–9 merely made it more easily available. William Withy, a prosperous burgess of the 1310s and 1320s, held 10½ acres of arable in Wells Manor.[79] Walter Compton, a merchant, held part of 27 acres of arable and 2½ acres of meadow in the manor hamlet of Wookey Hole in 1334. The annual rent was 16*s.* for the whole package.[80] In 1400–1 Thomas Tanner expanded his property holdings by purchasing fifty-seven acres of land in Wells Manor.[81] The cathedral clergy also were always heavily involved in the rural economy. By the thirteenth century the pattern was already well established. For example, the vicar-choral John Surrey bought urban properties as well as three acres of arable in Stoberry Field (above the city) and the East Field of Wells Manor.[82] Before the plague grain for bread and gruel was probably what most townsmen grew on the land that they owned or leased. Wheat, the premier cash crop, must have been favoured. The pressure of population, which attained nearly disastrous proportions when combined with poor harvests in the 1310s, put grain prices and possibly profits at a premium.[83] Before the plague, there was strong demand for grain.

After the plague wheat and oat cultivation on burgess-controlled land seems to have declined, although it never disappeared. Increasingly, however, producing the raw material for ale and the pasture for sheep were preferred uses for land. The two occur simultaneously sometimes in the town records, when one man's sheep ate another's standing malt barley.[84] But at the end of the

[79] SRO DD/B, Reg. 1: 255[b]; and *CPR 1321–4*: 6. Unfortunately, no rental value is recorded.

[80] R III: 288.

[81] *CFR, 1399–1405*: 13.

[82] WCAC 126. There are a great many other examples from all periods, see e.g. WTD 91 (1338), WTD 100 (1341), and WCAC 381 (1366), in which John Aunger, a canon, purchased Moniers Lane for over £100.

[83] Ian Kershaw, 'The Great Famine and Agrarian Crisis in England 1315–22', in R. H. Hilton (ed.), *Peasants, Knights and Heretics* (Cambridge, 1976), 85–132; Henry S. Lucas, 'The Great European Famine of 1315, 1316, and 1317', in E. M. Carus-Wilson (ed.), *Essays in Economic History*, ii. (London, 1962), 55–6, 59–61, 68–70 and 71–2; Postan, *Medieval Agriculture*, 14, 201 ff. But see above, Ch. 2 n. 38, for the population problem.

[84] e.g. CBI: 21 and 48.

fourteenth and into the fifteenth century wheat and oats were still being cultivated by burgesses on their land outside the city.[85] Food was always a good business.

The burgesses who bought land and raised sheep near the city were quick to take up the most modern and sensible methods of maximizing their profits and production. By the 1420s several of them had already—without the bishop's consent—enclosed their Wells Manor plots. Three weavers—Richard Trote, William Wicks, and Thomas Gross—were among those who saw how best to provide themselves with cheap supplies of wool, the primary stuff of their trade, in order to give themselves a competitive edge over the less well-endowed or farseeing weavers. Indeed, of those called to account by the bishop for having illegally enclosed their land that year (1424), seven out of nine were burgesses. One of the other two was the prior of the hospital of St John in Wells.[86] Thus, urban and industrial demand for wool had a clear impact on the countryside, altering its land use from arable to pasture, from open fields to enclosed. Burgesses and clergy took up land and grazed their sheep in sizeable numbers. John Roland, a cathedral canon, had 400 sheep at Chelcote in the manor in 1429.[87]

The burgesses of Wells invaded the countryside whenever and wherever they thought that they could benefit from controlling basic food and industrial supplies. The animals, grains, and wool-fells that drove the victualling, hostelling, cloth, and leather industries came mainly from the countryside. Some food came from further afield, of course; a little from within the town itself. This was the result of the high and increasing concentration on sheep-farming within the region.[88] But, to gauge from the burgesses' trades, these industries comprised about 60 per cent of the city's economy. To these local imports we must add the peat, wood, and stone that came from the region, and which do not seem to have been in any way under the control of Wells businessmen. The region surrounding Wells did not belong to the city, a vassal or

---

[85] e.g. CBI: 129, 142, 168, and 184.

[86] LPL ED 1187/6. On enclosure, see H. S. Fox, 'The Chronology of Enclosure and Economic Development in Medieval Devon', *ECHR*, 2nd ser., 28 (1975); M. M. Postan, *The Medieval Economy and Society* (Harmondsworth, 1975), 58–9 and 76–7.

[87] LPL ED 1187/6. CBI: 113, 129, 136, 191, and WCAC 145, provide other examples.

[88] This was a long-standing development: see above, p. 15.

colony like the hinterland of Italian cities. Furthermore, because of the industrial aspect of much of the country, and the slightly rural flavour of much of the city, they were in many ways competing rather than complementary entities. This was the fate of many a smaller town.[89] Their survival as significant centres of marketing and industry was never assured. Yet Wells did survive the challenge of the villages.

4. TRADE

The evidence of Wells's trading ventures and trends is relatively plentiful, but anecdotal. To follow the trade in and out of the city, one must of course follow the merchants, whether they are called such or chapmen, mercers, grocers, or drapers. But just as it was with the cloth industry, so it was with trade. The quick-witted, independent craftsman, whatever his particular art, took advantage of any merchandising possibilities that presented themselves. In the Middle Ages one never knew what would be offered for sale in a shop from the craft displayed on the sign.[90] On the wholesale level, too, one would fine a glover such as Edward Godtyde selling a consignment of wool in 1404.[91] Thomas Piggesley is variously described as a tailor and a chapman, plainly the small-town counterpart of the great merchant tailors of London, both maker and trader.[92]

Above the level of shop trade were the markets and fairs, whose original and abiding purpose was to make an event of themselves and thereby attract buyers and sellers to a particular place. In Wells the market which had been established in the twelfth century no longer opened on Sundays, but, as it does today, on Wednesdays and Saturdays.[93] It was essentially a provisions market, where grain

[89] *Colchester*, 141–58, 246–61; Bridbury, *Clothmaking*, 47–59; Gottfried, 14–23; Nicholas, *Town and Countryside*.

[90] S. L. Thrupp, 'The Grocers of London: A Study in Redistributive Trade', in Postan and Power (eds.), *Studies in English Trade*, 262–84.

[91] CBI: 162.

[92] CBI: 12 and 26.

[93] PRO C3/262/7. On markets, see Bryan E. Coates, 'The Origin and Distribution of Markets and Fairs in Medieval Derbyshire', *Derbyshire Archaeological and Natural History Society Journal* 85 (1965), 92–111; R. H. Britnell, 'The Proliferation of Markets in England, 1200–1349', *ECHR*, 2nd ser., 34 (1981), 209–21.

and other foodstuffs would be offered for sale to the town's victuallers and population. The market's regulation aimed at two things: to provide tolls for the lord's profit; and to limit the possibility for anyone, especially millers and bakers, to corner the vital grain supplies.[94]

The burgesses of Wells had no very great advantage in their own market-place. The tenants of the bishop, the dean and chapter, and of Glastonbury's twelve hides all went toll-free,[95] as did many others from towns to which the king had given freedom from tolls and exactions throughout the country.[96] In fact, the bishop took in very little money from market tolls: about 24s. in 1308–9; a derisory 2s. 7d. in 1491–2; and 6s. 8d. in the mid-sixteenth century.[97] The region had several other weekly markets in Glastonbury, Axbridge, and Shepton Mallet, so the small traders would have travelled this local low-toll circuit.[98]

The twelfth and especially the thirteenth centuries also produced a large number of fairs. Within comfortable riding distance of Wells, there were perhaps three dozen different fairs established by 1350, but very few became even moderately successful.[99] The majority had the most marginal of existences. Many quickly disappeared altogether. By the beginning of the fourteenth century Wells possessed grants for five fairs a year.[100] There were many other fairs in nearby towns and villages.[101] But of these late medieval fairs vying to attract merchants, cloth-sellers, and wool-

[94] PRO C3/262/7; PRO SC6/Henry VIII/3075; Phyllis Hembry, *The Bishops of Bath and Wells, 1540–1640* (Lonson, 1967), 35–6. Wheat, barley, malt, beans, dredge, or any other grains were taxed at a rate of 1 pint per bushel, or one-sixty-fourth on smaller amounts.

[95] WCC 5 and 9; and CCR 1327–31: 177.

[96] In 1466, for instance, the burgesses of Cardiff asked the burgesses of Wells to record a royal charter granted to the Welsh burgesses (CBII: 55).

[97] PRO SC6/1131/4, SC6/Henry VII/1806; and Hembry, *Bishops of Bath*, 259; cf. M. W. Beresford, *New Towns of the Middle Ages* (London, 1967), 65–7, bearing in mind that his figures include fair tolls, which were often the more lucrative.

[98] On the question of one market's proximity to another, see R. H. Britnell, 'King John's Early Grants of Markets and Fairs', *EHR* 94 (1979), 90–6.

[99] N. F. Hulbert, 'A Survey of Somerset Fairs,' *SANHS* 82 (1936), 87–117, provides a list; on fairs generally, see E. W. Moore, *The Fairs of Medieval England* (Toronto, 1988); Michael Reed, 'Markets and Fairs in Medieval Buckinghamshire', *Records of Buckinghamshire* 20 (1978), 563–85; C. Verlinden, 'Markets and Fairs', in *Cambridge Economic History of Europe*, ii, ed. M. M. Postan, E. E. Rich, and E. Miller (Cambridge, 1965), 119–53; and Coates, 'Markets and Fairs in Medieval Derbyshire'.

[100] WCC 2, 3, and 4.

[101] Hulbert, 'Somerset Fairs', 87, 98, 100, 101, 106–8, and 117, for the local

men to northern Somerset, eight had greater regional importance.
None was on the scale of the great twelfth-century fairs of St Ives,
Winchester, or Champagne. Later medieval towns were numerous,
and fairs were superabundant.[102] Furthermore, there was an
increasing tendency in the later Middle Ages for the capital's trade
to be conducted through London itself. The drapers of Bristol
called the eight main regional events 'general fairs'. They were
Norton St Philip, Queen's Charlton, Priddy, Bradley, Cosham, and
two of the Wells fairs.[103] To this list, evidence from Wells suggests
that Bristol's St James's fair should be added.[104] Cosham fair does
not seem to have been important to Wells, presumably because it
was nearly thirty miles away, on the other side of Bath. Salisbury
fairs, however, were occasionally mentioned in the Wells records,
and were certainly attended by some, notwithstanding the distance.[105] In the fourteenth century, during the age of cloth, these
fairs constituted a sort of cycle.[106] The Bristol and Norton St Philip
fairs were held for several days in May;[107] Priddy fair in mid-
August;[108] Wells's St Calixtus's fair in October, and St Andrew's
fair at the end of November. The timing of the Charlton fair can be
assigned to the early spring,[109] while Bradley's was probably in the
autumn.[110] All seven of these fairs were well attended by the cloth-
making and trading population of Wells and north Somerset, as
well as the merchants of Bristol. They were used by the courts in
Wells as convenient places and times for the payment of debts,
because it was known that virtually all cloth-making businessmen
would be there, and that a large amount of cash would be available
to them.[111]

fairs at Bath, Midsomer Norton, Binegar, Shepton Mallet, Congresbury, Priddy,
Axbridge, Bishop's Lydeard, Cheddar, and Glastonbury. For local Wells references
to some of these fairs, see CBI: 140, 100, 106, 108, and RI: 116.

[102] Moore, *Fairs of England*, 217–22, whose arguments for the decline of the
great national fairs seem to apply, *m.m.*, to the smaller fairs.

[103] *Little Red Book of Bristol*, ed. F. Bickley, (Bristol, 1900), ii. 53–4.

[104] CA, 1455–6.

[105] CA, 1446–7.

[106] There was still a cycle of national English fairs as late as 1300: *Westminster*,
99.

[107] For Norton St Philip's, see Hulbert, 'Somerset Fairs', 92, and CBI: 62 and
153.

[108] CBI: 15, 24 and 62; and Hulbert, 'Somerset Fairs', 107–8.

[109] CBI: 26.

[110] CBI: 137.

[111] e.g. CBI: 15, 16, 26, 137, and 145.

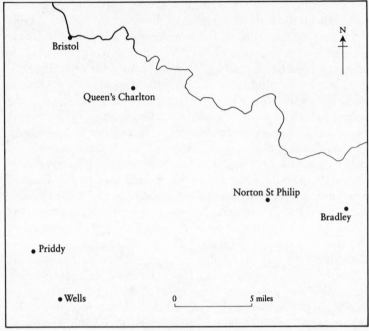

MAP 5. Regional fairs

Wells itself was early to get involved in the business of fairs, all of
its grants having been given by 1201. Yet only two of its fairs had
considerable success in the later Middle Ages. The thirteenth
century must in fact have been a period of decline for two to five of
the fairs. No more were added, because it was plain that no more
could have been supported. St Calixtus' and St Andrew's fairs
probably only expanded again with the development of the cloth
industry in the 1330s. It was only in 1334 that they were extended
from three-day fairs to eight-day fairs.[112] In 1292–3 St Andrew's
fair netted 13s. 4d. in tolls on goods and horses, but 200 years later
the profit had risen sharply to 47s. 6d.[113] In the 1490s the St
Andrew's and St Calixtus' fairs were worth about four times as
much as Wells's two lesser fairs, and the gap between them grew in
the sixteenth century.[114]

---

[112] CCR 1327–41: 306.
[113] PRO C44/1/13/5, and SC6/Henry VII/1806.
[114] PRO SC6/Henry VII/1806; and Hembry, *Bishops of Bath*, 33.

The presence of fairs did not necessarily assist the resident merchants of Wells. Markets which they might have commanded on their own were thrown open by the fairs to the well-organized, well-financed merchants of towns larger, richer, and further afield. The drapers of Bristol took advantage of the fairs to extend their business.[115] Fairs contributed to the success of outside merchants in Wells and in the many other smaller centres across the country. In other parts of the country foreign trade was effectively removed from English control, but the natives of the West Country did do better, even as their share of the nation's trade declined.[116]

Before examining the trading activities of Wells merchants, we must note two features of Wells's situation. First, the occupational structure table (Table 2) indicated that Wells had a comparatively low proportion of traders.[117] Part of this was attributed to the local idiosyncrasy of neglecting to state the occupation of merchants, especially in the city's freedom lists. And, of course, the high proportion of textile workers depresses all the other occupational categories. Nevertheless, compared to the 13.2 per cent share of merchants in Bury St Edmunds, Wells's 6.7 per cent represents a lower level of real commercial activity. The comparison is apt, because both towns were inland cloth centres.

Secondly, a great deal of the trading from Wells was carried out by the citizens of other towns, especially Bristol, Salisbury, and London. Attracted by cloth, they limited local merchant activity. Certainly, several Wells merchants did very well, but there were few in the later fourteenth and fifteenth centuries who made as much of a mark as their counterparts in other towns. The most obvious proofs of great wealth are lacking. Few burgesses progressed into the ranks of the gentry from trade.[118] Not many chantries were established in the town by burgesses, and the few that there were came mainly from the fourteenth century.[119] With the exception of Thomas Tanner and Richard Vowell, who, though not a merchant, owed his position to his father's mercantile success, no Wells

[115] *Little Red Book*, ii. 53–4.
[116] Carus-Wilson and Coleman, *Export Trade*, 80–125, outlines trade volumes by port, and the shares held by foreign and denizen merchants. Despite the growth of the export trade, Bristol's share declined, and Exeter's did not in anyway compensate.
[117] See above, Table 2.
[118] See below, p. 153 ff.
[119] See below, p. 268 f.

traders after 1380 made any mark on national politics, even by the humble standards of provincial burgesses.[120]

Merchants from outside the city always maintained a good share of the business of collecting wool and cloth from the area. The inland city of Salisbury, although forty miles away, cast a broad net to draw cloth to itself, and centred its activities on Somerset.[121] Like the merchants of Bristol, the Salisbury traders were in Wells often enough to become involved in the property market.[122] Salisbury men such as John Croscombe were buying rayed cloth in Wells in the later fourteenth century and sending it down to Wiltshire by a Salisbury carter.[123] Wine and dye unloaded at Southampton would have been brought to Wells via Salisbury.[124] In 1399 a Wells cook was outlawed for failing to answer a charge of debt for £44 made by John Wallop, a Salisbury draper.[125] Another Salisbury trader, Thomas Teyntrell, was on close enough terms with the Wells weaver Stephen Windford to stand as his pledge for a debt to a Wells fuller in 1398.[126] Both the cook, who we know also made cloth, and Windford were plainly selling their products, possibly on contract to Salisbury merchants. Some of Wells's entrepreneurial capital may have come from outside the city. Throughout the fourteenth century Salisbury merchants had been coming to Wells frequently enough for them to direct the king in 1345 to send letters patent to Wells outlining the mercantile privileges—freedom from tolls and other duties—possessed by the city and its burgesses.[127]

Without question, however, Wells's relationship with Bristol was its most valuable. To some extent, Wells's mercantile activity was an extension of Bristol's—and Wells was Bristol's mercantile suburb. The trade routes sought most often by Wells traders were those of Bristol. Merchants from the two cities would sometimes create partnerships for overseas ventures. A 1377 deal involved three merchants of the two towns freighting ships from Brittany to

---

[120] For Tanner, see *Rotuli Parliamentorum (1272–1503)*, ed. J. Strachey *et al.* iii, (London, 1767), 477. Vowell was escheator for Somerset and Dorset: CBII: 98, and *List of Escheators for England and Wales*, List and Index Society 72 (1971), 141.

[121] Bridbury, *Clothmaking*, 71–3.

[122] e.g. WCAC 400 and 408; and WTD 123, 147, and 176.

[123] Bridbury, *Clothmaking*, 71.

[124] Colin Platt, *Medieval Southampton* (London, 1973), 160–1.

[125] *CPR 1396–9*: 398.

[126] CBI: 115.

[127] SRO DD/B, Reg. 2: 242.

England, Wales, and Ireland.[128] When Wells took its charter of liberties on tour—to show its privileges where it mattered most—it did not send the charter to London or even to Salisbury, but to Bristol and the Somerset county court.[129] Even in the thirteenth century Wells merchants were exploiting the proximity of Bristol, and following that city's trade routes to Gascony. In 1250 John Francigena, a burgess of Wells, owed £24 to two men of Bordeaux.[130] Peter Moniers was lading cloth for export through Bristol and Dartmouth in the 1340s.[131] Overseas venture partnerships were made in the 1330s between Walter Middleton of Wells and Henry Russell of Salisbury.[132] Whether or not this particular partnership set out from Bristol, Wells was to some extent acting as a port city rather than a smaller town located well inland. Foreign merchants like Peter Moniers, originally of Amiens, and the French immigrant Peter Botoyr were attracted to Wells because of its cloth-exporting possibilities, and they enriched the city by further extending and expanding its trading ventures, mainly through Bristol.[133]

After the plague Wells merchants continued to operate with overseas trade in mind.[134] Strikingly, in 1390 Bristol's port-books refer to a ship called the *Marie* 'of Wells', even though the vessel could never have entered its home 'port'. The ship's master, John Lockier, was a burgess of Wells, as were most of the merchants who had consigned cloth to the vessel. These included Wells's greatest contemporary merchant and cloth-maker, Thomas Tanner, a regular cloth-exporter through Bristol.[135] But he was not alone. Four months later, in January 1391, the *Katherine* of Bristol carried cloth from Tanner, Richard Gross, and Thomas Jay, each of whom were substantial cloth-makers.[136] The destination of the vessel was—in this and most cases—Portugal, where cloth would be traded for wines, winter fruit (figs, raisins, and dates), and other

---

[128] *CPR 1377–81*: 77.

[129] *CBI*: 18 and 159.　　　　　　　　　　　　[130] *CCR 1247–51*: 366.

[131] *CCR 1346–9*: 561.　　　　　　　　　　　[132] *CPR 1334–8*: 506.

[133] Botoyr was Wells's richest citizen, according to the 1327 lay subsidy: *Kirkby's Quest* for Somerset, ed. F. H. Dickinson, SRS 3 (1889), 272; *CPR 1324–7*: 23; and *CPR 1334–8*: 427.

[134] For general current of trade, see Carus-Wilson and Coleman, *Export Trade*, 142–3; Gray, 'English Foreign Trade', 1–38.

[135] *The Overseas Trade of Bristol*, ed. E. M. Carus-Wilson, Bristol Record Society 7 (1957), 193; PRO E101/343/28.

[136] *Overseas Trade of Bristol*, 196; PRO E101/343/28.

luxury goods, as well as metal and leather products.[137] Merchants like Thomas Horewode returned from Brittany with wine.[138] Other men plied the coastal English trade in *batellae*, smaller ships. In 1406 the baker Thomas Jeve and William Halston bought such a boat in Wales.[139] Wells merchants also followed the armies. William Tanner went to Scotland in 1300 to provision the army, while about one hundred years later Robert Ashby went on campaign with the Earl of Somerset in Picardy, never to return.[140]

Although these merchant ventures were varied and continuous, there were rather fewer references to overseas ventures in the fifteenth century than in the fourteenth. This may be a peculiarity based on the episodic nature of the records. But it seems probable that the trading activity of Wells contracted in range and possibly in scope. The focus seems to have shifted to inland trade, with Wells the quasi-port returning to its land-locked self, its traders concerned more with English trade. If this is correct, it may well have been part of a national trend which left overseas trade in the hands of fewer merchants, particularly those from the capital.[141]

London merchants made their principal appearance in this sphere of domestic trade, and Wells merchants and chapmen played at least some role in most of their transactions. Much of this trade was directed towards London and was carried by what are often called chapmen. The chapmen dealt with the overseas merchants, with anyone who had anything to sell. They bought goods and then moved them from one town to the next, selling a great variety of items, but they were much better funded and more ambitious than mere pedlars.[142] The term 'chapman' is used in Wells as an overlapping term for merchant. A great overseas trader would never be called a chapman, but there are people who are called both—merchants in the local records, but chapmen by the records of central government. Generally, I take a chapman to have been a merchant of only moderate business who dealt with the domestic market.

[137] Carus-Wilson, 50–1.
[138] *CPR 1429–36*: 608.
[139] e.g. CBI: 170.
[140] *CPR 1292–1301*: 522; and *CPR 1405–8*: 16.
[141] Cf. Swanson, 175.
[142] Cf. *Winchester*, 308. For analytical purposes, e.g. Table 1, above, chapmen are but one category of merchant. See Hilton, 'Lords, Burgesses and Hucksters', 7, for a discussion of the pedlars; Margaret Spufford, *The Great Reclothing of Rural England* (London, 1984), discusses the early modern chapmen in detail.

The London trade consisted primarily in acquiring goods imported by London grocers. There were few men in Wells able to specialize in such varied dry goods, although there were a couple of fifteenth-century grocers and an apothecary who had come to the city from Salisbury.[143] One of the great fourteenth-century merchants was called John le Roper, and he was probably something of a grocer, since ropers were one of the divisions of London grocers. The inland trade in dyes, mordants, and the highly valued spices often forced traders from Wells and other provincial towns to go to London, since the grocers there increasingly tried to concentrate the nation's trade in the city to save themselves the costs and to enrich London's economy. They forbade their members to go out of the city even for fairs.[144] Henry Selwood, a Wells chapman, was buying goods in London in 1438 from the grocer Thomas Lane.[145] William Langford was also in London dealing with a different grocer in the same period.[146] The grocers' requirement that buyers come to them did not stop the consumer of these products from buying direct. Wells dyers such as Thomas Chynnok were in debt to London grocers, and were sued in a London court, in the middle of the fifteenth century.[147]

On their way to London, the chapmen went laden. Mainly they seem to have been selling cloth and hides. Merchants such as Thomas Tanner played a part in this trade in cloths, lucrative enough not to be left to lesser men.[148] But most of the evidence relates to chapmen supplying London drapers with West Country cloth, possibly receiving some fine imported fabrics in return, like the silk ribbons often noted in the cathedral accounts.[149] William Wicks, Richard Tesdale, and John Hunt were but three Wells traders who moved cloth along the Wells–London route in the fifteenth century.[150]

Wells traders also headed out along other paths. There was much business in Salisbury. But it is remarkable how little activity of any

[143] The grocers were Hildebrand Elwell and William Garet, the apothecary (CBII: 80) was Richard Bakeswell. There were almost certainly a few others. On the components of the grocers' craft, see Thrupp, 'Grocers of London', 248–50; *Winchester*, 262–4.

[144] Thrupp, 'Grocers of London', 247–77.

[145] *CPR 1436–41*: 111.

[146] CBI: 285 (ii).

[147] *CPR 1429–36*: 20.

[148] *CCR 1399–1402*: 207.

[149] e.g. CA, 1416–17, 1446–7.

[150] *CPR 1452–61*: 138; and *CPR 1436–41*: 205.

kind is recorded with nearby smaller centres to the north or south; there is rarely a mention of Bath, Taunton, or Bridgwater. For each lesser town such as Wells, the lines of trade remained simple. One smaller town had little to offer another. Each saw its trade arrive and depart along the roads to the larger cities. For some of the other Somerset towns, Exeter played the part of Bristol. In turn, much of the minor trade that connected the rural to the urban, and which existed for the most part below the level of the records, was strictly local, centred on the small to middling towns themselves.[151] Even if somewhat reduced in the fifteenth century, Wells exerted a continuous and fairly strong attraction on both its local region and the great cities with which it traded. In the fifteenth century, however, Wells's overseas activity faltered somewhat, following Bristol's into decline.

5. LABOUR

One of the striking facts about Wells's economy and society before 1500 was the lack of craft-guild organizations. Notwithstanding the fact that Wells was a great industrial town, there is not a trace of their existence at that time. The craft-guild is no longer to be taken as an assured part of a town's medieval landscape. In many towns the situation was similar to Colchester's: only in the fifteenth century did 'rudimentary gild organization' emerge.[152] Even where the craft-guilds' roots go deeper in history, the period of their semi-independence, of their advance from simple socio-religious groups, often came only towards the end of the Middle Ages. It is only from the fifteenth century that the characteristic regulation and restrictive practices really develop outside of London, often in the face of a weakening economy.[153]

---

[151] Some glimpses of the trade in food can be seen in LPL ED 1188/10, a court leet of 1432. On the role of this vital trade, see Postan, *Economy and Society*, 221–6; R. Hilton, *A Medieval Society: The West Midlands at the End of the Thirteenth Century* (London, 1966), 177–83.

[152] *Colchester*, 139 and 263.

[153] Perhaps the best account of the emergence of the later medieval craft-guilds *from* the parish guilds is Caroline M. Barron, 'The Parish Fraternities of Medieval London', in Caroline M. Barron and C. Harper-Bill (eds.), *The Church in Pre-Reformation Society* (Woodbridge, 1989), 15–17; *Colchester*, 238–40; Gottfried, 102; *Winchester*, 332–3 found numerous crafts from the 12th cent., but noted that their most 'striking feature . . . is their apparent insignificance'; Colin Platt, *The*

Wells's particularly slow development in this respect is consistent with the pattern of the small town rather than of the medium-sized to larger centres. In Colchester, Bury St Edmunds, Coventry, and Southampton the craft-guilds did eventually develop, all active in these towns by the 1450s.[154] The first possible indication of some sort of organization by occupation in Wells comes from 1515. In that year wardens of the altars and fraternities of St Katherine, St Nicholas, St James, and St Anne were entered in the city's records alongside the other, usual elections. The occupations of the wardens of each altar were written down—an unusual procedure—and every fraternity's offices were dominated by only one craft, respectively mercers, butchers, bakers, and brewers. For two further years the wardens of the St Katherine and St Anne guilds were recorded, and the new men—one per altar each year—came from the same occupations as their predecessors.[155]

It was not until 1555, however, that there was another, more definitive reference to the crafts. The master of the city required a list of all the craft-masters, and duly received an account of the crafts and their officers.[156] They were organized differently from the hypothetical, religious 'craft-guilds' noted in 1515. There were seven organizations in all: hammermen, cordwainers, butchers, weavers, fullers, mercers, and tailors. Together with butchers were the glovers, tanners, and chandlers, trades united by their use of animal carcases. The weavers subsumed the dyers and, rather oddly, the barbers. The fullers were combined with the shearmen and cappers. The mercers were combined with bakers, brewers, and innkeepers. The omissions are as puzzling as the odd combinations. Were the smiths and the allied metal trades included with the

English Medieval Town (London, 1976), 112–18, dates the guilds' emergence from about 1300, but exaggerates their concern with restricting the market; Swanson, 111–14, sees the craft-guilds as tools by which merchant élites could control the crafts.

[154] See above, n. 153, for Colchester and Bury; Platt, *Medieval Southampton*, 177. S. L. Thrupp, 'Gilds', in *Cambridge Economic History of Europe*, iii, ed. M. M. Postan, E. E. Rich, and E. Miller (Cambridge, 1963), 243 and 245, notes the lack of guilds in small towns; as does J. L. Bolton, *The Medieval English Economy* (London, 1980), 262–3; R. Hilton, 'The Small Town and Urbanisation: Evesham in the Middle Ages', *Midland History* 7 (1982), 1–8, 'Lords, Burgesses and Hucksters', and *The English Peasantry in the Later Middle Ages* (Oxford, 1975), does not report any guild formation in the very small towns.

[155] CBII: 275, 277, and 282.
[156] CBIII: 8ᵛ, 9, and 9ᵛ.

hammermen, or left out entirely? Was there a reason why the mercers were united with some of the victuallers? Had 'mercer' come to represent all the merchants of the city? Plainly, even when Wells did establish guilds, it did so with difficulty. The small numbers sometimes forced odd combinations of crafts, thus stressing vividly that these were by no means large organizations. Furthermore, some of the components cannot have had very similar economic aims. This makes it unlikely that their interests were primarily economic. Large towns often developed a variety of trade guilds for social and political reasons as well as economic ones. Beyond a certain size, a town's population could not meaningfully be included in a single guild. Furthermore, different social groups would tend to seek their own corporate bodies, especially if they resented or wanted to set themselves apart from other groups. To some extent, these needs were absent from the small town, where the independent population could be comfortably accommodated within the single burgess guild and the various religious fraternities.'[157] After the Black Death especially, pressure on the job market was low, and the desire to restrict access to the urban labour pool was weak. The need for craft-guilds, where they had not existed from the twelfth or thirteenth centuries, was virtually non-existent, and so they did not develop in the small towns. A further disincentive to their early development in Wells was that the town guild particularly valued and needed solidarity as a weapon against its powerful and not always friendly overlord.[158]

The medieval economy was still very rudimentary. Traditionally, by its very nature, it reduced the need for paid labour. For most potential employers in the city—the masters of the crafts—their own labour and that of their wives fulfilled the greater part of their needs. The family model was so supreme. Apprentices and often other servants (journeymen included) were housed, fed, and ruled by the master as if they were his own children.[159] On the one hand,

---

[157] See below, Ch. 4, sect. 5, and 8, sect. 3, for the town's guilds.
[158] See below, Ch. 4 and 6.
[159] See below, p. 146; and *Coventry*, 221–48, on the household's membership and size. Cf. J. C. K. Cornwall, *Wealth and Society in Early Sixteenth-Century England*, (Henley-on-Thames, 1988), 198–215, who takes the term *serviens* as a more precise term than it probably was; for Wells servants, see PRO E179/169/156. On apprentices, see Françoise Michaud-Fréjaville, 'Bons et loyaux services: Les Contrats d'apprentissage en Orléanais (1380–1480)', in *Les Entrées dans la vie:*

this kept his labour subservient and compliant. On the other hand, it created an environment in which some masters became extremely fond of, and favourably disposed towards, some of their workers. Apprentices were unpaid, of course, and were bound to the master for a strict amount of time, giving him an assured and cheap source of labour. Masters probably treated their apprentices as well or as poorly as they did their own children. But there are many wills in which the apprentices and servants were remembered by their masters, proof that there often was a real affection or at least solicitude between the master and the non-family members of his household.[160]

Prior to the plague apprenticeships were probably most assiduously sought by those parents who were trying to place their children in good circumstances, rather than by employers. Relatives and business associates were in an advantageous position to acquire such cheap labour. The merchant Peter Moniers, for example, brought a kinsman of his, William, from France to enter an apprenticeship in Wells in 1345.[161] There was probably a slight shift of enthusiasm after the plague, when the prospects for all working people, rural and urban, improved. Then it was masters who were more anxious to enlist the apprentices. Nevertheless, it was always one of the few decisions that parents could take to try to help their child's future prospects.[162] Even the less successful apprentices would end up as journeymen, earning a good wage when they had work, and with the chance of setting themselves up as independent masters, eventually becoming citizens. When labour was in short supply, the masters were very anxious to tie their apprentices to a long period of service. At least seven years was the fifteenth-century norm, and sixteenth-century terms could extend to eleven years.[163] This labour was truly captive. When William

Initiations et apprentissages (Nancy, 1982), 183–208; Bronislaw Geremek, *Le Salariat dans l'artisanat parisien aux xiiie–xve siècles* (Paris, 1969); 54; also S. Thrupp, 'Medieval Industry 1000–1500', in *Fontana Economic History of the Middle Ages*, ed. Carlo M. Cipolla (London, 1972), 247 and 267; and J. C. Russell, 'Population in Europe, 500–1500', ibid. 49–50.

[160] *SMWI*: 6–8, 55, 74–5, 389–91; *SMWII*: 17–18. Cf. P. J. P. Goldberg, 'Female Labour, Service and Marriage in the Late Medieval Urban North', *Northern History* 22 (1986), 23–5.

[161] *CPR 1345–8*, 20.

[162] Another, education, will be discussed below, Ch. 8, sect. 7.

[163] CBII: 106 and 124; *London*, 193, but see p. 11 for a 14th-cent. term of 14 years. For Wells's terms, see WTD 225, 228, 229, 235, 236, and 237.

Roper of Wells ran away from the service of Richard Setter in 1421, his new employer was fined £24.[164]

The late fourteenth and fifteenth centuries were characterized across Britain by labour shortages.[165] These were especially acute in the towns. Mortality rates were higher there, and immigration was the mainstay of population stability, the principal source of new labour and future burgesses.[166] But at the same time land was relatively cheap and productive because the rural population had not regained its later thirteenth-century levels. The result was that the attraction of the countryside, the fact that agricultural and industrial jobs were available there, could rarely be overcome by the towns, which lost population as a result. We have seen how population in Wells in the fifteenth century probably fluctuated widely, and we can now see why apprenticeships and the contracts with one's employees were thought extremely important.[167] Only by these means could a master ensure that he would have the labour to do the work, fill the orders, and make the profits available to him. The Ordinance and Statute of Labourers (1349 and 1351), unsuccessful attempts to restrain wages and the mobility of workers, stand as the greatest indication of the speed with which the Black Death revolutionized the labour market.[168] By the end of the century, when Wells records begin to provide some details, labour was in demand.

From the 1380s we find individual employers at loggerheads over a particular worker, a *serviens*, a term which could apply to both a wage-earner and an apprentice. One master would be accused of enticing another's servant away. The burgesses sued each other, but the town court was little more than sympathetic. It warned that it

[164] *CPR 1416–22*: 166.
[165] See Postan, *Medieval Agriculture*, 190–4, 199–202, and his sources; John Hatcher, *Plague, Population and the English Economy* (London, 1977), 35, 48–51; E. H. Phelps Brown and Sheila V. Hopkins, *A Perspective on Wages and Prices* (London, 1981), 4; W. Beveridge, 'Wages in the Winchester Manors', *ECHR*, 1st ser., (1936–7), 22–43.
[166] J. M. W. Bean, 'Plague, Population and Economic Decline in the Later Middle Ages', *ECHR*, 2nd ser., 15 (1963), 430; Hatcher, *Plague, Population*, 25; E. A. Wrigley, *Population and History* (London, 1969), 957; but see B. Gottfried, *Epidemic Disease in Fifteenth-Century England* (Leicester, 1978), 138–9 who argues that only London had a sufficient density of population to affect plague mortality.
[167] See Table 1, and Fig. 1.
[168] *Statutes of the Realm*, i (London, 1810), 34; Penn and Dyer, 'Wages and

should not happen again, but it did not attempt to set matters right, or even to assess a meaningful fine or compensation.[169] All the burgesses understood that they were caught in an inflationary labour situation, and that a good businessman would have to do what he could. Most of the cases come from the 1380s and 1390s, at least in part because thereafter it became more obvious that it was ineffectual to complain. It especially affected cloth-makers. Tuckers, weavers, and brewers, and butchers who also made cloth were among those who went to court over poaching employees.[170] It went beyond cloth, however. There were also cases involving a pair of bakers, for instance.[171] Whether true or not, some burgesses accused other masters of kidnapping. Richard Woodford, a cloth-maker of some sort, accused the butcher and cloth-maker William Bugworth of forcibly carrying off his servant in 1395.[172] The fishmonger Richard Lichfield made the same charge in 1407, accusing John Romsey, a weaver.[173]

There are cases later in the fifteenth century as well, enough to make it clear that, periodically at least, the labour market was not much easier for employers. Cases of enticement were still brought to the burgesses' court in 1454.[174] Employers could take other steps to combat defection. Higher wages were paid, of course. But there was sometimes the offer of some sort of partnership. In 1406, for instance, the baker Thomas Jeve rented a New Street messuage and included his servant John Fowles on the lease.[175] In 1471 the fuller Thomas Corset similarly gave an employee a similar stake, alongside himself and his wife, in a lease of a close and a paddock.[176]

An important component of the labour market at any time is the degree of participation by women. We have no local pre-plague evidence with which to contrast women's later activities, but there

---

Earnings'; B. H. Putnam, *The Enforcement of the Statute of Labourers* (New York, 1908), esp. 220–1; Phelps Brown and Hopkins, *Wages and Prices*, 16–19, whose data indicate the slower rise in *real* wages because of inflation; and A. R. Bridbury, 'The Black Death', *ECHR*, 2nd ser., 24 (1973), 578–81.

[169] Cf. *London*, 112–13; Hilton, 'Lords, Burgesses and Hucksters', 13.
[170] CBI: 12, 64, 89, 92, and 117.
[171] CBI: 68.
[172] CBI: 117.
[173] CBI: 173. On enticement, cf. Penn and Dyer, 'Wages and Earnings', 365.
[174] CBII: 12.
[175] CBI: 168.
[176] CBII: 86.

can be no doubt that they were important in the years of post-plague labour shortage.[177] Their participation did not develop because of any change in ideas about a woman's proper role. Nor did their function change, but the work that they did became more diverse and more essential to urban industry. More women became involved. Women came to the towns in numbers that exceeded male immigration.[178] If this was also the case at Wells, it would have been obvious to employers where extra labour could be found. Furthermore, since women were generally paid less than men, this constituted an additional economic benefit from the employers' viewpoint.[179]

While women had always worked and engaged in all manner of small trading and certain crafts like spinning, the later medieval period is striking for the fact that, for a time, women were filling economic positions that were considered male preserves. The merchant John Horewode had a female employee at the beginning of the fifteenth century, but in this case and others it is unclear whether the woman was more than a favoured domestic servant.[180] But after the 1466 borough ordinance which made apprenticeship in the city a mode of privileged admission to the freedom, we get a glimpse of what must have been the tip of the iceberg of women's technical work, an iceberg that was probably already melting when we learn of its existence. From this date we learn of men like John Pache, Peter Goldsmith, John Petit, and William Selman gaining the freedom of the city by virtue of their *wives* having been apprenticed in the town.[181] Women were given the chance to acquire considerable skills because labour was in such short supply. It must have been difficult even to attract apprentices, certainly the sort who would stay with the master who trained them. Interestingly, all four of the above wives were apprenticed to merchants or drapers

---

[177] Power, *Medieval Women*, 57–70; P. J. P. Goldberg, 'Women in Fifteenth-Century Town Life', in J. A. F. Thomson (ed.), *Towns and Townspeople in the Fifteenth Century* (Gloucester, 1988), 112–13; Martha C. Howell, *Production and Patriarchy in Late Medieval Cities* (Chicago, 1986); we shall discuss women at greater length below, Ch. 7, sect. 5.

[178] Cf. low sex ratios in towns like Colchester, Kingston-on-Hull, and Carlisle in 1377 (Russell, 'Population in Europe', 58); see also Goldberg, 'Female Labour'; David Herlihy, *Medieval and Renaissance Pistoia: The Social History of an Italian Town, 1200–1430* (New Haven, Conn., 1967), 83–4.

[179] Power, *Medieval Women*, 60.

[180] *SMWI*: 74.

[181] CBII: 100, 146, 147, and 154. The by-law is at CBII: 58. Cf. Swanson, 115.

who may also have made cloth. It is difficult to know exactly in which aspect of the business they were trained. When the merchant and cloth-maker John Atwater died in 1500, he left bequests to three female employees, including Alison Loveney, to whom he gave some blue cloths and some woad.[182] Difficult though it is to gauge, women had come to occupy an important place in the later medieval urban economy, occupying positions which, in an earlier and a later time, would be reserved to men. There are no female apprentices recorded for the last decade of the fifteenth century, so it is possible that, in Wells as elsewhere, men were beginning to restrict the role that women could play.[183] For most of the fifteenth century, however, there simply were not enough men for the available work.

6. CONCLUSION: QUALIFYING URBAN DECLINE

In the later Middle Ages Wells suffered three periods of decline,[184] separated by at least two periods of considerable recovery. After the fragile stability that probably endured until the appearance of the Black Death, the population and the overall economy fell to that scourge in tremendous proportions. However, the cloth industry's successes grew most impressively in the plague's wake. Despite the continuing high mortality from disease, especially until the 1370s, industry and trade expanded, bringing new people to the city. By 1380 the town's population had recovered to perhaps three-quarters its pre-plague level.

Fifteenth-century population and aggregate wealth went into a

[182] *SMWII*: 389–91.

[183] See below, Ch. 7, sect. 5.

[184] A good recent summary of the great debate on urban decline, attempting to see the whole picture, is D. M. Palliser, 'Urban Decay Revisited', in Thomson (ed.), *Towns and Townspeople*, 1–17. Some other important contributions are Bridbury, *Economic Growth*, and 'English Provincial Towns in the Later Middle Ages, *ECHR*, 2nd ser., 34 (1981), 1–24; R. B. Dobson, 'Urban Decline in Late Medieval England', *TRHS*, 5th ser., 27 (1977), 1–22; S. H. Rigby, ' "Sore Decay" and "Fair Dwellings": Boston and Urban Decline in the Later Middle Ages', *Midland History* 10 (1985), 47–61; id., 'Urban Decline in the Later Middle Ages: The Reliability of the Non-Statistical Evidence' *UHY* (1984), 45–60; 'Urban Decline in the Later Middle Ages: Some Problems in Interpreting the Statistical Data', *UHY* (1979), 46–59; *Winchester*, 86–105; Susan Reynolds, 'Decline and Decay in Late Medieval Towns', *UHY* (1980), 77–9; *Colchester*, 163–268; and Gottfried, 248–50.

gentler, but undeniable decline, from at least the 1420s. The city's physical decay and falling rents, the decline in the number of burgesses, were outlined in Chapter 2. The town fell on its hardest times with respect to overall size between 1445 and 1465, from which time a rally, which can only be attributed to recovered competitiveness in industry and trade, ensued. From the viewpoint of the later Middle Ages, terminal decline followed from the 1480s, although the town's population and economy appear to have stabilized in the early sixteenth century. There were fewer than 1,300 laymen in 1524, roughly half our estimate for the year 1300.

While aggregate economy follows population change fairly closely, the same cannot be said for relative wealth and per capita wealth. The subject of personal wealth has not been addressed extensively in this chapter. We have made clear, however, that there was no time when the demand for labour or Wells cloth dried up. Business generally was in good shape from the 1340s, notwithstanding several significant fluctuations in the export market for cloth, and the consequences of war and competition. Entrepreneurs, investors large and small, were paying more for labour because they had to compete against each other and, more critically, against the lure of the countryside, to which both industry and agriculture enticed craftsmen and labourers. Personal income went up because of this labour shortage. Standards of living went up still more because of the fall in the cost of accommodation which had taken place in the fifteenth century.[185]

We have indicated the scale of the cloth industry, noting both the extent of the wealth that it added to the city in the fourteenth century and how out of proportion to population growth this advance was. Cloth-making was buoyant even when the town was in some of its periods of decline. Its added value helped to make individuals richer by distributing wealth drawn from outside the county, from overseas, among Wells traders, businessmen, and working men and women.[186] For ordinary people, urban decline would have been a meaningless, incomprehensible notion, at most a reference to the growing number of vacant or ruined urban properties.

[185] See Bridbury, *Economic Growth*, 54–6; Hatcher, *Plague, Population*, 47–53; but also Christopher Dyer, *Standards of Living in the Later Middle Ages* (Cambridge, 1989), 210.

[186] Postan, *Medieval Agriculture*, 196–8.

For much of the late fourteenth and fifteenth centuries Wells was losing its relative share of industry and trade, especially outside the cloth industry. This meant that there were fewer men of great substance, fewer overseas traders, fewer—although possibly richer—cloth-makers. As we shall see, the key positions of civic government were limited to a small group of men not because of any policy of exclusion, but because of a lack of men with suitable wealth—one of the universally acknowledged criteria of leadership—in the city.[187] These and other factors suggest Wells's relative decline in importance in the fifteenth century. As far as population and economic size are concerned, it certainly fell several notches on the all-England table. Moreover, it had become distinctly subordinate to larger towns and their merchants.

A small to middling town in 1300 and 1380, Wells in 1350, 1450, and 1500 was a definitely smaller one. It had become more provincial than ever, and only the abiding influence of the cathedral and the effect of the proximity of Bristol on its economy and culture kept the town as diverse as it was. Wells in 1500 could never have been confused with Bristol, York, or even Bury St Edmunds, but nor could it have been mistaken for Axbridge or Evesham. Its decline was real and varied, but it was tempered by the cloth industry and by the greater personal wealth that it brought for the average person.

Our examination of the early history, population, and economic development of Wells has now prepared the way for our study of the social and cultural issues of the community. The demographic, geographic, and material factors remain available as contexts for appreciating other developments, sometimes as causes, sometimes as limiting factors. What is perhaps most striking is the degree of diversity and variability apparent in the size and character of the town and its people. It will be just as striking, then, to see that, from a social and cultural viewpoint, a considerable unity emerges from all this variety, frequent change, and occasional disruption.

[187] See below, Ch. 5, sect. 4.

4

The Balance of Authority

According to standard surveys of the English medieval town, the
great advances in urban privileges and independence took place
before 1300.[1] Aside from the formality of incorporation and the
dignity of county status, the great series of rights that made towns
independent in their day-to-day affairs, which freed them of all but
a monetary rent to their landlords, were victories of the late twelfth
and early thirteenth centuries. The ability to deal with the central
authorities had been attained with such privileges as the return of
writs, free selection of a town's own mayor and coroner, and the
right to pay the king his due rents directly (fee farm).[2] At the same
time, all thoughts of a more thorough independence, of the power
of the city-states of Italy or Germany, if they had ever been
entertained, were entirely forgotten, even by London.

Understandably, historians of the later Middle Ages have
increasingly turned away from these constitutional and jurisdictional concerns. They received so much attention in the first
decades of this century that they are only rehearsed today as
necessary but uncontroversial background. More recently, and
most fruitfully, interest has grown in the social and economic fabric
of the towns and the composition of their body politic, the
distribution of power in the city, and, particularly, in whether, and
to what extent, the towns were oligarchies.[3] But before we look
into such questions about the internal dynamics of the burgess
leadership of Wells or of any town, there are good reasons to look
once again at prevailing constitutional arrangements and confron-
tations. These must have affected the internal power structure and

---

[1] Colin Platt, *The Medieval English Town* (London, 1976), 125–38, esp. 136;
Susan Reynolds, *An Introduction to the History of English Medieval Towns*
(Oxford, 1977), 91–117.
[2] *British Borough Charters 1042–1216*, ed. Adolphus Ballard (Cambridge,
1913), *passim*; Charles Gross, *The Gild Merchant*, 2 vols. (Oxford, 1890), ii.
115–16, prints Ipswich's full charter.
[3] See below, Ch. 5, sect. 5.

organization of all towns, and they often do not agree with the summary picture of civic authority and independence outlined above.

First, at least half the chartered boroughs of England were not royal towns and had not achieved the level of independence and self-assurance that the more famous towns attained.[4] When granting privileges to such a mesne borough, the king was constrained to limit his constitutional gifts to those powers and rights which did not infringe on the jurisdictions that the lord of the town possessed: there were few of these. At the beginning of the fourteenth century, and still at the end of the fifteenth, there were scores of towns whose privileges were limited and static. Wells was one of these towns.

Second, these legal privileges, and the dry, juristic manner in which they have often been treated, deserve to be reviewed in the context of social history. They are not interesting to us for the light that they throw on English legal history. That issue has been faced, and, if it has perhaps been understood too precisely, as if modern concepts of law and legal language prevailed in the Middle Ages, it is more or less a known quantity now. The real interest is in seeing how and why such constitutional elements were sought after by groups of people, and what they were trying to attain. The late-flowering towns are best for this investigation, because their fights often occurred in the brighter documentary light of the fourteenth century, when the struggle for constitutional authority can be seen as an attempt to achieve increased community integrity. This is the significance of the collective grasp for power of later medieval towns.

Long ago, Professor Trenholme pointed out that the monastic boroughs of England, towns like Abingdon and Bury, Cirencester and Dunstable, spent much of the fourteenth century in conflict with their ecclesiastical overlords.[5] In the 1320s long-simmering troubles in Bury and Abingdon overflowed into violence in which lives on both sides were lost.[6] At the time of the Peasants' Revolt

---

[4] Rodney Hilton, 'Towns in Societies: Medieval England', *UHY* (1982), 9; see the discussion in James Tait, *Medieval Manchester and the Beginnings of Lancashire* (Manchester, 1904), 50 ff.

[5] Norman M. Trenholme, *The English Monastic Borough* (University of Missouri Studies, 2/3; Columbia, Mo., 1927).

[6] Trenholme, *Monastic Borough*, 41–4 for Abingdon; M. D. Lobel, 'A Detailed Account of the Rising in Bury St Edmunds in 1326–27 and the Subsequent Trial', *Proceedings of the Suffolk Institute of Archaeology* 21 (1932), 215–31; and

there were further disruptions in some monastic and seigniorial towns.[7] The essential point is that it was the seigniorial boroughs which were most dissatisfied in the fourteenth century, that their burgesses were generally unable to attain the privileges that they thought were their due, and that independence was a feature of only some of England's towns. The less privileged towns included the greater part of the smaller towns of England, whose history has so far been underrated. When we turn to the two most recent general histories of the medieval town, we find an awareness of the 'retrogressive' position of the mesne boroughs, but as little more than a qualification in Susan Reynolds's account.[8] And while Professor Platt is more conscious of the plight of the mesne boroughs and of its national importance, I would argue that a rounded picture of the English medieval town requires that places like Wells and their political regimes be moved closer to the centre of historical awareness, offered as examples of the norm rather than as the unusual or the exceptional.[9]

While it is useful to view towns as either seigniorial or royal, constitutionally advanced or regressive, the reality of power-sharing is better measured on a graded ruler. Wells comes somewhere in the bottom half of the scale of independence. It was a seigniorial borough, and the townsmen had distinctly fewer powers than the burgesses of many seigniorial and even some ecclesiastical boroughs, but it was nevertheless a royal town. By virtue of a charter of King John, frequently confirmed, the men of Wells always had some recourse to the king.[10] Even if he generally favoured the cause of the bishop of Bath and Wells, the burgesses of Wells cherished the right to call themselves the king's burgesses, and at least one of their bishop-lords resented it.[11]

Memorials of St Edmunds Abbey, ed. Thomas Arnold, RS 92, (London, 1892), ii. 328–40; and Thomas Walsingham, *Gesta Abbatum Monasterii Sancti Albani*, ed. H. T. Riley, RS 28, 3 vols. (London, 1867–9), ii. 155–8.

[7] Trenholme, *Monastic Borough*, 55–67; R. B. Dobson (ed.), *The Peasants' Revolt of 1381* (London, 1970), 239–94; and A. F. Butcher, 'English Urban Society and the Revolt of 1381', in R. H. Hilton and T. A. Aston (eds.), *The English Rising of 1381* (Cambridge, 1984), 84–111; and R. B. Dobson, 'The Risings in York, Beverley and Scarborough, 1380–81', ibid., 112–42.

[8] Reynolds, *English Medieval Towns*, 114–16.

[9] Platt, *Medieval Town*, 136–42; unfortunately, much of Platt's discussion is connected to an excessively legalistic argument, concerned with such dubious legal privileges as incorporation. Cf. *Westminster*, ch. 7, which examines the co-operative government of a town that was neither a borough nor discontented.

[10] WCC 4; see above, Ch. 1, sect. 2.

[11] See below, Ch. 4, sect. 4.

At Wells and elsewhere one of the main causes of friction in the later Middle Ages was the growing gap between the burgesses' urban ideal (embodied in other, freer cities) and the perceived reality of their own town. The seigniorial burgesses could see that they were not as privileged, as free, as many other boroughs, because they did not have the king as lord. Wells had been founded solely on the wishes of its bishops, 'for our profit', as Bishop Savaric's charter of *c.*1200 had bluntly phrased it.[12] By 1300 there was obviously an assumption among the lords of towns that adding to the privileges of their burgesses would not do their incomes any good. The flow of new urban privileges dried up. Wells received no new chartered privileges at all in the thirteenth century or later. It was a town whose pursuit of the ideal was to be thwarted.

I. THE BURGESSES' POWER, *c.*1300

Throughout the thirteenth century the townsmen had their eyes open to the possibility of expanding their power, and, if only as a logical consequence, reducing the authority of the bishop. When the eyre session judges passed through Somerset in 1242–3, they found their jurisdiction over a disputed property challenged by the 'burgesses of Wells', who claimed that no one outside of the city had the right to judge such a case.[13]

The first concrete indication that the men of Wells were really unhappy about their lack of independence, and were willing to go to some lengths to improve their situation, comes from the late thirteenth or early fourteenth century. This was an age of great growth in Wells. Its population, its wealth, its modest importance had all increased quickly. In the trail of such success, such new confidence, the burgesses of the city had presented the king with a petition to have their charter confirmed. Although the charters were nominally granted in perpetuity, it was common practice for the current monarch, especially at the time of his accession to the throne, to renew their privileges. Wells Archives include such a charter of 1290, granted by the lately crowned King Edward I.[14]

---

[12] WCC 3.
[13] *Somersetshire Pleas from the Rolls of the Itinerant Justices*, ed. C. E. H. Chadwick Healey, SRS 11 (1897), nos. 418 and 422.
[14] WCC 6.

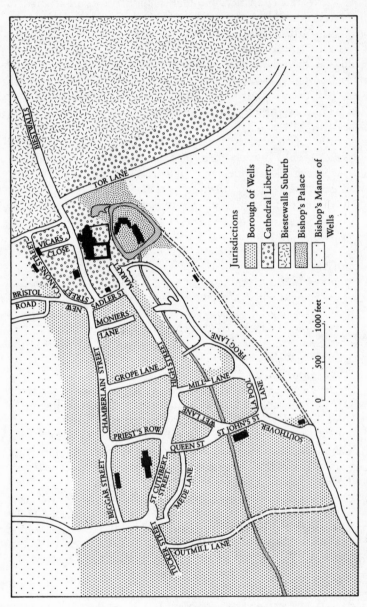

MAP 6. Wells: Jurisdictions

Very possibly, then, the undated petition was submitted in 1307, when Edward II had become king.[15]

But what the burgesses presented under the cover of a routine confirmation was nothing less than a considerable expansion of their rights. They asked that their civic guild be given the privileges of the merchant guild of nearby Bath and of Winchester, and that they be granted full commercial exemptions from tolls and public works. Furthermore, they sought the right to select a proper mayor, whom they would present to the bishop and coroners to deal with the king's government, thereby cutting out the bishop's right to control some issues of the Crown.[16] Since their request for confirmation went well beyond anything contained in King John's brief charter,[17] it was treated by the Crown as an application for a new charter, and an inquiry was called to determine whether the privileges should be given. Nothing more is heard of the issue. Obviously, it was found, as two later inquiries were also to do, that the extension of the townsmen's rights entailed an unwarranted reduction of the bishop's influence and income.[18] The bishop's rights were, for the whole of the later Middle Ages, the broad moat that the burgesses could never overleap.

Notwithstanding their lack of paper rights, the burgesses and people of Wells were not wholly without power and influence in their city. As Gervase Rosser has argued most convincingly lately, the existence of the legal privilege or the desire to expand one's town's authority is no absolute gauge of an urban community's strength or even its organization.[19] Human beings living in close proximity to one another will always organize themselves. Furthermore, in the medieval world they were already organized by the Church. So custom, including the notion of community, and the

[15] *Yearbooks of the Reign of King Edward III: Year XVI (First Part)*, ed. Luke Owen Pike, RS 31 (London, 1896), pp. xlii–xliii; Pike's introduction, pp. xxiv–xciv, is a detailed legal account of a number of Wells's constitutional developments. Royal towns were also alive to the possibility of expanding their jurisdiction by stealth and encroachment. See for e.g. *Colchester*, 31.

[16] *Yearbooks of King Edward III*, pp. xlii–xliii.

[17] WCC 4: King John's charter granted a new fair and confirmed existing fairs and the market.

[18] See *Yearbooks of King Edward III*, p. xliii. The other charter failures occurred in 1341–2 and 1574–5.

[19] Gervase Rosser, 'The Essence of Medieval Urban Communities', *TRHS*, 5th ser. 34 (1984), 91–112, repr. in Richard Holt and Gervase Rosser (eds.), *The Medieval Town: A Reader in English Urban History, 1200–1540* (London, 1990), 216–37.

parish organization always gave people some limited authority. No matter what powers were invested in the hand of the overlord, there were residual, modest rights which the local community maintained.[20]

Throughout the fourteenth century in Wells, there were two structures through which the townsmen participated in city administration. First, there was the parish. Wells was a one-parish town, so the collective selection of the churchwardens and the control of the fabric account gave the Borough Community an unusually concentrated authority in the city.[21] This was especially important in the period before the burgesses had much civic authority: the guild controlled the parochial organization (from which it may historically have emerged) before it controlled anything else.

Second, there were the manorial structures. Under the aegis of the lord of the town, the city retained officers and duties which were usually found in village or manorial circumstances. They existed in towns as vestiges. Probably they were the original government of the twelfth-century urban community, shaped by the assumptions of the bishop-lords. For as Professor Hilton has stressed, especially with respect to the smaller towns, the manorial and the 'feudal' were not excluded from the city in practical terms.[22] Rather, they were excluded from the urban ideal to which all townsmen subscribed. From the point of view of the townsmen, this administrative 'rusticity' was a great part of the problem.

The townspeople selected reeves to oversee their responsibilities to the lord and to represent them before the lord's courts. The reeves were almost certainly selected by the burgesses, but they were confirmed in office by the bishop.[23] All over England these men occupied a notoriously uncomfortable position between town and lord, but at least in the early fourteenth century—the office did not survive the disquiet of the 1340s—the men selected in Wells

---

[20] See e.g. Edward Britton, *The Community of the Vill* (Toronto, 1977), 94–102; Susan Reynolds, *Kingdoms and Communities in Western Europe, 900–1300* (Oxford, 1984), 148–52; and Helen Cam, *Lawfinders and Lawmakers in Medieval England* (London, 1962), 71–84.

[21] See below, Ch. 8, sect. 2.

[22] Hilton, 'Towns in Societies,' 11–12.

[23] On the role and selection of reeves and similar officers in town and village, see J. A. Raftis, *Tenure and Mobility* (Toronto, 1964), 95–6; Trenholme, *Monastic Borough*, 78–80; Tait, *Medieval Manchester*, 51; Reynolds, *Kingdoms and Communities*, 133 and 145.

were prominent and rich burgesses, men like John Markaunt and Robert Lovington, who were plainly and obviously the town's men, not the agents of the bishop's bailiff.[24]

The 'manorial' legal machinery of the town also included the juries and verderers who made presentments to the bishop's courts along with the bailiff's own accusations. Every street in the town had two of its residents appointed as verderers, a strange title for an urban office, but possibly one which displays the office's origins in a rural or manorial circumstance or tradition. These men were the town's pettiest presenting officers. They appeared at every sitting of the bishop's courts, and declared upon oath what infractions of the peace or of trespass had taken place in their streets, or whether anybody had raised the hue and cry.[25]

The juries wielded more authority than the verderers. It is sometimes forgotten that juries were originally representatives of the 'better and more honest' type of men of the area. To medieval eyes, they were the country, the people. We do not know exactly how they were selected in Wells. Those members of juries whose names we do know from the later fourteenth and fifteenth centuries were among the more influential and wealthy.[26] The jury's responsibilities entailed more than simply rendering verdicts. They made inquiries, received complaints, and brought the indictments. The hundred and bishop's borough court system functioned to a great extent on the basis of these juries. The jurors had a place of honour among the townsmen which persisted at least into the fifteenth century. They were almost always selected from among the burgesses, and must be viewed as a manifestation of burghal power even as they went about their business in the bishop's court's service. To swear at one of the twelve jurats, or to impugn his reputation, was a charge that the burgesses' own private guild court took seriously throughout the fourteenth century.[27] Clearly, then,

---

[24] RIII: 432[d]. These men served in 1333. Our information about the reeves of the borough is very limited. There are mentions of 13th cent. reeves (WCAC 35 and 36; RI: 34.), but it is not clear whether the borough had its own reeves, distinct from the manor, at that time. See also LPL ED 1188/11 for a reference to the reeve of Wells Manor.

[25] The work of the verderers can be seen in LPL ED 1181, 1186/9, and 1188/10.

[26] For lists of the Wells juries, the 'jurats' or 12, see ibid. 1097, 1181, 1182, 1186/8, 1186/9, and 1188/10.

[27] On juries, see William Holdsworth, *A History of English Law*, i (London, 1952), 312–27; Britton, *Community of the Vill*, 94; R. Lennard, 'Early Manorial Juries', *EHR* 77 (1962), 511–18; F. Pollock and F. W. Maitland, *The History of English Law before the Time of Edward I*, 2nd edn. (Cambridge, 1911), ii. 625–7.

the inhabitants of Wells did have some role to play in the government of the town.

Nevertheless, the central and reigning truth of government *circa* 1300 was the authority possessed by the bishop of Bath and Wells. All the courts that affected the lives of the laymen of Wells were in the hands of the bishop, with the single exception of the court Christian of the dean of Wells. The bishop's bailiff held weekly courts, and his steward held quarterly hundred and leet courts. Infringements of the petty assizes, disturbances of the peace, and all manner of business and personal trespasses would be presented and heard in these forums. The bishop also had the right to return all royal writs, and to hang apprehended murderers and thieves.[28]

The episcopal authority went further. Because the bishop had created the town, carving it out of a manor, he had kept in place not only parts of manorial government, but some manorial dues. But they were charges that the burgesses, highly sensitive to the taint of the manorial and servile, resented. The men of Wells had, for instance, to pay a due called 'tolsester', which was the bishop's right to a part of every brewing at an advantageous price.[29] Throughout the thirteenth century and possibly into the fourteenth the burgesses of Wells also had to grind all their grain at one particular mill of the bishop's, the 'out-mill', while the rural tenants of the manor used the 'in-mill'.[30] Both of these exactions were the kind that could become the cause or symbol around which serious dissension could arise. The suit of mill was near to the centre of the contemporary troubles in St Albans, where the abbey tried to suppress the hand-mills that the people were operating in order to avoid paying to use their lord's mill.[31]

Such petty issues were, of course, in addition to the extensive power that the bishop held over the regulation of the economy. He

---

[28] WCC 7; *Rotuli Hundredorum*, ed. W. Illingworth and J. Caley, ii (London, 1818), 134; *Placita de Quo Warranto Edward I–Edward II*, ed. W. Illingworth, ii (London, 1818), 703; On hundred courts and the usual local legal arrangements, see Helen Cam, *The Hundred and the Hundred Rolls* (London, 1930); for a summary of other mesne boroughs, see Trenholme, *Monastic Borough*, 78–9.

[29] WCC 7; this due was certainly being collected, since it helped to cause some of the friction between town and lord in 1343: see below, Ch. 4, sect. 2.

[30] CBII: 180.

[31] *Gesta Abbatum*, ii. 54 and 149. On towns and the 'soke', see Tait, *Medieval Manchester*, 98–102; on the development of the suit of mill outside of towns, especially with reference to the lord's interests, see Richard Holt, 'Whose Were the Profits of Milling?', *P & P* 116 (1987), 3–23.

owned the market and the town's four fairs. Only he had the right
to levy tolls. All of these were rights that he used, privileges which
were worth about £10 in 1300 (including the profits of his
courts).[32] This figure would grow to around £25 in the fifteenth
century.[33] Though these seem like modest sums, and were certainly
only a small proportion of the bishop's income, they were
important. After all, the greater part of the bishop's revenue was
composed of similarly small sums. He derived his income from
several different boroughs and more than a dozen manors. He also
possessed the courts in all these jurisdictions, including the hundred
courts.[34] When Bishops Reginald and Savaric granted a court to the
town in the twelfth century, they were legally separating the
borough from the manor. They were not granting the ownership or
control of the court to the burgesses.[35] To yield to the demands of
one community for legal or economic jurisdiction would have been
a bad example to the others, and yet the division was meaningful,
an acknowledgement of the separate status and different community of the borough.

But we must guard against believing that such customs, powers,
and exactions were exceptional, to be found only where lords were
unusually oppressive. The facts of the case show otherwise. Once
again, the picture of the later medieval town that was developed to
fit the case of the royal boroughs misleads us when we turn to the
many mesne boroughs. Every town had its customs, and these often
included exactions which the citizens felt detracted from their
dignity and sometimes from their wealth.[36] Like the dues at Wells,
they limited the liberty—understood as freedom and privilege—of
the burgesses. If the urban ideal was developed from the reality of
many royal towns, we must keep in mind that the reality of most of
the medium and smaller towns was otherwise. For them, the battle
for authority was still being waged, and it would be fought under
the banner of the collectivity.

[32] PRO C44/1/13, and SC6/1131/1 and 4.
[33] PRO SC6/Henry VII/1806.
[34] LPL ED 224ᵇ; PRO C44 1/13/5; PRO SC6/1121/1, 6, and 9 include episcopal
accounts of the 14th and 15th cents.
[35] WCC 1 and 3; in the same fashion the bishops granted fairs to the town (WCC
2 and 3), but always maintained control and ownership of these fairs.
[36] Rodney Hilton, 'Lords, Burgesses and Hucksters', *P & P* 97 (1982), 12; Tait,
Medieval Manchester, 48, notes restrictions on the freedom of movement of
Manchester burgesses; *Gesta Abbatum*, i. 410 (hand-mills). In the event, the men of
Wells had probably become free of suit of mill by the 1330s.

2. THE MOMENT OF CRISIS

The burgesses attempted a more direct path to increased authority in the 1330s and 1340s. First, they negotiated with the bishop to be allowed to hold most of the authority in the city in exchange for a composite rent of 100 marks per annum.[37] Unfortunately, we are unable to date this arrangement precisely. It is mentioned only in the aftermath of the troubles which developed in the 1340s. Since the composite rent was not noted in the episcopal accounts for 1329, during the vacancy following Bishop Drokensford's death, we can assign this development to the period between 1330 and 1341, sometime during Ralph of Shrewsbury's episcopate.[38] It was later asserted that the twelve jurats had held the town 'for a number of years' before 1343.[39] A document of 1333 is witnessed by two reeves of the city of Wells and by a bailiff named Richard Atmore.[40] All three were burgesses who were heavily involved in the opposition against the bishop ten years later.[41] Since both before and after the period of expanded power and the subsequent troubles the bailiffs of the town were not generally burgesses but episcopal appointees, it would seem that in 1333, when Atmore was bailiff, the burgesses were already in control of the city, and the office of bailiff was now within their control. Very probably, then, the burgesses received their expanded authority in 1329, when Ralph of Shrewsbury became bishop.

The agreement between burgesses and bishop was written down in an indenture which has now been lost. But its effect was to give the burgesses a taste of the independence that they desired. And, as subsequent events suggest, the prospect of ever having to surrender their leased authority rankled. Possibly, the burgesses resented having to pay 100 marks to the bishop each year. Indeed, it is unclear from the surviving accounts how the town could be worth 100 marks per annum (£66 13s. 4d.). In 1343 the bishop's itemized profits from the town, including rents of assize, were only £23.[42]

---

[37] PRO C44/1/13/3, and WCC 7; cf. Reynolds, *English Medieval Towns*, 102–3; and *VCH Leicester*, iv, ed. R. A. McKinley (London 1958), 9–23 indicate that other mesne boroughs sometimes paid such a composite rent to their lord, possibly a seigniorial equivalent of a fee farm.

[38] PRO C44/1/13/5.   [39] PRO C44/1/13/3.

[40] RIII: 432ᵈ.   [41] RI: 241ᵈ., and WCC 7.

[42] PRO C44/1/13/3; C44/1/13/5 indicates partial income from Wells for 1292–3 and 1329, which point to similar total values. PRO SC6/1131/4 valued the town at £10 6s. 2d. in 1308–9.

The combination of financial pressure and increased independence inspired the burgesses to attempt bold solutions.

The burgesses of Wells went to the king in 1341 to ask him to enlarge some advantages, 200 years old, which the bishops had granted the town, to enlarge them to such an extent as to prejudice the value and prestige of the episcopal franchise, the very elements cited as motives for fostering the town.[43] The king had returned from the debt-producing, disastrous campaign in the Low Countries anxious for money, however little, and he had no interest in inquiring too closely into Wells's constitutional history.[44] The burgesses were his men, and they sought to cease being the bishop's by the peaceful action and the permanent solution of a new royal charter—in short, to use the king to free themselves of the bishop.

On 17 July 1341 Edward III, having received £40 from the burgesses, reconfirmed their ancient charter and added a detailed list of constitutional privileges, commercial quittances, and freedoms from tolls and works on castles and bridges. The privileges represented the urban ideal achieved: self-government, independence, and direct relations with the Crown, freedom almost as complete as any burgess in England possessed or desired. The men of Wells were to have a mayor, bailiffs, constables of the peace, and coroners of their own choosing to oversee the town's affairs. All cases relating to Wells property and inhabitants were to be tried by the mayor and bailiffs, excepting pleas of the Crown. They were to have direct relations with the Exchequer, and the return of writs. No officer of the king—sheriff or bailiff—was to meddle in their affairs. Furthermore, only Wells burgesses would be liable for jury or inquisition duty in affairs concerning property or business within the town. Edward also granted a gaol, and the right to build a wall of mortar and stone, crenellated, and surrounded by a moat. The community would have become jurisdictionally and even physically self-contained.[45]

[43] WCC 3.

[44] M. H. Keen, *England in the Later Middle Ages* (London, 1973), 122–31; G. L. Harriss, *King, Parliament and Public Finance in Medieval England to 1369* (Oxford, 1975), 231–312: p. 276 reports that Edward owed £200,000 when he returned.

[45] CCR 1341–1417: 6–7; control of the gates was an important political issue in the disputes recounted in 'Depraedatio Abbatiae Sancti Edmundi', in *Memorials of St Edmunds Abbey*, iii. 332.

In effect, the burgesses were trying to steal the town from the bishop. They had no right to circumvent his authority by appealing directly to the king; and they contrived to have the charter issued without an inquisition *ad quod damnum*, a necessary procedural step to determine whose rights were being infringed. It was this process that would have revealed the damage done to the bishop. Perhaps as critical to the outcome of the town's gamble was that the burgesses did not curry enough favour with the king. For although they were extricating themselves from their dues to the bishops, they managed to avoid committing themselves to any fee farm or other regular payment to the king. Had they not done so, the conclusion of the dispute might have been more favourable.

The provisions of the new charter were implemented immediately. A mayor was elected; a new court was established. Walter Middleton was called the mayor of Wells in documents dated 4 December 1341 and 1 January 1342.[46] But very shortly after, within three months, questions were being raised in Chancery and the Exchequer about the prudence and legality of the charter. Bishop Ralph of Shrewsbury was certainly—but discreetly— behind some of the Crown's doubts and legal activity, concerned with his newly discovered losses of revenue and prestige. Although it is not known for sure if the borough had decided to cease or to reduce its composite payment to the bishop, he was clearly no longer assured this 100 marks per annum, since the king had intervened to replace Ralph as the main patron of the town. During the subsequent proceedings Wells did *not* defend itself by claiming that the bishop was receiving his rent and therefore had suffered no loss, from which it would appear that they were intending to pay rent neither to the bishop nor to the king. Politically, it was a mistaken policy, because it left the burgesses without allies.[47]

On 16 November the king issued a writ of *scire facias* to the sheriff of Somerset, summoning the burgesses of Wells to explain why they should not lose their charter. The Crown claimed that the bishop of Bath and Wells held the town and numerous privileges, the value of which would be lost to him—and to the king in a time of vacancy. Furthermore, the grant of a gaol was to the prejudice of the farmer of the county gaol in Somerton, since he would lose part

---

[46] WTD 100, and WCAC 264.   [47] PRO C44/1/13/1–3.

of his £24 annual income. Legally, however, the omission of the process *si sit ad damnum* was the most important point.[48]

A Chancery trial date was set for Hilary 1342, but in the mean time Wells continued under its new regime. The burgesses had begun to levy murage—a toll to support the construction of city walls—which the king had granted them for five marks in July 1341.[49] In March 1342, probably just before the trial, a commission of inquiry composed of several prominent West Country lords and justices arrived in Wells to establish the privileges of the bishop of Bath and Wells and to assess their value, all of which they did accurately, and therefore to the burgesses' damage.[50] Predictably, the Hilary proceedings went against the town. Since its lawyer failed to show that the burgesses had been correct to proceed without acquiring the writ of *ad quod damnum*, the issue was decided on the question of prejudice, the town being unable to refute the facts that the bishop and the farmer of the gaol would suffer permanent loss, and that the king would lose whenever these positions were vacant. Judgment was given against the town in Michaelmas term 1342.[51]

By that time Wells had enjoyed fifteen months of full borough privileges, and the burgesses were not anxious to revert to their old status. When the charter was cancelled, resentment hardened town opinion. They had lost the generous provisions of the new charter, including its potential economic benefits. They had lost the ability to select their own bailiff and to be in control of the bishop's franchise, as they had been since at least 1333. They were poorer by the £40 paid for the charter, the five marks paid for the murage, and the unknown but substantial legal costs. Furthermore, they knew that the bishop of Bath was the power behind the action against them, for, as their lawyer complained, not without truth: 'All that is assigned for damage is damage to another person, who does not complain, and therefore it is strange.'[52] It must be remembered that the legal challenge against the charter came from

---

[48] WCC 8 contains the writ and related documents, as does PRO C44/1/13.
[49] *CPR 1340–4*: 248; WCC 8; and PRO C44/1/13/3.
[50] PRO C44/1/13/2 and 3.
[51] *Yearbooks of King Edward III*, 109–20, where the report of the case is printed; cf. PRO C44/1/13/5; WCC 8.
[52] *Yearbooks of King Edward III*, 120.

the Crown, not from the bishop or the farmer of the gaol at Somerton. The charter cancellation ended the first phase of the troubles of the 1340s. To this point, the issue had been purely a legal and constitutional fight.

In the aftermath, however, the town tried to retain whatever advantages it could, and, one way or another, to end episcopal control of the town. By July 1343 Bishop Ralph did launch a legal complaint by initiating a lawsuit against his burgesses.[53] The bishop's legal action was now facilitated by the cancellation of the insurmountable obstacle of the royal charter that had sanctioned the burgesses' powers. The suit was necessary because of the continuing rebelliousness of his burgesses.

During the subsequent unrest Wells offered an instance of serious civil agitation and confusion, but not a case of violent revolt. The town acted with the authority of the charter that they had been forced to surrender and of the agreement, now suspended, to hold the town at a sort of fee farm from the bishop, quietly attempting, in the failure of its *de jure* jurisdiction, to continue it *de facto*. In order to reassert his authority after the revocation of the royal charter, the bishop and his bailiff would have had to put down the burgesses' court and officers and to reassert customary dues. The burgesses, however, refused to acknowledge the renewed episcopal jurisdiction.

In January 1343 the burgesses formed a sworn commune to oppose the bishop, gaoling three men, employed by the bishop, who refused to go along with them. In January and February 1343 they disrupted the bailiff's hundred courts. On 30 April they did the same to his view of frankpledge. They rescued any distraints that the episcopal officers attempted to make, and refused to render the tolsester demanded of them. While rescuing distraints in May, they injured some of the bishop's servants. They continued to run a court of their own, and compelled everyone to do suit there.[54] In effect, the conflict was between two established courts—the burghal and the episcopal—each distraining, fining, and arresting the suitors of the other.

The burgesses also refused to pay any more of the bishop's customary dues. These were of two kinds. First, there was tolsester,

[53] RI: 240–3; WCC 7.   [54] WCC 7, and RI: 242[d].

the bishop's right to buy five flagons out of every brewing in Wells for a set, low price. The second sort of custom concerned duties that were assessed at the four annual fairs in Wells. Bishop Ralph claimed that these were his fairs, and that the burgesses owed him toll, stallage, and numerous other duties, apparently as much money as any 'foreign' trader without a royal exemption. The burgesses had ceased to pay the duties at the fairs, and several of them led a revolt against tolsester. The citizens forcefully took over the collection of the tolls and amercements at the St Andrew's and St Calixtus' fairs in 1342. The complaint charged that they backed up their claims with drawn swords and bows and arrows.[55]

When judgment was given against the town in August 1343, the bishop was awarded £3,000 damages. In their dispute in the 1320s the men of Bury St Edmunds had been fined £140,000, nicely reflecting the relative severity of the two disturbances.[56] The crux of the difference was the lack of serious violence, of bloodshed, at Wells. There was force applied there, but no wanton violence, pitched battles, or deaths. The fine was presumably held over the heads of the individuals cited in the suit, since no corporate body was recognized, and there is no record in the cathedral documents—where Bishop Ralph asked for the proceedings to be enrolled—of any agreement about a schedule of payment. It gives the impression that the bishop wanted to re-establish his authority, but not to antagonize the town further.[57]

In the past the bishop's suit has always been thought to have been incited by 'riots' at Wells, but it is important to place events in their proper context.[58] They must be seen in the light of the arrangement to control the town that the burgesses had made with Bishop Ralph in the 1330s, and with an eye to the royal charter, however suspiciously acquired, which gave authority to the townsmen. The nature of Wells as a discontented mesne borough must be placed in a continuum between a borough like Leicester, where there were occasional disagreements with the lord but no serious defiance, and

[55] RI: 242^d, and WCC 7.

[56] RI: 243; and Lobel, 'Rising in Bury St Edmunds', 230; *Memorials of St Edmunds Abbey*, ii, app. A.

[57] RI: 243.

[58] *Register of Ralph of Shrewsbury, 1329–63*, ed. Thomas Scott Holmes, 2 vols. SRS 9–10 (1896), i, p. xxvi; Phyllis Hembry, *The Bishops of Bath and Wells 1540–1640* (London, 1967), 33, follows N. F. Hulbert, 'A Survey of Somerset Fairs', *SANHS* 82 (1936), 112 ff., in a fanciful view of the troubles of '1334'.

a borough like Bury, where the violence of 1326–30 left dozens on both sides dead and required the king's military intervention.[59] Since there were no criminal proceedings against any of the individual burgesses in Wells, it is plain that the violence was limited to a confusion of armed illegal arrests, forced court appearances, and the minor assaults that go with them.[60] 'Uprising' or 'rebellion' does not seem an entirely appropriate term for what occurred.

We can attempt some very rough analysis of who was involved in the events of the 1340s. Unfortunately, the detailed series of burgess court records and the freedom lists do not go back that far. The judicial records name sixty-two individuals: twenty-nine in the first instance; thirty-three added later by the local jury.[61] The first group of names comprised mainly the senior men of the town who must have constituted the town jury, possibly some of the twelve jurats who had negotiated with the bishop to control the town in the 1330s. In this group we find Walter Middleton, Wells's only medieval mayor, Richard Atmore, the town bailiff under the episcopal 'fee farm' arrangement, as well as two reeves, Robert Lovington and John Markaunt. Also cited were Hugh Somerton, Thomas Salter, and Thomas Mertok, who, along with Markaunt, were among the wealthier burgesses named as far back as the 1327 lay subsidy.[62] Men such as these would have been the principal losers—in terms of honour, power, and money—from the failure of the drive for self-government. Fifteen of them are mentioned repeatedly in the town charters of the period as both witnesses and property owners.

The town's protagonists did not come from this élite alone. Alongside the rich jurats in the first group are fourteen others who make no more than one or two appearances in the documents, six of them occurring nowhere else in the surviving documents. Some, like the former mayor's brother, John Middleton, were plainly better connected than well off. He was one of two cited who had no property by which he could be guaranteed.[63] It is clear that some of the men who were active enough in the disorder to be cited first

---

[59] Lobel, 'Rising in Bury St Edmunds', 214–19; *VCH Leicester*, iv. 12.
[60] RI: 240.
[61] WCC 7.
[62] *Kirkby's Quest for Somerset, etc.*, ed. F. H. Dickinson, SRS 3 (1889), 272–3.
[63] RI: 241ᵈ.

were not members of the town's merchant and proprietary élite, were not normally close to the centre of any decision-making. Thomas Chaloner and barber John Lange, for instance, made no mark on any other existing record.

The names added to the indictment by the local jury confirm that there was some popular participation.[64] Among these men, only eight out of thirty-three appear in any other extant documents. There were even two members of the clergy who were charged along with the burgesses. They were William Jordan and Nicholas Atwood, chaplains, who were possibly employed in St Cuthbert's church, and had taken the side of their employers, the parishioners and burgesses of Wells.[65] The evidence is inconclusive, but it suggests that the support for civic independence was fairly broad and probably popular.

The bishop's complaint said that his peace had been obstructed by a commune, a sworn confederacy.[66] Such communes were infamous, and the bishop was certainly trying to evoke the terrible events of previous uprisings, such as that of Bury in 1326, twelfth-century London, and the many Continental examples.[67] It was in a certain sense an accurate claim in Wells's case. Even during the trial it was plain that the townsmen conspired not to defend themselves. They asked the court's leave to discuss their position, won a recess, and never returned.[68] Furthermore, throughout the fourteenth and fifteenth centuries the burgesses of the Community continued to take an oath not to use the bishop's or even the king's court against one another without a borough licence.[69] In Wells the Community did function as a commune, a sworn fraternity which illegally attempted to limit the lawful authority of the lord of the town.

The one punitive excommunication that was declared fell on Walter Middleton. Bishop Ralph ordered that, until Middleton showed himself worthy of forgiveness, twelve priests in the

---

[64] Ibid; WCC 7; CPR 1343–5: 99.

[65] It may have been the same Jordan who was appointed vicar of Stokecury by the same bishop in 1348 (SRO DD/B, Reg. 2: 322.)

[66] RI: 240.

[67] A pointed discussion of the terms 'commune' and '*communitas*' appears in Reynolds, *English Medieval Towns*, 103–4 and 106–8; cf. Susan Reynolds, 'The Rulers of London in the Twelfth Century', *History* 57 (1972), 348–50; *Memorials of St Edmunds Abbey*, iii. 337; and *Gesta Abbatum*, ii. 155–7.

[68] RI: 243, and WCC 7.

[69] See below, Chs. 5 and 6, for details of the 'commune' of Wells embodied in the Borough Community.

cathedral and six in the parish church were to denounce him solemnly and publicly every Sunday before the gathered laity and clergy. He was charged with 'presuming to deprive the church of Wells of its liberties by malicious government'.[70] Since this all occurred in September 1343, however, after the bishop had won his damages and when Edward's charter was long gone, it must be considered further proof that the townsmen remained collectively recalcitrant.

Restricted in scope and frequency of meeting, the borough court—and the commune that it represented—would continue to rival, quietly oppose, and, ultimately, work with the bishop's courts throughout the later Middle Ages.[71] The town was defeated in its fight for more power, but it was not crushed. A community has resilience. And the strength of the burgesses' solidarity after their failure was instrumental in presenting the Borough Community with a surprising growth in responsibility in the aftermath of their greatest defeat.

It is not necessary that the burgesses of Wells should have been especially oppressed by the bishops; rather the contrary. It is notoriously the rising, prospering group which is the first to feel the prick of small degradations and legal inequalities. The 1327 lay subsidy and the prominence of Wells as a cloth-making town attest to its wealth. It was precisely in the period from 1330 to 1380 that Wells grew most prodigiously and wealthily, even overcoming to some extent the damage produced by the plague.[72] The prominent burgesses were rich enough and free enough to scheme, and the end of their thinking was to urbanize themselves more fully, to separate themselves as completely as possible from their manorial, unfree past, from their seignior. The bishop's dues and rights offended the burgesses more in 1340 than they had done when the borough was created around 1140, and the townsmen's ambition to approximate their ideal of a proper burgess probably had as much to do with their reasons for seeking the offending charter as any more substantive causes.

The defeats of the early 1340s demonstrate how difficult it was for an urban community to improve its constitutional position without the wholehearted support of the lord of the town.

70 SRO DD/B, Reg. 2: 283.
71 See below, Chs. 5 and 6.
72 On this subject, see above, Chs. 1, sect. 2, and 3, sect. 2.

Nevertheless, urban unrest in England was common in the fourteenth century. The several serious revolts of the 1320s to 1340s did not contain the agitation, and rebellions more severe than Wells's disturbances continued in the middle and later decades of the fourteenth century.[73] Constitutional weakness notwithstanding, townsmen were on the rise; business boomed, and their economic power grew nation-wide.[74] But in the event of significant conflict and the disruption of the peace, the king was sure to take the side of the offended lord. Ultimately, it was the unusual power of the English monarchy that allowed abbeys and bishops to stifle the governing aspirations of many townsmen.

But there are other lessons to be learned from Wells. First, it is plain that the town could work with the bishop, could bargain with him to advance their authority in the city on an *ad hoc* basis. They had at some point won the withdrawal of the suit of mill.[75] Prior to the new royal charter the jurats had negotiated responsibility for the town.[76] This was an advance in authority that their ill-advised coup destroyed. The composite rent, and the privileges that it bought, were never heard of again.

The crucial point was that the bishops were concerned with their own interests, especially their income. They had no desire to be hard on the burgesses for malice's sake. Bishop Ralph of Shrewsbury effectively protected his rights and safeguarded his income in the 1340s, but he had moved against the citizens with

[73] See Trenholme, *Monastic Borough*, 1–77; there were also intermittent disruptions in Salisbury, including during the 1340s and 1350s: see *VCH Wiltshire*, vi, ed. Elizabeth Crittall (London, 1962), 95–102; see also Dobson, 'Risings in 1380–81'; Butcher, 'English Urban Society'; Platt, *Medieval Town*, 140.

[74] The establishment of the borough representation in Parliament was one 14th cent. indicator of townsmen's importance, especially in providing taxes; F. T. Plucknett, 'Parliament, 1327–36', in E. B. Fryde and E. Miller (eds.), *Historical Studies of the English Parliament*, i, *Origins to 1369* (Cambridge, 1970), 217, notes that burgesses made up 160 of the 514 members of Parliament and the majority of the commons; also A. R. Bridbury, *Economic Growth: England in the Later Middle Ages* (London, 1972), 77–82, 112–13, modified by J. F. Hadwin, 'The Medieval Lay Subsidies and Economic History', *ECHR*, 2nd ser., 36 (1983), 212–13, and supported by D. M. Palliser, 'Urban Decay Revisited', in John A. F. Thomson (ed.), *Towns and Townspeople in the Fifteenth Century* (Gloucester, 1988), 12–13, argued for the relative increase in townsmen's wealth through the 14th and 15th cent.

[75] We cannot date this precisely; it was probably by the 1330s, but in 1493 the manorial custumal for Wells stated that the burgesses had once owed suit of mill, but were now freed: CBII: 180.

[76] See above, Ch. 4, sect. 2.

moderation. He and subsequent bishops were ready to extend further *de facto* authority to the townsmen, but they were not prepared to grant legally binding perpetual rights without heavy compensation, heavier than the burgesses were willing to pay before the reign of Elizabeth.[77] The burgesses wanted their independence, but they wanted it without burdensome costs. They had perhaps learned a lesson from some of their freer sister cities: the fee farm or an equivalent annual payment could be an onerous burden for a large town like Coventry; a crushing oppression for a small one like Droitwich.[78]

Although their rebelliousness in the 1330s and 1340s must have greatly undermined the bishop's spirit of accommodation, the townsmen's stubbornness and increasing economic clout were soon to win for them a power which was never recorded in any charter, never actually acknowledged by any court of record. Strength came to the citizens of Wells through fraternal solidarity. A sense of community was one of the ineradicable cultural features that underlay the body politic. It found its constitutional expression in various ways, but one potent urban manifestation was the guild or *communitas*. We shall have a lot more to say about the Borough Community and its particular strength and nature.[79] By the fourteenth century it had become the chief conduit of burgess and city aspirations and authority. In the wake of the cancelled charter, the failed rebellion, it was through the Community that the burgesses staged their rally. They had failed to wrestle legal power away from the bishop, so what they now did was to give more of their own capabilities to the Community. They bound themselves to use its court rather than the official courts. And they gave their wealth to the Borough Community, so that it could become an economic and landowning power in the city.[80] In adversity and further adversity, the burgesses fashioned small victories.

[77] *Wells City Charters*, ed. Dorothy O. Shilton and Richard Holworthy, SRS 46 (1932), pp. xix–xxi, discuss the 16th-cent. approach to independence, finally achieved in 1589 (WCC 29 and 30).

[78] Mary Bateson, 'Droitwich Borough', in *VCH Worcester*, iii, ed. J. W. Willis-Bund (London, 1913), 74–8; *Coventry*, 35; A. R. Bridbury, 'English Provincial Towns in the Later Middle Ages', *ECHR*, 2nd ser., 34 (1981), 6–7, on the disadvantages of the fee farm.

[79] See below, Chs. 5 and 6.

[80] See below, Ch. 6, for a discussion of burgess solidarity; WCC 7 for the bishop's accusation of a sworn conspiracy; and n. 46 above.

3. THE COMMUNITY'S RESOURCES

The relation between property and power in the later Middle Ages was unusually close. Furthermore, the combination of property and community was an assured way of gaining authority. From fairly early on, the burgesses of Wells succeeded in amassing a sizeable portfolio of property in the city. The practice of donating houses and land to the Borough Community seems to have begun in the thirteenth century. A fragmentary fourteenth-century account, probably written *c*.1370, describes some properties as once belonging to the burgess Henry Winchester, who seems to have been prominent around 1300.[81] But that same document also confirms that the majority of properties with identifiable former owners were donated after 1340. Indeed, twenty-eight out of thirty-eight former owners can be assigned to the post-1340 period.[82]

The power that the townsmen accumulated in the mid- and later fourteenth century was largely the result of the fact that the membership was committed enough to give property to the guild. When, shortly after the events of the 1340s, the plague struck Wells, the *esprit de corps* among the burgesses was still high, and the awful flood of death brought a beneficial flood of bequests, helping to accelerate the transformation of the Borough Community into a key player in the government of the town.[83] It would appear that there was a quite deliberate plan, a strategy, to make a good fortune for the collective out of the deaths of its individual members. The plague revealed many grants by triggering the bequests, but they had already begun to occur earlier, especially after the troubles of 1341–4. We know that many of the original grants have been lost, but we can outline some of them from this period and the later fourteenth century.

The burgesses involved in the dispute with the bishop were prominent among the donors. William Cheleworth, probably the

---

[81] WTA 86; WTD 26 and 27 (1298–9).

[82] See John Blair, 'Religious Gilds as Landowners in the Thirteenth and Fourteenth Centuries: The Example of Chesterfield', in P. Riden (ed.), *The Medieval Town in Britain* (Cardiff, 1980); and Levy Fox, 'The Administration of Gild Property in Coventry in the Fifteenth Century', *English Historical Review* 55 (1940), 634–47.

[83] Only a proportion of the grants of civic property have survived, but the first year of the plague was the most conspicuous for the number of extant grants.

son of wealthy Adam Cheleworth,[84] was cited for his opposition to
the bishop in 1343.[85] He was only mentioned after this in the past
tense, and was certainly dead by 1353.[86] He left the Community a
tenement worth 16s. per annum.[87] John Lange, a dyer, another of
the activists of 1343, left the Community land and a tenter-yard
worth 9s. per annum.[88]

The most concentrated group of donations for which the grants
are actually extant started in August 1348 and continued through
February 1349.[89] Plague came early to Somerset.[90] In August
Thomas Testwode granted a tenement worth 9s. per annum to the
Community.[91] A former master of the Community and a rebel of
1343, Richard Eyr, left various lands in the town and the manor to
the Community in mid-November.[92] Robert Fordham left a
tenement later worth 8s. per annum.[93] Walter Atputte donated a
tenement and two messuages.[94] In 1349 Alice Pirton, widow of
burgess William, surrendered all her rights in a tenter-yard and plot
of land in Tucker Street to the master of the Community.[95] It was
yielding 4s. per annum in the last decades of the century.[96] On 6
October Hugh Somerton, a leader in 1343, gave the Community all
his lands in Wells and his native Somerton. Included among these
lands were two tenter-yards.[97] Remarkably, none of these grants

[84] Adam Cheleworth was the city's fourth richest inhabitant according to the
1327 lay subsidy: see *Kirkby's Quest*, 272.

[85] WCC 7.

[86] RIII: 118–19. His son and wife were still alive; he may have died in the plague,
or possibly earlier.

[87] WTA 86; at the time of the account it was dilapidated and worth only 9d. p.a.
when occupied.

[88] WTA 86.

[89] See WTD 117–22, 124–6.

[90] SRO DD/B, Reg. 2: 325: on 17 Aug. 1348 the bishop issued a letter on the
plague, then raging in France, but it had in fact already entered England; J. F.
Chanter, 'The Court Rolls of the Manor of Curry Rivel in the Years of the Black
Death, 1348–9', *SANHS* 56 (1910), 88; E. H. Bates Harbin, 'The "Black Death" in
Somerset, 1348–49', *SANHS* 68 (1917), 91; J. F. D. Shrewsbury, *A History of the
Bubonic Plague in the British Isles* (Cambridge, 1971), 37–40.

[91] WTD 117; see WTA 86.

[92] WTD 119; the curtilage on La Pool was worth 3s. p.a. in the 14th-cent.
account (WTA 86); see also CBI: 227 for this property in 1421.

[93] WTD 121 (Nov. 1348); and WTA 86.

[94] WTD 120 (1 Dec. 1348); WTA 86. Cf. WTD 152, which refers, like Atputte's
grant, to a tenement called 'le Bakhouse' which was worth 4s. p.a.

[95] WTD 125.

[96] WTA 86.

[97] WTD 118 and 125; WTA 86.

mentioned or can be associated with any religious benefaction or other compensation. Most were certainly too small to establish anything more lavish than an annual mass. This is not to say that there was no religious requirement imposed by some other, now lost, document, but it cannot have amounted to much, and very probably did not exist. The benefactor was probably added to the bede-roll—the list of those for whom to pray—of the Trinity chaplains.

Some other grants from the same period did include a provision for religious services. On 6 December 1348 John Littlewyn's widow, Alice, gave the Community and St Cuthbert's church a tenement on condition that 5s. of the rent be given for prayers to the Virgin.[98] John Scriven's will was proved on 6 February 1349. It gave a tenement to the master and 'his fellow churchwardens' in support of the light of Corpus Christi in the church.[99] Nothing in this grant spoke of the Community, but the association of parish and Borough Community meant that the latter became the overseer of religious acts—and the *de facto* owner of the property. In contrast, Thomas Devonish plainly intended to support both religion and his burgess guild. He left the master and Community and the churchwardens a tenement and five shops, but required that they acquit his wife of all future tallage, and that they find a chaplain to hold an anniversary service for Thomas and his family.[100]

These and several other properties were left by people who disappear from the records at the time of the plague. But although there was never again such a concentrated outpouring of grants to the Community, the support continued, sometimes on a very generous scale. In 1394 the former town master Nicholas Cristesham granted eighteen properties to the Community 'in relief of the Community and in aid of the support of the charges incumbent on it'. Cristesham had had to pay a hefty £20 to the king for the mortmain licence.[101] In 1406 four burgesses who had served as masters of the town paid twenty marks for a mortmain licence to give the master and Community four messuages and four shops.[102]

---

[98] WTD 122; it would seem that this property was 'an empty place', yielding only 2s. p.a. in the 1370s and 1380s (WTA 86).

[99] WTD 124.   [100] WTD 108, 115, and 116.

[101] WCC 13, and *CPR 1391–6*: 515.   [102] WCC 17, and *CPR 1405–8*: 160.

Again, there is no evidence that either of these gifts carried any financial burdens for the guild. To this extent, the grant of five properties by Thomas Tanner's executors was different, since the former master's wealth was to be used to fund a chantry and other pious works.[103] The authority of the burgesses would nevertheless have been strengthened by all such grants, by any and every expansion of their corporate economic strength in the city. By the end of the Middle Ages the burgesses of Wells owned about 25 per cent of the city's real estate, about 120 properties in 1430, and 150 in the mid-sixteenth century.[104]

There are many questions about these donations that cannot be answered because relatively few of the grants have survived. Most properties are recorded in the two extant pre-1500 rentals and in the leases enrolled in the later Convocation Books. We do not know, for instance, whether the grants were solicited by the Community, or whether it was simply a recognized option, especially when a burgess did not have a son to succeed him. Moreover, few of the bequests that have survived contain details of the value of the properties being granted, and the fourteenth-century account is partial and thus of limited assistance.

The acquisition of property met with no real opposition from the local or royal authorities. It is significant, however, that the later fourteenth and early fifteenth centuries witnessed substantial mortmain payments which probably acted as a deterrent to donations on the scale of the 1340s. Prior to 1391 the mortmain statute had not been applied to guilds or towns.[105] The licences were expensive rather than difficult to obtain, and certainly contributed to the decline in bequests during the fifteenth century.[106]

The impact of the donations can best be seen by giving a rough idea of the income of the Borough Community in the early fifteenth century. It must be reiterated that the Community had no share in

---

[103] WCC 15 (1402), and *CPR 1401–5*: 165: this mortmain licence cost 50 marks. The chantry foundation document is WCC 16.

[104] SRO DD/CC 111736, and WTA 86 (1550–1).

[105] *Statutes of the Realm, 1377–1509*, ed. A. Ludens *et al.* ii. (London, 1816), 79–80; for some grants which did receive the royal licence, see e.g. WCC 13, 15, 16, and 17; see Sandra Raban, *Mortmain Legislation and the English Church, 1279–1500* (Oxford, 1982), 104–5, 170.

[106] But see Helena Chew, 'Mortmain in Medieval London', *English Historical Review* 60 (1945), 1–15, for an alternative opinion based on earlier material; see also Raban, *Mortmain Legislation*, 170–4.

the usual perquisites of urban government. They received no tolls, nothing from the three main courts of the town, nothing from foreigners who lived and traded in the city. Nor did they receive anything from the four fairs which were currently held in the city. These were the things that they had failed to wrest from the bishop in 1341–3. From the perquisites of the guild's private court, the master's court, they could expect maybe 40*d*. per annum in amercements, mainly assessed for failure to answer a summons. Monetary fines were very rarely collected at the end of disputes, although a few gallons of wine would have been levied and used for feasts. The admission of new burgesses was another—more significant—source of cash and wine. But with an average of about eight new members per annum, the guild received only about £4.[107] Making allowances for wine, Community income exclusive of rents stood at about £6 per annum. At about the same time, Colchester, a town of three times the population, possessed non-property revenues of over £82, more than thirteen times Wells's income.[108]

Without the income from the key administrative powers, such as market tolls and the profits of the main courts, the political strength of a town's burgesses was sharply limited. But property could make up part of the difference for the poorly enfranchised townsmen. Whereas the burgesses of Colchester received about £13 per annum from their fixed rents, 14 per cent of their income, the real property of the burgesses of Wells was worth just under £50 per annum, or about 90 per cent of their revenues. Aggregate income in the much smaller town of Wells was about £56 at that time, compared to the £95 of Colchester.[109] Through gifts of real property and the oversight of parochial lands, the burgesses had succeeded in making themselves a collective economic power in the city, one of the town's greatest landlords, and, through this wealth, a greater political force.

4. THE ACCOMMODATION

The Community soon found that the bishops and their officials were generally content to share the power and authority of the

---

[107] For details of admissions, see below, Ch. 5, sect. 1.
[108] *Colchester*, 70.
[109] Ibid. (1406–7); and for Wells income, SRO DD/CC 111736.

town. So long as their coffers were unaffected, it was often more convenient and simpler to allow the leading citizens of the town to take a hand in government. They knew the town better, they knew the people, and they could keep the peace among them more easily.[110]

In the years between 1346 and the early sixteenth century the men of Wells made no attempt to alter the written constitution of the town, and yet throughout this period they had a considerable authority and responsibility in the city. There were some administrative changes, presumably adopted by the bishop in the hope of appeasing the townsmen to a certain extent. The office of reeve of the city was eliminated.[111] There was no longer to be an officer who acted as an intermediary between the interests of the town and the bishop, a common feature of the reeves and bailiffs of mesne boroughs.[112] The bishop agreed that the leader of the burgesses should be whoever they chose to direct their guild, the master of the Community. It is his name and title that are to be found on so many of the post-1340 cathedral and private documents, his presence which was used to represent the fact that the Community of Wells had been apprised of any particular matter that concerned the town, whether a new law or a major property transaction. The master came to symbolize the sort of independent attitude recognized in the grant of a mayor to royal towns in the thirteenth century.[113]

But what most strikes the reader of these post-1340s documents is the division of responsibility and power between the town and the bishop. Furthermore, the changes were brought in with a minimum of formal acknowledgement of the evolution of authority. The Borough Community's place was never mentioned in the bailiff's court records. It was entirely up to the Community to maintain its small independence, and it relied on fraternal solidarity to shoulder the burden. There were no other tools available to it. Crucially, however, the bishop and his officers did not attempt to obstruct the court which the burgesses ran for themselves. In fact, the bishop's servants co-operated with the citizens in many of the essential and useful tasks that it was the business of local

---

[110] Cf. *Westminster*, 253–4, where co-operation came without any rancour.

[111] The office is not heard of after the 1330s.

[112] Cf. Gottfried, 135; Rodney Hilton, 'The Small Town and Urbanisation: Evesham in the Middle Ages', *Midland History* 7 (1982), 6, for Evesham.

[113] Cf. Reynolds, *English Medieval Towns*, 109.

government to provide. The one critical area where there was no power-sharing was in the commercial and economic spheres that might have affected the bishop's revenues. The market, the tolls, the other trading duties, and all their revenue remained exclusive perquisites of the bishop.

The court and the 'malicious rule' which Bishop Ralph accused the burgesses of holding illegally in the 1340s continued in gentler and friendlier guises. The court that they did hold was a private court, the court of their fraternity. Its sense of purpose and success were entirely based on the guild of burgesses. Technically, the burgesses were supposed to take all of their grievances—whether they involved land, business, or disturbances of the peace—to the bishop's weekly court. This was one of the powers that the bishops specifically claimed and had confirmed in 1281 and 1343: the right to hear all cases involving trespasses and contracts.[114] Nevertheless, the burgesses' determination to use their own court rather than the bishop's for all suits involving one another or members of their families was never challenged by the bishop or his bailiffs, not at any time in the period after the 1350s. This was the fruit of Walter Middleton's recalcitrance,[115] of the bequests of many dead members, and of the deep desire to establish the Community as a real, judicial, problem-solving power in the town.[116]

But elsewhere the bishop's connivance turned into co-operation. Each year the master of the Community appointed the two constables of the peace, the most senior positions within the Community, apart from the mastership itself. They were subordinate to the master within the guild, but they also possessed a broad authority. They held a regular court of their own, and this court's greatest distinction was that it was one to which both burgesses and the other inhabitants of the town owed suit. Whenever there was a disturbance of the peace, a brawl, a night-time disruption, or a non-fatal stabbing, the parties involved, together with the local verderers, would go before the constables, whose decisions and actions were recognized by both the bishop's bailiff and the Community.[117] The bishops were never disinclined

[114] WCC 7; and *Rotuli Hundredorum*, ii. 134.

[115] See above, pp. 121 f.

[116] For details about this court, see below, Ch. 6, sect. 2.

[117] None of the records of this court has survived. We can only infer its business from references in the Community court records. It is unclear what relation it had with the bailiff's court. See CBI: 117 (1395), 134 (1399), and Serel, 38 (1436). Cf. the village constable's duties: Cam, *Hundred Rolls*, 19.

to hand this sort of authority over to the Community. It relieved the bailiff of an important yet inconvenient charge. Furthermore, the bishop was in a sense acknowledging that the Community and its magistrates were better placed to assert the authority of moral persuasion and to enforce the communal desire for peace. The constables judged for the bishop, the Community, for the entire town. The burgesses' ordinances make their role clear, ordering them 'to trewly serve the Kinge and the Lorde of the Fraunchise [the bishop]'.[118]

The Community was almost as deeply involved in the daily administration of Wells as the burgesses of other, more privileged towns.[119] City governments were particularly concerned with the quality of life. Much of the responsibility for this jurisdiction was handed over to the master by the bishop. For example, the master chose two men to oversee the shambles, inspecting meat and fish and informing, as their oath specifies, either 'the Maister or the baylif' of any transgressions. Here two hierarchies, two opposing systems, are seen reconciled: an offending burgess was dealt with by the master; a foreigner was always reported to the bishop's bailiff.[120] Four men were also chosen to ensure that no swine wandered through the streets of the town, hungry and dangerous as medieval pigs often were. The bishop provided the pound in which the burgess street-wardens kept their prisoners.[121]

Like any modern municipal government, the Community was concerned with the water-supply. In 1451 Master William Vowell and Bishop Bekynton agreed to allow water to be piped from the springs in the palace grounds to the market-place, where it could then run through the streets for the use of the population.[122] This undoubtedly aided the sanitation of the city by washing sewage away and allowing fresh water to be drawn from the fountain for household use. The town constructed the piping, and appointed wardens to maintain the conduit and scour the pipes. All Bekynton asked for in return was for prayers to be said once a year at his tomb. The town had already been at work on the water system,

---

[118] Serel, 41.
[119] Cf. Platt, *Medieval Town*, 47–51; id., *Medieval Southampton* (London, 1973), 142–5; Rosser, 'Medieval Urban Communities', 98–101; C. Dyer, *Standards of Living in the Later Middle Ages* (Cambridge, 1989), 198–9.
[120] Serel, 38, 41.
[121] See the town's 'constitution', printed in ibid. 36–41.
[122] WCC 20.

buying and laying lead piping from at least 1448.[123] In the sixteenth century the town remained concerned with the city's water-supply. In 1537 they passed a by-law restricting the time of year and the number of people who could collect water in tubs 'in the hete of the yere'.[124]

The regulation and provision of water had its industrial uses, but it was not the only economic area in which the Community organized and funded important works. So long as they did not impinge on his franchise, the bishop was quite content to see the burgesses assist in building and maintaining the town's infrastructure. The Community always worked hard to keep its market and shops easily accessible to the countryside and the travelling traders, and to facilitate the journeys of its own merchants and pedlars. For instance, in 1401 the Porteway or Axbridge Road was being repaired, and was remembered as worthy of support in former master John Brown's will.[125] In 1458 the burgesses taxed themselves to raise funds to repair the southbound Keward Bridge.[126] In 1358 the Community had successfully prosecuted one of its members, Adam Carleton, for building his cookshop in the middle of the High Street, where, they complained, it obstructed access to 'all the taverns and butchers of the said town'.[127]

In the unlikely event that their property required more strenuous defence against the threat of invading armies, the Community took a number of measures to defend Wells. The threat was more real than it might now seem. While there were no large-scale foreign invasions, raids were common enough in the south of England, and once, in 1449–50, the town and cathedral were seriously preparing for an invasion by the French armies expected from the south. The cathedral was busy making secret compartments to hide its treasures, and hiring mercenaries.[128] More often, however, men from Wells were required to join the royal armies going to France

---

[123] CBI: 322 and 324.

[124] CBII: 395; many towns were looking to improve their water-supply: cf. 'Gloucester', in *The Atlas of Historic Towns*, ed. M. D. Lobel and W. H. Johns (London, 1969–75), i. 11; and Platt, *Medieval Southampton*, 144; *Westminster*, 239–40.

[125] SRO DD/WM 1/5.

[126] CBII: 25.

[127] *Select Cases in the Court of King's Bench, Edward III*, vi, Selden Society 82 (1965), 120–2.

[128] CA, 1449–50; for an idea of the impact that a raid and the threat of attack did have, see Platt, *Medieval Southampton*, 107–30.

or Scotland.[129] To aid such prospective troops and to keep the city in good military shape, the Community encouraged archery practice. In 1389 the town set aside an acre of land in West Culvercroft, north of Beggar Street, for bow and arrow practice for the sake of defence and sport.[130] The city also maintained a small arsenal, which in 1391 included helmets with and without visors, 'London plate' and 'Flemish plate' gauntlets, and coats of mail.[131] These military preparations, modest though they were, illustrate a strong commitment, a definitely perceived responsibility, on the part of the burgesses to see to the city's defence.

Defence was one of only a small number of areas in which the burgesses had direct dealings with the central government. These transactions were usually confined to tax assessment and collection and selecting their members of Parliament. While burgesses from Wells and other cities were frequently selected to oversee the Somerset tax collection, and almost invariably would report to the exchequer for Wells's share of the lay subsidies,[132] the real process of assessment and collection in the later Middle Ages was decided on, and executed by, the Community. Although the city's collective assessment had been set by the 1334 lay subsidy at £19, a new system allowed communities to apportion the payment among individuals, and in Wells they were assessed anew each time.[133] This is particularly understandable in an urban context, where the population was very volatile, and migration was constant and heavy. Two or more men were selected from every street in the town. They would assess the inhabitants, presumably according to ability to pay. The assessors would then present their results to two general tax collectors, who would make a circuit of the whole town. In turn, these men would submit the money to the official tax collector, burgess or otherwise.[134]

In terms of external presence and prestige, the right to have members of Parliament and to select those members was a privilege

---

[129] CBII: 140 and 146 (1484–5) records a grant from the burgesses to the king of 20 outfitted and provisioned soldiers for 21 days.

[130] CBI: 87; see also CBI: 79 for a possible earlier reference.

[131] CBI: 93.

[132] e.g. John Roper in 1371 and 1374 (*CCR 1369–74*: 297–8; *CCR 1374–7*: 1), and Thomas Weye in 1410 (*CCR 1409–13*: 135).

[133] R. E. Glasscock, *The Lay Subsidy of 1334* (London, 1975), 273; Hadwin, 'Medieval Lay Subsidies', 201.

[134] An example of this frequently conducted procedure can be found in CBII: 103 (1474) and 203 (1498).

of some magnitude for a small town. The burgesses were the main payers of the lay subsidies on which the fourteenth-century kings depended, the primary contributors to the military taxes, the official representatives of the city, and they had a very good and recognized claim to go to Parliament.[135] Wells sent members of Parliament from 1295.[136] However, in many communities it was common practice for the owner of the franchise to choose his own men to assume the seat. In times of political tension, the Church and the gentry were often very anxious to secure the seats of the towns, where interest in national politics was always duller.[137]

But actual control of the election was a different issue from who actually would hold the seat. Leading citizens were frequently selected in Wells even in the early fourteenth century, but actual control of the selection was in the bishop's hands. This is confirmed by the fact that on at least two occasions before 1320 the town was not represented because the bailiff chose not to answer the sheriff's writ.[138]

The situation had changed by the later part of the century. From as early as the 1330s burgesses were generally the returned parliamentarians, and from the 1370s at least the Borough Community was always the elector. The master probably made the selection himself. There is no evidence that the ordinary citizens of Wells had any say in the selection of the parliamentary burgess, as was the case in some other places.[139] Certainly, the sheriff had taken to issuing the writ to the master and Community in addition to the bishop's bailiff. In 1421 the parliamentary election was

[135] May McKisack, *The Parliamentary Representation of the English Boroughs during the Middle Ages* (Oxford, 1932), 11–17 and 30–8 discusses 13th- and 14th-cent. selection procedures, but she does not seem to have seen the local documents which would have indicated seigniorial control over the process.

[136] Representation was not unbroken, however, until about 1320.

[137] Hence the rise in interlopers among 15th-cent. parliamentary burgesses recorded in McKisack, *Parliamentary Representation*, 100–18; on the control of commons seats by magnates through their local clients, see K. B. McFarlane, 'Parliament and Bastard Feudalism', in id., *England in the Fifteenth Century* (London, 1981), 1–21; J. S. Roskell, *The Commons in the Parliament of 1422* (Manchester, 1954), 49, notes that in 1422 only a quarter of the parliamentary burgesses returned across the country were not resident; Patricia Jalland, 'The "Revolution" in Northern Borough Representation in Mid Fifteenth-Century England', *Northern History* 11 (1976), 27–51.

[138] *Parliamentary Writs and Writs of Military Summons, Edward I and Edward II*, ed. Francis Palgrave, i: (London, 1827), in 1307 and 1319.

[139] e.g. in Cambridge: see McKisack, *Parliamentary Representation*, 34–5; Roskell, *Commons in Parliament*, 28–35.

recorded on an indenture between the master of the town, Robert Elwell, and the bishop's bailiff, William Duddesham.[140] And when, in 1469, the sheriff sent the writ to the bailiff alone, the latter man turned it over to the master. The Community angrily and contemptuously refused to elect anyone, citing the incorrect addressing of the letter as the reason. The sheriff hastily sent out a new and correct writ.[141] The shift of control from the lord to the burgesses here speaks of the power of the concept of community, but also of the importance of wealth, for it was the need to raise taxes and to force loans from the burgeoning wealth of the men of Wells and of other cloth-making towns after 1340 which made their communities especially worth speaking to.

One result of the increased importance of the burgesses was the waning of the bailiff's position. His powers remained intact, but he was no longer accorded the greatest respect in the town. Such rank now belonged to the master alone. Indeed, we find one of the bishop's bailiffs coming to the master and Community in 1467 to seek membership in the burgesses' guild. William Edmond was accompanied by two of the bishop's other officers.[142] It was no coup of the bishop's, but rather a mark of the success and friendliness of the accommodation in those years. The Convocation Books make it clear that the bishop's officers were expected to follow the lead of the master and the rules of the Community. Edmond and the bishop's accountant even served as constables that year, under the direction of Master John Atwater.[143] It was an experiment in integration of the two authorities that was not repeated, but it was not resented.

It must be stressed that these bishop's officers played a conscientious but entirely typical role in the Community. Edmond and Thomas Smith, the bishop's apparitor, served as town councillors, but they were never selected as masters.[144] The Community would only accept them in the context of its own authority. It is very likely that the burgesses received further power—and certainly influence—from the bailiff in these years.

---

[140] CBI: 230; cf. CBI: 301; the same arrangement took place in other mesne boroughs at this period: see *VCH Wiltshire*, vi. 99.

[141] CBII: 76.   [142] CBII: 60.

[143] CBII: 65.   [144] CBII: 64.

The Community's dominance over the bishop's officers who had become its members is clearest from one incident of 1473. Smith was forced by the master in the Community's court to remove some fines that he had assessed against three burgesses while executing the bishop's jurisdiction.[145] If any change in the political balance had been achieved by governmental integration in these years of closest co-operation, the success belonged to the burgesses.

The administrative achievement of the burgesses of Wells was made possible not only by their solidarity, growing wealth, and the intrinsic usefulness of many of their endeavours; they flourished because the bishops of Bath and Wells were willing to give them authority. But since this was never a legally enforceable regime, the citizens' power was, in many respects, good only so long as the bishop and his bailiff remained well disposed towards the system. A hostile bishop or bailiff would have no difficulty in justifying a reassertion of the written rules and in suppressing much of the Community's independence. There is evidence to show that such a bailiff made life considerably more difficult for the burgesses for a brief period in the mid-sixteenth century,[146] while in 1493 the great accommodation that I have described was threatened by Bishop Richard Fox.

Shortly after beginning his short episcopate, Fox had his steward deliver four questions on the Wells constitution to the burgesses. Three of the four complaints were concerned with the master and Community's right to admit burgesses, and their claim that the king was lord of the town. These complaints were a bracing challenge to the Community. If the bishop's bailiff alone could create burgesses, as the bishop was suggesting, then the Community would have been critically undermined: they would never have been able to rise to the stature that they had achieved if they had not possessed the exclusive authority to control their membership. Their entire organization was threatened at its very roots.[147]

A further insult was contained in the last question. Here the bishop accused them of avoiding their obligation to do suit at his

---

[145] CBII: 95.

[146] CBII: 416 (1540).

[147] CBII: 178; interestingly, other 15th-cent. lords were making new troubles for some towns: cf. Alan Rogers, 'Late Medieval Stamford: A Study of the Town Council', in Alan Everitt (ed.), *Perspectives in English Urban History* (London, 1973), 23.

mill. Interestingly, the bishop did not offer a direct challenge to any of the powers or courts by which the burgesses helped to run the city. There was a considerable element of restraint in the bishop's unfriendly advance. He had, after all, only been asking questions—in effect, holding a kind of *quo warranto* inquiry, challenging the burgesses to justify some of their powers and practices or to risk having them removed or diminished.[148]

The burgesses replied fully, seriously, but with some heat. They were obviously upset at the boat being so unnecessarily rocked. 'The lordes articles', they answered, 'ben maters whiche have not been in argument among theyme nor spoken of in their days', adding that they intended nothing prejudicial to the bishop's franchise. They then proceeded to correct him on all points, at least insisting on the longevity of their practice and on the support of previous bishops. They sent along proof in the form of copies of royal and episcopal charters and extracts from some of the bishop's own custumals. The issues in question, they said, near to their conclusion, would 'not hurte ther saide lord a peny in a thousand yeres'.[149] The bishop found this reply a little too saucy,[150] but eventually he grudgingly surrendered the points, after threatening to take the matter to law.[151] However, he warned the burgesses to 'sette aparte all wilfulnesse and haultesse. And [to] be content to lyve under the righte of the Churche accordyng to your dutye.'[152] It can be categorically affirmed that wilfulness was to remain a primary and effective tool of Community policy and success. The accommodation continued, but it was under constant strain for nearly a hundred years, before a new charter and a large compensation fee finally freed the Community of the bishop in 1589.

5. CONCLUSION

Wells the mesne borough provides further evidence that the landscape of medieval English urban government was an astonishingly variegated one. Local custom, local history, were the principal determinants of the nature of town government. What we may call

[148] CBII: 178.
[149] CBII: 179–80.
[150] CBII: 180–1.
[151] CBII: 181.
[152] CBII: 180.

the national model, as represented by the fully enfranchised royal boroughs of places like Lincoln or Oxford, was more of an idea and an ideal in many of England's towns than a description of the working polity.

A general feature of English political circumstance also can get lost because of excessive insularity. There were probably few landlords who could have subdued their rebelling towns were it not for the power and authority of the Crown in England. Fritz Rörig's classic account of towns—especially of the struggle for independence of the German cities, which was successful in great part because of the lack of a strong central authority—forces one powerful comparative fact upon us: it was the existence of the royal power in England, lurking in courts and armies behind the scenes, which stopped the men of Wells from maintaining their stolen privileges in the 1340s, and the men of Bury and St Albans from freeing themselves of their abbeys in the 1320s or earlier.[153]

The accommodation achieved at Wells challenges historians to look beyond the outline of strict legality to the customs and practices of each community, preserved in its local documents. Power in a mesne borough was very probably never the sole possession of the overlord, even where that was a somewhat repressive abbey convent. England was a community of communities, a Church of parishes, and the people constituted an acknowledged and essential participant in government, broadly construing that term. In towns like Wells, the wealth of the citizens was enough to intensify the power that a community without paper rights could possess. Considered steps were taken to concentrate this power further by bequeathing wealth to the burgess Community. Gervase Rosser has demonstrated how far the men of Westminster were able to go without even the legal power or the guild structure of the men of Wells.[154] The burden of government was not one that the overlords of mesne boroughs were especially anxious to retain. The suspicion arises that, had more records survived, more attention to the question been paid, we would know of many other places where the increasing needs of late medieval towns led directly to greater authority for the poorly enfranchised

[153] Fritz Rörig, *The Medieval Town*, trans. Don Bryant (London, 1967; orig. 1932), 23; see also David Herlihy, *Medieval and Renaissance Pistoia* (New Haven, Conn.), 23–6.
[154] Rosser, 'Medieval Urban Communities'.

burgesses of those boroughs and of urban enclaves such as Westminster.

Seigniorial boroughs like Wells were also characterized by an unusually clear political structure. It appears to be the case that an overlord, perceived as repressive or at least restricting, united a greater part of the urban community than would otherwise have been probable. The political culture of Wells formed itself around the central fact of this opposition to the bishop. The Borough Community owed some of its strength and its unusually fraternal nature to this unity in opposition. Charles Gross noted long ago how mesne boroughs were unusually often dominated by their social and fraternal guilds.[155] They possessed no other suitable organ by which to organize and express their strength, and the particular strength of the fraternity, ideally a relationship of love, was best suited to the slightly subversive activities in which the burgesses of less privileged towns were often engaged while attempting to 'liberate' themselves.

While the unifying ethos and organization probably had broad popular support, we must not lose sight of the fact that the burgesses, the 'Community' of any town—Wells included—formed a minority group whose prominence was based on their wealth. From the vantage of the complete urban society, they were a thoroughly undemocratic institution. The greater body of the town's inhabitants (about 50–60 per cent of adult men were not burgesses[156]) played an insignificant political role and are hidden from the records. However, these invisible people were almost certainly more likely to hold the lord of the town in contempt, and to blame him and his ministers for their difficulties, than the Borough Community. The tension in authority in Wells, the polarization of lord and burgesses, gave to the entire society a greater degree of political unity than would have existed in many other towns. In most places where the national model prevailed, the townsmen would have played their largest political games against one another. The first faint indications of this only begin to reveal themselves in Wells in the mid-fifteenth century, once the accommodation between the Borough Community and the bishop had grown old enough to be a fixed and accepted thing.

[155] Gross, *Gild Merchant*, i. 75 and 90.
[156] See below, Chs. 5, sect. 1, and 7, sect. 2.

5

The Social History of the Borough Community, 1377–1500

The Borough Community was one of two groups into which the laymen of the town were divided. This was a division encountered in virtually all enfranchised towns across Europe. Simply put, it separated the privileged from the rest, those with a corporate identity and political authority from those who deferred to their rule. The importance of the Community did not derive from its relative numerical strength. More salient was the fact that it was an organized corporate body, comprising most of the important men of the town, whereas the numerous foreigners made up a fluid, amorphous social group, without any of the other attributes of a community which could readily be turned into authority or collective action. The foreigners were therefore no counterpart to the burgesses. The Borough Community of Wells was taken to be the town of Wells, its only representative body, its collective face, to which king and sheriff addressed themselves.

The burgesses were politically active and played a considerable part in the government of the town, but it must be reiterated that they were not collectively the effective lords of the town, as were the burgesses of so many other cities.[1] As the citizens of a mesne borough, they were subordinate to their lord's officers and courts. Their limited authority must be borne in mind when considering questions of oligarchy and political stability. The majority of the people of the town, the foreigners, would not have rebelled against the burgesses even if they had wanted to dissent.[2] The foreigners in particular were under the jurisdiction of the lord. The burgesses' independence was akin to that of a modern college of physicians: they retained a considerable degree of self-regulation and privileges which the higher authority acknowledged.

[1] See above, Ch. 4, sect. 4, for the burgesses' part in town government.
[2] See below, Ch. 7, sects. 1–2, for a discussion of the foreigners.

In the next chapter much will be said about the ideology and mentality of the Community, and the many activities that it organized on behalf of its membership. The business of the present chapter will be more structural and analytical, concerned to break down the corporate Community into its constituent parts. The membership's composition will be examined first. Then the analysis will be limited to those burgesses who took a more active part in the guild's affairs by serving in one of its offices. Finally, the élite of the guild—and, therefore, of the city—will be sketched, to outline the nature of Wells's governing social group and to face the vexed question of oligarchy in the later medieval town.[3]

I. MEMBERSHIP

Few questions about medieval town society demand as much attention as establishing the size of the privileged social group. It has not always been easy to answer. The records of the freedom lists are not always extant, and population estimates for medieval towns are especially difficult to produce. More to the point, it is particularly difficult to establish the number of burgesses in a town at a particular time. For Wells, the surest starting-point is the late 1370s. We have estimated the total lay population of the town in 1377 at *c*.1,800.[4] From the surviving Community court records and the freedom lists, we estimate that there were approximately 230 burgesses alive at this time. On this basis, the burgesses represented about 12.8 per cent of the total lay population, or about 25.6 per cent of all males. Of approximately 450 male adults, 51.1 per cent, or about half, were citizens, members of the Borough Community.[5] At about the same time, the burgesses of Exeter comprised only 3

---

[3] Cf. Ronald F. E. Weissman, *Ritual Brotherhood in Renaissance Florence, 1200–1600* (New York, 1982), 107–61, who has perhaps the most analytically sophisticated approach to individual fraternities and their memberships.

[4] See above, Ch. 2, sect. 3.

[5] I have estimated the number of burgesses alive between 1378 and 1385 by adding together the new admissions (75) and all the references to burgesses in these years in CBI (188), which records only transactions between burgesses. The combined total of 263 has been modified downward to account for the many deaths, which certainly outnumbered those burgesses who were not recorded but who were already members in 1377. See above, Ch. 2 n.95, on the use of such lists. The freedom list is printed (from its first survival in 1377) in *Wells City Charters*, ed. Dorothy O. Shilton and Richard Holworthy, SRS 46 (1931), 124–94.

per cent of that city's total population,[6] so Wells had an impressively high participation rate. The Borough Community has a good claim to represent the community of the town as a whole.

The foreigners, who, by strict definition, were outside the Community, can help to define those within it. Any group, such as the Community, that draws its membership mainly through voluntary subscription must be dynamic in order to thrive. There are deaths, rejections, vicissitudes in the pattern of admissions, always some development. Every new member of the Community, with the arguable exception of burgesses' sons, was a foreigner until the moment of his initiation. In an important sense, to become a burgess of Wells was to have achieved a certain stage of life, economically and socially secure, possibly more politically ambitious. Joining the guild was an option available at some time to the majority of the men who lived and worked in the city. For many who never did join, as well as those who did, it would have been a goal.[7] Since burgesses of Wells did not possess exclusive rights to trade or own a shop in the city, becoming a burgess was probably more a sign of success than the prerequisite for economic survival.[8] Since virtually all financial decision-making was the prerogative of the bishop and his bailiff, the economic lure of Community membership was the dullest attraction, pale in comparison with the social, political, and cultural features.

To a great extent, then, the timing of admission to the Community was left to the individual.[9] A foreigner like John Goldsmith could wait seven years or more after beginning to ply his trade in the city before deciding to seek Community membership.[10] When the mason John Norman finally became a burgess in 1421, his son, who was already a fully trained mason, was admitted on

[6] Maryanne Kowaleski, 'The Commercial Dominance of a Medieval Provincial Oligarchy', *Medieval Studies* 46 (1984), 356; *London*, 41–52, calculated a citizen % of 13.2 for London in 1501, although the figures must be considered somewhat speculative; R. B. Dobson, 'Admissions to the Freedom of the City of York in the Later Middle Ages', *ECHR*, 2nd ser., 26 (1973), 17 n. 1, expresses doubts about their utility as a population index.

[7] See below, pp. 222–6.

[8] See above, p. 119; elsewhere it was also the case that in fact, whether or not in law, foreigners were not as economically disabled as has sometimes been thought; see *London*, 3; A. F. Butcher, 'Canterbury's Earliest Rolls of Freemen Admissions: A Reconsideration', in F. Hull (ed.), *Kentish Miscellany* (Kent Records 21; 1979), 4–5.

[9] See below, Ch. 7, sect. 2.

[10] *CPR 1467–77*: 53; CBII: 108 (1475).

the same day.[11] His father was certainly middle-aged at the time. Men of much greater stature might also be admitted late, well into lives already filled with success. John Horewode, who was probably a merchant, had amassed his wealth by the time he was admitted in 1402. He paid his entry fine immediately rather than in the usual deferred instalments, and was master of the Community within two years.[12] Horewode's speedy ascent was bettered only by Nicholas Trappe, who joined the fraternity in December 1496, when he was already a well-established lawyer and a proctor of the court of Arches at Oxford University. He became master ten months later.[13]

But the Community was by no means an association of middle-aged and older men. The majority of the membership would have been drawn from those younger craft-masters who had completed their long apprenticeships in Wells or elsewhere, established a shop, and were able to spare the 10s. entry fee.[14] From 1473 those admitted on the basis of an apprenticeship in the city were specified in the admissions lists, and these men accounted for 17 per cent of all admissions over the next sixty years.[15] If we also included those who were apprenticed elsewhere but came to Wells to set up their shops, this figure would be still larger, thereby underlining the significant presence of the younger burgess.

The longevity of some burgesses after they had attained their freedom also points towards fairly youthful admission. Of the 500 men admitted between 1377 and 1442, about 18 per cent were active in the Community for at least twenty-five years. Thomas Chynnok, Thomas Sholer, John Sadler, and John Godwyn each lived for at least fifty years after entering the Community. On average, however, burgesses continue to be heard of for about thirteen years after they join the guild.[16] This cannot be taken to express the average number of years until death, especially since

[11] CBI: 229 (1421).

[12] CBI: 151 and 162.

[13] CBII: 198 and 201; A. B. Emden, *A Biographical Register of the University of Oxford to AD 1500*, 3 vols. (Oxford, 1957–9), 1890; *SMWII*: 107, is his will, written in 1507 and proved in 1510.

[14] That is, not directly upon completing their apprenticeships (Dobson, 'Admissions to the Freedom', 18).

[15] From CB II: 95; cf. Kowaleski, 'Commercial Dominance', 357, which gives Exeter apprenticeship admissions as 9% in the last half of the 14th cent.

[16] This average is based on occurrences in CBI and CBII as well as in other records. In a small number of cases the precise year of death was known and was used as a terminus.

humbler men—the majority—often had little reason to appear in the court records after their admission. But this period of activity strongly suggests that admission at age 21 was neither the rule nor even the norm.[17] Generally, men probably received the freedom of the city somewhere between 25 and 30.[18] The Community was a socio-political club of mature and economically stable men, but the lines between burgess insiders and foreigner outsiders were fluid, so that the two groups were not strictly opposed. Even among the 40-year old foreigners, there were men who would eventually join the guild and perhaps dominate it.

The lines that separated burgesses from foreigners were particularly indistinct and wavering wherever the nominally unenfranchised were members of a burgess household. Although it is not a term that is used much in the records, the household emerges as a significant social category of the town.[19] The Community's custom and policy was to extend second-order membership to the members of a burgess household, especially to his apprentices and his natural, immediate family. Preferential access to full Community membership was reserved only to those who had been part of a burgess household (or whose wife had been). To a less developed, less advantageous degree, even the actions of simple employees could come under Community scrutiny. A burgess's journeymen and labourers certainly possessed no rights in the Community, but any action that they took which might be thought damaging to another burgess could involve their employer in a lawsuit in the Community court. For example, in 1411 Adam Dodesdene complained of the affront that he suffered when Thomas Galeway's employee abused him.[20] In 1397, when Stephen Skinner lost money as a result of his employee being disabled by the blows of another burgess, he sought the Community court's help.[21] The defence of their employees was probably motivated more by self-interest than affection, but it serves to emphasize the sense in which even the members of the outer household were to be

[17] Jennifer Kermode, 'Obvious Observations on the Formation of Oligarchies in Late Medieval English Towns', in John A. F. Thomson (ed.), *Towns and Townspeople in the Fifteenth Century* (Gloucester, 1988), 105 n. 64, assumes that admission took place at age 21–2.

[18] *Coventry*, 124, suggests that a journeyman probably set up his shop when he was about 24. This implies an age of admission sometime later.

[19] Cf. Swanson, 6–8.

[20] CBI: 193.

[21] CBI: 128.

considered part of the Community—not as individuals, but as an extension of the burgess and his interests.

Apprentices were in a similar, but superior, position to employees, being more closely integrated into the burgess household.[22] Their masters were in effect their guardians. They lived under his roof, whereas the employees spent only their long days there. If apprentices had a harder, even less free working life than journeymen and labourers, they also had their prospects before them. As often as not, authentic familial feelings must have bonded master and apprentice, especially if, as was the case in Orléans for instance, apprentices were frequently orphans.[23] This helped to place these young people almost entirely on the inside of both the burgess's family and the Borough Community. This affinity was recognized in the Community by-law of 1466, which placed burgesses' apprentices in the same advantageous position as burgesses' sons when they came to seek admission to the Community.[24] Generally, the advance of an apprentice from foreigner to burgess was considered both natural and desirable.

A burgess's immediate family shared his citizenship to the extent that each of them carried in his or her blood, as it were, at least the potential for lifetime membership in the civic guild. The Borough Community was essentially a guild of father-centred nuclear families, in which apprentices were counted and treated as surrogate children. Understood in this light, membership in the Community stood at more than half the total population of the town. Burgesses' wives could not lose their memberships, even though a woman could not become a burgess in her own right. Her membership was always second-order and channelled through a man, either father or husband. Nevertheless, wives were members of the Community: they were unable to violate the oaths that their husbands had taken and the by-laws that he was bound to respect.[25] To the same extent as her husband, the Community court was her court of first recourse for life. Women were often involved

---

[22] On apprenticeship, see above, pp. 96 ff.

[23] Françoise Michaud-Fréjaville, 'Bons et loyaux services: Les Contrats d'apprentissage' en Orléanais', in *Les Entrées dans la vie: Initiations et apprentissages* (Nancy, 1982), 188.

[24] CBII: 58.

[25] This was embedded in borough custom, and was never made explicit, modified, or criticized. Such widows' rights existed elsewhere: see Dobson, 'Admissions to the Freedom', 13–14; Caroline M. Barron, ' "The Golden Age" of Women in Medieval London', *Reading Medieval Studies* 15 (1989), 35–58.

in litigation there. Margery Halyete, for example, made several appearances as a successful litigant between 1390 and 1405, during her widowhood.[26] She sued directly, without proxy, but she had never appeared in her own right while her husband was still alive. Wives were generally represented, or at least accompanied, by their husbands. Their cases were usually the same as those involving employees, being concerned with the household or the business, but their superior status in the Community is demonstrated not only by the widows' independent legal actions, but by the many cases where the wife's honour was particularly at issue. The prominent fuller John Newmaster was kept busy by his wife. In 1379 Newmaster sought satisfaction from the butcher John Bailiff because Bailiff's wife had accused Mrs Newmaster of having stolen a capon. Three months later the persecuted woman sent her husband back to sue another burgess, whose wife had also slandered her.[27] For all wives and widows, whether the disputed issues involved land or money, the use of the court was not simply a convenience. It was a requirement imposed by their Community membership. Edith Skinner learned this in 1409, when the master forced her to discontinue an action that she had brought against a burgess in the king's court.[28]

The membership custom of the Community was far richer and more complicated than most discussions of burgesses would suggest. This is because the burgess is rarely treated as a social classification so much as a political and economic category. Without denying the importance of these aspects of burghal corporate life, we can see that there was more to it if we examine this custom more closely. The total effect of the burgesses' membership custom was to encourage and recognize patriarchal nuclear families. This included the integration of new people into the Community through their relationships with an existing burgess, and the provision of incentives for the members of a burgess's immediate family to stay within the Borough Community. It was assumed that every Community household would be led by a burgess or his widow. Burgesses' daughters and female apprentices could find a permanent place in the Community only if their husbands joined. Paradoxically, widows would be 'restored' to

[26] CBI: 91 (2), 116, and 164.
[27] CBI: 41 and 42.   [28] CBI: 148.

complete status only upon the reduction of their personal independence when they remarried and their new husbands joined the guild. The customary means of encouraging the maintenance of the familial principle of membership was for the Community to waive the monetary fine for the new husbands of burgesses' widows, daughters, and female apprentices. But, again, the husband's membership was essential. For the members of a family or household to have a share of the freedom of the city, its head, a sort of paterfamilias, had to join the guild. If her husband had not been admitted, the burgess's daughter or widow would forfeit her rights in the guild. Only burgesses' sons were unable, through neglect or marriage, to alienate their birthright to privileged—that is free—membership. They had actively to assume the freedom, but they could do so at any time. It was entirely up to them whether they maintained their guild status, whereas their sisters' fates were more often determined by the decisions and status of their husbands.

The extent of Community membership was broader than it at first appeared. As a matter of policy and a fact of custom, the guild's patriarchal system brought families within its dominion. Wells's somewhat unusual regime is visible in part because of its limited constitutional authority. The Community court was only for burgesses and their relations, whereas the borough court in other towns would have had jurisdiction over all the inhabitants of the city, foreigners and burgesses both; the line between members of burgesses' families and others could not have been drawn so easily. But it may very well be the case that similar customary notions of membership existed elsewhere and may yet be discovered. Certainly, some of the basic elements of Wells's system, such as the widow's rights and the patrimonial rights of the son were common enough.[29] In Wells's case, the separate jurisdictions of Community and bishop's courts (which judged all cases in which at least one of the litigants was not a member of a burgess household) allow some of the burgesses' assumptions to become evident.

Medieval Borough Communities could be exclusive clubs, limiting access to their ranks. In York, for instance, access to the freedom list was cynically controlled by varying the admission fees over time, even case by case, depending in great part on revenue

[29] See e.g., Barron, 'Women in London', 39–45; and below, n. 44.

requirements.[30] In Exeter admission itself was at the discretion of the common council, who used this power, at least before the plague, to control the numbers admitted.[31] Although this does not necessarily mean that admission fees were tools of social oppression, it is worth asking further questions about Wells's membership policy. Generally, the concerns that R. B. Dobson raised about York can be set aside in Wells's case. The Community never altered its relatively low admission fee to affect the rate of admission, or for any reason. In 1377 it was 10s. and in 1520 it was the same.[32]

However, closer examination of the main plank of the membership policy, the principle of familial preference, does hint at some sensitivity among the guild's governors to the pace of admissions. Contrary to experience in Exeter, the numbers admitted in Wells were lower than the Community would have liked. Whereas before 1425 the Community sometimes closely scrutinized a candidate's claim to receive free admission, after that date it asked no more questions; it accepted whatever members it could get. Before 1425 Community concern over the proper application of custom was indicated whenever the records include the note 'to inquire whether . . . '—whether, for instance, the man's father truly was a burgess, or whether his wife was, as claimed, the daughter of a burgess.[33] The Community also wanted to assure itself that the applicant (in cases of patrimonial admission) or his wife (in cases of preferential admission because of marriage to a burgess's daughter) had been born in wedlock *and* after the father had himself been admitted to the freedom.[34] If the applicant could not satisfy both conditions,

[30] Dobson, 'Admissions to the Freedom', 18–20; below, n. 31.

[31] Kowaleski, 'Commercial Dominance', 357–60, but she has probably underestimated the impact of demographic changes after 1349 in arguing that the freedom of that city continued to become less available to newcomers.

[32] Dobson, 'Admissions to the Freedom', 20; A. F. Butcher, 'The Origins of Romney Freemen 1433–1523', *ECHR*, 2nd ser., 27 (1974), 25, where the fee was 2s.–10s.; Bristol fees could reach £10: see *Little Red Book of Bristol*, ed. F. Bickley, 2 vols. (Bristol, 1900), ii. 47–8; Steven Rigby, 'Urban "Oligarchy" in Late Medieval England', in Thomson (ed.), *Towns and Townspeople*, 70: the fee at Grimsby was 40s. until 1498; but Stamford's variable fee was tied to occupation, ranging from 2s.–20s: see Alan Rogers, *The Making of Stamford* (Leicester, 1965), 48–9.

[33] e.g. John Reed, CBI: 166 (1410), William Laly, CBI: 165 (1410), and Thomas Skipper, CBI: 155 (1403).

[34] e.g. Richard Davy, CBI: 35 (1380), John Leeve, CBI: 144 (1393), John Stokes, CBI: 155 (1403), Peter Bowyer, CBI: 249, 289, and 295; cf. *Report on the Manuscripts of the Corporation of Beverley*, Historical Manuscripts Commission 54 (1900), 39–40, where an identical requirement is noted; *Colchester*, 205, n. 68.

then he had to pay a fine. These hard decisions on borderline cases indicate that, up to the early fifteenth century, the Community still tried to enforce the correct application of its customary idea of a burgess's family. Unfortunately, we do not know the origin of these customary definitions.

While there is no reason to be unduly cynical about the motives behind them—especially when we have seen how deeply and comprehensively the principle of familial preference and membership was applied—it is possible that these customs arose and flourished in the long period of high immigration which started before 1300 and lasted until at least 1400.[35] In such circumstances the guild had no difficulty in attracting more than enough fee-paying new men to the fraternity. Consequently, it could afford to define preferential admission narrowly, and to examine candidate's claims closely. In pre-plague Exeter—indeed, across the country's towns—citizenship was more restricted in the thirteenth and first half of the fourteenth centuries than it was after the plague.[36] When Wells's extant admission lists begin in the late 1370s, the Community's income from admissions was over £3 a year, sufficient to pay most of a permanent chaplain's stipend, and therefore a real contribution to the Community's charges, although a small sum compared to those raised elsewhere.[37] From 1380 to 1419 the average annual admissions income had fallen to 54s. 9d., but during the next four decades income fell to only 61.6 per cent of the 1380 sum, a mere 33s. 9d. per annum, less than half of the late 1370s total. Overall admissions between the two periods fell to only 71.8 per cent of that of the earlier period.[38]

It was this decline which encouraged a moderate change in policy, intended to promote increased membership. This was a difficult goal, since the Community seems always to have had a basically open policy, requiring only a moderate admission fine compared to most other towns, and no set annual dues.[39] Their ineffectual actions consisted of an end to the close scrutiny of

[35] See above, Ch. 2, sect. 3.
[36] This is how I interpret Kowaleski, 'Commercial Dominance', 356–60; A. R. Bridbury, *Economic Growth: England in the Later Middle Ages* (London, 1962), 55–8, and the charts of admissions, 65–9.
[37] In 1442–3 York raised one quarter of its income, over £40, from admission fees alone: Dobson, 'Admissions to the Freedom', 20.
[38] Fuller admissions information is printed above, Ch. 2, sect. 5.
[39] See above, Ch. 2, n. 97.

borderline claims to free admission. The last case of this kind was in 1425.[40] This policy was enacted to encourage those who were able to contribute to the Community's expenses to join more quickly than they might otherwise have done. It was a difficult situation which occurred only in towns where men could prosper without being burgesses.

The Community took further positive steps to encourage membership from the 1460s. It passed the by-law extending free admission to burgesses' former apprentices.[41] While this may have expanded membership, it can only have depressed admissions income. In 1467 the Community placed a time-limit on free admission by virtue of marriage to burgesses' widows and daughters. From then on, these husbands had only one year in which to join the guild without paying the fine.[42] This by-law helped to make 1467 the single largest admissions year in the later Middle Ages. But there was little subsequent impact on admissions through marriage, and the ordinance was repealed in 1478, no doubt as it was then considered both an ineffectual and a cynical measure, opposed to one of the central ideas of the Community.

The separate acts of individuals combined to produce another change in the pattern of membership, hastened by the decline in admissions and the difficulty that masters had in finding apprentices and journeymen.[43] The share of admissions accounted for by burgesses' sons rose sharply during the fifteenth century. Indeed, even the 'raw' number grew. In the 1380s only 5.6 per cent of new burgesses entered via patrimony, but in the 1420s this figure jumped to 15.8 per cent and it continued to rise, reaching 27.4 per cent in the 1490s, and 28.6 per cent in the 1510s.[44] We have discussed the demographic implications of these figures,[45] but here it is significant to note that they meant that the guild's social character was being altered even more in favour of those with more familial connections to existing burgesses. To a great extent, it was

[40] See above, n. 34.
[41] See above, p. 146.
[42] CBII: 61.
[43] See above, Ch. 2, sects. 3–5, on population decline, and Chs. 2, sect. 6, and 3, sect. 5, on consequent labour shortages.
[44] Cf. Dobson, 'Admissions to the Freedom', 10–11, 19: before 1420 patrimony provided 8%, but this rose to 14% between 1479 and 1488; it is interesting to note, however, that in Exeter the patrimonial share was 7% from 1350 to 1400, but had been 21% from 1299 to 1349: Kowaleski, 'Commercial Dominance', 357, table 1.
[45] See above, Ch. 2, sect. 6.

a reaction to demographic shifts, but the movement was decisive. By the 1490s those who paid a fine represented only 29 per cent of all admissions. In the 1380s this group had accounted for almost three-quarters of the burgesses. By 1500 guild membership had become, in a social sense, less open, more parochial. But considerable discrimination and exclusion remained unknown.

2. SOCIO-ECONOMIC COMPOSITION

Considering the relatively high proportion of men who became burgesses, it is perhaps not surprising that the membership was drawn from a very broad socio-economic pool. Since so much of the analysis of the town's economy in Chapter 3 was based on the freedom lists and the Borough Community's records, it would be circular as well as untenable to argue that the trades of the city were accurately represented in the membership of the Community. If, however, the general economic division among masters, journeymen, and labourers was similar to that found in Coventry at the very end of the Middle Ages, then we have good reason for thinking that the guild was representative of the upper half of the town. In Coventry about 40 per cent of the households were led by independent men, by masters, while journeymen headed 33 per cent, and labourers, out-servants, and poor widows 27 per cent.[46] As previously noted, about 51 per cent of Wells men were members of the guild, and the court records make it clear that there was comparatively little involvement of journeymen and labourers, although it is difficult to distinguish masters and journeymen in many cases. Most master craftsmen and merchants were therefore members of the Community, and the admission lists confirm that the vast majority, over 95 per cent, of the burgesses were craftsmen and merchants. The cloth trades accounted for more than one in four burgesses; the victuallers for one in five; and the garment-makers and -sellers, leather-workers, and builders each accounted for one in ten. Merchants comprised at least 4.5 per cent of the Borough Community. The high level of general participation in the guild may explain why most of the existing social tension was either within the Community or, more usually and sharply, between the Community and its overlord.

[46] *Coventry*, 133.

On the other hand, there was no straightforward 'class' division in Wells, socially reflected in whether or not one was a burgess (employer) or a foreigner (employee). We have already seen, and will present more evidence to affirm, that men no different from the burgesses in wealth and trade might remain for many years, or for their whole lives, outside the guild. Furthermore, many of the masters enjoyed only a small business, and did not employ any journeymen.[47] The humbler trades like the carpenters, masons, and tilers, just skilled labourers with few opportunities to employ others or to amass wealth, were also represented. Carpenters were at least as numerous as merchants and chapmen.

In pressing the point that there was a modest but significant amount of socio-economic heterogeneity to the guild, we must note the place of the unskilled. There were two categories of burgess, fairly small but intriguing, without a trade. At the bottom were the two labourers who are known to have joined the Community, both before 1420.[48] One, William Laly, claimed to have married a burgess's daughter,[49] but we can be sure that the other, John Handyman, really wanted Community membership, because he paid the fine, the equivalent of thirty to forty days' wages.[50] Neither man was among that significant minority of burgesses who disappear as soon as they join the Community, never involved in litigation or office-holding. William Laly held a minor civic office, and both men were involved in their shares of litigation.[51] There may well have been other unskilled labouring burgesses among the many men with no stated trade. These men serve to mark the lowest boundaries of the realm of the possible, and to prove that the Community was not simply an association of the economic élite, capitalists or employers.

The other unskilled burgesses were the gentlemen. Aside from a 'king's servant', admitted in 1383, the age of the gentlemen began in the 1420s. They continued to play a significant part in the affairs

---

[47] Ibid. 104.

[48] Cf. Rogers, *Stamford*, 49: a 15th-cent. schedule notes that labourers, 'servingmen', wrights, and masons were to be admitted for only 2*d.*

[49] Laly was admitted in 1405 (CBI: 165).

[50] CBI: 31; 4*d.* was the prevailing building labourer's wage: see EA, 1417–18; E. H. Phelps Brown and Sheila V. Hopkins, *Perspective on Wages and Prices* (London, 1981), 4, fig. 2, gives labourers' wages as 3*d.* from 1380 to 1400, rising then towards 4*d.*

[51] Handyman, CBI: 19 and 87; and Laly, CBI: 169 and 171.

of the Community until the end of the century.[52] There were two basic types of gentlemen in the medieval town. There were those townsmen who acquired rural landholdings and won the style of either gentleman or yeoman on the basis of quite modest holdings. Generally, they continued to live in the town and to practise their trade, most often as merchants. Then there were those who came to the town after first being landholders in the countryside. In virtually all cases in Wells we are dealing with the very bottom rungs of the county gentry. There were about nine entirely non-commercial burgesses in Wells, and perhaps six who can be confirmed as gaining the title of 'gentleman' on the basis of business success and landownership. Together they constituted about 2.5 per cent of the Community. It must be stressed that, with the exception of the current section, 'gentleman' will be employed throughout this chapter to indicate the gentlemen burgesses who were not businessmen.

The appearance of such gentry among the burgesses of a provincial town is to be expected. The many boroughs of the country that sent members to Parliament constituted a great pool of seats, which were often available to the county gentry.[53] Towns are well known for allowing outsiders to represent them, although they retained more control over the elections than has sometimes been thought.[54] In fact, Wells had an unusually good record of self-representation. But the gentlemen interlopers did appear. Thomas Mundy was admitted to the freedom in 1448. His only other appearances were on his election to Parliament twice in 1449.[55] But this sort of burgess was rare. Most of the gentlemen displayed the commitment to the Community that was the mark of the inhabitant

---

[52] CBI: 14, identified as such in *List of Early Chancery Proceedings*, i (List and Index Society 12; London, 1827), 5/10. See J. Horace Round, *The King's Servants and Officers of State* (London, 1911), 311 ff. On the terminology of the gentry, see Nigel Saul, *Knights and Esquires: The Gloucestershire Gentry in the Fourteenth Century* (Oxford, 1981), 1–27; D. A. L. Morgan, 'The Individual Style of the English Gentleman', in Michael Jones (ed.), *Gentry and Lesser Nobility in Late Medieval Europe* (Gloucester, 1986), 15–35; and, more generally, London, 234–87; Rosemary Horrox, 'The Urban Gentry in the Fifteenth Century', in Thomson (ed.), *Towns and Townspeople*, 22–44.

[53] Mary McKisack, *The Parliamentary Representation of the English Boroughs during the Middle Ages* (Oxford, 1932), 106–17; Patricia Jalland, 'The "Revolution" in Northern Borough Representation in Mid Fifteenth-Century England', *Northern History* 11 (1976), 27–51; above, Ch. 4, sect. 4 and n. 137.

[54] Jalland, 'Northern Borough Representation'.

[55] CBI: 322, 324, 325.

of the city or locality. The guild offered the local gentry not only a possible parliamentary seat, but a venue in which to fulfil their natural desire for a sense of community and a share in authority. They served the guild only in the higher, wholly honourable offices: masters, constables, councillors, and members of Parliament. The first three each involved some judicial or quasi-judicial activity, and may have been especially attractive to these minor landlords, providing them with a fuller, more complete sense of the lordship to which they aspired. Contact with the urban in no way disgraced them. For instance, Mundy was elected to Parliament alongside another gentleman, Peter Shetford. It was his first such election, but he had already been a burgess for thirteen years.[56] The first burgess explicitly to be called a gentleman, Robert Elwell, received the freedom in 1421 and was immediately selected for Parliament.[57] But when Elwell returned from Westminster, he continued to play an active role in the borough's affairs until his death about ten years later, serving twice as constable and once as master.[58] William Gascoigne, who owned a third of the manor of Newton Plecy, never went to Parliament, but he was a long-serving member of the council and eventually a master.[59]

Sometimes the gentry's easy acceptance of urban life and its special honours and attractions was the result of their own urban antecedents. In William Gascoigne's case, for example, we know that he was the son of a very successful Bridgwater merchant.[60] The same process of transformation occurred in Wells. One of its greatest fifteenth-century merchants, William Vowell, succeeded in making his eldest son Richard into a gentleman, untouched by trade, vested with rural property, but also a master of the city and a substantial urban landlord.[61]

But, as we have mentioned, this group of fifteenth-century urban gentlemen contained another important component in men such as

---

[56] CBI: 292 and 324.

[57] CBI: 229 and 230.

[58] CBI: 233, 235, and 263.

[59] CBI: 312, 314, and 321, admitted 1444. For the manor, see AH 178; WCAC 669 and 670.

[60] AH 178; and *Bridgwater Borough Archives, 1400–1445*, ed. T. B. Dilks, SRS 54 (1938), index *sub* Gascoigne.

[61] For his landholdings, see *Calendar of Inquisitions Post Mortem*, 2nd ser., ii (London, 1974), 187; CBII: 97, 114, 137, 152, and 175; Vowell was escheator for Dorset and Somerset in 1474.

William Vowell himself, Richard Burnell, John Sadler—all merchants—and John Godwyn (a glazier), who were called gentlemen notwithstanding their continued mercantile and trade activity.[62] Other burgesses of great wealth and provenance were never so called, and the difference must have been the possession of rural property. Townsmen had always invested in rural property, but the recognition that this made them into a separate social type, perhaps having as much in common with the bona fide gentry as with their fellow burgesses, was a particular and distinctive fifteenth-century development. To this extent, then, I dissent from Rosemary Horrox's view that fourteenth- and fifteenth-century urban gentlemen were basically the same.[63] Notwithstanding the stimulus of the Statute of Additions (1413), which had required that legal documents should identify individuals according to their social and occupational status, the new terminology not only reflected, but helped to reinforce a new urban social reality, a new understanding.[64] The gentlemen burgesses did not comprise the élite of the town, but they were found among that élite, and they constituted a new, loose, and prestigious social subgroup, which existed comfortably within the fifteenth-century Community. The appearance of the gentlemen did not mean that the membership of the guild was shifting away from the humbler men and towards the socially superior landed families and the merchants. The Community was committed to a high level of membership and this necessarily meant continuing to admit men of all trades and of sharply varying levels of economic success. If part of the élite had begun to distinguish themselves more sharply by calling themselves gentlemen, they did so within the traditional structure of the guild. A real separation between body and head had not yet occurred.

---

[62] For sources of these styles, see Josiah Wedgewood, *History of Parliament, 1439–1509: Biographies* (London, 1936): Vowell, 912; Burnell, 110; Sadler, 734; for Godwyn, see *Register of Thomas Bekynton*, ed. H. C. Maxwell-Lyle and M. C. B. Dawes, 2 vols., SRS 49–50 (1934–5), 433. Cf. Horrox, 'Urban Gentry', 22–4; and *London*, 269–78.

[63] Horrox, 'Urban Gentry', 37–8.

[64] R. L. Storey, 'Gentlemen-Bureaucrats', in C. H. Clough (ed.), *Profession, Vocation and Culture in Later Medieval England* (Liverpool, 1982), 90–5; cf. Maurice Keen, *English Society in the Later Middle Ages* (Harmondsworth, 1990), 1–24.

3. PARTICIPATION AND OFFICE-HOLDING

The Community's vitality was due in great part to the relatively high levels of involvement and interest which the burgesses showed in the activities and issues of the guild. The Community court was responsible for much of this activity.[65] The burgesses had to appear at the Community's meetings if they had business at court, whether as suitor, arbiter, or witness. The guild meetings ('convocations') included all deliberations on by-laws, elections, and issues related to the Community's property, as well as the regular business of the court. The convivial aspect of many of the meetings also encouraged attendance, with wine being freely distributed after (perhaps while) the business was done. Because these elements all existed in the same forum, there was no sharp division of the business of decision-making from that of justice. An interesting ceremonial aspect of the guild was the custom of distributing the pairs of gloves that had been donated by new burgesses to all the members at a given meeting, and this sometimes allows us to see how many men were at such a meeting. In March 1393, for instance, there were six dozen pairs in the custody of the churchwardens, which were distributed at a meeting at the beginning of April.[66] Every pair was claimed, indicating a healthy attendance of more than seventy, at least 28 per cent of all the burgesses, at an entirely usual meeting. In the 1460s similar numbers were still attending the regular meetings.[67]

Of all those burgesses who were admitted between 1377 and 1476, at least three-quarters played a further part in Community business which was worth recording in the Convocation Books. Many of those who disappeared after admission were simply neither litigious nor ambitious; many would have been from the lower end of the socio-economic scale, but they may well have continued actively to support the guild, attending its functions and meetings. About a quarter of the burgesses eventually held some civic office, minor or major.[68] Put another way, one out of every eight men in the city held some form of municipal office. This high

[65] See below, Ch. 6, sect. 2(iv) and 2(v), for an extensive discussion of this court.
[66] CBI: 105.
[67] CBII: 71 and 73.
[68] About half of these served as street-wardens or shambles-keepers, both relatively unimportant offices.

level of active, conscientious participation further indicates the real and widely felt desire to participate in the responsibilities of the Community. There were as many men who showed great commitment as those who, according to the records, showed none. Indeed, one of the significant social functions that the Community fulfilled was to offer both its greater and lesser members the opportunity to hold public offices through which they could establish, or perhaps be rewarded for, their steady characters and relative social importance. It was essential that office-holders were considered financially stable, too, but this did not mean that they had to be rich. Lower offices involved men with less money, fewer years, less honour.[69] Everyone could participate.

The annual elections in Wells selected four to six street-wardens, two shambles-keepers, two rent collectors or chamberlains, two constables, and one master. In addition, several of the more prominent men would be appointed to audit the officers' accounts. There were occasional elections of councillors, who served for life, members of Parliament, and tax assessors and collectors. The annual elections took place on 29 September, and were written in the records in order of precedence and honour, the reverse of the order given above. Elections were not democratic. The master selected the other officers, presumably in consultation with other superior members of the guild, and probably in consultation with the candidate.[70] The higher up the scale a burgess went, the greater his influence and personal success in the social pyramid of the Community. But there was no *cursus honorum* comparable to that found in Tudor Coventry, with its quite strict ladder, each rung of which a future master would have to touch.[71] Wells was a smaller town and a mesne borough of limited independence, so the Borough Community had relatively few administrative powers and correspondingly few substantial jobs which already well-established, wealthy men were willing to do. Men could enter office higher up and pass over intermediate positions, but motion was always upwards. There were no examples of men moving down the scale. Once a burgess attained a churchwardenship, he would never

[69] For further discussion of the qualities needed or preferred for office-holding, see below, Ch. 6, sect. 1(iv).

[70] CBII: 219 provides some evidence of preselection of the candidate.

[71] *Coventry*, 124–8; cf. Kermode, 'Obvious Observations', 97–9; Kowaleski, 'Commercial Dominance', 360–2; D. M. Palliser, *Tudor York* (Oxford, 1979), 71.

again serve as shambles-keeper; once a master, never again a constable. The occasional position stood outside the strict scale. Councillors, auditors, and parliamentarians were positions that were open only to senior burgesses, while the complex business of tax collection involved a cross-section of the Community which seems to have been for the most part unrelated to previously attained honours or responsibilities.

A closer examination of the scale of honours and the office-holders will illuminate the Community's social and political activists and its élite. But it will also make clear the constitutional 'cleverness' of providing positions of responsibility for a great number of the guild's members at levels commensurate with their standing. Each office displays a unique profile in terms of the trades that its occupants followed, the time it took them to be elected, and their further progress to superior positions. As with so many other aspects of the Community, social cohesion was a continual by-product of the system. This is not to say that the system engendered social homogeneity, equality, and the levelling-out of the differences among burgesses. The aim was almost the opposite. Through the tenure of public office, a burgess both paid his 'dues' and was able to assert himself, enhancing his honour by achieving public recognition of his individual level of economic success and of his moral worthiness. For the most active men, the Borough Community was a great stage upon which they promoted their social prominence.

For the purposes of this analysis, I have traced only those office-holders who were admitted to the Community from 1377 onwards, and who held office before 1500. There was an unusually tight relationship between the magistracy and the constabulary, quite different from the pattern of other office-holding. The strong connection that existed between the occupants of these two positions, their steady pre-eminence in the town's affairs, justifies referring to this dominant group of former and present masters and constables as the 'judicial leadership'. These were the two positions that involved holding courts. Furthermore, there was a fairly strict requirement that a future master should do an apprenticeship in the other judicial office. Aside from the two men already mentioned who quickly progressed from foreigner to master, all the other thirty-two fifteenth-century masters had first served as constables.[72]

---

[72] See above, p. 144.

By comparison, only 45 per cent of constables served as rent collectors, the directly preceding office. Indeed, 36 per cent of the constables had never served in any other position. The apprenticeship as constable provided the potential master with a period during which to display his aptitude for Community leadership, his magisterial air. While he judged, he himself was on trial. He had to try to convince the judicial leadership and, to a lesser degree, the whole Community and city that he possessed the moral qualities of steadfastness, honesty, and patience, which were as important as economic substance or social standing in determining whether he would subsequently be offered the mastership. When we come to discuss oligarchy, we shall look for it among the judicial leadership.

In many cases, wealth and its attendant prestige paved the way to admission to the judicial leadership. Thus, gentlemen were offered the constable's chair almost as a matter of course.[73] None of the gentlemen ever held inferior offices; they all moved unusually quickly to the top. Successful merchants who joined the Community also did well. Among these men were the great middle-aged burgesses, men like the merchant and gentleman Richard Burnell, who was chosen as constable within a year of entering the guild. On average, it took these inexperienced men only 4.5 years from admission to reach this high office, more than eight years less than the average for the group of constables as a whole (see Table 5). It was a boon to the Community, in terms of its overall prestige and its coffers, to be able to entice men of substance with these two judicial offices.

TABLE 5. *Average duration between admission and first tenure of office (burgesses, 1377–1500)*

Office	Years
Street-wardens	3.0
Shambles-keepers	6.9
Churchwardens	10.7
Rent collectors	13.0
Constables	12.8
Masters	15.5

Source: CBI and CBII.

Significantly, however, the gentlemen did not have any advantage over the other members of the judicial leadership when it came to

[73] 7 non-trading gentlemen held the constableship.

advancing to the mastership. Only three went on to become masters, a success rate comparable to the merchants or any other occupational group. But whereas the gentlemen served a total of only seven years in the higher office, the five merchants logged a combined total of twenty-eight years. To some degree, this reflected the partially split allegiance of the gentlemen, who probably divided their time between town and country.[74] In any event, their social superiority did not translate into political authority when it came to selecting the Community's leader.

Table 6 suggests that longevity may have been a contributing factor in determining election to the mastership.[75] On average, a burgess would appear in the records for about thirteen years, but a man would generally have to wait closer to sixteen years to reach the highest position. Almost 26 per cent of the constables had been burgesses for more than twenty years before they were elected to their current office. The corresponding figure for the masters was 32.3 per cent. Thomas Horewode waited no less than forty-one years.[76] At the same time, some of those who rose so quickly to the judicial leadership could not have been very old. For example, after achieving the constabulary within six years of admission to the guild, Richard Setter survived for at least twenty-seven years, William Vowell for forty-six, and John Atwater for fifty-six. The average 'guild-span' of the judicial leadership was 28.3 years from admission, more than twice that for burgesses as a whole, and while prominent men were, without doubt, followed more assiduously in the records, there was probably a real difference in longevity involved. It was not that wealth and honour made them thrive, but that age provided them with more time to acquire money. And, as has long been suspected and has now been demonstrated by Maryanne Kowaleski, prosperity and economic security were necessary components of social and political success.[77] On average, the judicial leadership was older than the burgesses as a group, but it often included younger men who had made their fortunes quickly, through either business, marriage, or inheritance.

---

[74] But see Horrox, 'Urban Gentry', 26–7, who argues, correctly I think, that it was not the aim of burgesses to make their money and then flee from the towns for a country ideal.

[75] Cf. Kermode, 'Obvious Observations', 99.

[76] Admitted in 1425 (CBI: 247), elected in 1465 (CBII: 54).

[77] Kowaleski, 'Commercial Dominance'; see also Rigby, 'Urban "Oligarchy"', 64–6;

The looser relationship that existed between the holders of inferior offices and those of the judicial leadership was altogether to the Community's good. Occupying a lowly office by no means disgraced the holder, but it is proof of the relatively low probability of raising oneself through the ranks that comparatively few men advanced step by step. The time required to execute any civic office detracted from the time spent amassing the income which alone could make further advancement possible, although influence and new connections may have generated their own economic compensations.[78] Of those who worked for the Community in its humblest position, as street-wardens, only 24.7 per cent went on to any other office. As Table 6 illustrates, very few (only five) masters had served at the bottom of the ladder. Only one man actually served in every Community office: John Sadler, a merchant who was active in the Community for over fifty years, was elected street-warden in 1441, shambles-keeper in 1443, churchwarden in 1444, tax collector in 1448, constable in 1450, and, finally, master in 1463.[79] Although most of the men who served in the lesser offices went no further, and few went anywhere near the top, they were in no sense failures. They were among the one quarter of burgesses who served at all, and these men must have been both relatively successful at their trade and personally respected to have been selected to hold office.

TABLE 6. *Percentage of office-holders eventually becoming masters*

Office	%
Constables	38.0
Rent collectors	17.5
Churchwardens	7.4
Shambles-keepers	2.9
Street-wardens	3.0

Source: CBI and CBII.

The two lesser and the two intermediate offices can each be characterized differently with respect to their place in the guild

[78] See Kowaleski, 'Commercial Dominance', 363–9, although the advantages noted by her pertained to the oligarchs, not to the pettier office-holders.
[79] CBI: 304, 310, 315, 323, 326, and CBII: 45.

society and hierarchy. The particular social role of the street-wardenship, for instance, was to involve men only recently made burgesses in the government of the town, as responsible members of the Community. Unlike the other offices, the care of the streets required four to six men a year. A third of the street-wardens were selected at the first election after their admission, and the average was four years after admission. Chasing the pigs and controlling the pound may not have been attractive duties, but they were necessary, and tended to be performed by these younger members. Shamble-keeping was only a small step up.

By contrast, the churchwardens and rent collectors tended to be more established figures. These men had been in the guild for an average of ten and thirteen years respectively. In the period under discussion the churchwardens no longer took care of the real property of the church and the Community, but they concentrated on maintaining and expanding the fabric of the church, safeguarding some of the vestments and plate, organizing church ales and other social events, as well as arranging the seating within the church.[80] The churchwardens were remarkable for being committed to their job, and less concerned with further political advancement. Unlike the rent collectors, the churchwardens were never suspected of embezzlement. In the 1390s John Clothier served as churchwarden with John Ronburgh for nine successive years, and each man served additional years with others, Ronburgh for a total of fifteen years. Neither man moved further up the scale of honours, but they were certainly not just discharging a minimum commitment. Their years of tenure speak of real concern for St. Cuthbert's, and of the confidence that the judicial leadership had in them. In the fifteenth century such long service was unknown, but the churchwardens still tended to hold office more than once or twice.

The office of rent collector was more honourable than the churchwardenship, but increasingly difficult to carry out as the Community's rents fell.[81] Rent collectors were always well-established men, but those who served longest tended to be those who did not have the prospect of advancing into the judicial leadership, although some were made councillors. By the end of the fifteenth century the Community was having difficulty in filling the

[80] See below, Ch. 8, sect. 2.
[81] For the fall in rents, see above, Ch. 2, sect. 4.

post. Honest men did not want the time-consuming job, and the less honest defrauded the Community. Part of the fault probably lay with the Community which may have unrealistically expected the collectors to make good the long-lost arrears of decayed rents. Fewer rent collectors (36.8 per cent) advanced up the ladder after 1440 than had done before that date (48 per cent). The worst scandals occurred near the end of the fifteenth century, a time of great fiscal stress for the Community. William Wilmot, sole rent collector from 1475 to 1481, was ordered in 1482 to restore £9 in arrears.[82] In 1483 John Draper was ordered to return £8 that he had 'taken from the common chest' in 1472, when he had served as rent collector with Wilmot.[83] A stipend of 26s. 8d. per annum was introduced in 1484, but it failed to regularize the accounts.[84] John Beynton was caught misappropriating funds in 1495, and William Chamberlain in 1503.[85] Some of these men continued to hold other, and higher, offices, to be respected by the judicial leadership, after these shortfalls were discovered. Rents were a major source of the Community's wealth and power in the town, and rent collectors continued to be seen as holding a crucial civic office, but one which placed them in a difficult position. Towards the end of the fifteenth century those who sought the magistracy increasingly tried to avoid the difficulty and temptation of collecting the rents.

4. TRADES AND 'POWER'

We have already seen that one of the distinct characteristics of the Borough Community was the breadth of its base, the high level of participation from all socio-economic sectors. There were no craft-guilds in medieval Wells.[86] This lack may well have contributed to the generally harmonious conduct and ethos of the Community in Wells (and other small towns): power and authority were centralized within the single broadly based guild, in which all trades participated. The Community was an 'equal opportunity' organization in so far as there was no trade that was excluded or

---

[82] CBII: 134.
[83] CBII: 138.
[84] CBII: 143.
[85] CBII: 192 and 196.
[86] See above, Ch. 3, sect. 5.

made unwelcome. This was virtually universally true in fourteenth-
and fifteenth-century English towns.[87]

Anyone who could prosper sufficiently could stake his claim to
that variety of social power—influence and honour—which existed
within the Community. In practice, the membership fee meant that
most labourers were excluded from Community membership and
office-holding, although we have seen the exceptions from the
pre–1420 period. Financial weakness also contributed to the
effective exclusion of the humbler trades from the top echelons of
the guild and town, particularly from the judicial leadership.
Presumably, the less lucrative the trade, the greater the number
of its members to be found outside of the Community.[88] The
building trades were the poorest of the sizeable commercial groups
of the Community, accounting for about one-tenth of the Community throughout the later Middle Ages. (I have excluded glaziers
here, dealers in a luxury product.) On a strictly proportional basis,
we would expect them to have contributed at least two masters, five
constables, five rent collectors, and six churchwardens. In the event,
the highest position achieved by any of their members was rent
collector. In this office they had a 6.3 per cent share. Even among
the street-wardens they were barely represented (2 per cent). The
butchers held even fewer offices; Table 7 shows how they received
only 10 per cent of their proportional due, and elected no one to a
position of real authority. Bakers (not illustrated) did better among
the victuallers, but only the brewers won a large share of the
judicial offices. Tailors and weavers received approximately their
fair share, but were pinched back as they approached the judicial
leadership. Both were trades from which a good profit could be
made, but only exceptionally was business good enough to scale the
socio-economic heights. There were really prosperous tailors and
weavers, as well as tanners, dyers, and brewers, and all these trades
contributed masters, reminding us that, regardless of their share,
they all had access to the judicial leadership. There was no
overwhelming bias against any craft *per se*, no custom that only
merchants could rule.[89]

[87] Bridbury, *Economic Growth*, 58–63; Rigby, 'Urban "Oligarchy"', 71; cf.
Swanson, 109–10, who offers a different interpretation of the expansion of the
franchise.
[88] Swanson, 151–9, provides evidence of the relative prosperity of different
occupations.
[89] *Westminster*, 234 and 286, also found great diversity among the élite.
Swanson, 2, argues that this was a feature of smaller centres.

TABLE 7. *Select trade representation of office-holders (burgesses, 1377–1500)*

As % of	Builders*	Merchants**	Tailors	Butchers	Tuckers	Weavers	Gentry
Whole community	7.8	5.5	7.8	7.6	8.5	12.3	2.6
Street-wardens	2.0	2.3	5.4	2.7	14.0	24.8	—
Shambles-keepers	3.4	10.2	16.9	1.7	10.2	9.3	1.7
Churchwardens	4.5	18.2	9.1	—	6.8	19.3	—
Rent collectors	6.3	17.7	9.4	—	—	14.6	—
Constables	—	25.9	7.7	—	3.8	11.5	13.5
Masters	—	25.4	5.0	—	2.5	5.0	13.6
Average share	2.7	16.6	8.9	0.7	6.2	13.3	4.8
Average share as a % of due	35.0	302.0	114.0	10.0	73.0	108.0	185.0

Note: *Comprises carpenters, tilers and masons. **Comprises merchants, chapmen, mercers, and grocers.

Nevertheless, it was still true that the conspicuous successes in Community government went to the merchants and 'pure' gentlemen, both groups of which received high overall shares, especially of the judicial leadership, and notwithstanding their relatively small numbers.[90] They had almost five and six times their respective proportional dues among the élite. The gentry served in virtually no other capacity, apart from a fourteenth-century shambles-keeper. The merchants, by contrast, served at all levels, growing in strength towards the top of the ladder, as Table 7 shows. They provided more occupants of the upper three offices than any other trade: 17.7 per cent of the rent collectors; 25.9 per cent of the constables; 25.4 per cent of the masters. Their dominance at the top was greater still, since they tended to serve longer as masters, occupying that office for 42 per cent of the time between 1377 and 1500, compared to the gentlemen's 9 per cent share. The two groups were related, since, of the burgesses, merchants were more likely to become gentlemen later in life. But it would be overstating the case to see a merchant–gentry axis as controlling the town's superior offices. They predominated, certainly, but half the time some other trade provided the Community's chief officer. When the list of constables included a barber, a cordwainer, and a smith, it must be admitted that merchants and gentlemen were simply the most successful, the richest men in a system that rewarded wealth with socio-political recognition.

5. OLIGARCHY

The form of government of English medieval towns has long been one of the main subjects of enquiry and dispute for historians. For at least one hundred years, however, this question has settled around the issue of oligarchy.[91] For the most part, the argument has focused on the nature of political power, the organization of councils, the membership of the ruling body. Lately, and fortunately, Susan Reynolds has addressed another aspect of the difficulty: the term itself.[92] She has argued that 'oligarchy' is a

---

[90] See Table 7.

[91] See Charles W. Colby, 'The Growth of Oligarchy in English Towns,' *English Historical Review* 5 (1890), 633–53.

[92] Susan Reynolds, 'Medieval Urban History and the History of Political Thought,' *UHY* (1986), 14–23; ead., *An Introduction to the History of English Medieval Towns* (Oxford, 1977), 171; ead., *Kingdoms and Communities in Western Europe, 900–1300* (Oxford, 1984), 198, 203–4.

pejorative term, denigrating the moral fibre of the leadership and suggesting that they governed in their own, and not the community's, interest. She suggests 'aristocracy or moderate polity' as a more accurate replacement.[93] These entail difficulties of their own. The second is too vague to be useful, while the first—borrowed, like oligarchy, from Aristotle—has, for many historians, a sharper and more negative connotation than oligarchy itself, suggesting some presumption of the right to govern and the right to pass the privilege on to heirs. It is the concept that we must be clear about; we can keep the term 'oligarchy', shorn of any moral connotations. Reynolds's work has now born further fruit, conspicuously in Rigby's effort to reconcile the reality of power with the understanding that townsmen had of their governments.[94] In the rest of this chapter and in Chapter 6, we also shall try to view government in terms of social realities as well as ideas and institutions.

In this chapter 'oligarchy' is taken to mean a governing political regime in which only a small proportion of the population have real authority—an authority, moreover, that is bestowed neither by birth nor by popular election (not, that is, as in hereditary aristocracy or a modern democracy). Furthermore, this same group must be in a position to decide who holds political office and who can become a member of the political élite.

Another view of oligarchy has been mooted. P. J. Jones has argued in an Italian context that regardless of the name under which a regime operated—whether communal democracy or despotism—the practice was ever proof of oligarchy.[95] There is both an important point here and a major confusion. Jones has correctly pointed out, I think, that, beneath the structure of government, there is always a social system, customary relationships, which endure and which underlie the words and actions of both the regime and its opponents. In other words, political revolution does not entail social revolution or a transformation of *all* underlying ideas, even those about politics. Clans, for instance, do not disappear when a commune replaces an aristocratic despotism. But he goes on to argue that, because the social

[93] Reynolds, 'Political Thought,' 20–1.
[94] Rigby, 'Urban "Oligarchy"', which argues ultimately that the 15th cent. saw a reduction of the power of the community and an increased authority for the rulers.
[95] P. J. Jones, 'Communes and Despots: The City State in Late Medieval Italy,' *TRHS*, 5th ser., 15 (1965), 71–96.

relationships encountered among the rulers in different regimes are similar, and the complaints made by the people are often the same, there is no real distinction to be made among the two parties.[96] But, all that this really proves is that these parties operate within the context of identical social and cultural ideas. In fact, the communes and the despots can easily be distinguished, so long as we do not expect too much of them. The difference is first and foremost in ideology and attitude. This is in effect Reynolds's point again—and our point of departure in examining Wells's circumstances. Oligarchies cannot be condemned for not acting like modern constitutional democracies. They must be viewed according to their actions, but also according to their own and their culture's image of them. Despots and democrats were not confused. Historians will find the difference between them in their ideology, not necessarily in their sociology. We shall return to Wells's urban ideology in the next chapter. The present section will develop the social and factual account of the system that prevailed.

The means by which holders of civic offices were selected was rarely articulated in medieval towns unless it had become a contentious issue.[97] Even where by-laws were passed to give the issue firm expression, the records almost invariably hint at tacit revisions, later contradictions. There was very little open discussion of the subject in Wells's records, but the 1437 constitution does make it clear that all positions beneath the magistracy were selected by the newly appointed master, 'in open semblie, with counsel of his fellows being there present'.[98] The outgoing master had an authoritative say in the choice of his replacement, guided by the advice of his more substantial fellows, the judicial leadership, and the town council. In reality, selections were made before the election meeting, which was mainly concerned with proclaiming the elected men, revealing them to the broader community. The selection of office-holders was certainly determined by those men who were already at the top of the social pyramid. Aside from the formal process of ratification at the general meeting, the body of the membership had no direct say in selecting the leadership. There were, furthermore, no clear instances of even an attempt on their part to change the official, imposed officers.

[96] Ibid. 74–96.
[97] e.g. Kermode, 'Obvious Observations,' 89–92; Rigby, 'Urban "Oligarchy"', 67–70; cf. *Colchester*, 118.
[98] Serel, 38.

At the same time, the nature of the oligarchy was the principal internal political issue faced by the guild in the period. As in other towns in the fifteenth-century, there were concerns that the oligarchs were insufficiently responsive to the interests of the lesser burgesses.[99] The evidence for this change in Wells is indirect but persuasive. There was never any question of electing a different sort of man to run the borough, nor does there ever seem to have been any resentment of the merchants and gentlemen. The means by which people proposed to cope with the problem of overweening oligarchy was not democracy but the check provided by the advice of others, by a functional town council.[100]

From the late fourteenth century there was a desire for a traditional and constitutional oligarchy to guide the community and city and to watch over the masters. In 1384 fifty burgesses gathered to choose twelve 'of the better men to govern and rule the Community'.[101] The number of electors suggests that the council was being established by the Community as a whole, possibly by fifty burgesses especially chosen for the task, and not just by the judicial leadership. Nevertheless, it was still thought sufficient to select men of only the 'better' kind to provide a check on the master and to represent the Community at large. Whether this council of twelve satisfied the Community is doubtful, since in 1408 a new, expanded council of 24 was elected.[102] Although this was the standard size for a late medieval council, it represented more than one in ten of the burgesses of a small town such as Wells.[103] The hint of dissent was more pronounced now, since, unlike its antecedent, this council was to be composed of 'twelve of the greater and twelve of the middling burgesses'.[104] In theory, at least

[99] Cf. Rigby, 'Urban "Oligarchy"', 68–77; Kermode, 'Obvious Observations,' 94–5; Bridbury, *Economic Growth*, 58–60.

[100] Bridbury, *Economic Growth*, 60–1, was the first to make much of the timing of their development; but see Rigby, 'Urban "Oligarchy"', 74–5, who notes that town councils in Grimsby and Leicester were used to restrict the power of the general assembly; see also Reynolds, *English Medieval Towns*, 172–6; *Coventry*, 124.

[101] CBI: 24.

[102] CBI: 176.

[103] Reynolds, *English Medieval Towns*, 173; e.g. *Colchester*, 118; Alan Rogers, 'Late Medieval Stamford', in Alan Everitt (ed.), *Perspectives in English Urban History* (London, 1973), 19–20; in Exeter the expanded council of 24 came in 1435: B. Wilkinson, *The Mediaeval Council of Exeter* (Manchester, 1931), 6.

[104] CBI: 176.

this was a more pointedly populist expansion of the counterweight to the masters, indicative of previous and continuing abuse.

Throughout the next seventy years the councillors frequently failed to replenish their numbers. Sometimes the council seems to have disappeared entirely. Yet there was no immediate reaction to this, let alone anger from the rank and file. The suspicion of undue dictatorial influence grew up slowly. In 1437 dissatisfaction peaked again; the town's customs were re-established and written down, and the council of twenty-four was selected anew, suggesting that it was one of the 'laudable ordynances' that had become 'somewhat withdrawn and negligently demised and not used'.[105] The breadth of the dissatisfaction was plainer in this case, reflected, however, not by any revolutionary constitutional alterations in the civic regime, but in the four men who were selected by the Community to choose the new councillors. They were William Dyer, Simon Wilde, John Trappe and Robert Bullock, respectively a chapman, a shearman, a tucker, and a mason.[106] These are trades representative of the Community as a whole, not its leadership. None of these men had ever been or would ever become even a rent collector, let alone a constable or a master. Two were eventually churchwardens. Wilde served humbly as a long-time shambles-keeper, and the mason, typical of his trade, never held any office and was otherwise little heard of.

Remarkably, however, at least half the men that they selected to become councillors and all of those actually named in the document were all members of the judicial leadership. The appointments were for life. Even at moments of confrontation, there was apparently agreement within the Community as to the qualities required of those in positions of authority. The lesser men who made the elections produced no surprises among these twelve. These characteristics and assumptions of the Community, its ideology, will be elaborated in the next chapter, but here it is worth noting how committed the guild was to the rule of the superior men, checked mainly by other superiors.

This council endured. Furthermore, it did display a composition that went beyond and below the judicial leadership. To this extent, the 1437 reform movement was successful. In 1444 the council,

[105] Serel, 36.
[106] Ibid. 37. Trades have been established from CBI; Serel transcribed 'Trappe' as 'Crappe'.

which must in the main have been the one selected seven years earlier, contained six men who were not currently part of the judicial leadership, four of whom never would be.[107] They were not humble, but solid, well-thought-of men, without wealth. One of them, John Grene, a hostler, eventually ended up in the almshouse.[108] Nevertheless, the council continued to dwindle—the result of natural attrition and the failure of the surviving councillors to appoint successors. In 1467 there were only five left. When the council was refilled that year, five of the chosen men were outside the élite.[109] To the extent that a council was conceived of as a check on arbitrary and dictatorial action by the master, Wells became less of an extreme oligarchy in the fifteenth century than it had been in the later fourteenth. Furthermore, by 1437 the abortive attempt (1408) that the broader Community had staged to achieve permanent representation on the council had been fulfilled, and remained so through the rest of the century.[110]

While the details of the common burgesses' grievances are unknown, the legitimacy of their complaints can be corroborated. Part of the difference between later fifteenth- and fourteenth-century office-holding lay in the prospects for high office of successful burgesses. Wells was, with the notable exception of the rent collectors, generally immune to the late medieval disease of office-avoidance, which was so conspicuous elsewhere.[111] The judicial offices were unaffected, because they combined great honour with limited expenses. The constabulary involved no outlay, while the Magistracy's was limited and, in the sixteenth century at least, the master's expenses were in great part met by the Community.[112] These offices were always attractive.

---

[107] CBI: 314.

[108] This is not to suggest that he was not prosperous at the time of his appointment (CBII: 108).

[109] CBII: 64.

[110] See CBII: 64 (a 1472 council list); CBII: 120, 145, 264 provide a few other names of councillors up to 1511. Representation from outside the judicial leadership continued.

[111] J. I. Kermode, 'Urban decline? The Flight from Office in Late Medieval York,' *ECHR*, 2nd ser., 35 (1982), 179–98, is sceptical of its relation to decline; S. H. Rigby, 'Urban Decline in the Later Middle Ages: The Reliability of the Non-Statistical Evidence,' *UHY* (1984), 52–4; Palliser, *Tudor York*, 204–5; J. W. F. Hill, *Medieval Lincoln* (Cambridge, 1948), 300–1, provides 14th-cent. evidence; R. B. Dobson, 'Urban Decline in Late Medieval England', *TRHS*, 5th ser., 27 (1977), 13–14; Charles Phythian-Adams, 'Urban Decay in Late Medieval England,' in P. Abrams and E. A. Wrigley (eds.), *Towns in Societies* (Cambridge, 1978), 164, 175.

[112] *Wells City Charters*, p. xxx, records the 1540 ordinance.

In the later fourteenth century the dominance of the few was quite pronounced. Often the same man would hold a position for more than one year, although rarely for consecutive years. The most powerful men held the magistracy as many as ten times. Nicholas Cristesham, Thomas Tanner, and John Blithe were all masters at least seven times in the 1370s and 1399, and although the reigns of such fifteenth-century men as William Vowell, John Atwater, John Godwyn, and John Tyler were as lengthy, these men needed more years to amass their equally impressive numbers. In the 1380s and 1390s only two men joined the ranks of the masters; only five new constables were selected. In the fifteenth century, however—indeed, from 1400—these figures rose. On average there were 3.6 new masters every decade in the fifteenth century, and 7.2 new constables.

The contrast was really more marked, because immigration and guild membership were higher in the late fourteenth century than they were in the fifteenth (except between 1463 and 1478). The 1390s, when the first signs of discontent are visible, was the period during which the great immigration wave of the post-plague years was maturing.[113] At that time there were more men who felt that they had a claim to office, or were owed at least a share in the decision-making. Their desire for participation, and their sensitivity to abuse were aggravated by their personal success. The post-plague period was a time of considerable economic expansion and success in the city, driven by an expansive cloth-making industry. But there were not as many men of substance in the town in the fifteenth century, and there were many fewer burgesses.[114] Masters Godwyn and Vowell held office so often between 1433 and 1466 (sixteen times between them) in part because suitable candidates were in short supply, and few others could either compete with them or spare the time to do the office and the Community as much honour.[115] In fact, access to this élite was more open than ever before.

The weakness of the élite family, the rarity of sons succeeding fathers, helped to make Wells's oligarchy more open and benign than those in Italy, for instance.[116] Resentment could not fasten on

---

[113] See above, pp. 150 f., and Ch. 2, sect. 3.
[114] See above, Chs. 2, sect. 5, and 3, sect. 4, pp. 150 ff.
[115] Cf. Rigby, 'Reliability of Non-Statistical Evidence,' 50.
[116] Jacques Heers, *Le Clan familial au Moyen Âge: Étude sur les structures politiques et sociales des milieux urbains* (Paris, 1974); David Herlihy, *Medieval and Renaissance Pistoia* (New Haven, Conn., 1967), 190–9; Jones, 'Communes and Despots,' 83.

particularly powerful families, leaving the élite to be accused of establishing an urban nobility. Every burgess family was encouraged to remain within the Community, but few families were conspicuously successful.[117] None of the pre-1377 masters known to us had a son who was also a master, nor were any of the names of the late fourteenth-century masters and constables repeated in the fifteenth century. In all, only two masters' sons succeeded their fathers. The first father–son pair was John and Thomas Horewode. Thomas, the son, was very slow to become master, not acceding until forty-one years after his admission, certainly a case in which the respectability of age aided his selection more than the influence or wealth of his father, who had been dead for forty-nine years. By contrast, Richard Vowell's success owed much to his father William. Richard Vowell became master in 1473, only seven years after returning to Wells from London to become a burgess, and only three years after his father had served his ninth magisterial term. Whatever his abilities, Richard, 'the gentleman of London', entered the élite on the basis of the wealth generated by his father, and his expectation of inheriting much of it.[118] But no other masters succeeded both in business and family survival, as William Vowell.[119] The Cutte family extended over several generations, attaining the constableship in two, the mastership in one, and still possessing considerable wealth in the next generation. But there was no other case of three- or four-generation participation in the judicial leadership.[120] There was no question of the right being

---

[117] Cf. *London*, 191–206; Gottfried, 59–63 and 137; but Kermode, 'Obvious Observations,' 95–6, and Edward Miller, 'Rulers of Thirteenth-Century Towns: The Cases of York and Newcastle upon Tyne,' in P. R. Coss and S. D. Lloyd (eds.), *Thirteenth-Century England*, i. *Proceedings of the Newcastle upon Tyne Conference 1985* (Woodbridge, 1986), 130, make more of the successful dynasties than of the general trend; of course, circumstances in the 13th cent. were decidedly different.

[118] *CPR 1467–77*: 589.

[119] The family's subsequent history included a canon of Wells, a prior of Walsingham, another master of Wells, and removal into the Norfolk gentry: see *SDNQ* 18 (1926), 10.

[120] 6 men of this family are known to have reached maturity in the city: 4 were burgesses, 2 were university-educated clergy. John Cutte I was admitted in 1401 (CBI: 144), served as rent collector in 1407 and 1408 (CBI: 172, 176), and as constable from 1409–11 (CBI: 179, 186, 193), and was a member of Parliament in 1416 (CBI: 212); his son, John II, was admitted in 1411; another son, William, was admitted in 1423 (CBI: 237), later becoming a councillor and master of the town (CBI: 314, 315, CBII: 19). His son and heir, John III, was a less conspicuous burgess, possibly short-lived (admitted 1474, CBII: 98). His son, John Cutte IV, was admitted in 1507 (*Wells City Charters*, 165), and was one of the town's richer men

passed from father to son. It was as much a freak of nature in the later Middle Ages: two long lives in the same family, lived one after the other.

Part of the reason why families played such as small role was the tendency, especially in the fourteenth and fifteenth century, for sons to be apprenticed outside the city. But even when, throughout the fifteenth century, more burgesses' sons did take up their patrimonial right, they were not remarkably more successful in demographic and economic terms. The unstable economic situation, urban ill health, and epidemic disease combined to keep the sons down, even when, in the mid- and late fifteenth century, they came to constitute 15 or 20 per cent of the Community.[121]

Factions or parties played no more of a role in the Community's oligarchy than the natural bond of families. While friendships or personal alliances can be found among the common run of burgesses—in their mutual support in court cases for instance, no parallel system of factions or association has been among the judicial élite. So far as the records reveal, there was at all times, certainly down to the 1490s, that striking level of unity of action and purpose so associated with oligarchy. Even though the presiding master was the main elector of the other office-holders, no master had a 'team' of regulars with whom he can be associated, whom he tended to choose during his terms. Nor can an opposition camp, a group of men whom he avoided, be discerned. The same names do sometimes occur, but no more often than when some other master was making the selections. This same blindness to favourites extended down to street-wardens, strengthening the possibility—suggested in Chapter 4—that most of the time the Community was a party or faction unto itself, an impressive social unity.[122]

At the top, however, the solidarity was especially pronounced. The individual members of the judicial élite were involved in

in 1524, being assessed in that year's lay subsidy on goods worth £13 (PRO E179/169/156). Robert and another William, respectively described as 'acolyte' and 'deacon', both with bachelor's degrees, had attained these positions by 1464 and 1452 respectively (*Reg. Bek.*, i. 547 and 497, and Emden, *Oxford University*, 531).

[121] See above, pp. 150–2 and n. 44; cf. Gottfried, 59–64, which probably overestimates the family failure rate; John Hatcher, 'Mortality in the Fifteenth Century: Some New Evidence', *ECHR*, 2nd ser., 39 (1986), 19–38; and, for contrast, Herlihy, *Pistoia*, 91.

[122] See above, Ch. 4, sect. 2, and below, Ch. 6, sect. 1(ii).

surprisingly few lawsuits, and very few indeed against one of their companions. Part of the reason for this was no doubt a question of character, and the desire to avoid the appearance of strife at the top.

The solidarity of the oligarchy was inextricably connected with the integrity of the Community as a whole. Whenever an individual burgess challenged the Community's hierarchy, its structure—usually by insulting the master—the case would be judged by a selected group of well-established men, usually councillors. Even if the rebellious man was a town councillor himself, he would be treated the same as a common burgess, punished with ejection or a fine.[123] But on the one occasion, in the early sixteen century, when an issue did arise which threatened to split the élite, a great deal of patience and moderation was used to avoid a deep, damaging division. John Welshot, himself a future master, refused to accept the office of rent collector when he was elected by 'all and single burgesses' in 1501. Not only this, but he refused to pay a penny of the £1 fine levied on all recusants. At this stage Welshot should have been discommoned, but he had become the symbolic leader of a group opposed to Master Nicholas Trappe and especially to the impressment of town councillors and others as rent collectors. That same year William Chamberlain, Henry James, John Elys, and perhaps others had already refused to serve.[124] Slowly, carefully, the dispute was resolved through compromise. Welshot was not discommoned.[125] After a year an ordinance was passed which relieved all members of the council, and others who successfuly petitioned the council, from both service as rent collectors and the fine.[126] This dispute allows us to see the élite's solidarity cracking, and factions and animosity developing. But because the core of the Community, its leadership, was involved, compromise was preferred to more extreme, divisive measures. It took a great deal of personal discomfort, of bad blood, to sunder the guild's one-party system, and it was actually pressure from the top rather than from the bottom that gave it its worst moments.

[123] e.g. CBII: 117 and 142.
[124] CBII: 219.
[125] This case is discussed at greater length below, Ch. 6, sect. 1(iv); CBII: 220, 224.
[126] CBII: 224.

6
The Culture of the Borough Community,
1377–1520

I have argued that the sort of oligarchy that was admired and desired by the burgesses was highly traditional and constitutional. This view requires further development, since it exposes the roots of the Community, the essential ideas and customs upon which all of its collective action and complex social life were based. The 'constitution' or regime of the guild was typically English, an accumulation of time-honoured, unwritten national and local assumptions and a handful of written by-laws. For the cultural historian, the records of actual practice are as informative as the more formal ordinances and the 1437 constitution. In the minutes of the Community court the city's customs and mentality emerge with a credibility rarely inspired by the self-conscious by-law. Reading this constitution provides insights into the customs and ideas by which the rule of the few was legitimated and made workable and acceptable in the eyes of the many. The constraints and expectations placed on the city's leadership also emerge vividly. Furthermore, the Community mentality encouraged each burgess to understand himself in part as a necessary element of a significant collectivity. The result was a real and unifying *esprit de corps*. Of course, every burgess was very much his own man, proud and protective of his achievements and business, as the hundreds of often trivial disputes, and the several more serious ones, in the Community court show. But the Borough Community had traditions and notions which helped to dispel and resolve tensions, and which gave members ideas—eyes to see the world, and words to understand their place and role in it. In short, the Community gave its members an identity and a culture.

The issues that this chapter will raise have not often been discussed by historians of the medieval English town, and so it is appropriate to acknowledge the important contribution of Susan

Reynolds in raising, often in a general but stimulating way, the question of the political theory of the towns—and, indeed, of all communities. The path was indicated long ago by Sylvia Thrupp's *The Merchant Class of Medieval London*, but, as in the case of so many of her fine experiments, there were few followers until lately.[1] In the present chapter I shall follow up many of their hints and give a more concentrated account of a single guild, the Wells Borough Community. I shall outline some of the concepts to be found in the constitution that played a large part in defining and organizing Community life, before going on to discuss the specific social and cultural functions and projects undertaken by the burgesses. In these explorations, far away from personal economic considerations, will be found the bright lures that enticed men to join the Wells civic fraternity, and to remain inside its fold.

I. THE COMMUNITY IDEAL

(i) Order and Tradition

There is a noble ideal embedded in the language of the borough records. It flashes forth frequently, on grand and trivial occasions, to justify, interpret, explain, and condemn words and actions. Naturally, the reality of burgesses' lives failed dismally to conform to the ideal. But even transgressions and failures were, from the standpoint of ideology, occasions to confirm the sure path by proscribing the offence and its perpetrator. The existence of a ready language of praise and blame was one of the durable strengths of the Community. Other cultures and communities, even within fifteenth-century England, would certainly have described borough society and activities differently. The political realities could have been depicted more cynically, more dispassionately, but the citizens' own political and social culture should be a part of any judicious account. Mentality is no ornament or afterthought, but part of the essential formative structure. Life is caught in the web of belief.

Pride of place among the Community's statements of ethos belongs to its most self-conscious and lengthy document, the 1437

[1] Susan Reynolds, 'Medieval Urban History and the History of Political Thought', *UHY* (1986), 14–23; and *London*, 14–27.

constitutional statement. Despite its deliberation, it seems closer to the burgesses' minds than some of the other charters and by-laws. It bears the signs of a more legitimately popular document, the fruit of consensus, written in accessible English rather than the Latin of almost all other Community and town records. Chapter 5 has already noted its simultaneously reformist and conservative nature.[2] It was the highly traditional document that was produced by both the disaffected commons and the élite, the only tangible proof of widespread unhappiness with aspects of the borough regime. It was fundamentally inspired by the burgesses' cardinal virtue: order. Everyone—indeed, everything—had his place and his duties, and an obligation to act appropriately. I shall discuss the concept of a borough hierarchy more specifically below, the sense of rank and relative worth, but one of the implicit moral themes of the 1437 document was that only when every member realized the requirement of acquiescence in the general order of things would the Community remain harmonious and workable.[3]

The scope of the conception was grander than this. To be durable, credible, and true, the borough regime had to be part of a greater whole which subsumed all people, all things. The Community's proper nature, the validity of its organization, its customary ways, were seen as an extension and as a base reflection of the cosmic order, of God's creation.[4] At the head of the document, the burgesses invoked the most concordant and disciplined individuals—ideals, impossible models: 'In Honour of the most puissant, high, mighty, glorious, and eternell Lorde, Our Lorde Jeshu, the most blessedful Virggine Moder and Maide Marie, Saynt Andrewe, Saynte Cuthberte, and all the Holy Company of Heaven . . . '[5] In a sense, these supreme powers were being called to witness, guarantee, and oversee the burgesses' sincerity and the aptness of their regime. If the document was imperfect or drawn up in bad faith, then something like blasphemy was being implied: the holy dealt only with the good and true. This much-abused principle of sanctification was an important feature of medieval life. Most

[2] See above, Ch. 5, sect. 5.

[3] Cf. *London*, 16–17; and Reynolds, 'Political Thought', 15.

[4] See Otto von Gierke, *Political Theories of the Middle Age*, trans. F. W. Maitland (Cambridge, 1900), 7–8 and 101 n. 2; and F. H. Du Boulay, *An Age of Ambition* (London, 1970), 148–51.

[5] Serel, 36. This document is discussed above, p. 10.

frequently encountered in the form of the oath, it served, with variable success, to deter people's faithlessness, errors, and misdeeds by binding them to God and the saints.

The invocation was not one which any town could have used. Wells's particular place in the cosmic scheme of God, saints, and common people was reflected by the explicit inclusion of Andrew and Cuthbert, saints of local prominence as the dedicatees of the cathedral and parish churches. In the mythology of the town, these patron saints were mediating between heaven and the burgesses in an analogy to the way in which their churches physically brought the town closer to the celestial beings. In this vision, Wells and the Borough Community have a clear, even important, place in the larger picture. The town seal reinforced pictorially part of the order. On the reverse, the burgesses had chosen a legend which paid homage to Saint Andrew, while the design depicted a stylized city and cathedral (Wells) beneath an ascendant Christ.[6] It would have been consistent with the Community world-view for the common burgesses to have been encouraged to see themselves as the humble element in the chain of being, exalted only through their obedience and the respect that they paid to those superior to them—civic leaders, saints, and Godhead.

A conscious sense of belonging to a tradition was as important as heaven and the grand design in contributing to the ideal of the well-ordered polity. Ideas from customary law may have aided and fostered the development of a reverence of the past, but more probably it was this reverence itself that allowed the tried and vindicated to gain the stature of law. In Wells's case, ordinances, ideas, and institutions which were repeated year after year for their usefulness achieved an almost superstitious weight of virtue. The explicit purpose of the 1437 constitutional restatement conveys this sentiment honestly and rather feelingly:

For that we, Burgeises of the Cite of Wells now beinge of this present tyme, have conceyved, seyne, and in our cense ripelye felte how worshipfully and discreetlye oure antecessoures Burgeises ordayned, compownded, and made by theyre sage and wyse descrecons diverse convenyent ordinances which be used and contynewed among us until this day: [these should] be

---

[6] Both were crudely drawn in 1494 in CBII: 186, but they were in use in the first part of the 14th cent. see *Wells City Charters*, ed. Dorothy O. Shilton and Richard Holworthy, SRS 46 (1931), pp. xxii–xxiv.

had among us, our successoures and heires, burgeises of the saide Cite, worlde without ende.[7]

To read these documents for expressions of feeling—or at least to see what was critical to the burgesses—is to appreciate their rhetorical convention of stringing synonyms together to convey emphasis. The wisdom of their predecessors, the continuity of their present with the good and formative past, the promise to bequeath the advantages of their customs to posterity, all these things involved the burgesses in a living relationship with tradition. The citizens were given both a blessing from the past and a responsibility to the future.

Of course, the pretext of this document was the need to restore to the Community its true and ancient regime. For some of the tradition had fallen into neglect: 'for the whiche greate losse and dysease for the defawte of undewe and inconveniente rewle hathe happened and fall among us burgeises more than was of old tyme'.[8] To neglect the past was to court the sad spectacle of disorder. Although the Community set out both to renew, add, and, conceivably, delete by-laws, their mental model remained that of an ideal non-specific past, 'old tyme', which it was incumbent upon them to recover. These notions found their way into practical justice and decision-making. In 1414, for instance, the Community justified its final judgement in a particular lawsuit with the claim that it was according to 'ancient usage'.[9] During their dispute with Bishop Fox in 1493 the burgesses defended their right to create and expel burgesses by pointing to custom, saying: 'the space righte wyth of 300 yeres passed they have used to make burgeises as they nowe do'.[10] Even when they did amend ancient custom—reducing the number of forgiven failures to respond to a summons in a suit of debt, for example—they did so with obvious difficulty; it took three long debates, no doubt with much off the record pleading.[11] And should a by-law or custom ever be repealed, the constitution required that a record of the old laws be kept 'for a memorye that all suche ordinaunces hathe bene hadde before this time'. The past, a functional part of the undying Community, was not to be forgotten. Four times a year the clerk was to breathe on the embers

[7] Serel, 36.   [8] Ibid.
[9] i.e. 'antiquo usitate', e.g. CBI: 205.   [10] CBII: 179.
[11] CBI: 158 and 159 (1404).

of tradition by publicly reading through the constitution and by-laws.[12]

The burgesses did not have a well-developed sense of history *per se*. The city clerk rarely took the time to consult the old records or to read the civic charters. During the great dispute of the 1340s the bishop made many charges that would have seemed ridiculous to anyone who had read Bishop Savaric's charter of *circa* 1200, but the town did not contest these points.[13] Their lawyer did not show any knowledge of the town's early constitutional documents during the Chancery trial in 1342, at which the king cancelled his recently granted charter.[14] It was not until the sixteenth century that a search of the old records, apparently a real historical enquiry, suggested to the burgesses that they had privileges that they had failed to exercise. In 1525 and 1540–1 the examination of some early charters (1174–1201) convinced them that they owned two of the town's fairs that had been claimed by the bishop in 1341, and that they could hold a regular court for their tenants.[15] A little earlier, in 1493, Bishop Fox's claims were rebuffed by reference both to old documents and to customary practice.[16]

Myth and a sense of custom grew to maturity earlier than local history.[17] The image on the city seal displayed a consciousness of origins: the springs and cathedral which were thought to have spawned the town were prominently featured.[18] But the memory of the living, encapsulated in the folk phrases 'time out of mind' or 'not spoken of in their days', remained in addition to practically and orally conveyed custom, the main civic remembrance.[19] The burgesses knew that their Community had come a long way, but they were vague about the details. Possibly this attitude influenced their choice of the Jesse tree as the carving for the reredoses in the

---

[12] Serel, 40.

[13] WCC 8; *Yearbooks of the Reign of King Edward III: Year XVI*, ed. Luke Owen Pike, RS 32 (London, 1896), 109–20.

[14] *Yearbooks of King Edward III*, 109–20.

[15] CBII: 325, 422, 428, and 441.

[16] CBII: 178–81; see above, pp. 137 f.

[17] While true everywhere, some other towns were quicker to develop the historical and investigative clerical interests, and possessed better developed civic myths. See *Six Town Chronicles*, ed. R. Flenley (Oxford, 1911); Coventry, 171–2; Colchester, 122; *Croniques de London*, ed. G. J. Aungier, CS, 1st ser., 28 (1844); see also George Holmes, 'The Emergence of an Urban Ideology at Florence c.1250–1450', *TRHS*, 5th ser., 23 (1973), 111–34.

[18] See above, n. 6.

[19] e.g. CBII: 179.

church in 1470. The town participated in the selection of the
subject, going so far as to include fairly exact specifications in the
contract with the mason, a burgess himself.[20] In their art the
Community opted for the represented past, the genealogy of Christ.
They admired not only the nobility of the family, but the idea of a
long descent. But, as represented, this past was schematic,
symbolic, and abstract. It was handsome, but it was nevertheless a
stylized past, a long way from history.[21]

(ii) The Fraternal Ideal

The fraternal ideal was perhaps more powerful and more essential
to the success of the Community than the more abstract orders of
cosmology and tradition. The fraternity was the most widespread
form of association, adopted across Europe by even the humblest of
laymen. Its roots run deep into Germanic civilization.[22] Among the
burgesses of Wells, fraternity was expressed in many concrete
practices, reinforced by several social institutions and civic
ceremonies. Everything that the burgesses did was thought to 'turne
with the ayde of the Trinitie, in whose name the sayde Burgesses
and fraternitie be founded'.[23] The Community very probably began
as a parish or socio-religious fraternity in the twelfth or thirteenth
century, perhaps, as at Chesterfield, with special reference to the
business and rights of the newly enfranchised burgesses.[24] Even in
the fifteenth century, however, the Community of Wells was
unusual among civic guilds in the degree to which it was informed
by the customs and notions of the brotherhood. Guilds played

[20] CBII: 89.
[21] On the history and meaning of the Jesse tree, see Émile Mâle, *The Gothic
Image: Religious Art in France of the Thirteenth Century*, trans. Dora Nussey (New
York, 1958; orig. French edn., 1913), 165–70.
[22] On the context and history of the fraternity, see E. Coornaert, 'Les Ghildes
médiévales', *Revue historique* 199 (1948), 22–55 and 206–43; Susan Reynolds,
Kingdoms and Communities in Western Europe, 900–1300 (Oxford, 1984), 66–78;
Richard Mackenney, *Tradesmen and Traders: The World of the Guilds in Venice
and Europe, c.1250–1650* (London, 1987), 47–50, provides fine details; as does
reading the guild returns in L. Toulmin Smith (ed.), *The English Gilds*, EETS 40
(1870); see also R. F. E. Weissman, *Ritual Brotherhood in Renaissance Florence,
1200–1600* (New York, 1982), 80–98, 99–105; H. F. Westlake, *The Parish Gilds
of Medieval England* (Oxford, 1919).
[23] Serel, 37.
[24] Toulmin Smith (ed.), *English Gilds*, 165: Chesterfield's guild of the Blessed
Mary was instituted shortly after the town became a chartered borough. The guild
had the express purpose of both stimulating a religious life and 'the better to assure
the liberties of the town'.

important, even dominant, roles in other towns: the Trinity guild in Coventry, the Corpus Christi guild in York, the aldermen's guild in Bury St Edmunds, were all true clubs, with social and cultural as well as political functions, but none of them constituted the entire body of burgesses, as did Wells's Community.[25] Distinctive, the Community court functioned to preserve and enhance the bonds which existed among its members.

The Community possessed many of those characteristics which have traditionally been associated with the dangerous fraternity, the commune, typically described as a bellicose twelfth-century organization of local independence and unrest. Susan Reynolds has done much to take the sting out of this inflammatory term, to blend it with the unobjectionable *communitas* (community). She has pointed out, for instance, that 'Associations bound by oaths were commonplace and not in themselves subversive.'[26] Nevertheless, whatever we may choose to call these sworn associations, it must be recognized that they retained a potentially rebellious aspect well into the fourteenth century. The idea of men binding themselves before God to each other called into question their loyalty to the law and to the king. In 1326 the uprising at Bury St Edmunds seems to have involved a sworn confederacy of burgesses against the abbey, whether or not the term 'commune' was used.[27] Richard II's motivation in requiring all fraternities to register with the government and to justify their purpose and activities was at least partly born of fear of rebelliousness and secretive societies. To quote George Unwin on the return of London's guild of St Bride, the fraternity 'nervously admitted that there had been something of a livery (parliament had lately banned liveries "given under colour of gild fraternity or any other association",) but urged that it was "not out of any wicked intention of maintaining a confederacy . . . . They had no oaths, congregations, conventions, meetings, or assemblies." '[28]

[25] On these guilds, see *Coventry*, 119–22; Toulmin Smith (ed.), *English Gilds*, 165–6; Gottfried, 181–8.

[26] Reynolds, *Kingdoms and Communities*, 174; and ead., *An Introduction to the History of English Medieval Towns* (Oxford, 1977), 103–9.

[27] See M. D. Lobel, 'A Detailed Account of the Rising in Bury St Edmunds in 1326–7 and the Subsequent Trial', *Proceedings of the Suffolk Institute of Archaeology* 21 (1932), 215–31.

[28] George Unwin, *The Gilds and Companies of London* (London, 1908), 125; Reynolds, *English Medieval Towns*, 165, agrees that 'suspicion of secret societies', was in part the king's concern, but she does not connect the civic guilds which had to file reports with any particular potential for urban revolt.

It was also at about this time that the Statute of Mortmain was extended to guilds of all kinds, presumably because, like the Church a hundred years earlier, they had acquired a worrisomely large amount of property.[29] The acquisition of property had been essential to the advance in authority achieved by the Borough Community in the fourteenth century.[30] The 'commune' had seemed especially real in Wells in the 1340s, when the burgesses had tried to remove the bishop's authority.[31] That mild commune or *conjuratio* was the burgesses' fraternity, the Community. Throughout the Middle Ages the Community retained a high level of unity as a defence against future encroachments. It required the spiritual closeness of brothers for the burgesses to force the bishops of Bath and Wells to allow them increased autonomy. Fraternities and communes were sometimes rightly confused.

The unity that was generated or strengthened by the events of the 1340s was written into the Community statutes and customary law. Burgesses and their families were required to sue other burgesses in the Community court, where no foreigner could ever sue. They denied themselves immediate recourse to the king's or the seigniorial courts. Some men tried to overlook their obligation to the Community court, driven by expediency or impatience with a slow-moving case, but to fail to use the court was to risk the very real threat of permanent expulsion from the fraternity. Burgesses were also forbidden to support a foreigner against another burgess. Those who did oppose the interests of a brother in this way would be sued before the master. In 1379 Ralph Tucker was summoned for aiding the outsider John Clifford in a case against a burgess in the bishop's court.[32] In the same year Nicholas Baker sued Henry Gage for supporting an outsider whom Nicholas had accused of damaging his porch.[33] These customary demands on the legal lives of its members had the important effect of drawing a sharp line around the Community, separating the brotherhood from the rest of the city, fostering its sense of specialness, defiance, and superiority. Any breach of this line was taken fairly seriously. The Community often chose to describe the crime as perjury, thereby

[29] See Sandra Raban, *Mortmain Legislation and the English Church, 1279–1500* (Oxford, 1982), 170–4.
[30] See above, Ch. 4, sect. 4.   [31] See above, Ch. 4, sect. 2.
[32] CBI: 44.   [33] CBI: 46.

highlighting the moral and religious failure of the offending burgess.[34]

The Community's confraternity was underlined by the nature of its meetings, and the difference between these and public town-hall gatherings. Anyone who was a burgess was expected to appear at the main annual meeting, or face a fine.[35] Non-burgesses were virtually never allowed entry, whereas the presence of foreigners at a gathering of the borough of Colchester, for instance, could develop into a political problem.[36] Henry James tried to attend a meeting in Wells over two years after having been expelled, but he was immediately and ceremoniously shown the door.[37] When, in 1409, Lawrence Tucker revealed 'secrets of the Community' to the bishop's steward, he was summoned to the master to be questioned thoroughly, although he seems to have avoided discommoning.[38] William Weye almost incurred the ultimate civic penalty of permanent ejection for simply doing his job. On watch and ward one night in the autumn of 1429, he raised the alarm against a group of burgesses which apparently included the master.[39] Plainly, the solidarity of the guild was extended outside the hall, and entailed each man showing his brother special treatment.

(iii) Unity

The tendency to manifest and enforce unity did not stem from social club camaraderie alone. Order was thought to derive in great part from solidarity.[40] Unanimity, the lack of dissent, legitimized action or decision in a way that a mere majority, implying opposing individuals or factions, could not. From the same soil that gave life to oligarchy sprang the ideal of unity, the distrust of 'democratic' parties and all divisiveness. Even after a very messy, obviously

---

[34] e.g. CBI: 57 and 106. Perjury was a religious crime tried by the consistory court. It accounted for one fifth of the instance business of the consistory court in Wells: see R. W. Dunning, 'The Wells Consistory Court in the Fifteenth Century', *SANHS* 106 (1962), 46–61, esp. 59.

[35] CBII: 121.

[36] *Colchester*, 220–1.

[37] CBII: 219 and 234.

[38] CBI: 178; on the secrecy of fraternities, cf. Unwin, *Gilds and Companies*, 97.

[39] CBI: 267.

[40] Reynolds, *Kingdoms and Communities*, 188–92; Charles Phythian-Adams, 'Ceremony and the Citizen: The Communal Year at Coventry, 1450–1500', in Peter Clark and Paul Slack (eds.), *Crisis and Order in English Towns, 1500–1700* (London, 1972), 69–74.

controversial, election, the records report that 'each and every burgess in unison and with unanimous assent' proclaimed the choice.[41] The political historian would sceptically challenge all such accounts of unanimity. But it is worth recalling that it is common practice in modern political conventions in Canada or the United States for the divisions and animosity produced in a hard-fought election, especially when tempers and manners had not been at their best, to be symbolically healed by having the loser ask his followers and the official recorder to make the vote unanimous. In a medieval urban context, a successful, healthy 'election' was thought to need the strength of unanimity. There was little appreciation of the tolerated, even comfortable, existence of opposed elements within the polity. Of course, such an attitude was especially important in Wells, where the Community's collective rights were poorly grounded and often opposed to the interests of their powerful lord. As Sylvia Thrupp wrote of London and its lord: 'Unity before the king was the city's prime need.'[42]

In the political theory of the borough, legitimation required unity. For instance, when selecting the four men who would reappoint the town council, the Community did so 'by one assente, consente, frewill, and full agreement'.[43] One can sense that they were protesting too much, but the ideal is only reinforced by the fact. As Steven Rigby has noted: 'Consensus . . . did not simply exist; it had to be created and maintained.'[44] The principle extended downward to cover even comparatively trivial issues like the granting of Community property to a new tenant, or the election of a new almsman to the hospital.[45] New ordinances always pointed to their authority in the 'unanimous assent of the Master and the entire Community'.[46] On the one hand such proclamations reveal the concern of the burgesses and the leadership to avoid both the appearance and the fact of the abuse of power which could result whenever the master or others would act on their own, possibly favouring their friends or themselves. But they also make clear that any initial dissent was probably raised

---

[41] CBII: 219.

[42] *London*, 100. cf. S. H.Rigby, 'Urban "Oligarchy" in Late Medieval England', in J. A. F. Thomson (ed.), *Towns and Townspeople in the Fifteenth Century* (Gloucester, 1988), 66–7.

[43] Serel, 37.   [44] Rigby, 'Urban "Oligarchy" ', 67.

[45] e.g. CBI: 13 and CBII: 123.   [46] e.g. CBII: 58.

and debated before the more public meetings were held; and by then it had been washed away in the waters of reconciliation.

The burgesses showed as much sensitivity to a public proof of disharmony as to a private embarrassment. For instance, in 1383 Master Nicholas Cristesham arraigned Henry Sparkeford for gross verbal disrespect, committed in the master's High Street shop. The offence was aggravated by the 'presence of diverse foreigners', who might have suspected the Community of being fragile, divided, and weaker than it wanted to appear.[47] Often enough they would probably have been right. In language and ceremony, the Community was often straining for effect.

(iv) Virtues and Vices

It should be sufficiently clear that proper behaviour was fairly well circumscribed in the Community mentality. But a closer examination of the language of praise and blame, civic virtue and sin, will show just how thorough and coherent the burgesses' ideology was.[48] The qualities sought in the leadership were noted or implied at numerous places in the Convocation Books. The criteria for election to the mastership were pithily summed up: the master was to be 'bonis temporalibus, bonis moribus', to have money and morals both.[49] The required level of wealth was never precisely defined in Wells. Moderate minimum requirements had already been set in fourteenth-century Exeter, and fifteenth-century Colchester expected office-holders to have a 'lyvelode in rente [of] forty shillings'.[50] But perhaps in the much smaller town of Wells it was feared that an excessive figure would only serve to deplete the modest pool of eligible men almost to exhaustion.[51] In 1437 the

[47] CBI: 15.

[48] Cf. Reynolds, 'Political Thought', 22, where she draws attention to the version of Brunetto Latini's 'Li Livres dou Tresor', in *Munimenta Gildhallae Londoniensis: Liber Custumarum*, ed. H. T. Riley, RS 12/2, i (1860), 16–24; *London*, 14.

[49] CBII: 37.

[50] Maryanne Kowaleski, 'The Commercial Dominance of a Medieval Provincial Oligarchy', *Medieval Studies* 46 (1984), 361; *Colchester*, 221; cf. *London*, 14–15 and 100–1; Edward Miller, 'Rulers of Thirteenth-Century Towns', in P. R. Coss and S. D. Lloyd (eds.), *Thirteenth-Century England*, i. *Proceedings of the Newcastle upon Tyne Conference 1985* (Woodbridge, 1986), 133.

[51] See above, pp. 173 f; cf. Jennifer Kermode, 'Obvious Observations on the Formation of Oligarchies in Late Medieval Towns', in Thomson (ed.), *Towns and Townspeople*, 93.

word used to describe the councillors' desired economic status was 'sufficiente', and either this or 'self-sufficient' best captures the sense that the burgesses intended, the 'virtue' that they sought.[52] The politically responsible man had to be truly independent. He could still work and run his business, but he should no longer be a desperate slave to money. Such men would be able to neglect their business to a certain extent, so that they could execute their sometimes time-consuming superior offices. Furthermore, the Community hoped that richer men could avoid the seduction of bribery or of showing 'partialitie for dread', that is, succumbing to psychological or economic intimidation.[53] There was also an expectation that the master of the town would be generous to his brothers—and to the king if called upon to contribute to a forced loan—and these purely practical concerns helped to make a degree of financial stability inseparable from leadership.

While it is sometimes difficult to believe that character was scrutinized as closely as wealth when candidates were chosen, it is nevertheless impressive to see how much space was devoted to a discussion of the ideal character of a leader. Candidates for the council or the judicial leadership were to be 'sworn not corrupte, but being of sadde and goode rule, havyng insyghte, conscience, and trewe conceyte, dredyng God'.[54] 'Discrete' was another favourite adjective.[55] Such terms are often difficult to distinguish. Again we are facing the rhetorical device of repetition to convey emphasis. But they do indicate a certain manner of man. Susan Reynolds has recently noted the inclusion of Brunetto Latini's advice on choosing a leader in the *Liber Custumarum* of London, where the fifteenth-century Anglicized Latini elucidates on what some of these qualities meant. He advises the mayor to keep himself from drunkenness, pride, anger, anguish, avarice, envy, and lust, 'for each of these sins is mortal before God'. He must learn not to speak too often, nor to laugh too loudly, 'like a child or a woman'.[56] In Wells, as elsewhere, the leader was to be a man who added consideration, self-possession, and decorum—in a word, *gravitas*—to his fear of God.

[52] Serel, 37; cf. *London*, 14.
[53] Serel, 37 and 40; cf. Toulmin Smith (ed.), *English Gilds*, 350; *Liber Custumarum*, i. 18.
[54] Serel, 37.
[55] Ibid. 38; cf. Reynolds, *English Medieval Towns*, 98.
[56] *Liber Custumarum*, i. 22.

The social virtues which the Community expected to emerge from these personal qualities were honour for the guild, and impartiality and sensitivity in justice and administration. The 1437 constitution makes this specific. Good character and the guidance of 'trothe' would, they reasoned, lead to 'just and equall governance'. Whether 'pore or ryche', every burgess was to be treated fairly, and any previous relationship with the leadership should not affect his treatment. Specifically, fear, love, hatred, and 'affinitie' were to be set aside.[57] The councillors' oath of office prominently featured a pledge to deem and do 'evenlye and indifferentlye'.[58] Impartial objectivity, patient consideration, has always been the judiciary's ideal. But it was the idea of the fraternity, of the brotherhood, that made equality before the magistrates a natural and workable idea.

Doubtlessly hidden from the orthodox records are the many cases in which the leadership was seen to have failed the common burgesses. The fact that the town council was often allowed to atrophy was an indication of this, because the council was, in effect like a city parliament. As we have argued, the burgesses saw its existence as a check on the arbitrary power and influence of the master.[59] Nevertheless, the aim was for the master to be a man likely to act well, and the evidence, which I shall detail below, does to a great extent confirm that, generally, a sort of justice was achieved. Unity required masters to compromise. Ideology exhorted them to consider the complaints of any burgess who came to 'fele hymselfe agreved, vexed, damaged, hurte, or oppressed in anywyse unresonablye'. The master and council then had to make amends, presumably at their discretion, within fifteen days of the complaint.[60] A master in any way approximating the ideal would not hesitate to heed the interests of any burgess who was suffering because of an unnecessary or foolish judgement or ordinance.

Nevertheless, the Community ideal of order was ultimately far stronger than any egalitarian element of the constitution. An

[57] Serel, 37; cf. *London*, 98; whether affinity here means a familial relationship or a political connection through the patronage of a lord, the intent is the same; on the connection to a lord, see K. B. McFarlane, *England in the Fifteenth Century* (London 1981), 23–43; and Kate Mertes, *The English Noble Household, 1250–1600* (Oxford, 1988), 59–63, 133–6, 165–7.

[58] Serel, 40.

[59] Ibid. 37; see above, pp. 170 ff.

[60] Serel, 37.

individual had to communicate his concerns privately, quietly, and constitutionally, showing due respect for the master and Community. Like the cosmic order, the Community was divided into degrees of power and precedence. In effect, every burgess was endowed with as much respect as his political position, wealth, and character merited. The fifteenth-century trend was, if anything, to give added stress to these differences, even at the very time that the lesser burgesses were winning increased political consideration. Simpler than the degrees of the angels, the burgesses' social hierarchy was a rough division between the *meliores, mediocres*, and, presumably as elsewhere, the *inferiores*.[61] In one place foreigners were called *plebs*, a patronizing or condescending term, rich with the burgesses' pride in their own exclusiveness and superiority.[62] One by-law required burgesses in the presence of the bishop or another great lord to make due reverence to one another 'after ther estate, degree, and faculte'.[63]

It is easiest to see the importance that was placed on status by looking at the admittedly special case of the place of the master in the social hierarchy. The qualities required of a master were the same as those expected in a councillor, but the wealth, the impressiveness of personality, were to be larger in every respect. The master was the head of the civic body. His leadership was as much social as it was administrative. The master's duties were generally supervisory. His share of the actual judgement at court was much less than a constable's; his custodianship of the Community funds was less direct than the rent collector's. But, as a political figure, he represented the burgesses of Wells. He might well be thought of as one of the Community's emblems, the successful and imposing display of which maintained and even enhanced the Community's sometimes fragile stature and honour. He alone was specifically charged in his oath of office with sustaining the living tradition of 'laudable customes, usages, and ordynaunces of the Cite of Wells'.[64] The master had the greatest share in assuring the continuance of the regime by being responsible for the appointment of all the junior officers and, more crucially,

---

[61] CBI: 176; and for inferiors, see e.g. Colin Platt, *The English Medieval Town* (London, 1976), 119.

[62] CBII: 80; cf. *London*, 15. The context in the Wells example was charitable, not political.

[63] Serel, 39.   [64] Ibid. 41.

his successor. From the perspective of the small borough ideal, the master was a sort of icon, to be awarded the same reverence as the burgesses owed to the fraternity.[65]

His emblematic quality was essentially a public one. Within the guildhall he was authority, but outside he was the Community. It was customary, for instance, for the master to be at the High Cross whenever a proclamation was being read out by the bailiff or the steward, symbolically to receive the law on behalf of the burgesses.[66] At weekly services in the parish church, and on feast-days, the master went out with the priest at the end of the service, the rest of the council following behind to emphasize his superiority and to indicate their own intermediate position.[67] In such a display the religious and the secular mingled, the one authority reinforcing the other. There would have been no doubt as to the ascendancy of the Community in the city; burgesses and foreigners would both have seen their places in the Wells order confirmed. For some foreigners it may have initiated the desire to join the guild. To others, the procession was possibly the cause of a moment of quiet resentment.

Whatever his previous status or trade, once a man became master he was transformed by honours, rituals, and attentions.[68] Disrespectful behaviour towards constables and councillors did exist, and was serious enough to find its way into the courts, but the wrath of the Community was reserved for trespasses against the master. The reasons for this are now obvious. To attack him was simultaneously to attack the ideals of fraternity and unity. Furthermore, it was also seen as a sad proof of the unruliness of the offending burgess, who was exhibiting the very qualities which were the antithesis of the ideal leader. Such moral failure was thought to be at the root of disorder and instability. The Community term for this social disease was 'rebellion'. The charge was common enough in the records, and often seems to have involved little more than harsh language or anger directed at the master. Sylvia Thrupp has noted a similar sensitivity to insults, which were 'thought of as sin rather than misdemeanor', on the part of London magistrates.[69] The 1437 constitution named the

---

[65] Cf. *Liber Custumarum*, i, 16–24.   [66] *Wells City Charters*, p. xix.
[67] CBII: 251.
[68] On the trades of the masters, see above, Ch. 5, sect. 4, and Table 7.
[69] *London*, 18.

source of this sin: a 'stoburne and prowde herte', 'wilfulness'.[70] Typically, rebellion would occur during a session of the Community court, arising from a debate or litigation. The angry man would refuse to yield to the master's 'rewle'. Procedure at this point was clear: 'and after that he is ones or twice *commanded* by the Maister for to kepe silence and peace, which but yf he do *obedientlye*, he shal be discomyned for ever [my emphasis]'.[71] Yielding to the master was showing that one knew one's place, understood who one was in the civic world. By contrast, failing to do so, and compounding one's error by abusing the master, was repulsive and irrational to the burgesses. So Thomas Hampton's 'vile' attack on Master Richard Vowell was described as originating in 'pure malice' and 'instructed by the Devil', the ultimate lord of misrule.[72]

The doctrine of respectful obedience built a conservative and authoritarian element into the guild regime. For although we have noted that the master was charged to be sensitive to the problems of any of his brethren, and have observed that there were other moral and constitutional checks on the master, the requirement of obedience constituted a form of political closure. The proper balance between authority and obedience was a major theme in medieval political theory which found its echo in the custom of Wells.[73] But neither at Wells nor elsewhere could there be any real question of the authority of the chief magistrate or the monarch being undermined. To show oneself to be stubborn and impatient, rebelliously disobedient, was to become 'contemtable'. The entire Community was enjoined to treat such a man with due disrespect, possibly with a limited form of social ostracism, even when he was not yet discommoned. In two places the 1437 constitution says that the delinquent should 'falle in a greviouse contempte amongst the Master and burgeises'.[74] In the eyes of the Community, obedience, which might mean giving up the point, was the way of virtue. Political restiveness and defiance were inherently unworthy of a good man. Oligarchy thrived in this moral atmosphere.

The firm line that the Community took on obedience to the master was greatly mitigated by the considerable amount of

[70] Serel, 39.   [71] Ibid. 39.   [72] CBII: 142.
[73] See Walter Ullmann, *Medieval Political Thought* (Harmondsworth, 1975), 102–14; *Coventry*, 137–40.
[74] Serel, 38–9.

flexibility and understanding documented in the Convocation Books. Wells's was a traditional and constitutional oligarchy, and this meant that there were distinct limits to the harshness with which a burgess would be treated. To acknowledge error was generally to receive forgiveness. We shall return to this later, but an example will make clear the importance that was placed on due humility when seeking readmission or reconciliation. It was essential that the social 'sinner' manifest his inferiority to the master and Community—in effect, his acceptance of his place in the society of degrees. Some time after William Fox, previously a town councillor, had been discommoned in 1478, he returned to the common hall to seek renewal of his oath and membership. He succeeded because his appeal was made 'kindly, humbly, and affectionately'.[75] In all such cases the repentant man 'placed himself completely at the mercy of the Master and Community'.[76] On other occasions the offender was said to 'submit himself' to his former brethren.[77] There is evidence that, in many cases, some behind-the-scenes arbitration succeeded in winning a reprieve for the offending man, or an improved settlement to the dispute which had angered him in the first place. But the terms of the reconciliation were always similar and unequivocal, a triumph of the fraternity over the individual.

A closer examination of one extraordinarily detailed and unusual case will sharpen many of the ideas that I have been discussing, and will help to bring alive the personal qualities either admired or despised by the burgesses. The account that the city clerk, John Beynton, provided of the disagreement between Master Nicholas Trappe and John Welshot was highly supportive of the master. Beynton was an older man, and had served as town clerk for over twenty years. He was, in a sense, the keeper of the civic order and regime, so his position is understandable, his orthodoxy helpful and revealing. Since we are relatively unconcerned with the political facts at this point, Beynton's prejudice only makes the civic ethics stand out more clearly.[78]

On 6 October 1501 the Community had a small crisis on its hands. It had been unable to persuade anyone to accept the position of rent collector. General elections had been held the week before,

[75] CBII: 119.
[76] e.g. CBI: 34.
[77] e.g. CBII: 27, 31, and 129.
[78] Cf. above, p. 176.

but Master Trappe's approaches had been refused by all. Since most of the Community's income was dependent on the execution of this office, the deadlock had to be overcome quickly. At the next convocation, 'each and every burgess, including John Welshot, with one assent, conceded' to the master the right to select a rent collector then and there, without the nominee's previous consent. The clerk narrated how Trappe gave the matter a lot of thought, in depth and 'out of affection', and elected Welshot. Welshot immediately became inflamed. He was 'very angry in the presence of the Master,' the councillors, and all the burgesses: 'He violently struck the table with his fist and said in a loud voice in English: "I sette not a pynne by the mayster. He hath caused more stryfe in this halle than ever was before." ' He went on to brag of having locked the master in the hall at a recent convocation, in the hope that Trappe would have to leave the first-floor chamber through a window and at some risk of injury. Welshot reiterated his refusal, and thus incurred the fine of 20s., which was assessed by the master 'with the assente of the whole hall'. Failure to pay, Welshot was told, would lead to his expulsion from the Community. In this one day of defiance, we already have before us the anger, disobedience, and inflammatory action and language which the ideology declared to be a threat to the Community's very nature. There was to be more.[79]

The sequel makes it plain that real solidarity was lacking. Welshot had some supporters, at least among the other men who had refused to serve as rent collector and who were anxious to avoid paying the fines which had been assessed against them.[80] Furthermore, Welshot's social prominence won him some special consideration. For our purposes, however, the fact that he was not expelled and that the case was prolonged is fortunate because it provided an occasion for Trappe to act in an impressively magisterial manner. Quiet, unsuccessful diplomacy laboured behind the scenes until 5 December, when, at a meeting, 'Welshot said plainly and expressly in a loud voice that he was not willing to pay one penny of the fine.' At this point Trappe was all reserve and due process. He had the relevant ordinance found and read aloud to the assembly. Still Welshot pushed him, adding provocation upon defiance, goading Trappe to expel him. Welshot said that he would prefer to be discommoned rather than to pay any of the fine. Trappe's patience remained intact, and he adjourned the issue until the next meeting later in the month.[81]

Shortly before Christmas Trappe called upon Welshot to satisfy the Community one way or the other, with money or commitment to office. He spoke to him not in the 'loud voice' that Welshot used, but 'with deliberation and in a pleasant [literally, a suave] voice'. He offered one of the subtle forms of peacemaking that the Community preferred. The master pointed out that one of the other men who had refused to occupy the office, John Broke, had lately been reconciled. Broke's case had in fact been dealt with earlier on in the meeting. Beynton described how Broke 'humbly submitted himself to the Master, of his own free will and without being ordered to', placing the 20s. fine on the table. Master Trappe and the burgesses were so impressed by Broke's action and attitude that they had returned the money. The implication was that they were anxious to do the same for Welshot. He was unmoved, however, and vowed his steadfastness—in the Community's eyes, his stubbornness. Attacking the Community's constitution (*regimen*) this time, Welshot 'suddenly and angrily and stubbornly' left the hall, without the required permission of the master. Once again, Trappe resisted the temptation, no doubt then being pressed upon him by some of his brethren, to expel Welshot immediately. Instead he adjourned the meeting.[82]

After this, Welshot, a man with considerable social connections, tried to bring pressure to bear from outside, threatening the involvement of the king and council through his uncle, Thomas Cornish, a suffragan bishop and the vicar of St Cuthbert's. By involving outsiders, telling them of the affairs of the hall, Welshot was only aggravating his already considerable offences.[83] On Trappe's side, patience prevailed. It was not until 30 September 1502, fully a year since the fracas had begun, that Welshot was persuaded to submit on the same terms as Broke and others, the very terms that he had rejected so fiercely nine months earlier. As a final compliment to Trappe, the 'model' master, the clerk was careful to write that the restitution of the fine was granted by the whole Community, but 'at the request of the Master'.[84]

[81] CBII: 219.
[82] CBII: 220.
[83] CBII: 220.
[84] CBII: 224.

This vividly depicted case puts flesh on the conceptual bones that I have been describing. The Community ideal, the burgesses' views of virtues and character flaws, are all here as features which allowed the clerk, Beynton, to appreciate and understand events and individuals. Trappe was portrayed as patient to a fault, considerate, reasonable, and filled with due gravity. In this ideal rendering he was a hero among burgesses, the magisterial ideal achieved. As Brunetto Latini prescribed, quoting Cicero, the ruler must have justice not malice; he must keep his temper lest he seem the fool, unable to recognize truth or to give correct judgements.[85] By contrast, Welshot's disobedience, obstinacy, hot anger, and barbed tongue nearly exhausted the list of premier character failings that the civic scribe knew could plague a man and the Community. Another, more balanced political account could be given. Chapter 5 has indicated how this case revealed serious trouble within the oligarchy.[86] Without question, Welshot was given special treatment, not the fairness that the Community purported to admire. He had influential friends upon whom other men could not rely. He was a very rich man, a future master, and he had allies in the Community.[87] He avoided the expulsion that many other men would have incurred, and he was forgiven absolutely. Moreover, the unanimity and solidarity of the guild was shaken, at least to some extent. One hopes that somebody later saw the irony in the fact that Welshot went on to become a rent collector as early as 1505, and master twice before he died. His later success, however, might indicate that his anger in 1501 was thought by many to have been somewhat justifiable and out of character. But, regardless of these issues, in their conception of these events the burgesses subordinated what we would call political considerations to the moral language of the Community ideal.

2. THE INSTITUTIONS OF COMMUNITY

(i) Initiation

The burgesses of Wells had diverse ways in which to put flesh on the conceptual bones of their fraternity. Men were attracted to the

[85] *Liber Custumarum*, i. 17–18.
[86] See above, p. 176.
[87] An idea of his wealth may be gauged from his will, *SMWII*: 199–202 (1519).

Community—and bound to it—by a series of rituals and activities which provided them with a social network, possible help in times of personal hardship, a congenial problem-solving mechanism, increased religious life, and a firm corporate identity of which they could be proud.

However different their pasts, or diverse their futures, each man began his fraternal life in the same way, by going through a rite of admission. The ceremony was symbolic, traditional, but not unduly solemn. In the Convocation Books this rite of passage jumps out at the reader. A gauntlet was drawn beside every admission record, for an offering of gloves was part of the ceremony. The idea of supplication was central to the process. Although money was often tendered to the guild, the freedom of Wells was granted, not sold. One recurrent phrase was that the freedom of the city was 'humbly sought' by the outsider. From the first, therefore, the new man was thereby required to acknowledge to the leadership and the Community his subordinate and humble position. It was he who was being honoured. This is the message that the act of admission conveyed.

The new man bound himself to the Community by his holy oath, by gifts, and through the act of conviviality. It is difficult to convey the importance of the holy oath in medieval life.[88] But it is worth repeating how often disobedient burgesses were charged with perjury, the stinging spiritual offence. The rebellious man had broken faith, and set himself against the social and spiritual order of things. The burgesses' oath, which was taken at the ceremony, was a central moment for these men, when the supplicant gave himself and his will 'to the Master and to all the burgesses', and was thereby transformed into one of them, a member of the city's élite.[89] He promised to commit his worldly resources to the Community's needs, to honour his fellows and their constitution, and to be obedient, 'help me God and holidome'. This avowal was given in front of his brothers, and they now took him for one of their body. But it was more like a religious conversion than joining a modern social club or even a political party. The oath effected a transformation, because afterwards the man could not leave the

---

[88] In urban context, see Phythian-Adams, 'Ceremony and the Citizen', 59–61; *London*, 19–21; Weissman, *Ritual Brotherhood*, 97–8, notes that in Florence the guilds prohibited oaths lest they be broken and imperil souls.

[89] CBII: 1.

Community of his own will, nor could he neglect its rules. The only way out was ejection. Even a man who moved from Wells could not be sued by another burgess without first receiving the master's consent.[90] Every initiate brought wine and gloves, while those who had been admitted without a fee substituted wax. In any event, money was not generally handed over at the ceremony; that came later. These were the tangible offerings which went along with the personal undertaking that the man had made. The gloves and wax were both useful. The dozen pairs of gloves would eventually be distributed among the membership at a future meeting, or would be given to the poor. The two pounds of wax were usually given to the churchwardens, sometimes to the proctors of the Trinity altar, for use in the parish church. The offerings were thus both religious and fraternal.

Wine was an altogether more effective tool for fostering community spirit. It was valued for the pleasure that it brought, especially for the way in which it could bring about friendship between newcomers or the estranged. Some of its other civic functions will be discussed below. It was, however, the cap on the initiation. Accepted by the company as a brother, the new burgess was then given the honour of treating the house. Each man brought four gallons of wine, and usually more than one man was admitted at a given ceremony so that there was enough to go round.

(ii) Conviviality

The place of conviviality in medieval confraternities can hardly be overestimated. For many of the simpler parish guilds, the annual feast was the one great occasion of the year when all the members would come together to renew pleasurably the corporate spirit.[91] But all fraternities, whether craft organizations, parish or borough guilds, had their calendars marked by feasts and drinking-parties. It has plausibly been argued that guilds owe their beginnings to simple pre-Christian drinking-clubs.[92] At Wells there were three regular kinds of Community feasting. Most frequent were the 'potacions', straightforward drinking-parties at which the initiates'

[90] CBI: 187, 191.
[91] Unwin, *Gilds and Companies*, 193–200; Gervase Rosser, 'The Essence of Medieval Urban Communities', *TRHS*, 5th ser., 34 (1984), 105; Toulmin Smith (ed.), *English Gilds*, 58, 92, 101, 104, and 117.
[92] Coornaert, 'Ghildes médiévales,' 31–2, 35–6.

gifts or other reserves were drunk once the official business was concluded. Whatever the origins of the custom, it made civic participation less painful. In so far as it encouraged attendance, drink helped to keep the Community lively, its members in personal contact with each other, friendlier. The stocks of wine were carefully replenished by additional levies. It was common for fines to be assessed in wine. For example, in 1433 John Forde was ordered to pay a fine of one cask of wine for obstructing the tax collectors.[93] The minimum statutory fine for contempt was six gallons of wine.[94]

Twice a year the wine flowed more liberally, accompanied by food. The Master's Dinner was held for all the burgesses in October, at the start of the Community's year, shortly after the annual elections. The money for this feast came out of general receipts to some extent, but the occasion was, in effect, the new master's inauguration, the first act of communal generosity over which he presided.[95] Again, certain standard fines were really ways of providing wine for this feast. A 1478 ordinance laid down that anyone who missed the general election meeting had to bear the cost of a gallon of wine, to be paid at the dinner.[96] In 1499 William Poulet's rent for a Community house was paid partly in cash, partly as an 8*d*. gallon of wine provided for the dinner.[97]

The second large affair effectively ended the communal year, and was an even more expensive and inclusive event. In August the outgoing master treated the burgesses to a meal in the common hall, while his wife entertained their wives at her house. At the beginning of the sixteenth century, when the Community income was low, and the church and many civic properties were in need of repair, this annual festivity was suspended. But after several years the old custom was renewed.[98] On other occasions in the early sixteenth century (for example, in 1522) the masters were eager to reduce their expenses, but the feasts survived. In 1540 the masters had allowances for a dinner for the burgesses and their wives, a

---

[93] CBI: 282.   [94] Serel, 39.
[95] CBII: 142.   [96] CBII: 121.
[97] CBII: 207[c]; Margery K. James, *Studies in the Medieval Wine Trade* (Oxford, 1971), 53: 8*d*. was the standard price of Bordeaux at this time.
[98] CBII: 239; sometime after the law was passed, 'vacat' was written next to the entry.

Christmas feast, and a party when they left office in the summer.[99]
The Yuletide festivities, although not mentioned elsewhere, were
probably also a medieval custom; 1540 was an improbable time to
begin a Christmas celebration, since Calvinism and Puritanism
were already starting to gain ground. The persistence of the
dinners, possibly against the wishes of the increasingly isolated and
pretentious sixteenth-century masters, confirms that, without this
core of conviviality, the lifeblood of the broadly based medieval
Community might slow and threaten to stop altogether.

The development of an initiation ceremony for the town
councillors by the beginning of the sixteenth century suggests that
this process of narrowing the Community was well under way.
Upon his election to this prestigious lifetime appointment, the new
official would treat his fellow councillors to a feast.[100] Such ritual
generosity was a common attribute of medieval corporations. Aside
from the Community's own initiation, the Wells Cathedral chapter
rather notoriously practised a similar, if more extravagant custom,
known as an 'oyster feast', each one of which cost between 150 and
200 marks.[101] Once the council began to assume the traits of a
guild of its own, however, its relationship to the Community at
large began to change. Hindsight allows us to see here the stirrings
of increased conciliar authority and separation from the common
burgesses. In the fifteenth century there were already other signs of
such a reorganization of the guild. From the 1480s the title of
'master' had become a lifetime distinction for any man who had
ever held the office.[102] This distinction spawned a constitutional
amendment in the 1589 royal charter which gave Wells its political
independence. The new charter provided for a government by a
mayor, aided by six masters and sixteen other councillors.[103]

The political side of other rituals suggests further evidence. The
Trinity guild, of which all burgesses were *de jure* members, was

[99] CBII: 309; and *Wells City Charters*, p. xxx.

[100] CBII: 264.

[101] *Calendar of Entries in the Papal Registers Relating to Great Britain*, v. *Papal
Letters, 1396–1404*, ed. W. H. Bliss and J. A. Tremlow (London, 1904), 400; and
Kathleen Edwards, *The English Secular Cathedrals in the Middle Ages* (Manchester,
1949), 63–4.

[102] This convention may have originated somewhat earlier, but was only
sporadically reflected in CBII prior to the 1480s; good examples, contrasting the
masters with others, are the various lists of auditors, e.g. 1501 and 1502 (CBII: 218
and 223.)

[103] WCC 29.

overseen by proctors. We can identify only a limited number of them, just five before 1455. Of these, only one, John Blithe, would later become master. However, the honour attached to the office appears to have grown towards the end of the fifteenth century. From 1473 to 1498 fourteen different men occupied the position of proctor, of which there were two each year, and of these none was ever to become master of the Borough Community. But the situation changes thereafter. Of the fourteen who held the office between 1498 and 1510, fully half had become masters of the Community by 1520. The guild was apparently acquiring at least a politically symbolic role *circa* 1500. Its officers had entered the *cursus honorum* of the Community in a position comparable to that of the constables. The transformation may well be seen as part of a shift towards increased differentiation of the judicial leadership from the full body of the Community, and therefore representative of a considerable change in the nature of the Community. The evidence is ambivalent, however, because the Trinity was apparently a guild for the entire Community, not the judicial leadership alone. But it was becoming at least another way in which the leadership could set itself off from the full body of the group, in which the powerful could feel and appear distinguished from the rest.

Multiple rites of initiation, and separate feasts for various subsections of burgesses, are signs of fracturing. The differentiation of élite from commons was a developing feature of the period 1475–1600. Its growth signalled the end of the kind of guild that we have been describing, and similar developments can also be discerned across the towns of later fifteenth-century England.[104]

(iii) Manifestations of Unity

For most of the period under discussion conviviality was a tool of Community cohesion, an internal activity, but the Community was also anxious to display its unity and its social and political position to the outside world. Many of the ways in which it presented itself were practical, designed to assert its legal privileges. A medieval borough was always fighting for recognition and confirmation of its rights, and Wells, a legally disadvantaged town, was especially concerned to maintain its position. One of the main duties of the

[104] See e.g. Rigby, 'Urban "Oligarchy" ', 74–7.

Wells member of Parliament at the first session of a new reign was to have the king confirm the city's charter.[105] The expenditure could be considerable. In 1377 the confirmation—and the master's expenses in procuring it—cost the city £21 6s. 8d.[106] The 1342 charter cost £40, excluding the subsequent legal fees.[107] From at least 1446 the Community paid a retainer of 20s. per annum to a 'man of lawe' to represent and counsel it.[108] When a new confirmation was in hand, the Community was careful to bring this rather uninformative symbol of their corporate legality and privileges to the attention of their neighbours and trading partners. In 1383 a committee of distinguished burgesses was sent to Yeovil, then the county town, and to Bristol to proclaim Wells's borough status.[109] In 1404 the master and several others went to the courts of the mayor and bailiffs of Bristol to perform a similar function.[110] This was not unique to Wells, of course. It was up to every town to tell the relevant jurisdictions of its commercial privileges. Thus a copy of Cardiff's 1466 charter can be found in the Wells records.[111] In Wells's case, however, the charters themselves did not enumerate a single specific privilege beyond announcing their fairs.[112]

Similarly functional were the borough's seals. They were used not only for the borough's own business, but also to authenticate a wide variety of documents. Burgesses sought the seal's authority most often, but whenever a property in the borough or its suburbs was being conveyed, it was always a good idea to show that the borough knew of the transaction. There is even a quitclaim from the cathedral treasurer to the sub-treasurer which is sealed with the borough seal.[113] Local gentlefolk such as Christina Bithemar also sought the collective approval of the borough to verify real-estate transactions.[114] There were two seals throughout the fourteenth and fifteenth centuries: the more frequently used 'common seal of the borough of Wells'; and the 'seal of the steward of the borough of Wells'. The reputation of the town was affected by the reliability

---

[105] See e.g. *CPR 1422–9*: 225; WCC 6, 11, and 14; see also May McKisack, *The Parliamentary Representation of the English Boroughs during the Middle Ages*, (Oxford, 1932), 145.
[106] CBI: 56 and *CPR 1377–81*: 74.
[107] See above, Ch. 4, sect. 2.
[108] CBI: 318 (1446), and CBII: 116 (1478).
[109] CBI: 18.
[110] CBI: 159.
[111] CBII :55.
[112] See above, Ch. 4, sect. 1.
[113] RIII: 122[d].
[114] CBII: 189.

of these seals, and consequently their use was strictly controlled. Twelve burgess witnesses had to be present, along with the master, before the town clerk could affix the borough seal; half that number were required when the master set his seal. In all cases, the by-laws urged that the clerk should read the document, and that 'the matter be suffycent and trewe', so that the Community's good name would neither be sullied nor diluted by the false or the frivolous.[115]

The Community projected its corporate unity in the flesh as well as through these emblems. For the most formal collective displays, the burgesses would appear in their livery. They probably always had one, but certainly in 1411 a committee was set up to improve the design.[116] They opted for a simple blue tunic or gown, most probably made from Wells's own cloth.[117] The Community was represented by this homogenous river of blue during religious processions such as the Corpus Christi parades, which began in 1404.[118]

The most important occasions for an impressive display of strength and solidarity were the entries of great lords and kings into the city. Such events, irregular as they were, were the acme of the civic calendar across fifteenth- and sixteenth-century Europe. If this ceremony flowered at its fullest and most spectacular in the cities of Renaissance France in the sixteenth century, the modest efforts of a small town were culturally just as significant.[119] When the town went to bring a great lord into the city, meeting him at the gates or the boundary line, it was symbolically asserting its independence as the 'free borough' mentioned in the royal charters. In fact, there

---

[115] Serel, 39; cf. Charles Gross, *The Gild Merchant*, 2 vols. (Oxford, 1890), ii. 121.

[116] CBI: 193; cf. Unwin, *Gilds and Companies*, 191–2.

[117] CBI: 311; the word used for the garment is 'joupa'.

[118] CBI: 159; on Corpus Christi, see M. K. James, 'Ritual Drama and the Social Body in the Later Medieval Town', *P & P* 98 (1983), 1–29; and Miri Rubin, *Corpus Christi* (Cambridge, 1991); the parade took place throughout England, see e.g. *Coventry*, 111.

[119] On the entries, see Lawrence M. Bryant, 'La Céremonie de l'entrée à Paris au Moyen Âge', *Annales: Économies, Sociétés, Civilisations* 41 (1986), 513–42; Bernard Guenée and Françoise Lehout, *Les Entrées royales françaises de 1329 à 1515* (Paris, 1968); for vivid details of 16th-cent. efforts, see Victor E. Graham and W. McCallister Johnson (eds.), *The Paris Entries of Charles IV and Elizabeth of Austria, 1571* (Toronto, 1974); and D. M. Bergeron, *English Civic Pageantry, 1558–1642* (London, 1971), 9–121.

was little question of Wells acting independently of the Crown, but the troubled fifteenth century did afford examples of towns aiding or opposing rebels. Towns were always politically and economically more important than their populations warranted. Indeed, in the 1497 Wells entry the town was acting as a loyal subject, hosting the king's army, in contrast to Taunton, which had given support to the rebel Perkyn Warbeck.[120] On a cultural level, the entry was always an ambivalent event, one in which integrity and even defiance were manifested at the same time as deep respect for the advancing lord.

The royal entries at Wells occurred on average every fifteen years. According to a by-law recorded in 1437, they were granted 'when it fallith that King, Prynce, Duke, Bishoppe of this Diocese, approache or come to this Cite of Wells'. The burgesses could appear in the procession either on foot or, if they could afford it, on horseback.[121] Even when dressed uniformly, the prominent men were distinguished from the lesser, their places in the procession reflecting their places in the polity: 'Every burgesse *after his degre* shall ride or goo with the Maister [my emphasis].' All burgesses were to proceed in an orderly, seemly fashion until dismissed by the master. In this way they would increase 'the honor and Worshipe of all the Towne'.[122]

(iv) Peacemaking

The continuous success of the Borough Community as a social organization owed a great deal to its ability to provide a means for the reasonable resolution of disputes and the orderly reduction of accumulated animosity. Notwithstanding the themes of unity and fraternity, the day-to-day business of the Community was defusing arguments and soothing the wounds that one burgess inflicted on another. Of course, it was in the interest of unity that peace should be made.[123] In an imperfect world, harmony and solidarity were things to be worked at, achieved with difficulty.

[120] The Wells clerk says as much: CBII: 202; see *VCH Somerset*, i–ii, 193–5, ed. William Page (London, 1906–11), ii. which notes the especially heavy exaction that the king took from Taunton.
[121] CBII: 311; and Serel, 40.
[122] Serel, 40.
[123] This is a central theme of Weissman, *Ritual Brotherhood*, 1–105.

The Community court was the unique forum for conflict resolution. By the fourteenth century it had become the premier court for the burgesses, and yet it was still a fraternity court, private and technically unintegrated into the system of manorial and royal courts. Its influence derived from the importance of its suitors: the burgesses, the city's economic élite. But it had the same structure and social role as many of the parish guilds whose ordinances were collected by Richard II in 1389, like Norwich's Saint Catherine guild, for instance: 'if eny discorde be bytwen bretheren and sisteren, first that discorde shal be shewede to other bretheren and sisteren of the gilde, and by them acorde shal be made, if it may be skilfully. . . . '[124] Burgesses of Wells were required to take their business disputes and claims of trespasses to the master first, rather than to the bailiff or the king's court. The obligation to keep things local was one of the chief attractions of the Community. It allowed the burgesses of Wells to identify with the more privileged burgesses of other cities, who had the right to have all their judgments passed in their own town in front of their peers.[125]

The Community ran a lenient court, possessed of few coercive powers, and this added to its attractiveness in many situations. As a tactical manœuvre, or out of anger or exasperation, burgesses sometimes failed to sue here first. On three occasions in the fifteenth century general reminders were required.[126] But the numerous cases in which the Community court forced these oath-breakers to call off such illegal prosecutions are proof of the basic success of the system. Avoidance of the court was most likely to be achieved when both parties to the dispute wanted to face the sharper, firmer justice of a royal court.[127] But when the Community's interest was involved, or when one of the parties complained about the illegal prosecution, effective pressure could be brought to bear. Suing in the bishop's courts was not allowed, nor was suing the Community. In 1411 William Rydon went so far as to sue the master and Community in a Bristol court. We do not know what was involved,

[124] Toulmin Smith (ed.), *English Gilds*, 128; cf. Caroline M. Barron, 'The Parish Fraternities of Medieval London', in Caroline M. Barron and Christopher Harper-Bill (eds.), *The Church in Pre-Reformation Society*, (Woodbridge, 1985), 55–6.

[125] This had been one of the clauses granted to the burgesses in the revoked charter of 1341; see above, Ch. 4, sect. 2; cf. *British Borough Charters 1042–1216*, ed. Adolphus Ballard (Cambridge, 1913), 115–23.

[126] CBI: 205 (1414), CBI: 290 (1426), and CBII: 184 (1493).

[127] For a discussion of the various courts and jurisdictions in the town, see above, Ch. 4, sect. 1.

but the result was that Rydon broke off the suit and had to pay a fine.[128] Often enough, initiating a suit elsewhere must have served to speed up the procedure of the Community court and to indicate to the defendant how seriously the plaintiff took the issue.

When justice was given by the Community court, it was usually gentle. Fines were often threatened, ranging between one half and ten marks, but a sizeable payment was rarely made. When, for example, John Dounyng was found guilty of violating his oath by suing the shoemaker John Andrew for debt in the bishop's court, the substantial sentence issued by the Community court was that he had to repay whatever he had won as a result of the bailiff's judgment. In addition, he was fined £5, a very hefty sum for the barber, probably more than half his annual income, but the penalty was really a sign of the Community's dissatisfaction with Dounyng and of the severity of his offence. The sum was soon reduced to £2, and even this went unpaid. It was held over his head to guarantee his future good behaviour.[129] The reduction of fines, expected though it might have been, was a formal kindness which must have appealed to the burgesses and helped to reconcile the transgressor. Because the fine had actually been assessed, however, the Community made it clear that the man was in the wrong: it was only his brethren's graciousness that had saved him. As an added bonus, men like Dounyng were then free to prosecute the original case before the master.

The anger and antipathy that frequently developed between burgesses was often relieved in a particularly fraternal way, with the exchange of wine and kisses of peace. One or both were often traded according to the court's judgment. A long-running dispute between Adam and Hugh Baker was ended thus, with a fine held over each of them. The argument stemmed from an assault on one of the men's wives, and the enticement of an employee from one side to the other, so it was not just trivial problems that were settled in this ritual fashion.[130] A dispute over a horse between Robert Baker and Richard Lichfield ended with a kiss of peace and with each man giving the other a quart of wine.[131] We have already seen the role that wine played in Community ceremony, and it

---

[128] CBI: 190.
[130] CBI: 43.

[129] e.g. CBI: 13, 18, and 40.
[131] CBI: 163.

frequently comprised the fine that was levied on a burgess who had offended the master or who had seriously broken his oath. Wine was used more often than money. To be reconciled with the Community and received as a burgess once again, Robert Draper paid eight gallons of wine in 1484.[132] Nine years earlier John Hunt's readmission had cost him only four gallons, while in 1439 Thomas Chynnok's fine for breaking faith and suing in the king's court was set at four gallons, each to be worth at least 12*d*.[133]

(v) Arbitration

The process by which the many tensions were relieved, and these surprisingly effective and mild solutions were achieved, was in great part responsible for their success. The aim of the court was social harmony, attained at little cost, little risk. The best means of achieving this was to avoid the heavy sentence, often seemingly arbitrary, of the all-powerful judge. The Community court's method did this. It usually proceeded to arbitration rather than leaving matters to the possibly domineering or prejudiced judgment of the master. Politically, this was astute in so far as it prevented the master from acquiring too many enemies through his exercise of judicial authority. Assuming that the issue of a given suit was contested—sometimes the men agreed immediately—each party would usually name two other burgesses to take his side and to work with his opponent's nominees to produce a compromise solution.[134] Sometimes the master would intervene lightly to add a fifth and impartial arbiter.[135] Perhaps the bad feeling was particularly intense in such cases. In 1392 the master included two members of the judicial leadership to represent the Community's interests in a case, because the defendant had taken it to another

[132] CBI: 143.

[133] CBII: 209 and CBI: 299.

[134] Serel, 39; and, for further examples from among hundreds, see CBI: 196, CBII: 74 and 158; on arbitration, see below, n. 137, and Edward Powell, 'Arbitration and the Law in England in the Late Middle Ages', *TRHS*, 5th ser., 33 (1984), 49–67, which serves to show how different Wells's system of courts and arbitration was from the common-law model, in which arbitration was a *possible* resort, not the *necessary* one, as at Wells; but see his 'The Restoration of Law and Order', in G. L. Harriss (ed.), *Henry V. The Practice of Kingship* (Oxford, 1984), 70–2, which indicates the importance of reconciliation rather than harsh justice; see also Patrick J. Geary, 'Vivre en conflit dans une France sans état: Typologie des mécanismes de règlement des conflits (1050–1200)', *Annales: Économies, Sociétés, Civilisations* 41 (1986), 1107–34; and Barron, 'Parish Fraternities', 25–6.

[135] e.g. CBI: 18 and 111.

court without permission.¹³⁶ There is no doubt, however, that the men generally chose their own arbiters.

This system, which seems to have had its origins in the peacemaking customs of the early Middle Ages, in traditional law, allowed for the amicable defusing of difficulties.¹³⁷ Arbitration tended to moderate the outcome, often resulting, as some of the examples of sentences have shown, in each man assuming a part of the guilt. Unfortunately, the precise settlement was rarely spelled out, but in the case of John Curtis versus Thomas Rowse, in 1458, what must have been the common process is visible. The plaintiff had sought a payment of two marks, but was awarded a final settlement of three instalments of half a mark, 20s. in all, but the payments were spread over half a year.¹³⁸ Considerate compromise solutions were the standard end to burgess disputes. Furthermore, because the litigants were, through their nominees, the authors of the judgment, they found it difficult to argue (even when they were upset with the settlement) that they had been arbitrarily and unfairly dealt with. There were few instances of an arbitration settlement being wilfully violated. Since the burgesses could usually be sure of having their side of a dispute represented as they would prefer, and taken account of in the 'judgment', they were content to sue in the fraternity court, where the risks of complete failure (often compounded in some courts by the expense of lawyers) were distinctly lower.

The arbitration itself was held in private, some time after the convocation meeting, and it was very much an investigative as well as a bargaining process. Typically, the arbiters met within a week or two, and, depending on the circumstances, they would want to hear witnesses willing to support the litigants' claims, or to read accounts and contracts.¹³⁹ Reason and simple justice had their place, but the aim was 'peace'. The Wells clerks wrote *concord* or *pax* next to a successfully concluded case. As Patrick Geary has written with reference to the problem-solving apparatus of provincial France in the twelfth and thirteenth centuries, 'the ultimate goal

---

¹³⁶ CBI: 102.

¹³⁷ See F. Pollock and F. W. Maitland, *The History of English Law before the Time of Edward I*, 2nd edn. (Cambridge, 1911), 598–611; Reynolds, *Kingdoms and Communities*, 24–32.

¹³⁸ CBII: 25.

¹³⁹ On the timing, see e.g. CBI: 167 and CBII: 152; on the proof process, see CBI: 123, 133, 136, and 253.

of the negotiation is to reestablish a *pax* or *amicitia* between the two parties'.[140] This sort of group harmony and peacemaking was also important in late medieval Florence.[141] It was part of an older tradition of law, in which social harmony and the preservation of the polity, community, tribe, or family were more important and more attainable than abstract justice. Arbitration was as much a social process as a legal one.

Although a great deal more needs to be said about the Community court, there is only room here to focus on the ways in which the Community ethos shaped, some might say distorted, the system of arbitration.[142] In the first place, there was a distinct tendency for the 'superior' men to do a great deal of the arbitration. In most cases the litigants were certainly free to choose their own arbiters, but this means that they tended to choose men more prominent than themselves, generally preferring them to personal friends. It is certainly possible—in fact, probable—that the court would not accept certain poor or notoriously untrustworthy men as arbiters, but more often the lesser men would have preferred to have the influence of a couple of 'big' men on their side. A random survey of some three dozen late fourteenth-century burgesses shows that most of those who appeared in the records even a handful of times did do some arbitration. There is no question, then, of judgement *per se* being the exclusive privilege of the élite. A man like Roger Butcher, who had never held any politically important office and was not rich, was involved in eight suits—a typical number—three times as plaintiff, twice as defendant, and three times as arbiter.[143] William Butcher was similarly undistinguished, although more litigious. On nineteen occasions he was a party to a dispute, but only once was he called on to arbitrate.

At the opposite end of the scale were the burgesses who spent considerably more time judging than they did pursuing or defending their own interests in the courts. John Blithe, seven times master of the city, was a litigant on only four occasions, but an arbiter on forty-nine. Another master, John Broun, was called upon to mediate on thirty-seven occasions, but was only involved in nine

---

[140] Geary, 'Vivre en conflit', 1120: my translation.

[141] Weissman, *Ritual Brotherhood*, 89–93.

[142] I hope to discuss the system of arbitration, and the social relationships revealed by it at greater length in future work.

[143] CBI: 157, 161, 182, 190, 191, 209, and 210.

cases on his own behalf. There were also men whose court appearances were more balanced than my examples here. All conceivable variations were represented, from which one must conclude that the process was generally free and organic, not an imposition from the top to exclude and dominate those below. Most significantly, however, the one type that did not exist in the fourteenth century or later was the man who was highly litigious and who became a master of the guild. This stands as verification of the fact that masters were expected to be men who had a history of moderation and cool-headedness.

The predominance of the superior burgess in arbitration was not absolute, but it was striking nevertheless. There were other reasons to account for it. On simple, practical grounds, the politically dominant burgesses tended to be the richer men who could afford to take the extra time off work, which the lesser man could rarely spare. But it should come as no surprise that, in a hierarchical society such as the Community, justice was only workable if the litigants had some sort of basic confidence in the arbiters. From the point of view of the Community, it was essential that the process be respected. Short of ejection, there was little that they could do to the stubborn man. It seems very probable, therefore, that when men of unequal status were in conflict, there was a tacit understanding that the arbitration would only be successful if the four nominees were all respected by the more distinguished of the two litigants. Men who were too humble would not be able to impress their decision on a member of the judicial élite. It must be stressed that there is no evidence that a superior burgess ever rejected an arbitration in these circumstances. Neither was it a question of restricting the kind of man who could undertake arbitration in a given case. Rather, it was a pragmatic understanding of the court that, unless suitable people were chosen, the judgment might be challenged by one of the burgesses on the basis of the perceived status of one of the arbiters. Whether a particular burgess was suitable for a case, however, was a question of individual credit, of reputation. For example, in one of Master Blithe's four suits the relatively humble John Bennett was selected as an arbiter by Blithe's opponent.[144] Even in this case the three other men were all very prominent. Bennett must have been a man of acknowledged good

[144] CBI: 83.

character, because, although he only ever held the humble office of street-warden, he was chosen as an arbiter fifteen times.

Bennett's case proves that character was valued in the reality of the Community as well as in the ideal. Indeed, the records of litigation and arbitration provide further evidence that the ideology was taken seriously. We have seen that the men who were, or who would become masters were frequently trusted to arbitrate, to advance fairly the interests of a fellow burgess; but they were also able to negotiate with others and reach a reasonable and workable solution. They were apparently the sort of men who could bring people together. Furthermore, we have noted how rarely such men were involved in litigation themselves. To add to the evidence of Blithe's and Broun's cases, there was Henry Bowditch, who was a master four times. He was an arbiter on thirty-two occasions, a litigant on only six. Roger Chapman only served as master once in thirty-five years of Community activity, but he also was rarely involved in disputes. He never sued anyone, and was himself sued only six times, but he served as an arbiter twenty-nine times. By contrast, Richard Ferrour was wealthy (owning property in more than one diocese) and active enough in Community life to become a constable, but, despite a heavy load of arbitration, he never attained the mastership.[145] The obvious reason was his aggressive litigiousness, including something approaching a feud with one burgess. Ferrour sued other burgesses thirty-two times, but was himself sued only twice. He was part of the oligarchy, a councillor, but he proves that there were limits to how far wealth alone could take a man. The conclusion, therefore, is that the men who became masters were those who avoided lawsuits and yet were trusted by all the burgesses to reach a fair negotiated conclusion to disputes. Men of moderation, patience, and some honesty, able to reconcile their brothers—these were the masters, just as the ideal prescribed.

The interests of the Community did sometimes intervene to alter the system of arbitration. Whenever the master thought that the case involved a serious breach of a burgess's oath to the Community, or undermined the authority of the fraternity or its officers, he might step in to appoint the arbiters. Naturally enough, it tended to be the members of the council or the judicial leadership who served at such times. In 1486 Thomas Hethfield insulted

[145] His will was proved in the prerogative court of Canterbury: *SMWI*: 10.

Robert Grantham with such severity that he was accused of violating his oath to support and love his fellow burgesses. The master chose two men to make peace.[146] Similarly, in 1379 Richard Spray slandered Richard Ferrour, the town councillor, and felt the Community's anger as a consequence. The master appointed four prominent burgesses, all members of the judicial leadership, to arbitrate—in reality, to decide Spray's penance, the price of his reconciliation.[147]

Rebellious individuals who had made the master or Community the target of their scorn were judged either by men appointed by the Community, or the master and council. It must have amounted to the same thing. When men were expelled, the records are brutally curt. Manifest and unrepentant rebellion—that is, breaking the Community's solidarity—usually brought immediate rejection, a sentence determined by the master with the support of the councillors and the entire hall of attending burgesses. In 1380 William Webbe was expelled 'because of his rebellion', but we are told nothing further.[148] In 1379 two men were expelled for failing to answer their third summons.[149] The Community saw its very regime being scorned in such cases, and it was moved to act quickly and without the sense of considerable patience and fairness which characterized its more usual problem-solving mechanisms.

Perhaps more important than the thirty-odd discommonings and the authoritarian style assumed by the fraternity leadership in such cases is the fact that, in the great majority of instances, the expelled man was soon reconciled to the Community. Humble submission and sincere repentance were essential, but restoration followed almost as a matter of course, although often with conditions. Thomas Chynnok was twice ejected, once in 1437 and again in 1443. He took about two years each time to seek readmission, and we are told that he did so 'kindly, humbly, and affectionately'.[150] William Webbe 'submitted himself entirely to the grace of the Master and Community' several months after his discommoning. Henry Bowditch, William Churchstyle, and John Broun—members of the judicial leadership—decreed that he should pay 20s. if he ever acted badly again, presumably meaning against his oath and

[146] CBII: 152.   [147] CBI: 43.
[148] CBI: 33.   [149] CBI: 43.
[150] CBI: 296, 299, and 318.

the Community's regime.[151] In 1460 Robert Mors was readmitted under the stiffer threat of a £20 fine.[152] John Devenish was actually required to pay a fine of 6s. 8d. to rejoin the fraternity, while John Hunte junior was received after making a new oath and giving the Community four gallons of wine.[153]

A few men never returned to the fraternity, out of pride and anger, going on alone. Pride or simple cantankerousness was probably behind John Newmaster's late life expulsion in 1410. After at least thirty-three years of very active membership, including service as a town councillor, rent collector, and constable, he impleaded another burgess in the bailiff's court, refused to answer the master's summons, and was discommoned.[154] Other councillors were ejected, more likely than their humbler brothers to be assertive and proud individuals, unwilling to yield. In 1478 Councillor William Fox's strong resistance to Master Richard Vowell eroded a good deal of special consideration, and attempts by Vowell and others to bring peace, before Fox was ejected.[155] Fox was later readmitted to both the fraternity and the council.[156] Only Edward Goodgram's request for readmission is known to have been denied. Something withheld from the records must have made his case special, because the reason for his expulsion—suing in the bishop's court—was not unusual.[157] Perhaps, being a 'servant of the king', his submission to the guild was not given humbly or sincerely enough.[158] At any rate, when his son Thomas wanted to join the Community twenty-five years later, he became the only recorded example of someone who was denied membership for any reason, let alone lingering anger at one's father.[159]

The Goodgrams must be considered the exceptions that prove the rule—that, although the Community required submission to its regime and ideology, it was very concerned to foster reconciliation. I reiterate that the Community mentality saw the aim of any peacemaking as the re-establishment of concord and stability, the fresh assertion that the fraternity was a social, political, and religious unity. In 1509, just before Easter, the Community passed a new ordinance which stated that, henceforth, if any burgesses

---

[151] CBI: 34.   [152] CBII: 31.
[153] CBI: 313, and CBII: 108.   [154] CBI: 184 and 186.
[155] CBII: 117.   [156] CBII: 119.
[157] CBI: 156 (1403) and CBI: 74 (1408).
[158] This style is noted in the *List of Early Chancery Proceedings* i, List and Index Society 12 (1827), 5/160.   [159] CBI: 281.

'were out of love [*ex caritate*]' with each other during the week
before Easter, and if they did not succeed in reforming their ways,
they 'should not presume to receive the host', under penalty of
expulsion from the brotherhood.[160] This was a form of excommunication, one way or the other; internal unity was deemed that
important to the Community's survival, to its strength, to the
proper nature of Wells's part of the greater order. There is a
stridency in this ordinance which is more typical of the sixteenth
century than the fifteenth, but it expresses well the late medieval
Community's awareness that its true source of social and political
relevance was its inner cohesion.

[160] CBII: 253; the concept of love was prominent in the language and ritual (e.g.
the use of kiss of peace) of guilds elsewhere; see e.g. T. Bruce Dilks, 'The Burgesses of
Bridgwater in the Thirteenth Century', *SANHS* 63 (1917), 55–6, who prints the
later 13-cent. guild ordinances which claim to be ordained 'ad amorem et caritatem
inter nos nutriendos et lites et rancores reprimendo'.

7

The Social World Completed

1. THE FOREIGNERS: A NEGLECTED SOCIAL CATEGORY

The last three chapters have looked closely at the burgesses of Wells. The surviving records favour their history, and they were certainly the group of laymen who wielded the most wealth and authority in the town. Furthermore, the burgesses of Wells accounted for an unusually large proportion of the population, especially when we include, as we have argued that we must, their blood relations and households, who were accorded second-order membership.[1] Nevertheless, it is vital to say something about the other large social element of the town: the foreigners.

The term 'foreigner' is ambiguous;[2] its precise meaning has changed both over time and from one historical context to another. But it has always been used to determine who, on the most fundamental social and political level, belonged, and, more to the point, who did not. The medieval townsmen perceived citizenship in terms of privileged, legitimate participation in the governing social body, full involvement in the polity, and usually some economic privileges. It was not important to them whether a man came from France, Wales, or Scotland, or had been born and raised in Wells itself.[3] If he was not a member of the Borough Community, he was an outsider, without political rights or the perquisites of membership in the town's social élite. Of course, since the Borough Community held only a limited share in the government of the town, a foreigner's economic competence was not, by legal definition or regulation, heavily restricted.[4] Furthermore, this does

[1] See above, Ch. 5, sect. 1.
[2] *Forinsecus* is a synonym for *extrinsecus*, which was the term preferred in some other towns.
[3] Foreigners in the modern sense are discussed briefly above, Ch. 2, sect. 6. They were called aliens, for instance, in the 1523–4 lay subsidy return: PRO E179/169/156; and see Sylvia Thrupp, 'The Alien Population of England in 1440', *Speculum* 32 (1957), 262–73.
[4] See above, Ch. 4, sect. 2. See also an early 16th-cent. analysis quoted in Brian

not mean that he had no interests or rights within the town, only that he had no control.

What makes a discussion of these people all the more pressing is the fact that they have been neglected, notwithstanding the now large and growing literature on later medieval town life. Foreigners have generally been discussed (if at all[5]) under a rubric which was developed to explain political troubles in European towns or to fit medieval urban society into a particular ideological mould. They are usually included among either the 'proletariat' or the 'artisans' who were struggling against the 'merchant capitalists'.[6] Some other historians have divided society according to a contemporary perception, between the *meliores* and the *inferiores*, the *gros* and the *menus*, the *grasso* and the *minuto*. Such a division was common in medieval towns.[7] In practice, this means a simple and sometimes simplistic separation into rich and poor, patricians and people.[8] It was often not that straightforward. For instance, we have demonstrated the breadth of membership of the Borough Community, that is, of the socially ascendant group: it included carpenters and even unskilled labourers alongside the more successful craftsmen and merchants.[9] Yet there was no sharp division of the burgesses into opposing groups, the powerful against the populous, oligarchy versus commons. Nor could the political struggles of Wells be described as economic battles between Marxist or proto-Marxist classes. Urban revolt in later

Pullan, *Rich and Poor in Renaissance Venice* (Oxford, 1971), 99, and the subsequent discussion; elsewhere burgesses had some real advantages reserved to them: see *Colchester*, 24–5 and 33–8.

[5] Important studies—*Colchester* and Gottfried—do not mention them. The omission is worse in the latter case, since Gottfried's purports to be a complete study rather than an economic one.

[6] This is particularly so with overviews; the important English case is R. H. Hilton, 'Towns in Societies: Medieval England', *UHY* (1982), 7–13, esp. 10; a more refined version is in the same author's 'Towns in English Feudal Society', in *Class Conflicts and the Crisis of Feudalism* (London, 1985), 181–2; see also Bronislaw Geremek, *Le Salariat dans l'artisanat parisien aux XIIIe–XVe siècles* (Paris, 1969); Michel Mollat and Philippe Wolff, *Ongles bleus, Jacques et Ciompi* (Paris, 1970).

[7] For a similar scheme at Wells, see above, p. 170; cf. e.g. Jacques Le Goff, 'L'Apogée de la France urbaine médiévale', in Le Goff (ed.), *Histoire de la France urbaine*, ii (Paris, 1980), 324–33.

[8] Le Goff, 'L'Apogée de la France urbaine', 329–33, sets up the opposition of the *menus*, comprising 'surtout des artisans et des "laboureurs de la ville"', and the patricians, who alone are supposed to have wielded any power. On some of these concepts, see Susan Reynolds, 'The Rulers of London in Twelfth Century', *History*, 57 (1972), 337–57.

[9] See above, Ch. 5, sect. 2

medieval England did not usually have this industrial character.[10] Even in those European cities where it was an economic war against the oligarchies, it was generally a case of small capital fighting large capital, rather than capital versus labour.[11]

In fact, the foreigners were often part of the proletariat or the small masters, but they cannot be *identified* with either group. They deserve separate treatment, especially since the political circumstances that we have described do not suggest that we should see the foreigners as an unhappy, oppressed section of society. Dissent—the leadership in the revolts of the 1340s, for instance—came from the burgesses, great and small.[12]

If the average burgesses of the later medieval town have been neglected in favour of the greater, the foreigners, who constituted the majority of the population in every town, really have received no attention *per se*. The best treatment has come obliquely, from Bronislaw Geremek, for instance, in his study of the wage-earning population of medieval Paris.[13] But he, too, covered only the poorer of the foreigners, in a city whose circumstances, like London's, were far from typical, albeit most significant. Others have told us something about some of the foreigners in their discussions of women, but, again, women were not inevitably, not

---

[10] R. B. Dobson (ed.), *The Peasants' Revolt of 1381* (London, 1970), 13–18; and id., 'Admissions to the Freedom of the City of York in the Later Middle Ages', *ECHR*, 2nd ser., 26 (1973), 12–13, suggest that rebellion and frustration were often directed at ecclesiastical establishments; this was the case in Wells and elsewhere: see above, esp. p. 118; Gottfried, 250, concludes that in the monastic borough of Bury St Edmunds there was no class conflict element in the uprisings; Susan Reynolds, *An Introduction to the History of English Medieval Towns* (Oxford, 1977), 182, notes that the English proletariat was not the group at the head of civic agitation and rebelliousness in the later Middle Ages; as do A. F. Butcher, 'English Urban Society and the Revolt of 1381', in R. H. Hilton and T. H. Aston, *The English Rising of 1381* (Cambridge, 1984), 84–111, and R. B. Dobson, 'The Risings in York, Beverley and Scarborough, 1380–81', ibid. 112–42; see also Guy Fourquin, *The Anatomy of Popular Rebellion in the Middle Ages*, trans. Anne Chesters (Amsterdam, 1978), 101–2 and ch. 4 on the role of élites in rebellions; and R. H. Hilton, 'Popular Movements in England at the end of the Fourteenth Century', in *Class Conflict*, 152–64.

[11] Fourquin, *Anatomy of Rebellion*, 113–28; Dobson, 'Risings in 1380–81', 120–42.

[12] See above, Ch. 4.

[13] Geremek, *Salariat dans l'artisanat*; on the mobility of foreigners, see A. R. Bridbury, *Economic Growth: England in the Later Middle Ages* (London, 1962), 54–64; see also Samuel Cohn, Jun., *The Laboring Classes in Renaissance Florence* (New York, 1980).

essentially, outsiders in the same sense as the unenfranchised.[14] It is not that the poor or the workers, generally foreigners, have been neglected, but that this social stratum as a whole and as a type has been overlooked. Social groups based on economic activities have been preferred to the more obvious and comprehensive socio-political categories which were used by the writers of the time.

2. ECONOMIC AND POLITICAL SITUATION

At all times in the later Middle Ages the foreigners comprised the majority in Wells and in all the towns of Europe. There were fewer foreigners in Wells than in many other communities, especially in the great cities of Europe, but they still accounted for over 50 per cent of the lay adult male population at the end of the fourteenth century.[15] This proportion had probably risen to over 60 per cent by the early sixteenth century, due mainly to the fact that the conflicts with the bishop which had made the Borough Community so attractive and necessary an expression of opposition in the fourteenth century were long gone. Furthermore, we have noted how the judicial leadership had begun to assume the role of a separate corporation by the end of the fifteenth century, and this probably made the prospect of becoming a—politically insig-nificant—burgess less attractive to many foreigners.[16] It is also possible that a poorer urban economy simply made it more difficult to amass the necessary economic resources to join the guild, relatively small though they were.[17]

The inability to take part in government was one of the main limitations of the foreigners. The only positions that they could hold while they remained outside the Borough Community were petty ones. They could be verderers; these were the presenting officers in the bishop's leet courts.[18] It was a position with little to recommend it, and some foreigners tried to resist appointment, just as their social superiors in the guild tried to avoid being appointed rent collectors.[19] They also took part in the unpleasant duty of watch and ward.[20] These were offices that brought the foreigner

---

[14] See above, Ch. 5, sect. 1; for further discussion of women, see above, pp. 99 ff., and below, Ch. 7, sect. 5.

[15] See above, Ch. 5, sect. 1. [16] See above, Ch. 6, sect. 2 (ii).

[17] See above, Ch. 3, sect. 6. [18] See above, Ch. 4, sect. 1.

[19] Ibid. [20] LPL ED 1186/9.

little honour, much inconvenience, and even the occasional fine, for they often failed to satisfy the court that they had presented correctly or had been diligent enough.[21] A more important office which was open to them was that of jury member or jurat, in charge of more significant presentments and the more serious assize infractions. Jurats also judged the petty lawsuits of the court and other causes. But, in practice, foreigners seem never to have been entrusted with this more authoritative position.

We can evaluate the economic status of the foreigners to some extent by analysing the early sixteenth-century lay subsidy. The 1523–4 return for Wells allows us to compare the assessments of the foreigners with those of the burgesses. Such comparisons are the only way of learning much about those foreigners who were not poor, since these people had no associations of their own, no good records, and were not the objects of special concern, as were those in need.[22] We have limited the comparison to men, partly because it is difficult to determine whether the small number of women listed were burgesses' widows or *femmes soles*.[23] Furthermore, it must be borne in mind that a large proportion of the town was exempt from taxation, because of poverty.[24] This probably included many heads of households who had similar resources to those at the lowest end of the taxation list, but whose responsibilities, normally including a family, drove them into fiscal and 'working poverty'. The figures are nevertheless instructive, and are displayed in Table 8.

[21] At virtually every court session some verderers were found in mercy for failing to appear or for making false presentments. The latter infraction was rarer, see ibid.

[22] It has been one of the difficulties of the approach to the unenfranchised that an examination of the craft-guilds has frequently been the only means of finding out about them. The guilds, however, where they existed, included the enfranchised, who, naturally enough, tended to dominate proceedings. But see, e.g. Pullan, *Rich and Poor*, pts. 1 and 2; and Richard Mackenney, *Tradesmen and Traders* (London, 1987), 47–73, both of which discuss the Venetian *scuole*, religious guilds often affiliated with craft associations; and Heather Swanson, 'The Illusion of Economic Structure: Craft Guilds in Late Medieval English Towns', *P & P* 121 (1988), 29–48, who sees past the guilds to the journeymen and wage labourers, especially the women.

[23] See Caroline M. Barron, 'The "Golden Age" of Women in Medieval London', *Reading Medieval Studies* 15 (1989), 37, 39; Maryanne Kowaleski, 'Women's Work in a Market Town: Exeter in the Late Fourteenth Century', in Barbara Hanawalt (ed.), *Women and Work in Preindustrial Europe* (Bloomington, Ind., 1985), 146–7; and Eileen Power, *Medieval Women*, ed. M. M. Postan (Cambridge, 1975), 59.

[24] On using this tax, see J. C. K. Cornwall, 'English Country Towns in the 1520s', *ECHR*, 2nd ser., 15 (1962), 54–60 for methodological information; see also *Coventry*, 12; Bridbury, *Economic Growth*, 112–13; and n. 30 below.

Perhaps surprisingly, the foreigners' assessed wealth spanned all the categories, from less than £2 to over £40. Ten per cent of the taxed foreigners were financially quite sound. Several of them were distinctly wealthy. The richest (assessed at £60) was William Vowell, namesake and indirect heir of his grandfather, who was perhaps the town's most prominent fifteenth-century master. Another who was assessed at a high rate was also the heir of a prominent burgess.[25] Among the foreigners, then, were some heirs of citizens. Becoming a civic outsider could be a sign of social advancement. These men were no longer involved in trade or industry. Certainly, Vowell was styled a gentleman and owned much land in the area and in Norfolk, to which county, it would seem, the family ultimately moved.[26]

Here we see the heirs of burgesses pointedly leaving behind their commercial roots and associations. There had also always been gentry who lived in Wells or in the manor, but who never joined, and probably never considered joining, the guild.[27] But the substantial outsiders of the early sixteenth century were not all men

TABLE 8. *Tax assessment, 1523–1524*

Assessment (in £'s)	Foreigners (%)	Burgesses (%)	Total city (%)
Under 2*	24.7	0.0	14.7
2	57.2	38.8	49.7
3–5	7.7	18.8	12.2
6–9	1.7	10.0	5.1
10–19	6.0	17.5	10.7
20–39	1.7	7.5	4.1
40 +	0.9	7.5	3.6

Note: *This category comprises all those who were assessed in the Wells return according to their wages. The total number of relevant entries for this table and subsequent analyses comparing foreigners and burgesses was 197.

Source: PRO E179/169/156.

[25] Richard Aphowell, son of Thomas, a successful baker who served as civic rent collector and church-warden, was assessed at £20.

[26] He is mentioned as a deceased resident and gentleman of Long Ashton, Somerset, in a 1554 deed of his son and namesake (AH 362), so he must have spent less and less time in Wells; for an account of the family's distinguished progress, albeit with some errors, see *SDNQ* 18 (1926), 10. See above, Ch. 5, sect. 2, for more on gentry burgesses.

[27] Some of these men, like the attorney John Rewe, were certainly participants in Wells life, if only socially and through the bonds of the parish church (*CPR* 1422–9: 453, and *CPR* 1436–41: 172). Rewe (or possibly his son), for instance, was

with gentle pretensions. Others were like John Gregory, who was relatively well off (assessed at £5), a mason by trade, but was content to remain outside the Community for many years after he had acquired his modest wealth.[28] Our conclusion is that there was an 'élite' of substantial or wealthy foreigners, some of whom can be shown to have had gentle pretensions, while others were in business or following a craft.

But the more typical foreigner was a poorer man, distinctly poorer than his burgess neighbour. Over 80 per cent of the foreigners were assessed at £2 or less, twice as many as the burgesses. Furthermore, towards the top of the scale—those assessed on goods worth £10 or more—we find fewer than 7 per cent of the taxed foreigners, but almost one third of the burgesses. The median assessment of the foreigners was £2, whereas the median burgess assessment was £4. And, to demonstrate relative economic clout, we need only compare the *average* assessed wealth of the two groups, bearing in mind that there were many more unassessed foreigners than there were exempt burgesses, which would have brought the foreigners' average down even further if we had had precise figures to work on. As it is, the burgesses' average assessment was £11 6s., whereas the foreigners' was a paltry £3 4s. Moreover, although numerically superior, the foreigners commanded only about one third of the total assessed wealth in the town, and, individually, they were not even one third as prosperous. Of course we are working from a particularly imprecise tax assessment, but the general position of the foreigners is clear, as is the gap which existed between them and the burgesses. Nevertheless, the last word on this subject should be to stress that the largest group of both foreigners and burgesses fell into the £2 category.[29] The men included here have been described as 'a class of small craftsmen ... needing to work for day wages from time to

excommunicated in St Cuthbert's for moral offences (SRO DD/B, Reg. 6: 12). Others in a similar social position played an important part in Borough Community activities: see above Ch. 5, sect. 2.

[28] He was admitted to the Community only in 1533.

[29] Different areas of the country had different median levels of assessment, indicating either real economic variations or different methods of assessment. Cornwall, 'English Country Towns', 62, table 3, shows a median for the towns of Buckingham, Rutland, and Sussex of £1; Alan D. Dyer, *The City of Worcester in the Sixteenth Century* (Leicester, 1973), 175, table 10, found a similar result; but *Winchester*, i. 410–11, table 36, found the median assessment to be £2, as at Wells.

time', and elsewhere as 'the backbone of [a] town's economy . . . really too poor to be classed as part of the "middle class" but probably mostly self-employed'.[30] A great number of the foreigners of Wells, as well as more than a third of the burgesses, must be included among this group. Long-term economic stability was a problem for both burgesses and foreigners, and the social divisions between the two groups did not necessarily—did not in general—correspond to a difference in their economic circumstances.

It is important, therefore, that we should not separate the two groups into overly well-defined categories. A weakness of many social studies lies in their tendency to produce static pictures which give the impression—not always intended—that there were clear and permanent divisions among the various social groups. In fact, however, while there are inevitably group characteristics, some individuals are constantly moving from one category to the other, flourishing, declining, ageing, or dying. There was a large degree of fluidity in the medieval town.

The town was developed, after all, on the premiss of social change, on the promise that one could raise oneself in the towns. For many within the fourteenth- and fifteenth-century city, success meant being in a position to join the burgesses. This could take time. Most burgesses would have spent some time as foreigners; many more foreigners must have hoped—it would turn out, in vain—that they also could join the burgesses one day.[31] Such an association, albeit through hope rather than achievement, probably acted as something of a social adhesive so long as the foreigners believed that they had a fair chance at such advancement.

We have argued that the Community did remain fairly open.[32] We can affirm here that about one fifth of the foreigners *assessed* in 1524 would become burgesses one day.[33] (It is clear that the sixteenth-century burgesses formed a shrinking proportion of the town, smaller than their fourteenth- and fifteenth-century counterparts.) Furthermore, these individuals were already on their way at the time of the subsidy, in so far as they were distinctly wealthier

[30] Cornwall, 'English Country Towns', 63; and Dyer, *Worcester*, 174.
[31] We have touched on this issue above Ch. 5, sect. 1.
[32] Ibid.
[33] This is based on a correlation of PRO E179/169/156 and CBII's admissions lists.

than the rest of the foreigners (see Table 9). Fully a third of them were assessed at or above £3, and their average assessed wealth was £4. Some men, even some who would go on to become masters of the town, made the transition from foreigner to citizen rather late in life, while others awaited only the first favourable circumstance.[34] Thomas Lake, for instance, was assessed at only £2 worth of goods, but by the next year he had entered the guild on the basis of his marriage to a burgess's daughter.[35] John Bulman, a man worth a very respectable £10, made the transition in 1526, after he had married a burgess's widow.[36] Thomas Atwill (assessed at £2) purchased his membership, but only after almost another ten years on the outside.[37] This group of future burgesses was composed of men who were already craft-masters, but who, on average, waited, or had to wait, another 6.8 years before they joined the Community.

The economic status of the sixteenth-century foreigner cannot be compared very accurately with those from earlier times, but the suggestion that the picture we have described here is relevant to the later fourteenth and fifteenth centuries receives some support from other quarters. On the one hand, the fourteenth- and fifteenth-century leet courts consistently show that foreigners played a small role in the brewing industry, as reflected in the infractions against the assize.[38] Whereas they comprise almost half of the recorded tapsters, they represent only about one in ten of the brewers. And it was this latter trade which was the more lucrative. Similarly, the late fourteenth-century aulnage accounts confirm both that foreigners had their place in the making and marketing of cloth in the town *and* that they were dwarfed in numbers and scale by the burgesses. More than one third of the cloth-sellers in the 1395–6 account were foreigners, but they sold on average only about nine half-cloths, while the burgesses averaged over thirty-three.[39] The picture remains consistent. A sizeable group of foreigners succeeded in business in a smallish way, and there were always a few of them

[34] See above, pp. 143 f.
[35] *Wells City Charters*, ed. Dorothy O. Shilton and Richard Holworthy, SRS 46 (1931), 170.
[36] Ibid.
[37] Ibid. 172.
[38] For the following analyses, see LPL ED 1097, 1181, 1182, 1186/9, and 1188/10, which include courts from 1312 to 1432.
[39] PRO E101/343/28/4.

TABLE 9. Subsidy assessments by social group, 1523–1524

Assessment (in £'s)	Permanent foreigners (%)	Future burgesses (%)	Burgesses (%)
under 2	28.7	8.7	0.0
2	60.6	56.5	38.8
3–5	7.4	8.7	18.8
6–9	0.0	8.7	10.0
10–19	3.2	17.4	17.5
20–39	2.1	0.0	7.5
40+	1.1	0.0	7.5

who did very well. In the cloth industry, for instance, there was William Muleward, who delivered sixty-one half-cloths in 1395–6.

At the same time, the modesty of their trade or commercial activity did *not* distinguish them from many of the burgesses, those numerous lesser citizens whose economic situation was humble if not precarious, and no better than many of the foreigners. Throughout the later Middle Ages the crucial fact is that economic equals in occupation and income could be members of distinct socio-political groups.

In economic and social terms, the foreigners overlapped with the burgesses. They employed themselves as merchants, as weavers and dyers, bakers and brewers, both men and women. But fewer of them were independent businessmen; more often they were journeymen and labourers. About one quarter of those assessed in 1523–24 were wage-earners, and all of these were foreigners.[40] They were the poorest on the tax rolls, and there must have been many other wage-earners whose responsibilities made them too poor to be taxed at all.

The foreigners lived in all parts of the city, but certain areas were favoured, no doubt for their abundance of cheap housing. In 1523–4 58.9 per cent of the taxpayers were foreigners: taking this figure as 1, Table 10 illustrates their location. One of the striking features of the table is that, in several of the more peripheral streets of the city, such as Chamberlain/New Streets or Tucker Street, the foreigners were not very conspicuous. This was presumably the result of their inability to purchase the land in these areas because the burgesses, who saw its industrial, horticultural, and pasturing potential, were ready to pay a good price for it. On equally peripheral Southover, however, foreigners were dominant, and there we have fewer indications of any of these economic uses for the land. The High Street figures also deserve attention, because they confirm quite clearly that there was no strict or sharp segregation of the houses of the rich or socially superior from those of the less affluent or influential.[41] Over one third of the town's

[40] This proportion is much lower than in some other places, and again it would seem that idiosyncratic assessment, as much as any actual economic differences, was the cause. See Dyer, *Worcester*, 175, who records a proportion of over 2/5 in the £1 category; and *Winchester*, 411, table 36, which tabulated 46% of those assessed in the £1 category; Cornwall, 'English Country Towns', 63, table 4, had 26%–44% assessed at £1.

[41] See *Winchester*, 421–8.

taxpayers lived on the High Street, and they were a mix of rich and poor, burgess and foreigner.[42] The final conclusion, then, is that, while foreigners were certainly a distinct group, politically incompetent, and imperfectly integrated into the town's social life, they were also definitely part of the broader community, living and working next to the burgesses, sometimes content with their status, but often looking to improve their position.

TABLE 10. *Location of foreign taxpayers, 1523–1524*

Chamberlain St. New St.	0.75
High St.	0.96
Queen St. Wet Lane	1.08
Sadler St.	1.23
St Cuthbert St Priestrow	1.06
Southover St.	1.53
Tucker St.	0.34

Note: 1.0 = overall average occurrence of foreigners in town.
Source: PRO E179/169/156.

3. POVERTY

Discussions of poverty are almost always plagued by several technical difficulties and ambiguities. This is especially true in the context of the history of the pre-modern and, pre-eminently, of the medieval world. First there is the question of the meaning of the word. Even in modern usage it retains a confusion of flavours, including the pathetic and the worthy of sympathy. It also describes dire physical distress and need. To this common-sense list, social scientists have added more precise definitions based on subsistence, inequality, or relative adverse impact on society as a whole.[43] Some of the same notions contended in the medieval mind. In the thirteenth century poverty might mean only that a person was not one of the powerful or very rich.[44] Poverty could mean helpless

[42] In Winchester more than half the taxpayers lived in its High Street aldermanry: ibid. 411, table 36.
[43] For a brief summary, see Martin Rein, 'Problems in the Definition and Measurement of Poverty', in Peter Townsend (ed.), *The Concept of Poverty* (London, 1970), 46–8.
[44] Alexander Murray, 'Religion among the Poor in Thirteenth-Century France: Humbert of Romans', *Traditio* 30 (1974), 291.

destitution, true penury, and mendicancy.[45] Reduced status was one of the most important medieval meanings of poverty.

Increasingly, however, in the Middle Ages—and certainly by the fourteenth century—there was an understanding that those without independent or secured means to live were those upon whom God looked most favourably, and whom people should support. Nevertheless, it was soon recognized that further discrimination would often be necessary. Resources were limited.[46] Later medieval people tended to see those who were *physically* unable to earn a living as those who most deserved support. The able-bodied person was generally expected to fend for himself, and was consequently least likely to receive help.[47] The unemployed labourer or journeyman in search of work was regarded with suspicion, especially since this was a time of labour shortage.[48] Not surprisingly, employers and workers must increasingly have seen moral weakness and laziness in such poverty.

For our present purposes, which are to fill in some of the large spaces that we have left unmapped in Wells's social world, we plan to adopt an understanding of poverty as mainly tied to, and caused by, economic hardship of a severe rather than a chronic but manageable kind. We are adopting a loose, economic-subsistence definition of poverty.[49] If an individual or a family had enough to eat and could house themselves without relying on the alms of others, we prefer to think of them as vulnerable to poverty rather than poor. There would be times when many of those in this very large category, especially those who lived in the cities, would have fallen into poverty. But the two states should not automatically be equated.

4. THE SCOPE OF POVERTY

The number of poor people in medieval Wells cannot be accurately determined. The poor were inevitably omitted from the tax rolls which function among historians as the nearest thing available to

[45] See below, Ch. 8, sect. 6.
[46] Brian Tierney, 'The Decretists and the "Deserving Poor"', *Comparative Studies in Society and History*, 1 (1958–9), 360–73.
[47] Ibid. 369–70.
[48] See above, Ch. 3, sect. 5.
[49] Rein, 'Definition of Poverty', 48–60.

censuses. In Wells's case, this applies to the lay subsidies of both 1327 and 1523–4. Some of the poor might have appeared in the poll tax of 1377, but Wells's detailed return has not survived. But the poor were sometimes noted in the tax rolls of Europe and of later sixteenth-century England, usually as too poor to be taxed. Understandably, these figures must be used carefully and never with undue confidence, because the tax threshold varied from place to place, even within the same tax collection. The numbers of fiscal poor in medieval urban communities varied widely, but everywhere they certainly constituted a sizeable part of the population. In fifteenth-century northern France and the Low Countries the proportion ranged from 20 to 30 per cent.[50] In fifteenth-century Reims nearly half the households had virtually no grain reserves from which to make the rest of the year's bread.[51] More relevant to Wells, however, are the English cities. In early sixteenth-century Coventry, in the midst of some economic hardship, poor households have been estimated as consisting about a quarter of the city.[52] These figures can be reconciled with other (later) sixteenth-century English evidence, which shows urban poverty as ranging from a low in Salisbury of only 5 per cent, to about 22 per cent in Norwich.[53] Evidence from Worcester in the mid-sixteenth century suggests that serious poverty afflicted 2–20 per cent of the population, depending on the year.[54]

Wells most probably had a poor population in line with these English cities. This would have meant that up to one in five people were receiving some form of money or food-aid at any given time. Furthermore, there were local circumstances which affected the number and visibility of the poor in the city. First, as a cathedral

[50] Michel Mollat, *Les Pauvres au Moyen Âge* (Paris, 1978), 283–6, for these and other statistics, some of which indicate proportions of 80% (from Burgundy). Obviously, care must be used when approaching such indications of poverty and regional disparity.

[51] Pierre Desportes, 'La Population de Reims au xve siècle', *Moyen Age* 77 (1966), 504–6. These figures require careful use since we do not know enough about the purchasing patterns of wage-earners—whether they would ever have purchased large lots of grain, for instance; presumably they had to purchase it by the month or week. We prefer to think of these people as potentially vulnerable to hardship rather than clearly in difficulty.

[52] *Coventry*, 130, table 9.

[53] Paul A. Slack, 'The Reactions of the Poor to Poverty in England *c.*1500–1750', in Thomas Riis (ed.), *Aspects of Poverty in Early Modern Europe*, ii (Odense, 1986), 21; John Pound, *Poverty and Vagrancy in Tudor England* (London, 1971), 25–9.

[54] Dyer, *Worcester*, 166–7.

city, Wells was unusually well endowed with funerals and chantries, obits and anniversary services. As we shall see in some detail below,[55] it was a common part of these ceremonies for alms to be distributed to the poor. Moreover, Wells was a fairly small town with a fairly large cathedral establishment. It had more canons and vicars than many larger cities, so the cathedral's effect on the economy of poverty was more significant.[56] Very plausibly, this meant that the poor were attracted to the city at a greater rate than would have occurred in another town of comparable size, like Bridgwater in the fourteenth century, or Taunton in the fifteenth.

This is not to suggest that the population of the poor necessarily increased with the growth of chantry endowments, and as the overall size of the city fell.[57] There is no reason to doubt that most of those who lost jobs in the town returned to the countryside to find sustenance.[58] Fewer people moved to the city in the first place in the fifteenth century, and since labour was frequently in short supply, Wells probably had fewer poor labourers then than before.

The combination of these two considerations, neither of which can be gauged accurately, compels us to suggest that the proportion of the town's population afflicted by poverty in the fifteenth century was probably no higher than in the fourteenth century. The available charity may have attracted other paupers to the city, but probably only on an occasional basis.[59] And the countryside tended to lure those on the margin of economic independence away from the city.

One last speculation is worth mentioning in connection with the fifteenth-century poor. We have suggested that the burgesses were having difficulty replacing themselves in the fifteenth century.[60] Not only were many sons dying before they could succeed their fathers and establish families, but, more critically, fewer and fewer outsiders were being attracted to the city as immigrants. This suggests that the population was ageing. In a world without adequate old-age pensions, a world only disappearing in the West among the current generation of elderly, poverty tended to be

[55] See below, pp. 236 ff.

[56] On institutionally administered charity, see Miri Rubin, *Charity and Community in Medieval Cambridge* (Cambridge, 1987), 245–50. See below, pp. 233 ff.

[57] See above, Ch. 2, sect. 3.

[58] See above, Ch. 2, sects. 3–6.

[59] People would come a long way for the funerary distributions to the poor: see Mollat, *Pauvres*, 318–21.

[60] See above, Chs. 2, sect. 6, and 5, sect. 1.

correlated with age.[61] It is possible, then, that a politically neutral but socially distinct poverty developed in Wells, quite unlike that of the fourteenth century. The poor—those who needed support to survive—were not *primarily* urban labourers, unhappy with their prospects, but the old and the widowed, often once-respected citizens and journeymen, people who had lived full and relatively successful lives in the community.[62] This may have been why urban communities were especially willing to erect and support almshouses for their aged poor residents in the fifteenth century.[63] They were a group of people who were most worthy, helpless—and a known quantity. The canonists had said that you should first help those who were closest to you.[64]

Perhaps the best way to categorize the poor as a group is to follow the hints of the foundation charter of the town's almshouse (1436). This gives us the community's assessment of who deserved practical help. The hospital was established to support two categories of poor. First, half the places (twelve) were available to men and women whose poverty meant that they could no longer pay their rent or find accommodation. The second group of twelve comprised those in more dire circumstances, more advanced difficulty. These people, whose 'decrepitude' had made them unable to earn a living except by begging, were only eligible for the remaining places in the almshouse when they had deteriorated to such a point that they could no longer move around to beg from door to door.[65]

Once again, we have indications that many of the acceptable poor were probably old or afflicted by serious illness. So long as they did not have leprosy, the terminally ill must frequently have

[61] On the subject of old age pensions or retirement pension arrangements, see Elaine Clark, 'Some Aspects of Social Security in Medieval England', *Journal of Family History* 7 (1982), 307–20. There were some examples in Wells of retirement arrangements: see CBI: 199 (1413), CBII: 29 (1459), 145 (1485); and RI: 162^d. (later 13th cent.); *SMWI*: 64–6; *SMWII*: 129.

[62] See below, pp. 244 ff., for support for this claim.

[63] In later 16th-cent. Norwich old age ranked third among the causes of poverty: accounting for 16% of the poor, see Slack, 'Reactions of the Poor,' 27, fig. 1; see also the summary remarks of Richard M. Smith, 'Families and their Property in Rural England, 1250–1800', in R. M. Smith (ed.), *Land, Kinship and Life-Cycle* (Cambridge, 1984), 73–80; and Tim Wales, 'Poverty, Poor Relief and the Life-Cycle: Some Evidence from Seventeenth-Century Norfolk', ibid., 351–404. On the old, see Barbara Hanawalt, *The Ties that Bound: Peasant Families in Medieval England* (New York, 1986), 227–37; and Clark, 'Social Security'.

[64] Tierney, 'Deserving Poor', 370.

[65] AH 172/1.

found a final home in the almshouse.[66] The first group, however, represents those who had fallen on hard times, very probably also because of age or sickness. Thus, the aim of the almshouse and its ecclesiastical and civic founders was twofold. They wanted to reduce dire poverty by keeping a small group from ever having to face the torments and humiliation of mendicancy, to help these shamefaced poor. But they also wanted to ease the last days of some who had already suffered the great humiliations of begging and sickness or age. Two kinds of medieval poverty—fallen status and dire physical collapse—come a little bit closer to each other when seen in the light of this continuum.

The evidence of charity casts the only light which can reveal medieval poverty in Wells. Without the need for the cathedral, the bishop, and the town to record donations, we would only have the proof provided by charitable bequests in wills to indicate that there were any poor people at all. We have mentioned, and we shall return to, the provisions for poor relief presented by the almshouse, for we know most about it.[67] But it was only started in the 1430s. What was there before this? First, and most important, must have been the alms provided by individuals at their doorsteps.[68] The almshouse charter makes it clear that, for those without a place to live, and possibly for some who did have a residence, this was the main source of money or food.[69] Other aid was probably given by people, neighbours or relatives or the parochial staff, who knew somebody who was impoverished but was too proud to beg.[70] Among this group would have been those members of the working

[66] Although leprosy was no longer common in England, it was mentioned several times in the foundation charter. Lepers were presumably expected to go to lazar houses. See Rubin, *Charity and Community*, 115–16; Rotha M. Clay, *The Medieval Hospitals of England* (New York, 1966; orig. edn., 1909), 41–7, charts the disease's late medieval decline.

[67] See pp. 231, 244 ff.

[68] Rubin, *Charity and Community*, 267–9, makes an approach of sorts to this subject; Bronislaw Geremek, *La Potence ou la pitié: L'Europe et les pauvres du Moyen Âge à nos jours*, trans. Joanna Arnold-Moricet (Paris, 1986; orig. edn., 1978), 95, assigns it the key role in preserving later medieval society from disaster.

[69] AH 172/1.

[70] The role of the parish in charity is discussed by Rubin, *Charity and Community*, 237–44, esp. 244; J. Tits-Dieuaide, 'L'Assistance aux pauvres à Louvain au XVe siècle', in *Hommage au Professeur P. Bonenfant* (Brussels, 1965), 421–39; the actual process of donation and distribution—the parish table—is outlined by William J. Courtenay, 'Token Coinage and the Administration of Poor Relief during the Late Middle Ages', *Journal of Interdisciplinary History* 3 (1972–3), 285–6. See n. 71 below, for the shamefaced poor.

poor, especially larger families, who could not live on a labourer's insecure income.[71]

The scope of most institutionally administered poor relief was modest, although we must allow that defects in the records probably account for a good deal of the sparseness of the evidence of charity. Canon law required bishops to help the poor of their dioceses, and it was a charge that they executed to some extent.[72] For instance, in 1313 Bishop Drokensford ordered his bailiff of Wells and Pucklechurch to initiate what was obviously the bishop's customary support of the poor, along the lines prescribed by Gratian's *Decretum*.[73] Forty of the poorest people of the two towns were daily to receive a silver farthing or its value in food. At Michaelmas forty beggars were to receive 4s. each so that they could buy clothes and shoes. Those eligible for support were both impoverished priests and, especially, widows and tenants who had lost their holdings and had to take up begging.[74] The forty people were chosen from both towns; indeed, the Wells provision also made the people of the adjacent rural manor eligible. The number who actually lived in the borough cannot be determined.

Before the almshouse was built, the only institution in the town to care directly for the poor was the hospital of St John the Baptist.[75] The hospital was established in 1206, at the end of the first great period of European hospital foundations which had arisen to cope with the increased population and the growth in

---

[71] Slack, 'Reactions of the Poor', 21, notes the large number of complete families recorded among the 16th-cent. almspeople. On the shamefaced poor, see G. Ricci, 'La Naissance du pauvre honteux: Entre l'histoire des idées et l'histoire sociale', *Annales: Économies, Sociétés, Civilisations*: 38 (1983), 158–77; Rubin, *Charity and Community*, 72–3; and Geremek, *Potence ou pitié*, 55; Courtenay, 'Administration of Poor Relief', 289, discusses a mainly Continental system of channelling relief to the worthy, including the shamefaced poor. The category was certainly alive in Wells, as can be seen in the charitable arrangements of Canon Richard Bamfield in the 1290s (RI: 87, and WCAC 145).

[72] Brian Tierney, *Medieval Poor Law* (Berkeley, Calif., 1969), 70; Rubin, *Charity and Community*, 238, both of whom outline the devolution of the *practical* responsibility to the parishes; Dyer, *Standards of Living*, 241, offers other evidence of English episcopal charity.

[73] As outlined in Rubin, *Charity and Community*, 238.

[74] SRO DD/B, Reg. 1: 141ª.

[75] On the medieval hospital, see Clay, *Medieval Hospitals*; Rubin, *Charity and Community*, the heart of which (pp. 99–236) is actually a study of selected hospitals; and, among the many French works, J. Caille, *Hôpitaux et charité publique à Narbonne au Moyen Âge de la fin du XIᵉ à la fin du XVᵉ siècle* (Toulouse, 1978); and Nicole Gonthier, 'Les Hôpitaux et les pauvres à la fin du Moyen Âge: L'Éxemple du Lyon', *Moyen Âge* 84 (1978), 279–308.

business travel and religious pilgrimage.[76] Like most of its English
contemporaries it was always a small institution.[77] It probably
possessed fewer than the average thirteen beds.[78] But, before the
creation of the almshouse in 1436, it was the only place to house
the sick and the poor in addition to travellers.[79] The burgesses and
clergy of the town looked to it as a place worth supporting in order
to help those in need. Some of the money that the burgess William
Wythy gave to the hospital was destined ultimately to support poor
people.[80] In 1401 Thomas Tanner's will remembered the poor
people lying in St John's hospital.[81] And in 1407 Richard Gross
also made a bequest to the poor in its infirmary.[82]

For its part, the cathedral engaged in very modest institutional
donations. Aside from the alms that it administered through obits
and other trustee arrangements, the sums given by the church were
small even in times of difficulty. In 1428–9—a year of dearth, the
communar's account noted—the cathedral spent a total of 63s. of
its £600 income on the poor, only about ½ of 1 per cent, hardly the
traditional quarter or one third that the poor were once thought to
be due.[83] At least on one occasion it gave a small donation directly
to a burgess of the town who had fallen on hard times in the years
before the creation of the almshouse. In 1372–3 they paid William

[76] Cf. Robert Favreau, 'Pauvreté en Poitou et en Anjou à la fin du Moyen Âge', in
M. Mollat (ed.), *Études sur l'histoire de la pauvreté*, ii (Paris, 1974), 591; this
assignation does correspond to Clay's second period of hospital foundation in
England, of which the later 12th and early 13th cents. were certainly the years of
sustained growth: see Clay, *Medieval Hospitals*, 71–8; and also Mollat, *Pauvres*,
115–17.

[77] David Knowles and R. N. Hadcock, *Medieval Religious Houses* (London,
1971), 316. At the time of its dissolution in 1539 its income was £40.

[78] Clay, *Medieval Hospitals*, 156, found this to be the usual number of beds for
the smaller institution; Favreau, 'Pauvreté en Poitou', 595, found a similar average
of 12–15 beds.

[79] Knowles and Hadcock, *Medieval Religious Houses*, 316, mention the poor as
being admitted; *SMWI*: 26 proves that the sick were accommodated. It probably fell
into the category of hospital called a *syndochium*, a place for the poor and pilgrims,
by a 15th-cent. analyst: see Geremek, *Potence ou pitié*, 59.

[80] SRO DD/B, Reg. 1: 25^b (1326).

[81] *SMWI*: 8.

[82] *SMWI*: 26.

[83] CA, 1428–9; on the traditional third, see Geremek, *Potence ou pitié*, 25. It was
being practised—at the rate of one quarter to the poor and hospitality—in the 12th
cent.: see Giles Constable, *Monastic Tithes from their Origins to the Twelfth
Century* (Cambridge, 1964), 43–4 and 56; Rubin, *Charity and Community*,
246–50, outlines the occasional distributions of some religious houses, especially on
certain feast-days.

Wynd, who was once a churchwarden, a shilling.[84] Wynd was already a man of some substance in the 1340s, and was—in medieval terms—quite old, in his late fifties or sixties.[85]

The cathedral was really more of a help to the poor in its capacity as trustee of the monies assigned for that purpose by the laymen and clergy who had established chantries and annual memorial services.[86] For example, Wells Cathedral was the trustee of Bishop William de Bitton II's obit, which was established in the 1270s, and provided 3½ marks per annum to be distributed to the poor.[87] Similarly, in 1307 Dean Henry Husee awarded the cathedral 40s. per annum to distribute to the poor.[88] At about the same time, Bishop Robert Burnell had assigned 20s. per annum for poor relief, to be paid in two instalments.[89] The role of lay charity, administered by the churches, guilds, or towns, loomed larger in the later medieval period, when poverty became more pernicious in the urban context. Concurrently, however, there was the expansion of specialized institutions like the hospitals and almshouses, so the pressure for funding from cathedrals and monasteries was reduced.

The parish church was also the scene of regular, perpetual, and sometimes sizeable distributions provided by the last wills of burgesses. Here we find most of the lay townspeople's contributions. None was more generous than that of Thomas Tanner, established after his death in 1401. On St Catherine's day every year, 60s. worth of bread was to be distributed to the poor.[90] The churchwardens and the Borough Community fulfilled their promise to supervise this distribution. For instance, leases that the Community made with the bakers John Pyton and John London for a High Street bakery in the late fifteenth century required that they bake the bread for Tanner's alms.[91] Few burgesses were in a position to give as much as Tanner, but many, many more than the records show,[92] left something for the poor who attended their funerals. The grandest of these donors was John Welshot, who

---

[84] EA, 1372–3.
[85] He was active in the disturbances of 1341–3 (WCC 7) and a witness to property transactions, alongside other important burgesses, in 1346 (WTD 195).
[86] See below, Ch. 8, sect. 6. [87] RI: 62.
[88] RI: 521. [89] RI: 164.
[90] WCC 16. [91] CBII: 162.
[92] This is because we do not possess any wills of people who were not wealthy enough to qualify for Canterbury jurisdiction, or who did not actually make a bequest to the cathedral.

provided £10 in 1519 to be distributed on his burial day.[93] John Brown, a fairly rich man himself, ordered a halfpenny loaf for every poor person who attended his burial 'to seek the alms of Christ'.[94] Another master of the town, John Horewode, wanted £3 to be distributed to the poor at his funeral.[95] On a truly more humble level was Alice Swansee, who asked that 10s. be divided among the poor attending her final services in the plague year of 1348.[96]

We can provide some figures to estimate the total amount of institutionally administered perpetual support. There can be nothing but a rough accuracy to our numbers, because the possibility for omissions and cessations is high (see Table 11). We have mentioned the cathedral's donations, and we know that Bishop Drokensford was feeding and clothing about twenty people in the Wells area in the early fourteenth century.[97] The annual value of the bishop's gifts was perhaps £9 7s. 3d., the chapter's, say, 25s. Other assistance in place before 1350 was worth about £22 14s. 6d. per annum, giving a combined total of £33 5s. 10d. per annum.[98] Additional funds over the next fifty years were quite limited, even allowing for the inevitable and multiple ways in which information can remain hidden from us. Only about 45s. of new money per annum can be located.[99] Nor did this trend look up in the early fifteenth century. The 61s. of new annual support came almost entirely from Thomas Tanner's one grant.[100] There was

TABLE 11. *Foundations of permanent poor relief*

Year	New a/d	Aggregate relief
by 1300	n/a	£25 1s. 10d.
by 1350	£8 4s.	£33 5s. 10d.
by 1400	£2 5s.	£35 10s. 10d.
by 1450	£3 1s.	£38 11s. 10d.

Note: n/a = not available.

[93] *SMWII*: 199–212.
[94] SRO DD/WM 1/5.
[95] *SMWI*: 74–5 (1416).
[96] RI: 175.
[97] SRO DD/B, Reg. 1: 141ᵃ.
[98] CA, 1327–8, and 1343–4; RI: 33ᵈ; and *CPR 1343–5*: 571. There is no indication that Bishop Savaric's obit, which included the refreshment of 100 paupers once a year, was still being held (RI: 23, before 1205). We have assumed that there was no longer any payment being made.
[99] This came from four different people: CA, 1392–3; RIII: 134–6 (2); WTD 141.
[100] See below, pp. 251 f.

therefore little expansion in permanent relief until the foundation of the almshouse in 1436.

The above figures give rise to many doubts and problems. We have assumed that the level of support from the bishop and the cathedral was static, at cash values of £10 12s. 10d. per annum. The amount of money actually paid from each chantry could fluctuate, however, notwithstanding the founder's instructions. Economic hardship could intervene to reduce the rents upon which the poor relief was founded.[101] It is conceivable that later administrators might have exercised discretion, giving only to those people whom they thought deserving of help. We have very possibly missed or lost the documents which would have notified us of other arrangements, especially those founded by the burgesses. Nor have we allowed for the fact that inflation was probably reducing the real value of the distributions. Nevertheless, the trend is clear.

Relatively little money was given for permanent, public distributions in the period after the depopulation of the mid-fourteenth century. Furthermore, the new donations of bishops and others were actually greatest in the thirteenth century. There are several reasons for this shift. Once the population had fallen as a result of the plague, the resources were better able to cope with the need. Moreover, when the population fell, wages and the general standard of living in the town went up, and probably stayed there throughout the fifteenth century.[102] This may have suppressed the demand for increasing aid. On the other hand, the town was also a considerably smaller place after the plague, and especially in the fifteenth century,[103] so there were fewer burgesses to make the bequests, and those who did tended to make shorter-term provisions and more humble endowments, very probably reflecting the fact that industry and commerce in Wells were not as healthy as they had once been.[104]

Finally, there was the impact of the almshouse, established in the 1430s, which we have excluded from the above figures. From its

---

[101] This might explain the fluctuations in the amounts disbursed by chantries, for e.g. between 1327 and 1343. Henry Husee's chantry paid the poor 60s. in 1327, and only 20s. in the 1343 (CA, 1327–8, and 1343–4). One of the Godley chantries was vacant in 1391–2 because the assigned rents were insufficient (CA 1391–2).

[102] See above, Ch. 3, sect. 5 and 6.

[103] See above, Ch. 2, sect. 3.

[104] See above, Ch. 3, sects. 2(iii) and 5.

inception, it attracted much of the money which would otherwise have been distributed at funerals or even at anniversaries. To this extent, the almshouse in Wells—and presumably those elsewhere—could have had an ambiguous impact on poor relief, because, no matter how much money it received, it did not take in more needy people. Moreover, almshouses inevitably used more discretion in allocating their aid than did those who supervised the distributions which accompanied religious memorial services. Population and economy were smaller, and the almshouse provided other avenues of support, where discretion over who received help could be established more easily.

Indeed, the decline in alms distributed at memorial services must be seen in the context of the development of the almshouse. For, from its inception in 1436, it began to garner very considerable amounts of property and income. The burgess William Gascoigne gave one third of his manor of Newton Plecy to support the poor and to endow a chaplain to pray and to oversee the almshouse.[105] By the end of the fifteenth century the almshouse had accumulated property, which included both small manors and urban tenements, worth almost £20 per annum, and other donations and perquisites brought this total to almost £30 per annum.[106] The support of the poor in Wells had changed radically. Much was given to the almshouse, but the sometimes haphazard vehicle of the memorial-service distribution had faltered.

How significant were these perpetual donations? From the point of view of the donor's wealth, it is safe to say that, while Thomas Tanner's grant was generous, he assigned only about half as much to charity as he did to support a chantry priest.[107] This compares favourably, however, with the arrangements left by John Storthwayt, a cathedral canon, who in 1452 provided ten marks per annum for his chantry's priest, but only 6s. 8d. for the poor.[108] Indeed, as we shall argue below, the act of charity was an act of religion and the donors would not have separated one pious purpose from the other.[109] They were perhaps more interested in God than in the poor.

From the town's perspective, we have already suggested that the round of distributions which punctuated the year may have attracted permanent and itinerant poor people to the city,

---

[105] AH 178.
[106] AH 275 (1496–7 account).
[107] WCC 16.
[108] RIII: 306–10.
[109] See below, Ch. 8, sect. 6.

somewhat swelling the numbers of the indigent.[110] We can hazard some guesses as to the efficacy of these donations in actually helping the poor. Let us examine the mid-fifteenth century, assuming that the actual donations available in a given year were about £40 (see Table 11). In crassest terms, it would seem to have cost about £1 to keep a person alive, fed, sheltered, and clothed for a year.[111] This would have bought one hardy meal a day and a fair quantity of bread, the diet on which the people in the almshouse lived.[112] Basically, then, the distributions were enough to keep forty people comfortably alive, more if shelter was sacrificed. This would have been equivalent to *circa* 3 per cent of the town's fifteenth-century population. To assess the total poor relief, we would have to add the thirty-odd people who would have been living—for many of them, their last days—in the almshouse and the hospital of St John. Thus, about seventy people could have been supported, without taking into account the alms given in door-to-door and one-off funeral distributions. If the later fifteenth-century population of the town averaged about 1,500 people, institutional charity would have provided for about 4.5 per cent of the population, a figure slightly higher then, but on the whole commensurate with, the 3 per cent that Christopher Dyer has calculated for Worcester.[113]

Critically, however, the actual distribution of alms was not so orderly. Those who did not live in institutions would have had to compete for alms with many others, some coming from far afield. A twelfth-century obituary provision envisaged feeding a hundred people at the anniversary distribution.[114] Canon Richard Bamfield's arrangements, drawn up at the end of the 1290s,

---

[110] See above, p. 230.

[111] This rate is somewhere above the bare minimum of ¼d. a day and the more generous 1d. a day, on which a person could live well enough to eat some meat and ale with his bread: see n. 120 below; and Dyer, *Standards of Living*, 253; The average price of a cottage in Wells ranged between 3s. 4d. and 5s. on average. Cf. the similar results of *Winchester*, 123.

[112] Allowing for unfilled places because of death, we have based the almshouse food requirements on 22 people. The accounts used are AH 275 (1496–7), 276 (1497–8), 277 (1498–9), 289 (1501–2), and 303 (1522–3). The average annual per capita expenses were 4s. on bread, 4s. 7d. on ale, 4s. 5d. on meat and fish, ½d. on salt, and 2½d. on flour. The per capita total for this varied diet, fairly rich in protein, was 13s. 3d. p.a. This leaves the numerous donations out of account.

[113] Dyer, *Standards of Living*, 252–3. Indeed, part of the difference is on account of Dyer's use of a 1d. a day as the minimum a head (that is, 30s. 5d. p.a.), whereas we have used the considerably lower 20s. p.a.

[114] RI: 23.

provided a halfpenny for as many as 200 paupers.[115] The bishop, we recall, gave his special paupers only a farthing a day. We can now put all this generosity, and the surprising numbers who must have attended the obits of Dean Henry Husee and others, into perspective. His 40s. per annum would have provided a halfpenny loaf to 960 people.[116] Thomas Tanner's generosity filled the stomachs of at least 720 people for a day, perhaps provided enough for twice that number, or even gave a simple day's worth of bread to 2,880 people.[117] Wells itself never had a population large enough to justify such annual largesse.[118] These distributions must have drawn substantial numbers of the poor from the countryside and possibly from neighbouring towns, conjuring up a scene of vagrant poor moving from town to town, on the circuit of poverty, looking for the large hand-outs.

In the size of these annual distributions, which could be many times larger in other cities, we touch upon a circumstance which may have lain behind two important late medieval facts. First, the population of all but the smallest towns was extremely volatile, capable of wild fluctuations, with which no demographic estimates, based on tax rolls or hearths, can cope. The roads and towns were filled with beggars and with those labourers, journeymen, and servants who were moving from town to town in search of work.[119] Second, and as striking, is the worry that was heard especially from the fifteenth century and most loudly in the sixteenth, that vagrancy was alarmingly high and somehow dangerous, increasingly related to criminality.[120] The criminals of the post-plague years differed from those of the earlier period, at least in France, in the degree to which the perpetrator operated outside his home locality.[121] It is

[115] RI: 87.

[116] RI: 52, RIII: 277; and CA, 1327–8, and 1343–4.

[117] Dyer, *Standards of Living*, 253, views this sum, buying a 2lb. loaf, as the bare minimum. It was a figure frequently met with, and one upon which Bishop Drokensford and other bishops based their charity (SRO DD/B, Reg. 1: 141ᵃ.; Dyer, *Standards of Living*, 241).

[118] Some 15th-cent. European distributions attracted thousands, e.g. 2,400–3,000 in Poitiers, 6,000 in Perigueux: see Favreau, 'Pauvreté en Poitou', 600–1.

[119] Dyer, *Standards of Living*, 230–1, discusses workers' mobility; Pound, *Poverty and Vagrancy*, 27–30.

[120] Pound, *Poverty and Vagrancy*, 29–30; Favreau, 'Pauvreté en Poitou', 606–8, demonstrates how poverty turned into criminality; see John Bellamy, *Crime and Public Order in the Later Middle Ages* (London, 1973), 30–1 on the link between wandering, poverty, and criminality from the 13th cent.

[121] Jacqueline Misraki, 'Criminalité et Pauvreté en France à l'époque de la Guerre de cent ans', in Mollat (ed.), *Histoire de la pauvreté*, ii. 536–7.

possible that there were virtual armies of indigence crossing the countryside in hard times. It was not that there were necessarily more poor people in the later Middle Ages, but that relief, organized according to personal religious aims rather as poor relief *per se*, was increasingly located in the towns, especially in the cathedral cities. The unemployed and the alms-seekers were an alarming presence in the city, as they were unattached to the community, unknown elements in a state of chronic need. Townsmen across Europe eventually tried to drive out door-to-door beggars and the vagrant poor, establishing more direct and controllable means of supporting *their worthy* poor.[122]

The expansion of the almshouses was part of this well-considered late medieval response. In other places the fraternities intervened to help the 'respectable, resident poor'.[123] If the almshouses provided less complete and less effective aid than some sixteenth-century institutions like the well-known *aumône-générale* of Lyon,[124] they nevertheless had their advantages, and continued to be founded in Wells until the seventeenth century, and used and expanded until the present day. They served the community; they provided comprehensive support for a small but not insignificant number of people who were in trouble but were considered worthy of help by the local donor community. B. Geremek has called such people 'the aristocracy of beggars'.[125] The turn towards the almshouse, which garnered an increasingly large share of charitable bequests, represents a turn towards discretionary and local poor relief, and against indiscriminate almsgiving.

The hospital of the Holy Saviour in Wells was established by the executors of Bishop Nicholas Bubwith in 1436, twelve years after

---

[122] This appears to have begun in southern Germany as early as the later 14th cent.: Geremek, *Potence ou pitié*, 64; as early as the mid-14th cent. the London council thought that a great deal of the alms were wasted by being given to the vagrants: Clay, *Medieval Hospitals*, 6–7; see also Natalie Z. Davis, 'Poor Relief, Humanism, and Heresy', in *Society and Culture in Early Modern France* (Stanford, Calif., 1975), 17–64; Mollat, *Pauvres*, 326, 349–52; and Felicity Heal, *Hospitality in Early Modern England* (Oxford, 1990), 318–19. On the mobility of labour, see Simon A. C. Penn and Christopher Dyer, 'Wages and Earnings in Later Medieval England: Evidence from the enforcement of the Labour Laws', *ECHR*, 2nd Ser., 43 (1990), 363–5.

[123] Pullan, *Rich and Poor*, 98.

[124] On this, see Richard Gascon, 'Économies et pauvreté aux XVIᵉ et XVIIᵉ siècles: Lyon, ville éxemplaire et prophétique', in Mollat (ed.), *Histoire de la pauvreté*, ii. 747–60; and Davis, 'Poor Relief', 17–64.

[125] Geremek, *Potence ou pitié*, 62.

his death, during the second great period of hospital building.[126] It was a true community effort, the one joint project of the town and the cathedral. Selection of the paupers and administration of the funds were the joint responsibilities of the Borough Community and the cathedral chapter. The almshouse reflected the city; and, to a certain degree, so did the inmates. They were to be selected from the poor of the Borough Community as well as of the city, from St Cuthbert's out-parish, and from the tenants of the cathedral estates (virtually all of which were in Somerset). The townsmen were to select two paupers to every one of the chapter's nominees.[127]

It would be interesting to know something about the other inmates of the house. The chaplain certainly kept a list of all those who were accepted, but these have unfortunately been lost.[128] We have only the names of about thirty of the almspeople. Virtually nothing can be said about those who were not burgesses or burgesses' family members. The one exception is John Payn, a free mason. He had lived and worked in Wells for at least thirty years, renting a tenement from the Community in 1465.[129] He gave the almshouse a considerable donation to expedite his acceptance.[130] What such gifts prove is that demand for the twenty-four places was high, and most people of this status were competing only for the twelve superior positions.

There is one element of the composition of the almspeople which is striking and somewhat disturbing. Of the thirty-one almspeople whose sex can be determined, twenty-four were men; only seven—less than a quarter—were women. While sex ratios for the medieval city are hard to confirm, and vary from place to place, there can be no question that women were better represented among the elderly, among the eligible population, than in the almshouse.[131] Without doubt, the elderly were more often poor

---

[126] AH 172.

[127] Ibid. We have discussed the criteria for eligibility, above, pp. 231 f.

[128] AH 172.

[129] AH 275–78 and CBII: 52.

[130] AH 275–8 are accounts which note an income of 6s. 8d. from John Payn, presumably rent from a property that he owned. His example shows that non-burgesses could also induce early admission, see below, pp. 244 ff.

[131] On this vexed question, see J. C. Russell, *British Medieval Population* (Albuquerque, NM, 1948), 148–54; David Herlihy and Christiane Klapisch-Zuber, *Les Toscans et leurs familles: Un étude de* catasto *florentin de 1427* (Paris, 1978), 326–49, present evidence which supports Russell's claim that there were more men than in modern society; but both show that women predominated in some places; see also S. L. Thrupp, 'Plague Effects in Medieval Europe', *Comparative Studies in Society and History* 8 (1965–6), 475–8.

and disabled.[132] In Coventry there may have been as many as nine times more widows than widowers in the early sixteenth century.[133] Every account of poverty in the medieval and early modern period reflects the fact that widows comprised a large portion of the poor.[134] Furthermore, medieval ideas of poverty tended to lay emphasis on the true need of widows and orphans, those cast outside the economic strength of the paternal family. Bishop Drokensford's charity singled out widows and serfs as particularly worthy.[135] The church had long declared itself the special protector of widows.[136]

Nevertheless, possibly because there were simply so many poor of various definitions, and because the almshouse was so attractive—at least among the preferred and able-bodied group of almspeople—the men were allotted many more places than their numbers warranted. Women, it would appear, were regarded as lesser to begin with, lesser in achievement, and unable to fall as far, as tragically. They were, paradoxically, less able to be poor, according to one prevailing medieval definition.[137] A closer examination aggravates the impression of male prejudice in selection. At least two of the seven female inmates were admitted because their husbands had arranged for them to have a place as a condition of their granting lands or rents to the almshouse.[138] Another was undoubtedly accepted on the same basis as the men, namely, compassion towards her deteriorating circumstances. Joanna Sadler, the daughter of John, a master of the town, was a pauper towards the end of the fifteenth century.[139] By virtue of her father, she was apparently thought high enough in honour to fall far enough to be helped.

[132] Slack, 'Reactions of the Poor', 26, table 4; one of the recognized categories of hospital was the *gerontocomium* (see Geremek, *Potence ou pitié*, 59.)

[133] *Coventry*, 92; the Florentine *catasto* also indicates a high ratio of widows to widowers: Herlihy and Klapisch-Zuber, *Toscans*, 403, table 59; see also Desportes, 'Population de Reims', 502.

[134] Smith, 'Families and their Property', 77; Wales, 'Poverty, Poor Relief and the Life-Cycle', 366; Gonthier, 'Hôpitaux et les pauvres', 301, found hospitals which favoured widows; Slack, 'Reactions of the Poor', 21 notes that two-thirds of the recipients were women and children; but Favreau, 'Pauvreté en Poitou', 597, describes a hospital where men predominated over women.

[135] SRO DD/B, Reg, 1: 141[a].

[136] Rubin, *Charity and Community*, 238, notes that Gratian charged churchmen with special concern for widows; see also Tierney, 'Deserving Poor'.

[137] See above, Ch. 7, sect. 3.

[138] These were Joanna Salmon (CBII: 123) and Joanna Bevys (CBII: 145).

[139] See endorsement of AH 273[b].

The burgess almspeople tended to be elderly. Life expectancy in the fifteenth century was very short, especially because of the existence of plague. Indeed, it has been persuasively argued that expectation of life declined in fifteenth-century England.[140] Life expectancy at birth seems to have been about thirty years.[141] We can determine how many years passed between a future almsman's admission to the guild and either his admission to the hospital or his death while there. The seven men for whom the duration between the two admissions can be calculated yield an average of at least thirty-two years.[142] The foreigner John Payn appears in the almshouse records thirty-one years after he first rented a property from the Community, when he was already married and a master mason. Juliana Hanam was admitted forty years after her husband Walter had first joined the Borough Community. Furthermore, the four burgesses for whom we have a date of death present an average duration of thirty-three years between Community admission and death. Given that the age of admission to the civic guild was probably between 25 and 30, we can conclude that the average age of admission of those almspeople selected by the Borough Community was between 55 and 60, and some were certainly older.[143] This helps to confirm that the almshouse poor, and perhaps the poor of the city as a whole, were divided into two parts: the old and worn out, and the seriously incapacitated or dying.

Although there was possibly an abuse or two, the burgess members of the almshouse probably did deserve to be there. They were people in some financial trouble who could not have kept their homes for long. The affluent could find themselves reduced to poverty in other parts of later medieval Europe as well.[144] It has also been argued that many of them who were admitted to almshouses in Europe were not truly poor by any accepted standard or definition.[145] The practice of allowing the purchase of corrodies

---

[140] John Hatcher, 'Mortality in the Fifteenth Century: Some New Evidence', *ECHR* 2nd ser., 39 (1986), table 2, and pp. 31–3.

[141] Russell, *Medieval Population*, 173–93; Hatcher, 'Mortality in the Fifteenth Century', 32–3; Herlihy and Klapisch-Zuber, *Toscans*, 199–204, calculated 33 years for women, and 37 for men.

[142] For 2 of the men, what we have is not the date on which they were admitted to the almshouse, but the year in which they negotiated for the next available place.

[143] See above, Ch. 5, sect. 1.

[144] Mollat, *Pauvres*, 199.

[145] Ibid. 327.

has frequently been viewed as a form of corruption which entered the traditional hospitals, diverting some of their resources—space if nothing else—from the relief of the poor, but they were nevertheless common.[146] We have noted that several of the inmates of the Wells almshouse made some sort of a payment to be received, but, on reflection, these should not be considered as corrupt corrodies, even though the benefactor-inmate certainly secured an earlier place than he ought to have done. The difference between the Wells cases and the sort of corrody which was a sign of a reduced concern with the poor was that, notwithstanding the donation, the Wells benefactor-inmates were in considerable need.

The typical corrody was that of John Pakenham of Bury. He paid the St Saviour's hospital there twenty-six marks to be admitted, fed, and clothed.[147] This was ample money on which to live on one's own. By contrast, the Wells grantors gave property that was worth much less, definitely inadequate to support a person. John Payn's property was yielding only 6s. 8d. per annum (and the hospital was not granted the tenement in perpetuity).[148] In 1482 John Wyx was accepted when he granted lands to the almshouse which were worth 4s. per annum.[149] Three years earlier John Salmon had won the right to have himself and his wife installed in the next two available places in the almshouse by agreeing to a one-off payment of 10s. to the parish church fabric fund and 40s. to the hospital itself.[150] John Bevys granted a property worth 4s. per annum to the almshouse at the time of his admission in 1485. Like Wyx, he was to receive the annuity during his lifetime, after which his wife was to receive it until she should enter the almshouse. The property was eventually to be vested in the Borough Community.[151]

These cases may prove that admission to these much-valued places was not, strictly speaking, fair, but they do not prove that

---

[146] See A. H. Thompson, 'A Corrody from Leicester Abbey, AD 1393–4, with some Notes on Corrodies', *Transactions of the Leicestershire Archaeological Society*, 14 (1924), 114–34; Rubin, *Charity and Community*, 171–3 and n. 73 for bibliography; and R. B. Dobson, *Durham Priory, 1400–50* (Cambridge, 1973), 169. Clay seems to have been the first to note the effect of the corrodies: *Medieval Hospitals*, 212–25.

[147] E. Rowland Burdon, 'St Saviour's Hospital, Bury St Edmunds', *Proceedings of the Suffolk Institute of Archaeology and Natural History* 19 (1927), 271.

[148] AH 275, 276, 277, and 289.

[149] CBII: 133. Wyx was to receive this rent during his lifetime, presumably as pocket-money.

[150] CBII: 123.

[151] CBII: 145. See also the case of Thomas Hayne and his grant of rural property worth only 20d. p.a. (AH 477 (1498–9)).

ineligible, inappropriately affluent individuals were using the almshouse as a retirement home. It is very possible, considering the smallness of the sums, that these people were simply taking care of the property that they would be leaving behind. It was a rule of the almshouse that all property was to be surrendered to the hospital and administered by the chaplain.[152] These people were giving up control of their properties prior to admission. At the same time, they were trying to accelerate that admission, and, in some cases, to direct the property and its income for the future support of either a wife, the almshouse, or the Borough Community. We can also add that there is no record at Wells, as there is elsewhere,[153] of any of these (or any other) inmates receiving special treatment or exemption from the rules of the house. Indeed, the one person to be recorded as having been expelled for failing to submit to the rules was a man, John Grene, who had once been a town councillor.[154] The town's selections were often people of this calibre, that is, older burgesses with a little property, people who were worn out, weak, and who would lose the house in which they lived and be unable to rent another, without the almshouse. Although they were not perhaps in immediate dire circumstances, many of them may have been threatened with such a situation. Unlike William Wynd a hundred years earlier, they could turn to help more substantial and permanent than the cathedral's 1s. offering.[155]

The trades of the inmates also suggest that they were not selected from among the rich. John Payn was not the only mason,[156] and the other trades included an innkeeper,[157] a weaver,[158] and a baker.[159] As citizens, they were all fairly humble in the civic responsibility that they had held when in the prime of life, with the exception of John Grene. John Wyx once served as a street-warden (1458), Richard Baker was once a churchwarden (1450), and a couple of others held similarly modest positions, those offices for which one did not have to have even moderate private resources. The others, like John Haylesden, John Salmon, John Plummer, Thomas Butcher, and William Widecumb, never held any office or were in any way conspicuous in the town's political or economic affairs.

---

[152] AH 172.
[153] Rubin, *Charity and Community*, 172.
[154] CBII: 108.
[155] EA, 1372–3.
[156] John Norman.
[157] This was John Grene, a former town councillor (CBII: 108).
[158] John Wyx.
[159] Thomas Butcher.

The cathedral chapter probably chose more inmates, often foreigners, who were in dire circumstances than the town. But the
almshouse always reflected the society which produced it, in so far
as the burgesses and foreigners were both given support, but the
citizens were honoured, even in their poverty, above the foreigners.
They were given the better places, the better beds.[160]

The almshouse and its inmates remained very much part of the
Community. They were the town's favourite paupers, the town's
own. In the first place, many of the people in the town and the
parish must have hoped that they, too, might benefit from the
security and piety of life there. It was a relatively good way in which
to finish one's life. The accounts and cash-book show that, all year
long, the almspeople lived on a good diet, relatively rich in meat
and fish. The money for food was basically divided among bread,
animal protein, and ale.[161] Occasionally, there would be honey,
especially for those who were sick.[162] Moreover, it was a religious
life. The almspeople were required to say prayers for the many
benefactors of the house, and these grew quite numerous as time
went on. Upon entering the house, the new pauper took an oath
and had to yield all of his or her property to the chaplain; thus,
admission to the hospital mirrored the religious profession of a
monk or friar.

Members of the community gave property or money to the
hospital from the beginning. The Borough Community made an
annual donation, which was about £4 at the end of the fifteenth
century.[163] But there was a great deal of individual giving. Some of
this was stimulated by the almspeople themselves, who, from the
beginning of the foundation, were licensed to go out and seek
alms.[164] They did so in the town and in the rural parish.[165] Cheese
was a popular offering;[166] some gave flour or grain.[167] Residents of
the city gave such things as wax, wagon-loads of fuel, ale, and
especially fish.[168] In 1501–2 John Welshot gave some 'wet hake',

---

[160] AH 172.

[161] AH 275, 276, 277, 289, 303, and 305.

[162] AH 289. Other pains and expenses were also incurred on behalf of the sick. For
instance, 4s. was spent during the illness of William Widecumb in 1498–9 (AH 277).

[163] It was 73s. 4d. in 1496–7; 86s. 8d. in 1497–8; 91s. in 1498–9; and 72s. 5d.
ob. in 1500–01 (AH 275, 276, 277, and 289).

[164] AH 172.   [165] AH 275 and AH 277.

[166] AH 275, 276, 277, 289, and 305.   [167] AH 278, 289, and 305.

[168] AH 289.

while others gave dried hake, herring, and salmon.[169] This charity, which must have served to bind the wealthy or fortunate to the poor, must have flourished at Lent. The close integration of the almshouse and the town made it a wholly suitable and successful institution. But it was, we can be sure, never large enough to cope with all the eligible poor, especially the neglected old women, let alone the mass of suspected beggars.

5. WOMEN

Women have been treated in this book as an integrated part of the society. We have discussed some of their economic activities, their place in the Borough Community, and their participation in religious life.[170] Discussions of marriage, child-bearing, and -rearing—in short, of the family—have not been included. The evidence is poor, and others have been able to do more.[171]

For these reasons, we shall advance here only several reflections on their place in the medieval town. In political terms, the facts are clear and simple. Wells women played no official role. The master's wife was no doubt honoured, as the wife of the mayor or the bailiff is in most towns, but women were not admitted to the freedom of the city in their own right, only by virtue of one of several possible relationships to a man, a burgess.[172] From this, we are able to conclude that the male-dominated household was in many respects the main social unit of the town.

By the same token, it would be misleading to view women as forced to lead inactive, housebound lives. Those who were burgesses' wives, widows, or daughters were members of the Borough Community and, to a great extent, participated in its

---

[169] AH 289.

[170] See above, Chs. 3, sect. 5, and 5, sect. 1; and below, nn. 175, 178, 180, 193, 194, and Ch. 8, sect. 3.

[171] On English towns, none has been better than *Coventry*; elsewhere, see esp. David Herlihy, *Medieval and Renaissance Pistoia* (New Haven, Conn., 1967); Herlihy and Klapisch-Zuber, *Toscans*; and David Nicholas, *The Domestic Life of a Medieval Family. Women, Children and the Family in the Fourteenth Century* (Lincoln, 1985), whose introduction is a good survey of this field.

[172] The one exception was Elsa Gyllyng (CBI: 73); cf. P. J. P. Goldberg, 'Female Labour, Service and Marriage in the Late Medieval Urban North', *Northern History* 22 (1986), 35.

advantages, such as the use of the master's court, inclusion in the Community's social and religious activities, and access to the almshouse.[173] In the latter case, however, we have seen how contemporary ideas of poverty, together with simple male self-interest, conspired to limit unfairly the place that women found in that institution.[174]

Women were conspicuous enough, however, in the economic life of Wells and in western Europe generally.[175] They became apprentices and pursued a variety of trades.[176] A wife often assisted her husband in his work, whatever craft he followed, since wives were normally the only free labour available in addition to his own.[177] Women were active independently in the cloth trade.[178] They might act as hucksters—of lace, for instance—or seamstresses and laundresses.[179]

At least some women seem to have been truly independent as businesswomen, neither wives, servants, nor widows. Evidence from other places suggests that single women often lived in the same part of town, and were more likely than men to share a residence with a 'room-mate'.[180] Both married and single women were relatively prominent among the tapsters of Wells, less so among the brewers.[181] Others operated more independently still.

---

[173] See above, Ch. 5, sect. 1.

[174] See above, pp. 242 f.

[175] Outstanding on this burgeoning subject are Power, *Medieval Women*, 53–69; Hanawalt (ed.), *Women and Work*; C. Klapisch-Zuber, *Histoire des Femmes en Occident*, ii. *Le Moyen Âge* (Plon, 1990); Goldberg, 'Female Labour', and his 'Women in Fifteenth-Century Town Life', in John A. F. Thomson (ed.), *Towns and Townspeople in the Fifteenth Century* (Gloucester, 1988); David Herlihy, *Opera Muliebria: Women and Work in Medieval Europe* (New York, 1990); Edith Ennen, *The Medieval Woman*, trans. Edmund Jephcott (Oxford, 1989).

[176] See above, Ch. 3, sect. 5; although Kowaleski, 'Women's Work', 163 n. 56, found only one apprentice in Exeter, they were more common elsewhere; see K. L. Reyerson, 'Women in Business in Medieval Montpellier', in Hanawalt (ed.), *Women and Work*, 120–1.

[177] Natalie Zemon Davis, 'Women in the Crafts in Sixteenth-Century Lyon', in Hanawalt (ed.), *Women and Work*, 172–7, discusses this topic explicitly.

[178] See above, p. 172.

[179] The cathedral bought lace from a woman in 1446–7 (CA, 1446–7), and Agnes Shepster, possibly an employee of the tailor John King, was active in Wells and London in 1424 (SRO DD/B, Reg. 4: 209). The cathedral employed a laundress (CA, 1414–15). Female petty traders have received attention from Kowaleski, 'Women's Work', 148–9; R. H. Hilton, 'Women Traders in Medieval England', in *Class Conflict*, 208–15; and Goldberg, 'Female Labour', 29.

[180] Goldberg, 'Women in Town Life', 108–9, and 'Female Labour', 20; *Winchester*, 388–9.

[181] See below, p. 250.

Joanna Hostilar, for instance, probably ran a tavern. Some of the credit that she received was guaranteed by a prominent burgess.[182] There were other examples of men giving surety for foreign women, but why they did so—if it was not for pure, probably extraordinary profit—we do not know.[183] Some, burgesses' widows among them, could be highly independent businesswomen, and highly litigious. Edith Skinner fought at least eight court cases, all seemingly about business debts or merchandise, between 1409 and 1418.[184]

Women's participation was not always even. We can examine the ale industry a little more closely.[185] Extant leet court records for the years 1312, 1382, 1383, and 1421 tell us who was charged with violating the assize of brewing and tapping ale.[186] Based on so few records, our results can only be tentative, but they show that women's involvement here declined over the fourteenth century. In 1312 they accounted for nearly a quarter of those (7/31) charged with brewing against the assize, but in the two years between 1382 and 1383 their share was down to 4.6 per cent of the brewers (3/65), and 39.3 per cent of the tapsters (11/28).[187] The 1421 figures are similar.[188] In the three post-plague courts women's share of both brewing and tapping violations was 16.3 per cent per year, down 9 per cent on the early fourteenth-century result. In late fourteenth-century Exeter women's share was less still, only 9 per cent of the total.[189] We can speculate that part of the decline was caused by women's increasing involvement in other areas of the economy in the labour-starved post-plague world.

This period of positive change for women's earning power peaked and declined in the fifteenth century. P. J. P. Goldberg has argued that, in York, women's economic acme came after the Black Death and especially in the early part of the fifteenth century. When

[182] CBI: 116; the surety was provided by Steven Windford.

[183] CBI: 281 (1443) was such a case between two burgesses involving 10s. owed by a woman. We cannot rule out the possibility that the men were somehow related to the women whom they guaranteed, but we would expect it to have been noted.

[184] CBI: 178, 188, 190 (2), 208, 213 (2), and 218.

[185] On this subject, see Judith M. Bennett, 'The Village Ale-Wife: Women and Brewing in Fourteenth-Century England', in Hanawalt (ed.), *Women and Work*, 20–36; and Hilton, 'Women Traders', 209–10; Kowaleski, 'Women's Work', 151.

[186] LPL ED 1097, 1181, 1182, and 1186/74.

[187] The 1312 court submitted only brewing infractions, not tapping: ibid. 1097, 1181, and 1182.

[188] LPL ED 1186.

[189] Kowaleski, 'Women's Work', 151.

economic times worsened, from mid-century, women were squeezed by nervous guildsmen into limited and marginal opportunities.[190] In Wells the timing was somewhat different. Certainly, labour was in short supply after the plague, encouraging women's increased immigration and participation.[191] But, despite an economy which was less than robust for much of the fifteenth century, starting in the 1420s and 1430s, women's decline in the trades of Wells came more gradually. Women were being accepted as apprentices there at least until the 1480s, after which their participation declined.[192] The difference between Wells and the northern cities may in part have been the resurgence of the Wells economy in the 1460s and 1470s. But perhaps more important still was the fact that the men of Wells were not organized into craft-guilds at this time. There were therefore no specific groups to eliminate the women's role when work became harder to get. From the employers' point of view, women were still a cheaper source of labour in an economy that was having trouble attracting and keeping employees.

Other women found an increased freedom and responsibility in widowhood. To do so, they had to be financially secure. Some made their widowhood and chastity a religious fact. Elizabeth Biccomb made a religious vow of chastity.[193] Others, like Isabel Tanner and Margery Moniers, achieved secular influence and respect in the Community. Born a serf and not freed until 1393, years after her marriage, Isabel Tanner became one of the town's most prominent women.[194] She spent her last years executing the many charitable works and foundations upon which she and her dead husband, Thomas Tanner, had decided to spend much of their wealth. Many of the decisions about which religious houses they favoured were probably hers. His will, for instance, did not specify that the Carthusians were to receive as much as they did. They

[190] Goldberg, 'Female Labour', 35–6; and 'Women in Town Life', 122; Martha C. Howell, 'Women, the Family Economy, and the Structures of Market Production in Cities of Northern Europe during the Later Middle Ages', in Hanawalt (ed.), *Women and Work* 198–222; and Swanson, 'The Illusion of Structure', 29–48.

[191] See above, Ch. 3, sect. 5.

[192] CBII: 98 (1474), 146 (1485), 147 (1485), 154 (1487); and above, Ch. 3, sect. 5. These few women apprentices are only a small fraction of the total, visible only because of a change in the Borough Community's admission rules. The last reference to admission on account of marrying a woman apprentice was in 1487.

[193] SRO DD/B, Reg. 6: 235; see below, Ch. 8, sect. 8.

[194] *CPR 1399–1401*: 53–4 (1399).

received gifts to Henton and Wytham Priories of over 100 acres of land as well as some urban property.[195] Indeed, his will did not mention the chantry which was established in his name, nor the concomitant relief of the poor.[196] These, too, may have been Isabel's ideas as well as her work.

Margery Moniers lived in the mid-fourteenth century, and she may have been the greatest lay landlord in Wells at that time. In the 1340s she inherited the lands of her father, Thomas Testwood.[197] He, in his turn, had been one of the town's richest men, according to the lay subsidy of 1327.[198] She then married the immigrant merchant of Amiens, Peter Moniers.[199] He was active in the service of the Earl of Salisbury, and was one of the men of quick action who fostered the local cloth industry and saw to the export of cloth in the 1330s and 1340s.[200] He was dead by the early 1350s, and his wife also inherited his numerous properties.[201] We find her in control of a large part of the city's property, including an entire street that her husband had developed and which was sold for £155 6s. 8d. in 1369.[202] But the most striking proof of her importance, and of an influence at which we can only wonder, is that when the era's greatest burgess, Walter Compton, died in 1363, he made Margery an executor of his long will, steward of his great wealth.[203] He had a widow, yet she was not so favoured. Widows were frequently executors, but I know of no other woman who was given such a charge by another man, let alone a man of Compton's stature.

---

[195] *CPR 1405–8*: 370 (1407), and *CPR 1408–13*: 48 (1409); Tanner's will, proved 1401, does include other gifts to these houses: *SMWI*: 6–8.

[196] *SMWI*: 6–8; and WCC 16.

[197] WTD 142 names her as her father's executrix.

[198] *Kirkby's Quest for Somerset, etc.*, ed. F. H. Dickinson, SRS 3 (1889), 272; *CPR 1343–5*: 571, outlines his impressive religious arrangements, which included 25 chaplains saying mass; RI: 246[d] suggests his importance in the Borough Community; *Parliamentary Writs and Writs of Military Summons: Edward I and Edward II*, ed. Francis Palgrave (London, 1827–34), ii. 269; and *Accounts and Papers 17*, i. *Members of Parliament*, List and Index Society (1878), show that he was member of Parliament 4 times in the 1320s and 1330s.

[199] *CPR 1327–30*: 16.

[200] *CPR 1338–40*: 462.

[201] WCAC 324 (1352); SRO DD/B, Reg. 2: 401.

[202] WCAC 371 and 378; Margery had sold it in 1366 (WCAC 381) for at least £100; for other property transactions, see WCAC 324 (1352), 336, 340, and 368; WTD 155 and 178; the last transaction took place in 1387. See A. J. Scrase, 'Peter Monier and His Lane', forthcoming.

[203] WTD 141.

These were extraordinary women, extraordinarily lucky. For the most part, women were considered as members of a household. They were essential in the economy, playing a large role. But they were marginal labour. When the economy no longer needed as much labour, women were pushed into less attractive, simpler work, the sort that is hidden within the household or beneath the concern of most records.

6. CONCLUSION

This chapter has tried to complete the social world of later medieval Wells. It has failed to do so. We have had too little to say of several groups, although they may have fitted into one or another of our major categories of society. The lesser members of the family and household—the children and the domestic servants—have been neglected. Of necessity, we have had to pass over many important social topics. The dynamism of family life—marriage, death, and birth—has only been obliquely mentioned. Unfortunately, the Wells evidence (like that of most English towns before 1500) will not reply to some of the most important questions that historians want to ask.

This said, we have made important additions to the world of the burgesses. They can now be seen in their essential and dynamic relationships with the foreigners from whose ranks most of them came, and in relation to the poor. Burgesses, we have argued, could be poor; foreigners rich. A significant minority of outsiders would one day succeed in joining the civic élite, that is, the Borough Community. But the great majority remained socially and economically humble, if not impoverished. In this respect, too, many burgesses were no better off than these foreigners. For a large proportion of the foreigners and some of the burgesses, especially widows, poverty was a stage of life closely connected to old age or sickness.

In so far as it was a community problem, the town and the cathedral took steps to succour their poor. But the relief of poverty, was in most cases, a private affair, hidden from the records. Religious charity was significant but insufficient and disorganized, catering to the needs of the donor rather than of the beneficiaries, a wandering mass rather than the community. In the almshouse the later medieval city found its inadequate but helpful response to poverty. It allowed the town to provide some protection for its own; and because these paupers were their own—neighbours, if not friends or relatives—the entire community responded and supported the almshouse. But the suggestion remains, that the outsiders who approached for alms, especially at the great religious distributions, were not so welcome. Nevertheless, it should be stressed that there is no evidence from Wells of any by-laws to drive vagabonds and other unemployed wanderers or beggars from the city. These more extreme actions belong, along with more concerted schemes of poor relief, to the sixteenth century, to early modern civilization.

8

The Culture of the Church

By the later Middle Ages there was a view articulated by Ockham and, later, Erasmus, among others, that two Churches existed within the one: the Church as an institution, with policies, religious and administrative servitors, and political battles; and the church as the community of the faithful.[1] It would be fair to say that in the last one hundred years historians have been mainly concerned with the first Church.[2] Indeed, whatever interest there was in the early part of the century for the church of the people, had mainly disappeared by 1920.[3] It is only lately that the popular Church has once again become a main subject of enquiry.

A fashion in research should never be deplored. That which dominated the period 1920–75 has produced a great amount of important information. The place of the Church in the national polity has emerged clearly. The nature of parishes, the ecclesiastical hierarchy, the relation of prelates to the government, the provision of clergy, the religious orders, ecclesiastical finances, as well as the ideas by which churchmen lived, and over which they worried, have

---

[1] David Knowles and Dimitri Obolensky, *The Middle Ages* (New York, 1968), 411; and Desiderius Erasmus, *Sileni Alcibiadis, Opera Omnia Desiderii Erasmii Roterodami*, ed. Felix Henimann and Em. Kienzle, ii. 5 (Amsterdam, 1981), 184, as quoted in Norman Tanner, *The Church in Late Medieval Norwich, 1370–1532* (Toronto, 1984), p. xv.

[2] See e.g.—to name only some of the best by, and about, Englishmen—F. Makower, *The Constitutional History and Constitution of the Church of England* (London, 1895); G. Barraclough, *Papal Provisions* (Oxford, 1935); W. A. Pantin, *The English Church in the Fourteenth Century* (Cambridge, 1955); M. D. Knowles, *The Religious Orders in England*, 3 vols. (Cambridge, 1948–59); A. Hamilton Thompson, *The English Clergy and their Organization in the Later Middle Ages* (Oxford, 1947); Kathleen Edwards, *The English Secular Cathedrals in the Middle Ages* (Manchester, 1949); R. W. Southern, *Western Society and the Church in the Middle Ages* (Harmondsworth, 1970); and Dorothy M. Owen, *Church and Society in Medieval Lincolnshire* (Lincoln, 1971). This is not to mention the many fine works of ecclesiastical biography and intellectual history which were written in this period.

[3] See esp. F. A. Gasquet, *Parish Life in Medieval England* (London, 1906), and the less sentimental, but more literary, B. L. Manning, *The People's Faith in the Time of Wyclif* (Cambridge 1919).

to a great extent become well-marked paths. It has made the process of building up Church history from the ground of the people, of the social world, a job more easily accomplished, although it has still not been easy.[4]

Trends have been easiest to establish in this area by examining the evidence of chantry and obituary donations and wills in those larger urban centres where they have survived in sizeable numbers.[5] But, in the case of a small town like Wells, it is all the more difficult to provide numerically useful results, or definitive trends. Others have pursued these questions where the soil is more fertile, the body of wills and pious foundations larger and more detailed.

What we can do for Wells is to approach the Church as a cultural fact—the greatest one of the era—and to outline how it impinged on and shaped the lives and expectations of the people of the later medieval city, to suggest the manifold, sometimes surprising, ways in which it made itself essential and forceful in their day-to-day lives and thoughts. To do this, we turn away from theology, from detailed discussions of purgatory or sin, and deal with the opportunities for life that the Church provided, and the structure that informed what Alexander Murray has called a 'simple religion to understand and to practise, both in observance and morals'.[6] Many matters of importance will be omitted or mentioned only in passing, but an idea of how the Church and the townspeople were wed together, of how the second Church, the Church of the people, was a true church, may emerge in incomplete outline.

[4] First mention deserves to go to Francis Rapp, *L'Église et la vie religieuse en occident à la fin du Moyen Âge* (Paris, 1971). Other notable works include John Bossy, *Christianity in the West, 1400–1700* (Oxford, 1985); J. J. Scarisbrick, *The Reformation and the English People* (Oxford, 1984); Clive Burgess, ' "For the Increase of Divine Service": Chantries in the Parish in Late Medieval Bristol', *JEH* 36 (1985), 46–65; id., ' "A Fond Thing Vainly Invented": An Essay on Purgatory and Pious Motive in Later Medieval England', in. S. J. Wright, (ed.), *Parish, Church, and People* (London, 1988), 56–84; and id., ' "By Quick and by Dead": Wills and Pious Provision in Late Medieval Bristol', *English Historical Review* 92 (1987), 837–58; Caroline Barron, 'The Parish Fraternities of Medieval London', in C. Barron and Christopher Harper-Bill (eds.), *The Church in Pre-Reformation Society* (Woodbridge, 1985).

[5] See the articles by Burgess, cited above, n. 4; J. A. F. Thomson, 'Piety and Charity in Late Medieval London', *JEH* 16 (1965), 178–95; R. B. Dobson, 'The Foundation of Perpetual Chantries by the Citizens of Medieval York', in G. J. Cuming (ed.), *Studies in Church History*, iv (London, 1967), 22–38; Joel Rosenthal, *The Purchase of Paradise* (London, 1972) concentrates on nobles' chantries.

[6] Alexander Murray 'Religion among the Poor in Thirteenth-Century France', *Traditio* 30 (1974), 317.

I. THE CATHEDRAL

The internal religious life of the cathedral of St Andrew is not within our scope here. Fascinating though it is, its complexity demands fuller treatment than it can be given, and its relationship to the town is too obscure to warrant the space. The very question of who could generally be found praying in a cathedral church is not very clear.[7] We have already noted, in passing, the impact that the great church had on the size of Wells, and the very positive contribution that it made to the town's economy. What must be added here is a small point about its role in society, lest the facts of legal and physical separation from the borough mislead us as to the true state of affairs.

The churchmen were in fact a very prominent, visible feature of town life. Social interaction between lay and clergy was of a high order. Most of the clergy of Wells lived in the town, or at least in private houses in the cathedral liberty. We find them heavily involved in the property market with burgesses,[8] and the cathedral itself was one of the town's greatest landlords and often had laypeople as tenants.[9] The cathedral records make it very clear that it was not uncommon for the taverns and women of the town (married or not) to exert a definite influence on cathedral vicars, offering alcohol, sex, or simple company.[10] Nor was it easy to keep the businessmen outside the cathedral, when business was their only reason for being there.[11] There was a sharp legal division between the churchmen and the laypeople, but the social life was quite richly intertwined, especially since the church was staffed by secular priests with good incomes which needed spending. The cultural life of the town was certainly stimulated and enriched by their presence.

Bearing this in mind as the background of cultural diffusion and social interaction, I want to concentrate here on the church of the lay people, the place that it held in their lives. Naturally, this entails putting aside much interesting detail from the ecclesiastical records

[7] But see below, Ch. 8, sect. 5.

[8] e.g. WCAC 126, 341; WCC 107, 110, and 166.

[9] e.g. RI: 202^d., 252^d.; WCAC 354, 450, (vicars-choral), 730.

[10] e.g. RI: 64^d.–65, 70, RII: 61, 63, 65, and 67.

[11] Herbert E. Reynolds, (ed.), *Wells Cathedral: Its Foundation, Constitutional History and Statutes* (Leeds, 1881), 60; WCC 2.

in favour of continuing our pursuit of the profile of the lay community of a small town.

2. THE PARISH

In the most superficial terms, the church in the borough of Wells was simply organized. There was only one parish, St Cuthbert's, a parish so vast that it extended well beyond the city limits, reaching even beyond Wells Manor to contain other hamlets of Wells Hundred.[12] On an informal basis, St Cuthbert's was divided into an in- and an out-parish, the city and the country. Collections for the fabric account—say, when an aisle was being renovated—would be divided into two sections.[13] Nevertheless, it was essentially an urban parish. The churchwardens were officers entirely controlled by the burgesses of the city, and the majority of the parishioners were city people. In the one sphere of the lay church, this small English town held the kind of influence over the countryside that is more frequently met with in Italy or the Low Countries.

Moreover, we have already seen how the Borough Community's strength owed much to the fact that, through its control of the town's parish, it was able to develop considerable political authority.[14] The city of Wells grew most of all after the years of the proliferation of parishes. In the late twelfth and thirteenth centuries, when Wells grew larger, vested ecclesiastical interests were already in place to rebut any attempts to multiply parishes and to undermine their control and income.[15] There were no new parishes, no large religious houses or friaries, established in the town in the later Middle Ages. The only cracks in the cup of parish solidarity were the cathedral, the hospital of St John the Baptist, and the occasional private chapel, a luxury granted to only a

[12] See the useful collection of documents—some now lost—in Serel, *passim*; and, on the development of parishes generally in Europe, see G. W. O. Addleshaw, *The Development of the Parochial System from Charlemagne to Urban II* (London, 1948); id., the *Beginnings of the Parochial System*, 2nd edn. (York, 1959), 11–15; Susan Reynolds, *Kingdoms and Communities in Western Europe, 900–1300* (Oxford, 1984), 81–7; and Owen, *Church and Society*, 4–6.

[13] CBI: 178 (1409).

[14] See above, Ch. 4, sect. 3.

[15] Gervase Rosser, 'Communities of Parish and Guild in the Late Middle Ages', in Wright, (ed.), *Parish, Church, and People*, 33.

handful, generally older rich people too weak or sick to leave their houses.[16]

Since the twelfth century, the rector of St Cuthbert's had been the cathedral itself.[17] The chapter appointed a perpetual vicar, and his security of tenure may account for the fact that there never seems to have been any serious friction between the cathedral and the town over the parish church. Independent vicars helped to keep the cathedral at arm's length from the actual running of parish affairs. Both parish and cathedral lavished care on the buildings, and shouldered the great expenses involved in maintaining chancel and nave in splendid form.[18]

The only conflicts over the church developed between the cathedral and the vicars whom it appointed. Inevitably, the disputes were over the division of the revenues of the church.[19] In the 1390s the cathedral had been so upset by a series of headstrong and disobedient vicars that they had made arrangements for the installation of a removable priest rather than a perpetual vicar. The chapter never went through with the change, despite having the required papal consent.[20] Possibly, they yielded to an appeal from the town to preserve the status quo and a successful, relatively tranquil church. Despite their frequent difficulties with the bishop, the town remained on good terms with the cathedral throughout the Middle Ages.[21]

The later medieval parish church was very much a layman's church, increasingly so from 1200, and considerably more so than the parish church after the Reformation.[22] Responsibility for most

[16] For examples, see SRO DD/B, Reg. 2: 168; Reg. 6: 148 and 231; and *Register of John Stafford, Bishop of Bath and Wells, 1425–43*, ed. Thomas Scott Holmes, 2 vols., SRS 31–2 (1915–16), 113.

[17] RI: 31; and RII: 12 and 46.

[18] See above, Ch. 2, sect. 1, and CA, 1343–4, 1455–6, 1473–4; see Nikolaus Pevsner, *North Somerset and Bristol* (Harmondsworth, 1958), 323.

[19] RIII: 145[d].–147 (1356–7); RIII: 148–51 (1380–90s), RI: 286[d]. (1391–1420), and RIII: 162–4 (1436–7).

[20] RIII: 164.

[21] See above, Ch. 4.

[22] Scarisbrick, *Reformation*, 39, 164–8; Emma Mason, 'The Role of the English Parishioner, 1100–1500', *JEH* 27 (1976), 17–29, charts the rise of lay authority, esp. after 1300; Owen, *Church and Society*, 115–17; Gervase Rosser, 'The Essence of Medieval Urban Communities', *TRHS*, 5th ser., 34 (1984), 101–3; and id., 'Communities of Parish and Guild'; cf. *Churchwardens' Accounts of Croscombe, Pilton, Milton, etc.*, ed. E. Hobhouse, SRS 4 (1890); Tanner, *Norwich*, 16, certainly underestimates the lay people's importance because of the lack of churchwardens' accounts, which he assumes never existed. See also F. Pollock and F. W. Maitland,

of the fabric funds and repairs was the laity's, as was the supervision of chantry and altar endowments and of furnishings. Lay control in Wells reached into the provision and hiring of the staff of the church. Beyond the vicar, St Cuthbert's was served by parochial chaplains and chantry priests, most of whom were selected by the parish. In 1377 there were six chaplains and six clerks there.[23] On account of Wells's particular constitutional arrangement, this meant that the Borough Community—in effect, the master of the town—had the power to choose who served in these positions. This allowed a proportion of local men from both the city and the out-parish to be employed in their home town, as well as those who would win preferment from other sources.[24] The parishioners also appointed other minor officials such as the beadle.[25]

The authority that the laity wielded in the parish had to be backed up with money. The two inevitably went together in the medieval city. Churchwardens' accounts for the later Middle Ages are scarce. Parishes adjacent to St Cuthbert's are among the few from which accounts have survived, but only fragments of the Wells accounts exist.[26] These slim sources are augmented only by the occasional reference in the Community's record-books. Nevertheless, Wells's records are better than many. We have enough evidence to suggest that most of the money raised for the repairs and expansion of the church fabric—and the sums must have been considerable—came through the sort of voluntary donation that is still the mainstay of many parish churches.[27] Individuals and possibly the members of fraternities—to go by one somewhat obscure example—provided money and goods in time of need as well as on a regular basis.[28] The various altars of the church were adorned by gifts of fabrics or vessels of direct use to the chaplain and service. Other gifts—rings—were sold to raise cash.

The History of English Law before the Time of Edward II, 2nd edn. (Cambridge, 1911), 613–15; Thompson, *English Clergy*, 130; and Charles Drew, *Early Parochial Organization in Britain* (London, 1954).

   [23] PRO E179/4/1.
   [24] For examples of chantry grants, see CBI: 228, CBII: 105, 172. CBII: 165 shows the admission of a parish clerk by the Community.
   [25] CBII: 58–9, CBI: 240; and WCC 16.
   [26] *Churchwardens' Accounts*; WTA, 'Mr Goodall's Book'.
   [27] Goodall's Book, 32–7.
   [28] CBI: 16 notes a gift of 6s. 10d. from a certain 'societate'.

One of the interesting items to be discovered from the extant accounts is the way in which rings came to count as the basic 'currency' of the churchwardens. Rings do not feature as gifts to the church in any of the extant Wells wills, so we cannot be sure how the churchwardens acquired them. At any rate, at least a part of the parish's surplus was kept in this form. In 1440 the wardens presented their account to the master, saying that they had one gold ring and thirty-four silver rings, as well as sundry other metal vessels. The next year the wardens had thirty-seven silver rings in addition to the single gold band. The total went up until 1443–4, when four rings were used to purchase a silver arrow to adorn the weather-vane which crowned the church.[29] In the 1420s and 1430s, possibly before major repairs were undertaken, the number of rings held in a given year could be as high as 134.[30]

Whatever wealth the parish had, however, came mostly it would seem, from the bequests and gifts of individual parishioners, who gave of their own volition, as acts of piety. If the laity treated the church as if they owned it, it is no surprise. They appointed and paid for most of the ministering priests there, and they paid for the fabric of everything but the chancel. The pews, the lavish altar furnishings, the reredoses, the paintings, were all created and provided at the people's instigation, in so far as the people were represented by the Borough Community.[31] Through the parish, the laity played their greatest role in the government and direction of the church. They may only have been able to touch what seem like small matters—certainly to read the historical literature on the late medieval church—but, for the most part, these were the issues which touched them most as Christians, the things that they saw during mass, and the people whom they heard sing the service.

3. THE PARISH GUILDS

The fundamental business of saying mass was executed by the parish priest, the vicar, but a high proportion of the praying that took place in St Cuthbert's or any other parish church was more specialized. Everywhere, from the relatively small villages to the greatest cities of Europe, there were guilds whose main concern was

[29] Goodall's Book, 32–3.
[30] Ibid. 36–7.
[31] CBII: 266; Goodall's Book, 32–8; CBII: 89; and *SMWII*: 368.

to offer prayers with the specific purpose of benefiting their own members. The guilds, especially those with chantries and chantry priests, rounded out the routine of parish prayer. The parish's ability to accommodate this popular addition (guilds were not created by the church hierarchy or government, but by the laity) to the basic ecclesiastical structure was an important feature of the parochial system's own vitality and durability. The system was flexible.[32]

H. F. Westlake thought that the parish guilds of England were primarily religious organizations.[33] The guild ordinances that were collected in 1389 generally specify and emphasize this aspect, especially the desire to establish a corporation of prayer.[34] Supporting Westlake, Professor Scarisbrick has lately called the fraternities 'poor men's chantries'.[35] While there were certainly other elements to the guilds,[36] at heart they were very much religious clubs, and each of their useful functions—aid in times of hardship, or the return of a deceased member's body, as well as prayer—was simply a different expression of later medieval religion.[37]

We cannot be sure that we know of all the different fraternities which met in Wells during the later Middle Ages. The number must have fluctuated; new associations appeared to replace earlier guilds, following to some extent the fashion for a particular cult. Since most of the fraternities of which we are aware owned some property, it is a safe surmise that many others, like a large group recorded in the 1389 national guild returns, possessed no real property, and must elude historical enquiry.[38] There were about

[32] Cf. Rosser, 'Communities of Parish and Guild', 32–3 and *passim* on the nature of the guilds.

[33] H. F. Westlake, *The Parish Gilds of Medieval England* (Oxford, 1919), 43–4.

[34] L. Toulmin Smith (ed.), *The English Gilds*, EETS 40 (1870), *passim*.

[35] Scarisbrick, *Reformation*, 20.

[36] Others have argued that they were mainly burial societies or aid organizations for hard times, see Toulmin Smith (ed.), *English Gilds*, pp. xxviii–xxix; Gasquet, *Parish Life*, 256, calls them 'the benefit societies and provident associations of the Middle Ages'. Miri Rubin, *Charity and Community in Medieval Cambridge* (Cambridge, 1987), 254–5, has pointed out how frequently the element of charity in times of hardship was a component of urban fraternities; cf. Richard Mackenney, *Tradesmen and Traders* (London, 1987), 47 and 61–4.

[37] Barron, 'Parish Fraternities', 23–5, places the burial function to the fore again, persuasively, and not to the exclusion of other elements.

[38] Toulmin Smith (ed.), *English Gilds*, 14–42 and 45–109, notes 12 in Norwich and 26 in Lynn; while Gottfried, 188, notes 10 parish guilds in Bury St Edmunds in the 14th cent.

eleven fraternities in Wells towards the end of the fifteenth century, and probably the same number a hundred years earlier.[39]

But the guilds were numerous, considering the size of the city, and some were even of impressive prominence. Without doubt, their numbers grew after 1400, but at least some of them had their *recorded* beginnings earlier. The adoration of Mary was observed regularly from at least the late thirteenth century,[40] and this guild was to stand with the politically significant Trinity guild as one of the city's pre-eminent religious associations.[41] Around the same time, regular, privately supported devotions were being held at St Leonard's altar.[42] By the fourteenth century the fraternities of the Holy Trinity, St James, and Corpus Christi had been established.[43] In the fifteenth century we can add fraternities and guild services devoted to St John the Baptist, the Jesus mass, St George, and St Erasmus.[44] There is early sixteenth-century evidence to suggest the existence of fraternities devoted to St Anne and St Nicholas, but we do not know when they were founded.[45]

We have only some fragments by which to convey the place of these guilds in their members' lives. It was concern for the eternal soul and for the souls of all the Christian dead which seems to have prompted the greatest generosity and commitment to the guilds. We can see this best in the great donations that several wealthy burgesses gave to their guilds and to the altar that they supported. Thomas Tanner to the Mary guild, Nicholas Cristesham and John Roper to St James's, unnamed or numerous donors to the Trinity and St John the Baptist guilds—these people all provided their guilds with properties to support permanent chaplains or chantry priests.[46] But, for every such large grant, there were dozens of lesser ones, and, more importantly and invisibly, hundreds or thousands of masses said and attended by the members of the guild.

[39] See the civic election returns at the end of the cent. and into the 16th cent.: CBII: 223, 227, 235, 238, 286.

[40] WTD 23. In this and other cases it is difficult, and perhaps impossible, to know whether the established and endowed worship at a particular altar inevitably indicates the existence of a corresponding fraternity. I suspect it does. Chantry and fraternity were certainly used as overlapping terms in the Wells records.

[41] Trinity guild proctors often went on to high office.

[42] WTD 23.

[43] CBI: 298; WTD 141, 124.

[44] CBI: 250 (St John the Baptist, a guild which may have begun much earlier); SRO DD/B, Reg. 6: 232 (St Erasmus); CBII: 36 (St George), 155 (Jesus mass). See Westlake, *Parish Gilds*, 120–7, on dedications of guilds.

[45] CBII: 275 (1513).

[46] WCC 16 (Tanner's St Mary's bequest); and CBI: 228 (St James's benefactors).

Guild membership was broad. Women, possibly the backbone of late medieval lay religion, were prominent donors to, and, we can assume, frequenters of, a guild's services. The fraternity of Mary was particularly popular with the town's women.[47] Its inventories list only a handful of donors by name, but there were more women than men. This was also the case at St Catherine's altar.[48] Women were notable participants of other guilds, too, including that of St John the Baptist and the Trinity.[49] They gave money for obituary prayers,[50] simple furnishings like napkins and tablecloths, and more elaborate and expensive items, like the set of vestments that Agnes Forfall gave to the St John the Baptist guild altar.[51]

At least some clergy joined these essentially lay organizations. The priests who served as chaplains were, naturally, devoted members. Some, like Master John Blakedon, went so far as to purchase an eighty-year share of prayers at the Trinity chantry after his death.[52] But it is difficult, on the evidence that we have, to say who else belonged to the guilds and how many of them there were. The prominent men and women of the town were involved, of course; they were conspicuous in the Trinity guild, and most of the other guilds too.[53] Nevertheless, Wells provides little evidence for the breadth of participation. There is no sign, for instance, that the guilds of Wells attracted or invited the high-profile member-ship—kings, lords, and abbots even—of the great civic guilds of Coventry, Ludlow, or Boston, and as little to suggest that the local rural gentry were invited to play such a role.

One of the most tantalizing gaps in Wells history involves the Trinity guild. We only know enough about it to be sure that it had a special place in the town, especially with relation to the Borough Community. The Trinity is mentioned in the 1437 constitutional document as the Borough Community's patron, 'in whose name the

[47] Mary was the favourite saint of the various Maidens guilds to be found across the country: Westlake, *Parish Gilds*, 61.

[48] Goodall's Book, 33–7.

[49] Ibid.

[50] e.g. Lucy Lundreys in 1298, and Johanna Dryxon in 1510: RI: 128; and CBII: 260.

[51] Goodall's Book, 33–4 and 38.

[52] CBII: 206 (1498).

[53] See *SMWI*: 6, 26–7, 354, 369–70, and *SMWII*: 159, 200, 227. Wills are probably a poor indicator of guild membership, since a rich man who was already a long-standing member would be included in the guild's prayers anyway. He could best expand prayers for his soul by hiring another chaplain.

said burgesses and fraternitie be founded'.[54] It is possible that it was the parish guild which had provided the basis for the civic organization of the Borough Community. However, this is pure speculation. The first mention of the guild is only in 1363, by which time it was plainly already established. It would seem to be a purely religious guild, fostered and supported by the Borough Community. Its membership very probably mirrored that of the Borough Community, including their families. Its proctors were selected by the master of the town, so we can be sure that it was subordinate to the Borough Community, and not an élite guild which dominated the broader Community.[55] A document dated 1380 refers to the master of the town as the 'conservator' of the Trinity guild.[56] Its privileged and prominent place among the parish guilds is easily established. The proctors of this guild are mentioned regularly in the election lists of the Community long before the records of other guilds are included. And the Trinity guild had its own chaplain throughout the later fourteenth and fifteenth centuries. The lavish church work being executed in 1419 was the construction or refurbishment of the Trinity chantry, and this was apparently financed by the Borough Community as a whole.[57] Furthermore, the guild was the only association in the town, aside from the Borough Community, which had any significant property.[58] In addition, it had the most impressive altar goods. In 1446 these included various vestments of colourful, fine cloth, two silver candelabras enriched with gold, two gilt bowls, a missal with a silver clasp, another old missal, two silver cruets, and altar cloths. One of the altar cloths was appropriately decorated with 'an image of the Holy Trinity', while some curtains bore images of golden leopards. For the under-frontal of the altar, there was a cloth embroidered with a picture of the assumption of the Virgin.[59]

The Trinity guild was especially important to the Community, and was therefore well endowed and somewhat better recorded. Thus the picture that we are given of its activities and property

---

54 Serel, 37.
55 Ibid. 38; and the elections noted regularly from 1473.
56 WTD 168.
57 CBI: 220.
58 AH 92; CBI: 262, CBII: 132, 192, 195, 210, and 226.
59 Goodall's Book, 35–6.

suggests, a little more vividly at least, the potential activities and importance of all parish guilds.

4. CHANTRY AND COMMUNITY

As we have seen, the strength and wealth of many of the guilds, certainly those which were most prominent, owed much to the large endowments of individuals. Priests were employed on a regular, even permanent, basis to pray, to conduct services in memory of, and for, the future of the founder, usually with some members of his family and possibly some others, but inevitably they included all the faithful dead in their prayers.[60] There seem to have been at least four chantry priests at St Cuthbert's in the later Middle Ages.[61] At the cathedral, there were even more, eighteen by 1487, funded by some of the bishops and canons who had served the church.[62]

It has been argued that chantries did little for anyone but the founder, that they were simply an 'institutionalized form of private spiritual succour', possessing very little value for anyone else except the priests and artists hired to serve and adorn.[63] Such a picture does not do the institution justice, but it is an understandable mistake. The foundation grants make it extraordinarily clear—especially those of the nobility and gentry outside the towns—that the establishment of a chantry was in great part concerned with the soul of the founder. From this perspective, one can understand why Wood-Legh concluded that the process of establishing chantries and of multiplying masses seemed to reduce the spiritual to the merely material.[64]

But such a picture fails to place the chantry in its context, in the world that the benefactor knew and took for granted. The urban chantry was, at its heart, a provision for prayer, but the services at which these prayers were held were by no means private, a lone

---

[60] Burgess, ' "A Fond Thing Vainly Invented" ', 66–9.

[61] *The Survey and Rental of the Chantries, Colleges and Free Chapels, etc.*, ed. Emanuel Green, SRS 2 (1888), 153–5, notes only 3 chantry priests, calling them Trinity priests, mere chaplains who served without an endowed foundation. It would appear that the St James chantry had disappeared. John Welshot's desire to establish a chantry in 1519 seems to have come to nought (*SMWII*: 200–1).

[62] Reynolds (ed.), *Wells Cathedral*, 240[a].

[63] Rosenthal, *Purchase of Paradise*, 37.

[64] K. L. Wood-Legh, *Perpetual Chantries in Britain* (Cambridge, 1965), 312.

priest singing for a long-dead rich man. They were, as Clive Burgess has shown for Bristol,[65] 'increases in a divine service' which, we have to believe, was much sought after and generally well attended by people from the city. There is no question that people attended these services in Wells, guild members and others. It was fairly common for the founder to direct the chantry priest or the stipendiary chaplain to speak to the congregation of the chapel before beginning his service, to tell them *in English* for whom they should pray. William Gascoigne's provision for prayer at the hospital of St Saviour (the almshouse) directed the chaplain to say to the attending people:

ye shall pray for the good estate of the kynge, peas and prosperite of this reame, William Gascoigne of Wells and Johane his wife, Hugh Kene and Auneys his wife, the dean and chapter of Wells and the maister and cominalte of Welles . . . her fadre and moder soules, brether and suster soules and all the good doers soules of this place, and all cristen soules.

He also asked them to say the Hail Mary and the Lord's Prayer.[66] The donors wanted the prayers of the people, the people were anxious for the occasion to pray, and prayer and the experience of the mass or a *dirige* were plainly thought to gain something from each other. The Hail Mary and the Lord's Prayer were the hallmarks of the common person's devotion, although many of the laity were capable of much more than this minimum.[67]

The quality of religious services in the city was also improved by the provisions which brought new priests to the church. All the priests of St Cuthbert's, from the vicar himself, who was often a cathedral canon, to the parochial chaplains and chantry priests were required to be in attendance, singing, at every regular parish mass.[68] On Saturdays—when the civic Lady mass was held—and Sundays in fifteenth-century Wells the choir was filled by a choir indeed, about eight voices strong.

[65] 'Increase of Service', 46–65; Wood-Legh, *Perpetual Chantries*, 294, did note the place of popular participation in the chantry services.

[66] CCR 1441: 403; and AH 178; cf. Wood-Legh, *Perpetual Chantries*, 294.

[67] Manning, *People's Faith*, 42–5 and 44 n. 4; and Murray, 'Religion among the Poor', 298; for an idea of superior lay attainments, see D. L. D'Avray, *The Preaching of the Friars* (Oxford, 1985), 29–42.

[68] Burgess, 'Increase of Service', 54–9, has stressed the effect that chantry priests and anniversary chaplains had on the music of the churches. Wood-Legh, *Perpetual Chantries*, 176–7, discusses the musical qualifications and support of the parish choirs.

The establishment of chantries by the burgesses of Wells came at about the same time as in other towns, mainly in the fourteenth and early fifteenth centuries—although there was at least an attempt to establish one as late as 1519[69]—but not on so great a scale as in some of the large centres.[70] To Wells's five or six burgess foundations, York had about a hundred.[71] The clerical poll tax of 1377 shows that there were already seven chaplains attached to St Cuthbert's church in addition to the vicar.[72] From the middle years of the fifteenth century the economy and population of the town were in deep depression.[73] Under these circumstances, the community did not really need, nor could it afford, several new chantries. Individuals, however, were still concerned to put their money to work to lighten purgatorial punishment by the expression of their repentance.

Most, but not all, *post mortem* endowments by burgesses went to the parish church. Yearly memorial services (obits) were established by burgesses in the cathedral and in the chapel of the small hospital of St John the Baptist.[74] This is not to mention those endowments for prayer which some burgesses set up outside Wells, in various charterhouses and convents.[75] The provision of short- and long-term intercessory services continued here as it did in York and Bristol and across England, albeit on a somewhat more modest scale. For example, Henry Goddislond's will of 1473 provided eight marks for a chaplain to pray for his soul and those of his parents and benefactors.[76] In 1482 Walter Baker's (alias Smith) will

[69] John Welshot's will asks for a priest to pray at St Erasmus's altar (*SMWII*: 200–1).

[70] Cf. Dobson, 'Foundation of Chantries', 24–5, 32; for London's 200+ chantries, see *Valor Ecclesiasticus Temp. Henrici VIII*, ed. John Caley and Joseph Hunter, 6 vols. (London, 1810–34), i. 367–9 and 378–84; Burgess, ' "By Quick and by Dead" ', 840–55; Norwich, however, seems on the whole commensurable with Wells, having relatively few chantries endowed by burgesses between 1370 and 1500: Tanner, *Norwich*, 92–8 and app. 10, 212–19; see also Thomson, 'Piety and Charity', 178–95; Peter Heath, 'Urban Piety in the Later Middle Ages: The evidence of Hull Wills', in R. B. Dobson (ed.), *The Church, Politics and Patronage in the Fifteenth Century*, (Gloucester, 1984), 219–20.

[71] Dobson, 'Foundation of Chantries', 24–5.

[72] PRO E179/4/1.

[73] See above, Chs. 2, sects. 3–5, and 3, sect. 6.

[74] CPR 1343–5: 571; WCAC 396, 473, 709; RI: 105[d]., 128, 162, 265; SRO/B, Reg. 1: 255[b].

[75] e.g. Isabel Tanner's pious bequests on behalf of her husband: *Register of Nicholas Bubwith, Bishop of Bath and Wells, 1407–24*, ed. Thomas Scott Holmes, 2 vols., SRS 29–30 (1914), 86; WCC 16; CPR 1408–23: 348.

[76] WCAC 695.

asked his wife Isabel to find a priest to pray at St Nicholas's altar in the parish church for a year.[77] In John Coker's will, written in 1501, the failure of his heirs to produce children was to have triggered the establishment of a perpetual daily mass in the cathedral.[78] There were certainly many smaller donations offered to those celebrating daily mass in the cathedral and parish churches. Other richer burgesses who died in the early sixteenth century, such as Thomas Aphowell, John Tyler, and William Frampton, also left post-obit religious bequests which were substantial, if not on the scale of the early chantry founders.[79] Those wills that survive continue to include post-obituary pious provisions, but there was less money available for distribution than there had been at the end of the fourteenth century. The change was probably forced on the burgesses by economy rather than by a shift in their commitment to the intercessory prayer as a form of religious life.[80]

5. Prayer

We have already noted many of the arrangements and occasions—chantries and fraternities, in addition to basic parish worship—for prayer. But we need to look a little more closely at which prayers were said, which causes and individuals were deemed worthy of such attention.

The chantry and anniversary priests prayed for those whose primary concerns were their own souls. Frequently, however, as we have seen, they included relatives, especially spouses and parents, and their benefactors in these prayers;[81] those at the almshouse and in the cathedral mentioned a great many of the benefactors to their respective institutions. The almshouse records include simple documents which directed the almspeople, in a form similar to the

---

[77] *SMWI*: 237–8.

[78] *SMWII*: 17.

[79] *SMWII*: 36, 159, 227, respectively 1503, 1519, 1526.

[80] Dobson, 'Foundation of Chantries', 35–6. I have decided, in the face of the great body of work now available on memorial arrangements, not to detail more than a few of Wells's anniversaries, obits, and chantries. The number of extant wills is simply too small—about two dozen—to add a great deal to the much-better documented studies mentioned above, n. 5.

[81] See above, p. 267.

following example, thus: 'Yowe shall pray for the sowles of Thomas Jury and Crystyne hys wyffe, Jone hys daughter, all hys chyldryn sowlys, and for all crystyin sowlys.'[82]

But the Church also encouraged people to pray as individuals in their daily lives as Christians, not only to look to prayers for themselves and their families in death. Of course, the laity knew, and were encouraged when attending mass to say, the Lord's Prayer and the Hail Mary.[83] But the Church and the Crown also sought prayers from their congregations for more specific causes. In 1335, for instance, Edward III wrote to the bishop of Wells asking for the prayers of the clergy and people of the diocese (*clerum et populum*) so that the army's Scottish campaign would have better prospects of success.[84] His son, Richard II, also asked for prayers, masses, and processions of priests and people of the diocese in 1394, when he embarked with his army for Ireland.[85] Bishop Bekynton asked for prayers (including the Lord's Prayer and the Hail Mary), processions, and masses in the cathedral and parish churches in April 1447. These devotions were aimed in part at putting an end to the floods, storms, and wild and unhealthy weather that were threatening the planting season and, later, the harvest.[86]

There were also rituals of private prayer for the devout soul. The document outlining a regime of lay devotion which was published by W. A. Pantin says so much that one suspects, but can never prove, to have been prevalent.[87] Public prayer was, of course, important. We have seen that people attended chantry and guild services in the parish church. Probably townspeople as well as travellers attended some of the services in the cathedral. When Bekynton consecrated his tomb in the early hours of 13 January 1452, and, two days later, held the inaugural service of his chantry—fifteen years before his death—it was attended by 'very many other men and women', plainly laypeople, besides some of the cathedral clergy.[88] We know that the town councillors and the city officials were regular attenders at the parish church. They

---

[82] AH 282 and 283.
[83] See below, n. 87, for details of devout lay practice.
[84] SRO DD/B, Reg. 2: 125.
[85] CCR 1392–6: 28.
[86] SRO DD/B, Reg. 6: 60.
[87] W. A. Pantin, 'Instructions for a Devout and Literate Layman', in J. J. G. Alexander and M. T. Gibson (eds.), *Medieval Learning and Literature*, (Oxford, 1976), 398–422.
[88] SRO DD/B, Reg. 6: 237.

were expected to accompany the master when he followed the ministering priest from the church at the end of mass on Saturdays and feast-days.[89] Furthermore, there was, it seems, a large demand for any available pews in the church. An ordinance of December 1511 stipulated that no one was to have more than one seat or pew in the church, and that 'the residue shall be yielded up to the churchwardens . . . to sell them to such honest persons that have no seats'.[90] Town councillors had to give up their own pews when they were elected to take their place in those of the Borough Community.[91] The impression is one of a high level of church attendance and prayer. Norman Tanner speaks of 'considerable absenteeism' in Norwich, but he can find only nine people who were accused of not attending their parish church in a 1492 visitation.[92] In a city the size of Norwich (it had a tax assessment in 1524 that was twelve times the size of Wells's), this seems quite *inconsiderable*.[93] A similar proportion could probably be found in church in Wells, which seems to me to represent a very high level of attendance in an era with relatively little coercion to be present.

6. ALMS: THE GIVING

Alms and desperately needed hospitality were a great part of Church life, especially from the sixth to the tenth centuries, before the great expansion of the European economy in the eleventh and twelfth centuries.[94] There is no doubt that, by the time we reach the period under discussion here, there had been a sharp decline in almsgiving by the churches themselves, the monasteries in particular. At the same time, however, a greater number of laypeople were able and willing—for religious reasons (and growing need)—to aid and succour the poor.[95]

[89] CBII: 251, 266, and 567.

[90] CBII: 567.

[91] CBII: 567, dated 1511, but referring to the council's traditional seating arrangements, reflected also in CBII: 251 (1508).

[92] Tanner, *Norwich*, 9, 180, 183, 185, and 187.

[93] *Coventry*, 12 where Norwich is estimated to have had over 10,000 people in 1524, possibly 10 times as many as Wells.

[94] See above, Ch. 7, sects. 3–4, for a full discussion of the poor, and the scale and effect of alms in Wells. On its European development, see Michel Mollat, *Les Pauvres au Moyen Âge* (Paris, 1978), 53–72, 121–7.

[95] Ibid. 165–6.

The main reason for this was the doctrine of charity, of loving one's neighbour, which stood at the centre of religious thinking and acting.[96] But almsgiving also met a great and obvious social function: wealth was directed where it was needed most direly. Furthermore, the poor were kept in contact with the rich, an important social fact in a small community. As we have seen, medieval support was inadequate as a welfare system.[97] In great part this is because the Church was practising charity rather than relief. Nevertheless, the culture of the Church suffused the society, cemented it, and alms was one of the ways in which it achieved this.

The nature of the records forces us to focus on extraordinary almsgiving rather than on the ordinary sort, when people gave at their front doors. But we must bear in mind, as the churchmen always wrote and the preachers proclaimed, that there was no more religious validity, no more efficacy, in these gifts of the rich.[98] Rather the opposite: a rich man could no more go to heaven than a camel pass through the eye of a needle; and a merchant, said Gratian, could only rarely please God.[99]

Most of the acts of charity which are recorded are connected with funerary arrangements. Almsgiving in these cases was but another means for the rich man to try to please God by good works. His interest—regardless of the effect of his act—was not in poor relief *per se*. Often the attendance of the poor at the funeral itself was encouraged, because their prayers were thought to be purer, untainted by lives spent in the pursuit of riches. The merchant Richard Gros willed a penny or a penny loaf to any poor person who would attend his funeral in 1407. In future years the anniversary was to be marked with similar distributions to the infirm who lay in the hospital of St John the Baptist.[100] Edward Curtis made another such provision for the poor who attended his funeral service in 1413.[101]

Such examples highlight another facet of the Church's culture: its effect as a maker of social cohesion. In the medieval city there was something that the poor could do for the rich: they could pray for

---

[96] Rubin, *Charity and Community*, 54–92.
[97] See above, Ch. 7, sect. 4.
[98] See Rubin, *Charity and Community*, 83–7.
[99] Quoted ibid. 84, which does not cite the page of original; see ibid., 83–7, for a discussion of prevailing ideas on the alms of the rich.
[100] *SMWII*: 25–7.
[101] *SMWI*: 64–6.

them, contribute to the reduction of their purgatorial suffering. All
the rich man could do was ease the poor person's present, the pangs
of hunger; and, from a religious point of view, the important issue
of life was elsewhere, the eternity after death. In this context, the
poor man could provide much-needed support for the rich. Thus
institutions like the Wells almshouse were established not merely to
make the lives of twenty-four poor people easier, but to provide an
outlet for sincere, efficacious prayer for the souls of various
bishops, canons, burgesses, and their families.[102]

Relief of the poor and the sick was only one form of donation or
charity which was encouraged and organized by the Church. The
breadth of such projects underlines as well as anything the way in
which the Church embraced and informed secular society. This is
best seen by looking at some of the licences to seek alms and the
grants of indulgences which were issued by the bishops of Bath.
These documents, recorded in the bishops' registers, are a rich
source for anyone interested in seeing which subjects were thought
worthy of support, to which appeals people were likely to respond.
They record the changing fashion and needs of the later medieval
Church and society.[103]

Indulgences from penance were offered in return for aid to causes
which, to a modern way of thinking, were purely secular. It forces
us to expand our notion of the Church and religion when we see
that money given to the man who kept a Bristol public street in
good repair was worth forty days' indulgence from penance for the
people of the diocese.[104] In fact, the keeping of such a road or a
bridge was frequently an organ by which an illiterate man might
practise his religious vocation. Hermits helped to keep the public
ways, and were sanctioned to do so by the bishop.[105]

Most of the charity requested by the itinerant representatives to
Wells was for more clearly 'religious' purposes. First and foremost
were the contributions sought for the fraternity of St Andrew, the
diocese-wide guild whose sole function was to raise money for the
cathedral church.[106] Almost every other charitable need was

[102] AH 172.

[103] I do not know how common the recording of these licences was, but I hope to
investigate this practice more fully in future work.

[104] SRO DD/B, Reg. 6: 34 (1445).

[105] On hermits, see below Ch. 8, sect. 8 and n. 144.

[106] *Reg. Bubwith*, 220–2; RI: 143, 168, and 182[d].; WCAC 464, 625, and 717;
and FA, 1390–1, 1457–8, 1480–1, and 1492–3.

subordinated to this local and essential work. When money was needed most, in the 1320s for instance, all other alms-seekers might be excluded from the parish church. Everyone who contributed, and was duly confessed and repentant, received forty days' indulgence and had their name inscribed on the cathedral's roll of benefactors, who had a share in the prayers of the church.[107]

If the fabric of the cathedral church was placed at the centre of the institutional agenda on charity, there was a great variety of causes which competed for the rest of the alms. Aid for building projects in other churches was a constant of the later Middle Ages: for instance, Bath Cathedral and Athelney Abbey both asked for the support of Wells parishioners at various times.[108] Other Somerset establishments, such as Crewkerne's chapel of Sancta Regina and Cleeve's chapel, were also supported, as well as a surprising number of distant institutions.[109] St Mary Bethlehem of London, the famous 'bedlam', approached the people of Wells, as did such exotic places as the hospital of St Anthony in Vienne, or the hospital of Holy Trinity and St Thomas the Martyr in Rome.[110] Unfortunately, we do not know how the people responded to these advances. The alms-seekers would make their pitch to the people in the parish church on Sundays, and the letters that they bore would instruct the vicar to address the congregation similarly.[111] The bishops' registers give a flavour of the reasons advanced for support; many certainly concentrated on the depth of their need, on the good work that their church did.

Another class of supplications points to the place of sentiment in eliciting charity. It was not rare for the members of congregations to be faced with the sometimes dismally sad and even tragic story of an individual or group of people whose lives had been nearly destroyed. In 1448 a Winchester merchant was travelling the country in a last attempt to raise the ransom that he needed to regain permanently his freedom. He told his unfortunate, complicated story of how the death of a man for whom he had stood as surety had thrown him into the captivity of Acquitaine pirates.[112]

---

[107] SRO DD/B, Reg. 1: 242ᵃ. Many of the other grants that allowed questers to enter the parish church excluded all other donations with the exception of the cathedral fund.   [108] Ibid. 52ᵃ. and 173ᵃ.

[109] SRO DD/B, Reg. 6: 18 and 138–9.   [110] Ibid. 49, 15, and 6.

[111] e.g. ibid. 6.   [112] Ibid. 79.

Knights who had worthily attempted to arrest the advance of the
French or, even more nobly to medieval eyes, the Turks at
Constantinople or in Hungary similarly presented their reduced
state and their great need to the parish of Wells.[113] But the
parishioners' feelings also were played for humbler people. In 1460
a man from the nearby village of Draycote was able to seek alms to
rebuild his house, which had been destroyed by an accidental
fire.[114]

These requests for charity do at least help to indicate the breadth
of the medieval world, as broad as the Church itself. Whether or
not he travelled during his life, every individual would have heard
news and stories from across the country and the world. It would
appear that their charitable impulses were large enough to extend
well beyond their own locality, but, when they did choose to help
an ordinary person directly, it was probably someone whom some
of them might know.

Bekynton's register described one of the cases as 'piteous', and
the word fits many of them.[115] Pity and, even more, compassion
were emotions which were important to the religious and charitable
impulse. The Church knew this, and used its knowledge to help
worthy causes and so to lead its people through charity towards
salvation. In the process, it generated many new connections
among different Christians, redistributed wealth, and gave some
succour to those in difficulty. The call to alms—when it succeeded
in touching someone—can only have generated a little more piety,
a little more charity, a fuller love of God.

7. EDUCATION

The provision of education was one of the most important offices
that the Church filled for the later medieval world. There was no
education, no literacy which could be got outside the Church. First
and foremost there was the religious instruction that was deemed
necessary for every Christian, and which parish priests were
supposed to provide. Everyone was to know the Hail Mary, the
Lord's Prayer, and the Creed—was to know, in other words, to

---

[113] Ibid. 79, 70, 119, 246, and 222.
[114] Ibid. 269.   [115] Ibid. 79.

whom to pray and what they, as Christians, were to believe.[116] We have noted its fruits, in the requests of the chantry priests for specific prayers to be said by the laity attending the service.[117] Others have shown how these basic prayers (among others) were sometimes woven through the day of the exceptionally devout.[118]

A great deal of moral and religious education would have been provided through sermons, given either by the vicar of the church or by an itinerant friar.[119] A large parish like Wells was fortunate in its vicars. They included several cathedral canons and vicars, for instance Thomas Cornish, a cathedral precentor, chancellor, and suffragan bishop at the end of the fifteenth and beginning of the sixteenth centuries.[120] But the parish would also have received several visits a year from itinerant preachers, especially from friars who had been sanctioned by the bishop to preach in the diocese.[121] Further moral aid and guidance were disseminated by personal confessors. Frequently these were the parochial chaplains or chantry priests of St Cuthbert's, and the evidence of wills makes it clear how much they were valued as advisers and, presumably, friends.[122]

The full picture of more formal and advanced education across England has recently come into sharper relief, especially through the work of Nicholas Orme.[123] He has detailed much of the history of the schools of Wells. As in many other cathedral cities, Wells

[116] This was the case at least from the 13th cent.: see Murray, 'Religion among the Poor', 298–9; Manning, *People's Faith*, 42–50, notes that the 10 commandments were also thought essential by some; and James A. Corbett, *The 'De instructione puerorum' of William of Tournai, OP* (Notre Dame, Ind., 1955), 7–9.

[117] See above, Ch. 8, sect. 4 and 5.

[118] Pantin, 'Instructions for a Layman', 398–422.

[119] On the content, see G. R. Owst, *Preaching in Medieval England* (Cambridge, 1926), 279–384: merchants could receive special attention in sermons (p. 304); D'Avray, *Preaching of the Friars*, 205–59; and David R. Lesnick, *Preaching in Medieval Florence* (Athens, Ga., 1989), 93–185.

[120] For his will of 1513, see *SMWII*: 167–9; see also John Le Neve, *Fasti Ecclesiae Anglicanae 1300–1541: Bath and Wells*, ed. B. Jones (London, 1964), 7, 9, 41, and 42, for his career: he was a master of Arts. Throughout the 15th cent. it was usual for cathedral canons to be appointed, including a subdean once (John Wansford in 1487: *Reg. Stafford*, 148), another suffragan bishop (John Valens in 1471: ibid. 40), and at least one doctor of laws (William Mors in 1513: *Registers of Oliver King and Hadrian de Castello*, ed. H. C. Maxwell-Lyle, SRS 54 (1939), 163).

[121] See for examples, SRO DD/B, Reg. 1: 14ᵃ, 249ᵇ, Reg. 2: 298, 369, and Reg. 6: 15. These indicate that licences to preach in the diocese were granted mainly to friars from Bristol: Owst, *Preaching*, 52–62.

[122] e.g. *SMWII*: 36 and 199.

[123] Nicholas Orme, *English Schools in the Middle Ages* (London, 1973) and *Education in the West of England, 1066–1548* (Exeter, 1976).

possessed three cathedral schools: a song school, an intermittent theology school, and a grammar school. Only the latter was open to the public of the diocese.[124] There is no indication that the town possessed any other school.

Details of the grammar school are scant. It may have had upwards of fifty students in the 1370s. The clerical poll tax names thirty-four scholars, all of whom were over 14 years of age. Their names indicate that most of them were certainly Somerset people, and some are the family names of burgesses of Wells.[125] Many who attended the grammar school returned to the secular world to follow a trade and a more worldly life, their literacy a permanent advantage and tool. It is doubtful, however, that the school or education was used as a tool against the church, as has been suggested for Bury St Edmunds.[126] Richard Piers, a prosperous burgess, used his education to help the Borough Community collect its taxes in 1407. He accompanied the tax collectors to read to them the list of names and assessments.[127] The weaver and cloth-maker Thomas Chynnok owned a matins service-book of his own in the 1450s, while Robert Kyng, a burgess of no more than average standing, owned his own life of St George.[128] Most essentially for the city, it was Church education that gave them their civic recorders. Thomas Walsingham, council clerk from 1408, was actually a deacon; one of his successors was John Beynton, a simple clerk and draper, who must once have enjoyed a good Church education.[129] We cannot say what proportion of urban men in Wells went to school. It must have been a small number who ever learned Latin, but a sizeable minority were probably able to read, if not write, English.[130]

8. NEW LIVES

But these men with their smattering of education, while probably representing the majority of schoolchildren, were not, by the lights

---

[124] Orme, *Education in the West*, 80–7.

[125] Thomas Gurdel, John Mulborn, John Brighampton, John Rose, and the two John Haywards were from Wells families, (PRO E179/4/1).

[126] Gottfried, 288.

[127] CBI: 170. On the subject of urban literacy, see London, 155–63 which estimates an urban male literacy rate of 50%.

[128] CBII: 30 and 141 (1484).

[129] CBI: 179 (1409), and CBII: 99 (1474) note each man's first appointment.

[130] Cf. *London*, 156–8; and Richard W. Kaeuper, "Two Early Lists of Literates in

of the Church, the most successful, whatever their civic eminence and business success. They represent another facet of the way in which the Church served secular society, served it to shape it according to its own needs. One of the reasons why parents paid for the education of their child, however, was probably in the hope that he might find a vocation, and lead an affluent and respectable life, in the direct service of the Church. Within the Church, a merchant's son could maintain his economic position without risk, and improve his social and moral standing. This was many a merchant's dream—whether or not it suited their son's own aspirations.

Bishop Bekynton's register (covering 1445–64) includes the names of thirty Wells natives among its ordinands.[131] Some, such as Richard Norman and Richard Widcomb, are not recorded as advancing beyond the level of acolytes, and never took a university degree.[132] But others, the majority it would seem, went on to become priests, many gaining the degree which so enhanced their prospects for permanent and comfortable preferment.[133] Most famous among them was the minor literary figure Thomas Chandler, who edited a tribute to his native town.[134] After attending Wykeham's Winchester school, he eventually became a master of Arts, doctor of Theology, chancellor of Wells Cathedral, warden of New College, Oxford, and chancellor of the University.[135] But others also did well. John Oliver, almost certainly the son of the burgess and tailor of the same name, and a butcher's son, William Northern, were able to stay in Wells as cathedral vicars.[136] Robert Cutte, a son of one of Wells's most prominent and durable fifteenth-century families, went on to Oxford, where he received his

England, 1334, 1373', *English Historical Review* 99 (1984), 363–9; both suggest that 40% of the laity were literate in Latin, but London merchants and the sort of people who would count as witnesses and jurors were certainly among the upper half of urban society, and were more likely to have received above average education.

[131] *Register of Thomas Bekynton, Bishop of Bath and Wells, 1443–65*, ed. H. C. Maxwell-Lyle and M. C. B. Dawes, 2 vols., SRS 49–50 (1934–5), 466–550, is the ordination register.

[132] Ibid. 489 and 536.

[133] Peter Heath, *The English Parish Clergy on the Eve of the Reformation* (London, 1969), 35–8.

[134] *The Official Correspondence of Thomas Bekynton*, ed. George Williams, RS 56, 2 vols. (1872), ii. 320.

[135] *Fasti Ecclesiae*, 9, 32, 52, and 75, follows his cathedral career; and A. B. Emden, *The Biographical Register of Oxford University to 1500*, 3 vols. (Oxford, 1957–9), 398–9.

[136] *Reg. Bek.*, 482, 532, and 517.

bachelor of Arts degree.[137] A relative, William, possibly even a younger brother, achieved the same success about fifteen years later.[138]

Such advancement in the ecclesiastical establishment was not, of course, restricted to Bekynton's era. Cathedral canons of the fourteenth century such as John Orum, who lectured on the Apocalypse in the cathedral's divinity school, and Master John Vowell, who served in the cathedral in the stall of Cumba Quindecima at the end of the fifteenth century, are only the most successful examples from earlier and later.[139] Remarkably, these two, and others, contrived to spend much of their careers at home. Becoming a cleric did not necessarily mean leaving one's home town for good, especially if one came from a cathedral city.

The origins of the boys who were sent to school and encouraged to enter the Church were varied. We have already noted several burgesses' sons. Most of the ordinands do seem to have come from the Borough Community as opposed to the poorer foreigners of the city, but they were by no means from only the most successful burgesses. Indeed, the several successful Vowells are the only sons of masters of the town whom we know went on to serve the Church.[140] Sons were in short supply in this period, and the wealth of the masters was perhaps sufficient inducement for a boy to serve a secular apprenticeship and follow his father's business pursuits. This possibility is strengthened somewhat by the predominance of the sons of tradesmen, of middle-ranking burgesses, among those ordained. Wells thus confirms the trend of research in seeing the Church as an open institution by which the relatively humble might rise, and frequently did.[141] Most probably, the aptitude for books and the inclination to prayer, piety, or administration had as much to do with determining which burgesses' sons went into the Church as did secular career goals.

[137] Ibid. 497; Emden, *Oxford University*, 531.

[138] *Reg. Bek.*, 547; Emden, *Oxford University*, 531.

[139] *Fasti Ecclesiae*, 52; for Vowell, see ibid. 39; and Emden, *Oxford University*, 1951.

[140] Most successfully, John Vowell (d. 1502), a canon of Wells and vicar of Cheddar, and his nephew Richard, who was the last prior of Walsingham. See, for John, *Fasti Ecclesiae*, 39; and, for Richard, *SDNQ* 18 (1926), 100.

[141] Margaret Bowker, *The Secular Clergy in the Diocese of Lincoln, 1495–1520* (Cambridge, 1968), 40–1; Douglas Jones, *The Church in Chester, 1300–1540*, Chetham Society, 3rd ser., 7 (Manchester, 1957), 22–7, was more hesitant to determine social background, but tended to notice the ruling families as being conspicuous among those gaining preferment. Cf. Tanner, *Norwich*, 23–8.

There were other paths into the Church, less worldly ambitious, perhaps more clearly indicative of piety. The late Middle Ages witnessed a great growth in personal religious 'experience'. It was the time of mystics and religious enthusiasts, of such great vernacular moralists as Langland. Towns could be quite ambivalent about some of the new converts to various forms of religious life,[142] but, without question, townspeople were at the centre of the wave of activity.[143] There were no known mystics at Wells, but there are signs of the lay piety which played such a revolutionary role in later medieval religion. It was a public sort of piety. By becoming a hermit or a chaste widow, regular men and women who had not been able or willing to enter a religious life earlier, who often could not read, found an avenue along which they could lead a more intense and an overtly religious life.

The hermit's life was one path that remained attractive to some in the later Middle Ages.[144] In 1452, for example, Bishop Bekynton approved the religious profession of one John of Wells, a single man who sought to 'serve his creator in perpetual chastity after the rule of St Paul the hermit'. Hermit John signed his profession with an illiterate's 'X', and was then invested by Bekynton with a hermit's habit.[145] This was a token of his place in a Christian society, and a proof against the fraudulent beggar-hermits who were a problem in the later Middle Ages.[146]

The donation of one's body to God through chastity was an option that was taken up by many later medieval women across Europe. It was an issue which, rather vividly and directly, was a concern for such mystics as Margery Kempe, whose lifelong fight with herself and others to become chaste says much for the

[142] Anthony Goodman, 'The Piety of John Brunham's Daughter, of Lynn', in Derek Baker (ed.), *Medieval Women*, (Oxford, 1978), 355, has pointed this out.

[143] One thinks in England of Margery Kempe, Richard Rolle, Walter Hilton, and Julian of Norwich among mystics, as well as the devout heretics who professed Lollardy, about whom, see below, Ch. 8. 9; see David Knowles, *The English Mystical Tradition* (London, 1961).

[144] See Rotha Mary Clay, *The Hermits and Anchorites of England* (London, 1914). Tanner, *Norwich*, 58–64 and app. 7, 198–202; Ann K. Warren, *Anchorites and their Patrons in Medieval England* (Berkeley, Calif., 1985), 127–280, *passim*.

[145] SRO DD/B, Reg. 6: 145. This was the general rule for a hermit as opposed to an anchorite. Its ceremony of benediction, including the pledge of the new hermit, is printed in Clay, *Hermits and Anchorites*, 199–202.

[146] Clay, *Hermits and Anchorites*, 61–2, notes the difficulty of the 'vagabond hermits', who were perceived as something of a social nuisance and were made illegal by a statute of 1495; see also J. J. Jusserand, *English Wayfaring Life in the Middle Ages* (London, 1961; orig. edn., 1889), 66–71.

emotional and religious ferment that arose around this question.[147] The way in which one woman—actually from the adjacent parish of Croscombe—embraced religious chastity was more mundane, doubtlessly more typical. In 1459, after being widowed, Elizabeth Biccomb took her vow and was invested by the bishop with a habit to express the fact that she was religious in the most palpable terms.[148] By this profession she established a social fact—namely, that she was not a woman to be courted—as well as the religious fact that she wished to finish her life, or, better said, begin life anew, in God's service.

The Church thus provided a number of ways in which to pursue a new and more vigorously religious life. For some, it was undoubtedly thought of principally as a career, but for others—at all stages of life—there was certainly a calling. This was the case with these adult lay people. They sought to break with a past life of which they probably could no longer approve. They went beyond the usual, collective devotion of the parish church and guild, and found that the flexible Church contained places and regimes to succour, channel, and contain their religiosity.

9. HETERODOXY AND CONTROL

Not every religious impulse could be satisfied within the bands that the culture of the Church prescribed. As Gordon Leff has said: 'In the middle ages the road to heresy was paved with piety.'[149] Moreover, to give people literacy was sometimes a risky policy. Lollardy thrived among the sort of people who were sent to grammar schools, or who learned to read English to help them in business. The tradesmen of the West Country were, from 1400 onwards, perhaps the largest contingent of suspected heretics in England.[150] Wells was granted a general pardon in 1415 which

---

[147] See *The Book of Margery Kempe*, ed. Stanford B. Meech and Hope E. Allen, EETS 212 (London, 1940), 11, 21, and 23; Goodman, 'John Brunham's Daughter'; and Nancy F. Partner, 'Reading *The Book of Margery Kempe*', *Exemplaria* 3 (1991), 29–66.

[148] SRO DD/B, Reg. 6: 235. She signed the profession with an 'X'.

[149] Gordon Leff, *Heresy in the Later Middle Ages*, 2 vols. (Manchester, 1967), i. 12.

[150] See John A. F. Thomson, *The Later Lollards, 1414–1520* (Oxford, 1965), esp. 20–51; and Anne Hudson, *The Premature Reformation* (Oxford, 1988), who pay the most attention to the Lollards themselves; Leff, *Heresy*, ii. 494–605, covers Wyclif and the Lollards, mainly their ideas; as does K. B. McFarlane, *John Wycliffe and the Beginning of English Nonconformity* (London, 1952).

would seem to have been necessary because of the part that some in the town had played in the Oldcastle rebellion of the previous year.[151] In 1408 Bishop Bubwith issued orders forbidding anyone to preach heresy, thereby suggesting that somebody may have been.[152] Furthermore, many an accused and convicted heretic was brought to Wells and was forced to do a public penance in the city.[153] This was a common event throughout the fifteenth century.[154] Lollardy remained strong in the West Country. Nevertheless, it remains the case that we have no proof of anyone from Wells being convicted of the offence. Possibly, one of the effects of the large ecclesiastical establishment of the city was that anyone who had heretical beliefs in Wells kept them to himself. Few inhabitants of another cathedral city, Norwich, were tried as heretics, especially when one takes into account the heretical . activity in the diocese.[155] For any Lollards in Wells, Bristol was near enough to meet like-minded people.

Wells was not, however, even on the surface, a monolith of orthodoxy. Within the church itself, there was a degree of dabbling with magic and necromancy, not surprising in an educated milieu. These are, for the most part, hidden things, but we have found, in the form of a charm, proof of the existence of an only quasi-Christian belief in magic. Dating from the fifteenth century, written in a jumble of English and Latin on the back of a deed, the writing promises to protect the bearer from his enemies. It guaranteed that he would not die unshriven; that a woman who carried the paper would deliver her children alive and well; that the bearer would not be falsely damned.[156] In brief, it was an amulet, unorthodox and not concerned with anything demonic, but, nevertheless, a traditional tool of witches or of their educated counterparts.[157] It speaks

[151] WCC 18. It is quite a general pardon, addressed to the men of the town, listing every imaginable, but not necessarily any actual, crimes. On the 'revolt', see McFarlane, *John Wycliffe*, 160–85.

[152] *CPR 1405–8*: 476.

[153] See e.g. the rash of Bristol heretics towards the end of the 15th cent. in *Reg. King and Castello*, 39–43. Cf. Thomson, *Later Lollards*, 46–8.

[154] See, for examples, *Reg. Stafford*, 40–1 (1426), 266–8; and *Registers of Robert Stillington, 1466–91, and Richard Fox, 1492–94*, ed. H. C. Maxwell-Lyle, SRS 52 (1937), 107 (1476).

[155] Norman P. Tanner (ed.), *Heresy Trials in the Diocese of Norwich, 1428–31*, CS, 4th ser., 20 (London, 1977), 26–7.

[156] AH 28[b].

[157] Claude Lecouteux, 'Paganisme, christianisme et merveilleux', *Annales: Économies, Societés, Civilisations* 37 (1982), 707–8. Whether a charm was

of the fact that people were worried by death, especially of being taken unconfessed, in which case they were doomed. The concern about childbirth points just as clearly to this broadly held fear in a time of high infant mortality. This charm spoke to the greatest fears of a people. Who can say how many other such amulets were used to assuage people's anxieties?

With this charm, one touches a facet of medieval belief that was only partly formed by the Church, and which certainly existed beyond its control. There must have been a great many ancient pre-Christian rituals, a durable hardwood of ideas and prayers, now covered in a more Christian varnish, which functioned to mediate between the ideas that the Church gave the people and the other needs and fears that they faced. Witchcraft doubtlessly existed in this space, where people's needs were greater than prayer alone or medieval medicine could reach.

At least one Wells woman was convicted of witchcraft. Her name was Katherine Love, and she was accused in 1499. She used charms, and dropped wax from holy candles' into the stools of men and women of the town in order to 'annoy' and harm them. She probably offered positive services, too, to cure as well as to provide helpful charms, but, like most witches, Katherine Love got into trouble for perceived malice.[158] The presiding vicar-general assigned a penance requiring her to march, in her shift, at the head of the procession in St Cuthbert's church on a Sunday that year, bearing an extinguished candle in one hand, and a lit one in the other. Furthermore, she was banished from the city, and was not allowed to come within seven miles of it.[159] The role of the Church here was to enforce orthodoxy and to suppress the belief in superstition—clear and religious purposes, concerned with controlling what people thought. But there is also the cultural dimension. The guilty woman's errors are highlighted for the community to see—and to see defeated. Orthodoxy and the wronged community itself are restored and upheld. Furthermore, the trouble that she

Christian or demonic is not always clear, and it has been argued that charms—like so much else pagan—had been Christianized. Ours may be of this type, for it invokes biblical figures, not demons or elves. See Karen Louise Jolly, 'Anglo-Saxon Charms in the Context of a Christian Worldview', *Journal of Medieval History* 11 (1985), 279–93.

[158] See, e.g. Christina Larner, *Enemies of God: The Witch-Hunt in Scotland* (Baltimore, 1981), 138–43.

[159] *Reg. King and Castello*, 41.

caused, presumably stirring up members of the town against one another, was eradicated, purged through her removal. She took the guilt and the shame with her. The community was seen to be resurrected. Excommunication, which could be used for political as well as moral failures, was employed in similar circumstances, and was also performed in public.[160]

Clearly, one of the roles that the Church played through education, preaching, and the courts was to form the practice of the people in accordance with its own ideas.[161] Morality was enforced in these courts. Here the Church could reach beyond narrow religious rite and observance to control how people actually acted, its own ministers and laymen both. Even if most of the consistory court business does seem to have been concerned with the rights and dues of the vicars of various churches in the diocese, with the failure to pay mortuary dues or tithes, the element of moral control is perhaps the most significant. Policing the bonds of marriage was of crucial importance in imposing the Church's view of the family and marriage, the most fundamental of social relations.[162] Honesty in speech was also guarded. Townsmen brought their suits of libel and perjury to the consistory court, although many preferred, or were compelled, to do this business in other courts.[163] Through its ecclesiastical courts, the Church enforced the laws and customary practices by which it shaped the entire culture of the later medieval city. Orthodoxy and heresy, the lawful and the illegal, were separated.

[160] The political use can be seen in the excommunication of Walter Middleton, the leader of the burgesses in the 1340s dispute: see above, pp. 121 f. For excommunicated burgesses, see SRO DD/B, Reg. 1: 101[b], 240[a], 283[a]., Reg. 2: 250–1, 276, Reg. 6: 11; see also Elizabeth Vodola, *Excommunication in the Middle Ages* (Berkeley, Calif., 1986), esp. 44–69, on the impact on community life; and F. Donald Logan, *Excommunication and the Secular Arm in Medieval England* (Toronto, 1968).

[161] For a description of the function of these courts at Wells, see R. W. Dunning 'The Wells Consistory Court in the Fifteenth Century', *SANHS* 106 (1962), 46–61; and extracts in *A Wells Cathedral Miscellany*, ed. A. Watkin, SRS 56 (1941), 155–6. Generally, see Thompson, *English Clergy*, 40–71 and 206–46; and C. A. Ritchie, *The Ecclesiastical Courts of York* (Arbroath, 1956); for the following period, see R. Houlbrooke, *Church Courts and the People during the English Reformation, 1520–70* (Oxford, 1979).

[162] Dunning, 'Consistory Court', 59. See R. H. Helmholz, *Marriage Litigation in Medieval England* (Cambridge, 1974).

[163] The Borough Community's court was used for some of these cases. The two systems could come into conflict: for examples, see CBI: 182, and CBII: 112.

10. Conclusion

In concluding his excellent study of the later medieval Church in Norwich, Norman Tanner posed a worthy but difficult question: 'How Christian was late medieval Norwich? . . . how far had Christianity . . . become so reduced to a merely cultural phenomenon that it ceased to be Christianity?'[164] To a certain extent, these are idealistic questions which cannot be satisfactorily answered, especially on the evidence from small towns. The Church was certainly alive with new forms of worship in the later Middle Ages, fuelled by powerful emotions. I have tried to suggest that these forms, pre-eminently the institutions of worship (the lay-controlled parishes, guilds, and chantries), were only part of the Church's, of Christianity's, success. As important to its strength were charity and education, the continued successful recruitment of new ministers from the 'grass-roots', the way in which its ideas insinuated themselves into every moment of life. The cultural—that is, the non-theological, non-liturgical—features which, Tanner fears, 'reduced' the Church were, in fact, the bedrock of the Church. To an idealist, this may seem sad and unfortunate, a sign that all is not well, but I rather think that few people, at even the moments of greatest religious fervour, can live entirely in accordance with religious ideas and devotions. A successful faith requires a physical and temporal presence. It must have ways in which to touch the people everyday, to remind them of what they believe and of who they are. And then the people must pay attention, be involved. At Wells this was often the case. Individuals were touched and affected by the form of Christian culture, its ideas and institutions, by charity, by prayer, and by the knowledge that they lived in a Christian universe. They are therefore just as worthy of being thought of as Christians as any people have ever been. If this is depressing, somehow not providing enough, it may be worth recalling how hard it is to be disciplined, how hard is the life of the saint. There were few saints in the later medieval city, but a great number of active, interested, and committed Christians.

[164] Tanner, *Norwich*, 171.

Conclusion: The Complexity of Small Things

Although Wells was a town of, at best, medium size throughout the Middle Ages, it was a surprisingly complex place. Starting from nearly nothing in the twelfth century, the town's population fluctuated between about 1,200 and 2,500 people in the years 1300–1525, and yet it easily kept its identity, because of the continuation of institutions such as the cathedral and the Borough Community. Indeed, it may well be that the sort of volatility that is of the nature of towns, especially medieval towns, actually contributes to the tenacity with which such groups reinforce and strengthen their corporate bodies. Community may thrive most where the instability of the membership is most acute. In a town such as Wells, where demographic and economic realities produced a largely transient population—and a population faced with poor prospects for personal longevity—and where two local authorities vied for influence, the signs of the collectivity may well have loomed even larger. Thus the official mentality of the leaders of the town was one which fostered the importance of unity, tradition, solidarity, and the connection of surrogate brotherhood. Social complexity helped to father social and cultural unity. If this was so, then perhaps the variety of community that we have outlined had a very different character from that of a village community. In a small unstable town, it would be more dependent on notions and rituals than on the confidence built of blood ties and co-operation in the common fields.

I have concentrated on the dominant lay people of the city, the Borough Community, and, although this was a surprisingly large group, comprising about half the city, it is important to note that there were other important social players, not all of whom I have treated in equal detail. The cathedral and its staff have been treated more lightly, but we have seen that, in many matters, they stood apart from the lay town, and yet, on others, they worked closely with them. When the issue was political, particularly the great dispute between town and bishop in the 1340s, the cathedral played no known public role. Ultimately, legal propriety would have forced them to take the bishop's side, but not necessarily with enthusiasm. The town and cathedral both preferred to keep the bishop of Bath and Wells outside their own affairs, so we might consider that they were natural, if not actual, allies. Furthermore, there were areas in which the burgesses and the cathedral did work together. The cathedral was the rector of the parish church, the lay people its members and partial governors, and to this extent the religious life of the community was a co-operative effort. In the fifteenth century the almshouse became the main and most impressive instance of actual joint control of an institution, in which the money as well as the selection of the privileged paupers was placed under the guidance of the Borough Community and the cathedral.

Most of the impact of the cathedral on the town was less structured. We noted the favourable economic impact, especially on the victuallers of the city, whose high profile in the town, even relative to other places, suggests the effect that supplying over a hundred well-paid clergymen could have. No doubt, the hard economic stretches of the fifteenth century would have been harder still if the cathedral and its stability had not been at hand. But interaction was not limited to the economy. Throughout I have been at pains to stress the fact of social fluidity, and we have seen how the Church represented one of the options for the young of the town, particularly because of the presence of the cathedral schools. Lay and clerical mingled most freely where the one turned into the other.

A similar point can be made about the more frequent transformation of social status which took place when a foreigner became a burgess. One of the conclusions that a study of Wells forces on us is the need to pay more attention to those who were not citizens, and especially not to assume that they were a monolithic and belligerent counterweight to the burgesses. I hope it is clear enough that neither group was in fact monolithic, and, if they were distinguishable as groups, that their group identity was not easily read from the economic facts of an individual's life. Without being told who was a burgess and who was a foreigner, one could make a guess based on affluence, trade, or profession, and often enough one would be wrong. Even poverty was not itself a simple and separate social grouping, but one which existed among burgesses, foreigners, clergy, and strangers, not all of whom were deemed equally worthy of assistance.

I have suggested that, in such transformations of status, life cycle may very well have been an important factor. It plainly was part of what determined the timing of a decision to join the Borough Community, and it also had a role to play in determining advancement within the elite of that Community. What we have not been able to establish definitely is whether the role of age was really just a secondary sign of wealth: that is, it took time to become wealthy, so it took time to become master of the town, and so on. The correlation between old age and poverty underlines the reality of the fact that, for whatever reasons, social status and age frequently moved in parallel, upwards to a middle-age plateau, and downwards towards an impotent old age.

The complex social world was matched by the economic life of the town. There was a great variety of trades practised, and an impressively large cloth-making industry. For certain periods Wells sustained a considerable long-distance trade, and the town always had many domestic merchants. One of the questions that this raises concerns the nature of even smaller towns. Did they also have real diversity, even if fewer trades? The greatest problem in answering this question may be the quality of the sources. We can, at any rate, determine that, for towns of Wells's size, there was a critical role to be played in the later medieval economy. It was from here that goods from abroad and from the larger centres of the country were disseminated to the countryside. When this marketing function was combined, as at Wells, with important industrial and administrative or ecclesiastical functions, the life of the town took on a little more substance. But it seems perfectly possible that, even without these special administrative features, similar marketing and manufacturing functions could be executed by towns of possibly fewer than 1,000 inhabitants. The hope now must be that one of these small places yields rich enough records to test the hypothesis.[1]

The smaller towns of England were often mesne boroughs or even simple vills, so a study of them will frequently be approached through the records of the lords of the town. A recent study of Durham confirms how strikingly different the nature of those

---

[1] R. Hilton, *Class Conflict and the Crisis of Feudalism* (London, 1985), 175–204, gives some hints, but the records and or the treatment are too preliminary to be sure.

records will be.[2] In Wells we have been fortunate to find interesting non-seigniorial records for a seigniorial borough. It has provided a sharper picture of urban community in action and idea than is usually afforded us. In this picture the relationship with the overlord was as complex as everything else about the town. On the one hand, we have the disturbances, the corporate ambition of the 1340s. But, opposed to this, we have the perhaps more impressive fact that, in the periods preceding and subsequent to the open conflicts, the town and its lord had worked out ways to share power, to share responsibility, and to live civilly. Tensions before and after the 1340s were few and not very serious. There was, in effect, no real progression of animosity. The story of these social conflicts is not part of a great pattern of historical development, but mainly of local concerns. Without question, the general atmosphere of fourteenth-century urban rebelliousness contributed to the burgesses' boldness, but this did not establish a pattern of intermittent warfare or bickering. The town was not bitterly repressed or impoverished by its lord in the later fourteenth and fifteenth centuries. Both sides stood on their rights, and worked to keep the business of life in their town moving. Honour and pragmatism found their place together, as they seem to have done in other towns such as Westminster and possibly Durham.[3]

The conclusion to be drawn is not that medieval towns, even those under ecclesiastical lords, were harmonious and content places. It may rather be the case that moments of social function inevitably outnumber those of dysfunction by a great margin, and that historians have frequently been more interested in the radical moment of crisis, thinking it a turning-point, than in the regular state of affairs and slow evolution. There was anger, upset, and resentment enough in medieval towns, but, without a great amount of readily available police power, it is the case that legal structures, quiet arrangements, and a mentality which laid great stress on order and moderation generally managed to keep the peace. Later medieval English towns, Wells included, worked.

If no sure trends can be identified for the small seigniorial town's 'feudal' politics, its economic and demographic development show a somewhat clearer path. Wells's steady growth until the plague of 1348–9 was followed by a recovery fuelled in part by the

[2] Margaret Bonney, *Lordship and the Urban Community* (Cambridge, 1990).
[3] *Westminster*, 237–8; and Bonney, *Lordship*, 230–5.

expanding cloth industry. From the early fifteenth century a new and uncatastrophic decline had set in, which ended the Middle Ages by leaving the town a considerably smaller place in 1525 than it had been in 1380 or 1300.

For a demographer or an economist of aggregate economy, there is not much doubt that Wells is an instance of fifteenth-century 'urban decline'. But, for the historian, the case is not so simple. Very probably the life of the common labourer or tradesman was considerably improved, in so far as housing was affordable, and wage rates had gone up more than inflation. From the vantage of social or cultural history, it is not always clear that the concept of decline is very helpful. There was vitality enough in the reactions to oligarchy, to poverty, to the economic challenge of a restructuring cloth industry and of the vicissitudes of population change, to social status and identity, and to religious life, among others, to warrant increased historical attention. It is time to refuse to allow the haze of economic calculations and speculations to hide the other important features of later medieval urban life, the social diversity and cultural ferment of which beckon.

Wells Bishops

Bishops of Wells

Athelm	909–23
Wulfhelm I	923–6
Aelfeah	926–37
Wulfhelm II	938–55
Brithelm	956–74
Cyneward	974–5
Siger	975–97
Aelfwine	997–9
Lyfing	999–1013
Aethelwine	1013–23
Brihtwig or Merewit	1024–33
Duduc	1033–60
Giso	1061–88

Bishops of Bath

John of Tours	1088–1122
Godfrey	1123–35
Robert of Lewes	1136–66
Reginald	1174–91

Bishops of Bath and Glastonbury

Savaric	1192–1205
Jocelyn	1206–42 (only of Bath from 1219)

Bishops of Bath and Wells

Roger	1244–7
William Bytton I	1248–64
Walter Giffard	1265–6
William Bytton II	1267–74
Robert Burnell	1275–92
William of March	1293–1302
Walter Haselshaw	1302–8
John Drokenford	1309–29
Ralph of Shrewbury	1329–63
John Barnet	1363–6
John Harewell	1367–86
Walter Skirlaw	1386–8
Ralph Erghum	1388–1400
Henry Bowet	1401–7
Nicholas Bubwith	1407–24
John Stafford	1425–43
Thomas Bekynton	1443–65
Robert Stillington	1466–91
Richard Fox	1492–4
Oliver King	1495–1503
Hadrian de Castello	1504–18
Thomas Wolsey	1518–23

Stewards and Masters of Wells Borough

1336	Richard Eyr		1401	John Blithe
1341	Walter Middleton		1402	John Blithe
1347	John Roper		1403	Richard Gros
1348	John Roper		1404	John Horewode
1351	Walter Compton		1405	John Blithe
1355	Richard Stowey		1406	John Blithe
1357	John Roper		1407	Walter Baron alias Dyer
1361	John Roper		1408	John Wycombe
1362	Nicholas Cristesham		1409	John Wycombe
1372	Nicholas Cristesham		1410	Henry Maundeware
1374	Thomas Tanner		1411	Henry Maundeware
1376	Henry Bowditch		1412	John Horewode
1377	Robert Compe		1413	Thomas Weye
1378	Nicholas Cristesham		1414	Walter Dyer
1379	Thomas Tanner		1415	Walter Dyer
1380	Henry Bowditch		1416	John Horewode
1381	Richard Stowey		1417	Richard Setter
1382	Nicholas Cristesham		1418	Richard Setter
1383	Henry Bowditch		1419	Richard Hall
1384	Thomas Hore		1420	Hildebrand Elwell
1385	Nicholas Cristesham		1421	Hildebrand Elwell
1386	Thomas Tanner		1422	John Pedewell
1387	John Blithe		1423	John Godwin
1388	Nicholas Cristesham		1424	John Rocke
1389	Thomas Hore		1425	Richard Setter
1390	Nicholas Cristesham		1426	Simon Bailey
1391	John Broun		1427	John Godwin
1392	Thomas Tanner		1428	Robert Elwell
1393	John Blithe		1429	Richard Hall
1394	Thomas Hore		1430	?
1395	Thomas Tanner		1431	John Rocke
1396	John Broun		1432	John Weatley
1397	John Blithe		1433	John Godwin
1398	Roger Chapman		1434	John Rocke
1399	Thomas Hore		1435	John Colles
1400	Thomas Tanner		1436	Richard Dyer alias Wright

1437	Richard Dyer alias Wright	1480	Richard Burnell
1438	William Vowell	1481	Richard Burnell
1439	William Vowell	1482	Thomas Rowdon
1440	?	1483	Richard Vowell
1441	John Godwin	1484	John Atwater
1442	Richard Dyer alias Wright	1485	John Atwater
1443	Richard Mayne	1486	Richard Vowell
1444	William Cutte	1487	John Tyler
1445	William Vowell	1488	John Draper
1446	William Vowell	1489	John Smith
1447	William Gascoigne	1490	John Adam
1448	John Godwin	1491	Richard Burnell
1449	John Godwin	1492	Richard Vowell
1450	William Vowell	1493	John Tyler
1451	Thomas Nabbe	1494	John Tyler
1452	Thomas Nabbe	1495	John Smith
1453	Thomas Atwater	1496	John Tyler
1454	Thomas Atwater	1497	Nicholas Trappe
1455	John Godwin	1498	Richard Burnell
1456	William Cutte	1499	John Tyler
1457	William Vowell	1500	John Tyler
1458	John Atwater	1501	Nicholas Trappe
1459	Walter Baker alias Smith	1502	Nicholas Trappe
1460	John Atwater	1503	John Smith
1461	John Scholer	1504	John Ustewayte
1462	William Vowell	1505	Robert Grantham (died in office)
1463	John Sadler alias Davy		
1464	Walter Baker alias Smith	1505	Richard Burnell
1465	Thomas Horewode	1506	John Tyler
1466	William Vowell	1507	Thomas Fox
1467	John Atwater	1508	John Mawdleyn
1468	John Grype	1509	John Welshot
1469	Walter Baker alias Smith	1510	John Ustewayte
1470	William Vowell	1511	Walter Sarger
1471	John Sadler alias Davy	1512	Henry Cornish
1472	John Atwater	1513	Thomas Fox
1473	Richard Vowell	1514	John Mawdleyn
1474	John Atwater	1515	John Welshot
1475	Walter Baker alias Smith	1516	Walter Sarger
1476	Richard Burnell	1517	Henry Cornish
1477	Richard Vowell	1518	William Frampton
1478	John Atwater	1519	John Mawdleyn
1479	John Draper	1520	John Mawdleyn

Bibliography

MANUSCRIPT SOURCES

Wells Cathedral, Wells

Communar's Accounts, 1327–1505
Escheator's Accounts, 1372–1503
Fabric Accounts, 1390–1501
Register of the Vicars-Choral of Wells Cathedral
Wells Almshouse Charters
Wells Cathedral Charters
Wells Cathedral Register I (*Liber Albus* I)
Wells Cathedral Register II (*Liber Ruber* I)
Wells Cathedral Register III (*Liber Albus* II)
Wells Vicars-Choral Charters

Wells Town Hall Archives, Wells

Convocation Book I
Convocation Book II
Convocation Book III
'Mr Goodall's Book'
Wells City Charters, 1–22, 25–6, 29–30
Wells Title Deeds, 1–213, 228–30, 234–7.
Wells Town Archive, 86

Public Record Office, London

Subsidy Accounts

E179/4/1	Clerical, 1377
E179/235/60	Alien, 1452–3
E179/169/156	Lay, 1523–4
E179/169/36	Lay, 1377

Aulnage Accounts

E101/339/2	Gloucestershire and Bristol, 1395–6
E101/343/28	Somerset and Dorset, 1395–6
E101/344/3	3–4 Henry IV, Somerset and Bristol

E101/343/29   20–1 Richard II, Somerset
E101/344/2   2 Henry IV, Somerset
E101/344/4   4–5 Henry IV, Somerset
E101/344/6   7–8 Henry VI, subsidiary documents
E101/344/7   4–10 Edward IV

Chancery Pleas and Proceedings

C3/262/7
C44/1/13

Ministers' Accounts

SC6/1131/1   2–3 Edward I
SC6/1131/3   30 Edward I
SC6/1131/4   2 Edward II
SC6/1131/9   37–8 Henry VI
SC6/Henry VII/1806 7–8 Henry VII
SC6/Henry VII/584   6–7 Henry VII
SC6/Henry VIII/3075 26–7 Henry VIII

Customs Accounts

E356/7

Lambeth Palace Library, London

Estate documents (ED) relating to the see of Bath and Wells

Borough and Manor Court Rolls

ED 1097   1312
ED 1099/1   1510
ED 1176   1342
ED 1177   1353
ED 1178   1361
ED 1181   1382
ED 1182   1383
ED 1183   1384
ED 1184   1390
ED 1185   1394
ED 1186   1421
ED 1187   1424
ED 1188   1432
ED 1189   1440

Account Roll

ED 224[b]   Bishop of Bath and Wells estate, 1442

Somerset Record Office, Taunton

DD/CC 111736	1427–8 Borough Community rental
DD/WM 1/5	John Brown's will
DD/WM 1/7	Robert Southover's will
DD/SAS SE 5 C795	Deposition taken at Wells, 18 Elizabeth I, on town customs
DD/B, Register 1	Bishop Drokensford's register
DD/B, Register 2	Bishop Ralph of Shrewsbury's register
DD/B, Register 4	Bishop Bubwith's register
DD/B, Register 6	Bishop Bekynton's register

PRINTED PRIMARY SOURCES

Accounts and Papers 17, i. Members of Parliament, List and Index Society (1878).

Bede's Ecclesiastical History of the English People, ed. Bertram Colgrave and R. A. B. Mynors (Oxford, 1969).

The Book of Margery Kempe, ed. Stanford B. Meech and Hope E. Allen, EETS 212 (London, 1940).

Bridgwater Borough Archives, 1400–1445, ed. T. B. Dilks, SRS 54 (1938).

British Borough Charters, 1042–1216, ed. Adolphus Ballard (Cambridge, 1913).

British Borough Charters, 1216–1307, ed. Adolphus Ballard and James Tait (Cambridge, 1923).

British Borough Charters, 1307–1660, ed. Martin Weinbaum (Cambridge, 1943).

Calendar of Charter Rolls (London, 1903–).

Calendar of Close Rolls (London, 1892–1954).

Calendar of Entries in the Papal Registers Relating to Great Britain: Papal Letters, ed. W. H. Bliss, C. Johnson, J. A. Twemlow (London, 1893–).

Calendar of Fine Rolls (London, 1911–63).

Calendar of Inquisitions Miscellaneous (London, 1916–69).

Calendar of Inquisitions Post Mortem, 2nd ser., ii (London, 1974).

Calendar of Manuscripts of the Dean and Chapter of Wells, Historical Manuscripts Commission, 2 vols. (London, 1907–14).

Calendar of Patent Rolls (London, 1901–).

The Chronicle of Glastonbury Abbey, ed. James P. Curley, trans. David Townsend (London, 1985).

Churchwardens' Accounts of Croscombe, Pilton, Milton, etc., ed. E. Hobhouse, SRS 4 (1890).

Codex Diplomaticus Aevi Saxonici, ed. J. M. Kemble (London, 1846).

Croniques de London, ed. G. J. Aungier, CS, 1st ser., 28 (1844).

Dean Cosyn Manuscripts and Wells Cathedral Miscellany, ed. A. Watkin, SRS 56 (1941).

Domesday Book, 2 vols. (London, 1783).

Exeter Freemen 1266–1967, ed. M. M. Rowe and Andrew Jackson, Devon and Cornwall Record Society, Early ser., 51 (1973).

FINBERG, H. P. R., *Early Charters of Wessex* (Leicester, 1964).

GLASSCOCK, R. E., *The Lay Subsidy of 1334* (London, 1975).

GRAHAM, VICTOR E., and JOHNSON, W. MCCALLISTER (eds.), *The Paris Entries of Charles IX and Elizabeth of Austria, 1571* (Toronto, 1974).

'Historia Minor' and 'Historia Major', in *Collectanea I*, ed. T. F. Palmer, SRS 39 (1924).

Historiola de Primordiis Episcopatus Somersetensis: Ecclesiastical Documents, ed. Joseph Hunter, Camden Society, 1st ser., 3 (London, 1840).

Kirkby's Quest for Somerset, etc., ed. F. H. Dickinson, SRS 3 (1889).

Leland's Itinerary, ed. L. Toulmin Smith, 5 vols. (London, 1907).

List of Early Chancery Proceedings, i, List and Index Society 12 (1827).

List of Escheators for England and Wales, List and Index Society 72 (1971).

Little Red Book of Bristol, ed. F. Bickley, 2 vols. (Bristol, 1900).

MALMESBURY, WILLIAM OF, *Gesta Pontificum Anglorum*, ed. N. E. S. A. Hamilton, RS 82 (London, 1870).

—— *Gesta Regum Anglorum*, ed. W. Stubbs, 2 vols., RS 90 (London, 1887–9).

Memorials of the Reign of King Henry VI: Official Correspondence of Thomas Bekynton, Secretary to King Henry VI, and Bishop of Bath and Wells, RS 56 (London, 1872).

Memorials of St Edmunds Abbey, ed. Thomas Arnold, RS 92, 3 vols. (London, 1892).

Mendip Laws and Forest Bounds, ed. J. W. Gough, SRS 45 (1930).

Munimenta Gildhallae Londoniensis: Liber Custumarum, ed. H. T. Riley, RS 12, i. 2 (1860).

The Official Correspondence of Thomas Bekynton, ed. George Williams, RS 56, 2 vols. (1872).

The Overseas Trade of Bristol, ed. E. M. Carus-Wilson, Bristol Record Society 7 (1957).

Parliamentary Writs and Writs of Military Summons, Edward I and Edward II, ed. Francis Palgrave, 2 vols. (London, 1827–34).

Pedes Finium: Feet of Fines for the County of Somerset, ed. Emanuel Green, 4 vols., SRS 6, 12, 17 and 22 (1892–1906).

Placita de Quo Warranto Edward I–Edward III, ed. W. Illingworth, ii (London, 1818).

Register of John de Drokensford, Bishop of Wells, 1309–29, ed. E. Hobhouse, SRS 1 (1887).

Register of John Stafford, Bishop of Bath and Wells, 1425–43, ed. Thomas Scott Holmes, 2 vols., SRS 31–2 (1915–16).

Register of Nicholas Bubwith, Bishop of Bath and Wells, 1407–24, ed. Thomas Scott Holmes, 2 vols., SRS 29–30 (1914).

Register of Ralph of Shrewsbury, 1329–63, ed. T. S. Holmes, 2 vols., SRS 9–10 (1896).

Register of Thomas Bekynton, Bishop of Bath and Wells, 1443–65, ed. H. C. Maxwell-Lyte and M. C. B. Dawes, 2 vols., SRS 49–50 (1934–35).

Register of Walter Giffard, Bishop of Bath and Wells, 1265–66, and of Henry Bowett, 1401–07, ed. Thomas Scott Holmes, SRS 13 (1899).

Registers of Oliver King and Hadrian de Castello, ed. H. C. Maxwell-Lyte, SRS 54 (1939).

Registers of Robert Stillington, 1466–91, and Richard Fox, 1492–94, ed. H. C. Maxwell-Lyte, SRS 52 (1937).

A Relation, or rather, a True Account of the Island of England, ed. C. A. Sneyd, CS, 1st ser., 37 (1847).

Report on the Manuscripts of the Corporation of Beverley, Historical Manuscripts Commission 54 (1900).

Reprint of the First Edition of the One-Inch Ordnance Survey of England, Sheet 76 (Newton Abbot, 1970).

REYNOLDS, HERBERT EDWARD (ed.), *Wells Cathedral: Its Foundation, Constitutional History and Statutes* (Leeds, 1881).

Rotuli Hundredorum, ed. W. Illingworth and J. Caley, ii (London, 1818).

Rotuli Parliamentorum (1272–1503), ed. J. Strachey *et al.*, 6 vols. (London, 1767–83).

RYMER, T., *Foedera, Conventiones, Literae*, ed. J. Caley and Fred Holbrooke, 4 vols. (London, 1818–69).

SAWYER, P. H. (ed.), *Anglo-Saxon Charters: An Annotated List and Bibliography* (London, 1968).

Select Cases in the Court of King's Bench: Edward III, vi, Selden Society 82 (1965).

SEREL, THOMAS, *Historical Notes on the Church of St Cuthbert, in Wells, etc.* (Wells, 1875).

Six Town Chronicles, ed. R. Flenley (Oxford, 1911).

L. TOULMIN (ed.), *The English Gilds*, EETS 40 (1870).

Somerset Medieval Wills, 1383–1500, ed. F. W. Weaver, SRS 16 (1901).

Somerset Medieval Wills, 1501–1530, ed. F. W. Weaver, SRS 19 (1903).

Somersetshire Pleas from the Rolls of the Itinerant Justices, ed. C. E. H. Chadwick Healey, SRS 11 (1897).

Statutes of the Realm, ed. A. Ludens *et al.*, 2 vols. (London, 1810–16).

The Survey and Rental of the Chantries, Colleges, and Free Chapels, etc., ed. Emanuel Green, SRS 2 (1888).

TANNER, NORMAN P. (ed.), *Heresy Trials in the Diocese of Norwich, 1428–31*, CS 4th ser., 20 (London, 1977).

TOPHAM, J., 'A Subsidy Roll of 51 Edward III', *Archaeologia* 7 (1785), 337–47.

Two Cartularies of Bath Abbey, ed. William Hunt, 2 vols., SRS 7 (1893).

Valor Ecclesiasticus Temp. Henrici VIII, ed. J. Caley and Joseph Hunter, 6 vols. (London, 1810–34).

WALSINGHAM, THOMAS, *Gesta Abbatum Monasterii Sancti Albani*, ed. H. T. Riley, RS 28, 3 vols. (London, 1867–9).

Wells City Charters, ed. Dorothy O. Shilton and Richard Holworthy, SRS 46 (1932).

WILKINS, DAVID (ed.), *Concilia Magnae Brittaniae et Hiberniae* (London, 1737).

WORCESTRE, WILLIAM OF, *Itineraries*, ed. John Harvey (Oxford, 1969).

Yearbooks of the Reign of King Edward III: Year XVI, pt. 1, ed. Luke Owen Pike, RS 32 (London, 1896).

SECONDARY SOURCES

ADDLESHAW, G. W. O., *The Development of the Parochial System from Charlemagne to Urban II* (London, 1948).

—— *The Beginnings of the Parochial System* 2nd edn. (York, 1959).

ASTON, MICHAEL, 'The Towns of Somerset', in J. Haslam (ed.), *Anglo-Saxon Towns in Southern England* (Chichester, 1984), 192–4.

The Atlas of Historic Towns, 2 vols., ed. M. D. Lobel and W. H. Johns (London, 1969–75).

BAILEY, SHERWIN, *Wells Manor of Canon Grange* (London, 1985).

BARLOW, FRANK, *The English Church, 1000–1066* (London, 1963).

—— *The English Church, 1066–1154* (London, 1979).

BARRACLOUGH, GEOFFREY, *Papal Provisions* (Oxford, 1935).

BARRON, CAROLINE M., 'The Parish Fraternities of Medieval London', in Caroline M. Barron and Christopher Harper-Bill (eds.), *The Church in Pre-Reformation Society* (Woodbridge, 1985).

—— 'The "Golden Age" of Women in Medieval London', *Reading Medieval Studies* 15 (1989), 35–58.

BATESON, MARY, 'Droitwich Borough', in *Victoria History of the County of Worcester*, iii, ed. J. W. Willis-Bund (London, 1913).

BEAN, J. M. W., 'Plague, Population and Economic Decline in the Later Middle Ages', *ECHR*, 2nd ser., 15 (1963), 423–37.

BECHTEL, H., *Wirtschaftstil des deutschen Spätmittelalters, 1350–1500* (Munich, 1930).

BELLAMY, JOHN, *Crime and Public Order in the Later Middle Ages* (London, 1973).

BENNETT, JUDITH M., 'The Village Ale-Wife: Women and Brewing in Fourteenth-Century England', in Barbara Hanawalt (ed.), *Women and Work in Preindustrial Europe* (Bloomington, Ind., 1985), 20–36.

BERESFORD, M. W., *New Towns of the Middle Ages* (London, 1967).

BERGERON, D. M., *English Civic Pageantry, 1558–1642* (London, 1971).

BERRY, E. K., 'The Borough of Droitwich and its Salt Industry, 1215–1700', *University of Birmingham Historical Journal* 6 (1957–8), 39–61.

BEVERIDGE, W., 'Wages in the Winchester Manors', *ECHR*, 1st ser., 7 (1936–7), 22–43.

BLAIR, JOHN, 'Religious Gilds as Landowners in the Thirteenth and Fourteenth Centuries: The Example of Chesterfield', in P. Riden (ed.), *The Medieval Town in Britain* (Cardiff, 1980).

—— 'Local Churches in Domesday Book and Before', in J. C. Holt (ed.), *Domesday Studies*, (London, 1987), 265–78.

—— 'Minster Churches in the Landscape', in Della Hooke (ed.), *Anglo-Saxon Settlements* (Oxford, 1988), 35–58.

BLAIR, PETER, *An Introduction to Anglo-Saxon England* (Cambridge, 1956).

BOLTON, J. L., *The Medieval English Economy* (London, 1980).

BONNEY, MARGARET, *Lordship and the Urban Community* (Cambridge, 1990).

BOSSY, JOHN, *Christianity in the West, 1400–1700* (Oxford, 1985).

BOSWORTH, J., and TOLLER, T. N. (eds.), *An Anglo-Saxon Dictionary* (London, 1898).

BOWKER, MARGARET, *The Secular Clergy in the Diocese of Lincoln, 1495–1520* (Cambridge, 1968).

BRAUDEL, FERNAND, *Les Structures du quotidien: Le Possible et l'impossible* (Paris, 1979).

BRIDBURY, A. R., *Economic Growth: England in the Later Middle Ages* (London, 1962).

—— 'The Black Death', *ECHR*, 2nd ser., 24 (1974), 577–92.

—— 'English Provincial Towns in the Later Middle Ages', *ECHR*, 2nd ser., 34 (1981), 1–24.

—— *Medieval English Clothmaking* (London, 1982).

BRITNELL, R. H., 'King John's Early Grants of Markets and Fairs', *English Historical Revew* 94 (1979), 90–6.

—— 'The Proliferation of Markets in England, 1200–1394', *ECHR*, 2nd ser., 34 (1981), 209–21.

—— *Growth and Decline in Colchester, 1300–1525* (Cambridge, 1986).

—— 'The Towns of England and Northern Italy in the Early Fourteenth Century', *ECHR*, 2nd ser., 44 (1991), 21–35.

BRITTON, EDWARD, *The Community of the Vill* (Toronto, 1977).

BRYANT, LAWRENCE M., 'La Cérémonie de l'entrée à Paris au Moyen Âge', *Annales: Économies, Sociétés, Civilisations* 41 (1986), 513–42.

BURDON, E. ROWLAND, 'St Saviour's Hospital, Bury St Edmunds', *Proceedings of the Suffolk Institute of Archaeology and Natural History* 19 (1927), 255–85.

BURGESS, CLIVE, ' "For the Increase of Divine Service": Chantries in the Parish in Late Medieval Bristol', *JEH* 36 (1985), 46–65.

—— ' "By Quick and by Dead": Wills and Pious Provision in Late Medieval Bristol', *English Historical Review* 92 (1987), 837–58.

—— ' "A Fond Thing Vainly Invented": An Essay on Purgatory and Pious Motive in Later Medieval England', in S. J. Wright (ed.), *Parish, Church, and People* (London, 1988), 56–84.

BUTCHER, A. F., 'The Origins of Romney Freemen, 1433–1523', *ECHR*, 2nd ser., 27 (1974), 16–27.

—— 'Canterbury's Earliest Rolls of Freemen Admissions: A Reconsideration', *Kentish Miscellany*, ed. F. Hull, Kent Records 21 (1979), 1–26.

—— 'English Urban Society and the Revolt of 1381', in R. H. Hilton and T. H. Aston (eds.), *The English Rising of 1381*, (Cambridge, 1984), 84–111.

BYNUM, CAROLINE WALKER, 'Did the Twelfth Century Discover the Individual?', in *Jesus as Mother: Studies in the Spirituality of the High Middle Ages* (Berkeley, Calif., 1982).

CAILLE, JACQUELINE, *Hôpitaux et charité publique à Narbonne au Moyen Âge de la fin du XIᵉ à la fin du XVIᵉ siècle* (Toulouse, 1978).

CALHOUN, C. J., 'Community: Toward a Variable Conceptualization for Comparative Research', *Social History*, 5 (1982), 105–29.

CAM, HELEN, *The Hundred and the Hundred Rolls* (London, 1930).

—— *Lawfinders and Lawmakers in Medieval England* (London, 1962).

Cambridge Economic History of Europe, ed. M. M. Postan, E. E. Rich, and E. Miller, 3 vols. i, 2nd ed., (Cambridge, 1966), ii (Cambridge, 1952), iii (Cambridge, 1963).

CAMPBELL, BRUCE M. S., 'Population Pressure, Inheritance and the Land Market in a Fourteenth-Century Community', in Richard M. Smith (ed.), *Land, Kinship and Life-cycle*, (Cambridge, 1984), 87–134.

CAMPBELL, JAMES, *Essays in Anglo-Saxon History* (London, 1986).

CARUS-WILSON, E. M., *Medieval Merchant Venturers* (London, 1954).

—— 'The First Half-Century of the Borough of Stratford-upon-Avon', *ECHR*, 2nd ser., 18 (1965), 46–63.

—— (ed.), *Essays in Economic History*, ii (London, 1962).

—— and COLEMAN, O., *England's Export Trade, 1275–1547* (Oxford, 1963).

CHAMBERS, J. D., *Population, Economy, and Society in Preindustrial England* (Oxford, 1972).

CHANTER, J. F., 'The Court Rolls of the Manor of Curry Rivel in the Years of the Black Death, 1348–9', *SANHS* 56 (1910), 85–135.

CHENEY, C. R., 'Rules for the Observance of Feast Days in Medieval England', *Bulletin of the Institute of Historical Research* 34 (1961), 117–47.

CHEW, HELENA, 'Mortmain in Medieval London', *English Historical Review*, 60 (1945), 1–15.

CHURCH, C. M., *Chapters in the Early History of the Church of Wells, 1136–1323* (London, 1894).

CLARK, ELAINE, 'Some Aspects of Social Security in Medieval England', *Journal of Family History* 7 (1982), 307–20.

CLAY, ROTHA M., *The Hermits and Anchorites of England* (London, 1914).

—— *The Medieval Hospitals of England* (New York, 1966: orig. edn., 1909).

COATES, BRYAN E., 'The Origin and Distribution of Markets and Fairs in Medieval Derbyshire', *Derbyshire Archaeological and Natural History Society Journal* 85 (1965), 92–111.

COHN, SAMUEL, Jun., *The Laboring Classes in Renaissance Florence* (New York, 1980).

COLBY, CHARLES W., 'The Growth of Oligarchy in English Towns', *English Historical Review* 5 (1890), 633–53.

COLCHESTER, L. S., *Wells Cathedral* (London, 1987).

—— (ed.), *Wells Cathedral: A History* (West Compton, 1982).

CONSTABLE, GILES, *Monastic Tithes from their Origins to the Twelfth Century* (Cambridge, 1964).

COORNAERT, E., 'Les Ghildes Médiévales', *Revue historique* 199 (1948), 22–55 and 206–43.

—— 'Draperies rurales, draperies urbaines: L'Évolution de l'industrie flamande au Moyen Âge et au XVIᵉ siècle', *Revue belge de philologie et d'histoire* 28 (1950), 60–98.

CORBETT, JAMES A., *The 'De instructione puerorum' of William of Tournai, O.P.* (Notre Dame, Ind., 1955).

CORNWALL, J. C. K., 'English Country Towns in the 1520's', *ECHR*, 2nd ser., 15 (1962), 54–69.

—— *Wealth and Society in Early Sixteenth-Century England* (Henley-on-Thames, 1988).

COURTENAY, WILLIAM J., 'Token Coinage and the Administration of Poor Relief during the Late Middle Ages', *Journal of Interdisciplinary History* 3 (1972–3), 275–95.

DARBY, H. C., *Domesday England* (Cambridge, 1977).

DAVIS, NATALIE ZEMON, 'Poor Relief, Humanism and Heresy', in ead., *Society and Culture in Early Modern France* (Stanford, Calif., 1975), 17–64.

—— 'Women in the Crafts in Sixteenth-Century Lyon', in Barbara Hanawalt (ed.), *Women and Work in Preindustrial Europe* (Bloomington, Ind., 1985), 167–97.

D'AVRAY, D. L., *The Preaching of the Friars* (Oxford, 1985).

DESPORTES, PIERRE, 'La Population de Reims au xve siècle', *Moyen Âge* 77 (1966), 463–509.

DILKS, T. BRUCE, 'The Burgesses of Bridgwater in the Thirteenth Century', *SANHS* 63 (1917), 30–59.

DOBSON, R. B., 'The Foundation of Perpetual Chantries by the Citizens of Medieval York,' in G. J. Cuming (ed.), *Studies in Church History*, iv (London, 1967), 22–38.

—— 'Admissions to the Freedom of the City of York in the Later Middle Ages', *ECHR*, 2nd ser., 26 (1973), 1–22.

—— *Durham Priory, 1400–50* (Cambridge, 1973).

—— 'Urban Decline in Late Medieval England,' *TRHS*, 5th ser., 27 (1977), 1–22.

—— 'Cathedral Chapters and Cathedral Cities: York, Durham and Carlisle in the Fifteenth Century', *Northern History* 29 (1983), 15–44.

—— 'The Risings in York, Beverley and Scarborough, 1380–81,' in R. H. Hilton and T. H. Aston (eds.), *The English Rising of 1381* (Cambridge, 1984), 112–42.

—— (ed)., *The Peasants' Revolt of 1381* (London, 1970).

DREW, CHARLES, *Early Parochial Organization in Britain* (London, 1954).

DU BOULAY, F. H., *An Age of Ambition* (London, 1970).

DUNNING, ROBERT W., 'The Wells Consistory Court in the Fifteenth Century', *SANHS* 106 (1962), 46–61.

—— 'The Bishop's Palace', in L. S. Colchester (ed.), *Wells Cathedral: A History* (West Compton, 1982), 227–47.

—— 'Somerset Towns in the Fifteenth Century', *SDNQ* 29, 187 (1986), 10–12.

DYER, ALAN D., *The City of Worcester in the Sixteenth Century* (Leicester, 1973).

DYER, CHRISTOPHER, *Standards of Living in the Later Middle Ages* (Cambridge, 1989).

EDWARDS, KATHLEEN, *The English Secular Cathedrals in the Middle Ages* (Manchester, 1949).

ELLINGTON, H. D. W., 'The Mendip Lead Industry', in Keith Branigan and P. J. Fowler (eds.), *The Roman West Country*, (Newton Abbot, 1976).

EMDEN, A. B., *The Biographical Register of the University of Oxford to AD 1500*, 3 vols. (Oxford, 1957–9).

ENNEN, EDITH, *The Medieval Woman*, trans. Edmund Jephcott (Oxford, 1989).

EVERITT, ALAN (ed.), *Perspectives in English Urban History* (London, 1973).

FAVREAU, ROBERT, 'Pauvreté en Poitou et en Anjou à la fin du Moyen Âge', in M. Mollat (ed.), *Études sur l'histoire de la pauvreté*, ii (Paris, 1974), 589–618.

FINBERG, H. P. R., 'Sherborne, Glastonbury and the Expansion of Wessex', in id., *Lucerna: Studies in Some Problems in the Early History of England* (London, 1964).

The Fontana Economic History of the Middle Ages, ed. Carlo M. Cipolla (London, 1972).

FOURQUIN, GUY, *The Anatomy of Popular Rebellion in the Middle Ages*, trans. Anne Chesters (Amsterdam, 1978).

FOX, H. S., 'The Chronology of Enclosure and Economic Development in Medieval Devon', *ECHR*, 2nd ser., 28 (1975), 181–202.

FOX, LEVY, 'The Administration of Gild Property in Coventry in the Fifteenth Century', *English Historical Review* 55 (1940), 634–47.

FRANKLIN, M. J., 'The Identification of Minsters in the Midlands', in R. H. Brown (ed.), *Anglo-Norman Studies*, vii (Woodbridge, 1985), 69–88.

GASCON, RICHARD, Économies et pauvreté aux XVIᵉ et XVIᵉ siècles: Lyon, ville éxemplaire et prophétiques', in M. Mollat (ed.), *Études sur l'histoire de la pauvreté*, ii (Paris, 1974), 747–60.

GASQUET, F. A., *Parish Life in Medieval England* (London, 1906).

GEARY, PATRICK J., 'Vivre en conflit dans une France sans état: Typologie des mécanismes de règlement des conflits (1050–1200)', *Annales: Économies, Sociétés, Civilisations* 41 (1986), 1107–34.

GEREMEK, BRONISLAW, *Le salariat dans l'artisanat parisien aux XIIIᵉ–XVᵉ siècles*, (Paris, 1969).

—— *La Potence ou la pitié: L'Europe et les pauvres de Moyen Âge à nos jours*, trans. Joanna Arnold-Moricet (Paris, 1986).

GIERKE, OTTO VON, *Community in Historical Perspective*, trans. Antony Black (Cambridge, 1990).

—— *Political Theories of the Middle Age*, trans. F. W. Maitland (Cambridge, 1900).

GOLDBERG, P. J. P., 'Female Labour, Service and Marriage in the Late Medieval Urban North', *Northern History* 22 (1986), 18–38.

—— 'Women in Fifteenth-Century Town Life', in John A. F. Thomson (ed.), *Towns and Townspeople in the Fifteenth Century* (Gloucester, 1988), 107–28.

—— 'Urban Identity and the Poll Taxes of 1377, 1379, and 1381', *ECHR*, 2nd ser., 43 (1990), 194–216.

GONTHIER, NICOLE, 'Les Hôpitaux et les pauvres à la fin du Moyen Âge,' *Moyen Âge* 84 (1978), 279–308.

GOODMAN, ANTHONY, 'The Piety of John Brunham's Daughter, of Lynn', in Derek Baker (ed.), *Medieval Woman*, (Oxford, 1978), 347–58.

GOTTFRIED, ROBERT, *Epidemic Disease in Fifteenth-Century England* (Leicester, 1978).

—— *Bury St Edmunds and the Urban Crisis of the Later Middle Ages: 1290–1530* (Princeton, NJ, 1982).

GRANSDEN, ANTONIA, 'The History of Wells Cathedral, *c*.1090–1547', in L. S. Colchester (ed.), *Wells Cathedral: A History* (West Compton, 1982), 24–51.

GRAUS, FRANTISEK, 'Au bas Moyen Âge: Pauvres des villes et pauvres des campagnes', *Annales: Économies, Sociétés, Civilisations* 16 (1961), 1053–65.

GRAY, H. L., 'The Production and Exportation of English Woollens in the Fourteenth Century', *English Historical Review* 29 (1924), 13–33.

—— 'English Foreign Trade from 1446 to 1482', in M. M. Postan and E. Power (eds.), *Studies in English Trade in the Fifteenth Century* (London, 1966; orig. edn., 1933), 1–38.

GREENWAY, DIANA, 'The False *Institutio* of St Osmund', in Diana Greenway, Christopher Holdsworth, and Jane Sayers (eds.), *Tradition and Change: Essays in Honour of Marjorie Chibnall*, (Cambridge, 1985), 77–101.

GROSS, CHARLES, *The Gild Merchant*, 2 vols. (Oxford, 1890).

GUENÉE, BERNARD, and LEHOUT, FRANÇOISE, *Les Entreés royales françaises de 1329 à 1515* (Paris, 1968).

HADWIN, J. F., 'The Medieval Lay Subsidies and Economic History', *ECHR*, 2nd ser., 36 (1983), 200–17.

HALL, DAVID, 'The Late Saxon Countryside: Villages and their Fields', in Della Hooke (ed.), *Anglo-Saxon Settlements*, (Oxford, 1988), 99–122.

HANAWALT, BARBARA, *The Ties that Bound: Peasant Families in Medieval England* (New York, 1986).

HARBIN, E. H. BATES, 'The "Black Death" in Somerset, 1348–49', *SANHS* 68 (1917), 89–112.

HARRISS, G. L., *King, Parliament and Public Finance in Medieval England to 1369* (Oxford, 1975).

HARVEY, B. F., 'The Population Trend in England, 1300–48', *TRHS* 5th ser., 16 (1966), 23–42.

—— 'Work and *Festa Ferianda* in Medieval England', *JEH* 23 (1972), 289–308.

—— 'Introduction: The "Crisis" of the Early Fourteenth Century', in. Bruce M. S. Campbell, (ed.), *Before the Black Death* (Manchester, 1991).

HARVEY, JOHN, 'The Building of Wells Cathedral, I: 1175–1307', in L. S. Colchester (ed.), *Wells Cathedral: A History* (West Compton, 1982), 52–75.

HARVEY, SALLY P. J., 'Taxation and the Ploughland in Domesday Book', in P. H. Sawyer, (ed.), *Domesday Book: A Reassessment* (London, 1985), 86–103.

HATCHER, JOHN, *Rural Economy and Society in the Duchy of Cornwall, 1300–1500* (Cambridge, 1970).

—— *Plague, Population and the English Economy* (London, 1977).

—— 'Mortality in the Fifteenth Century: Some New Evidence', *ECHR*, 2nd ser., 39 (1986), 19–38.

—— and BARKER, T. C., *A History of British Pewter* (London, 1977).

HAVINDEN, MICHAEL, *The Somerset Landscape* (London, 1981).

HEAL, FELICITY, *Hospitality in Early Modern England* (Oxford, 1990).

HEATH, PETER, *The English Parish Clergy on the Eve of the Reformation* (London, 1969).

—— 'Urban Piety in the Later Middle Ages: The Evidence of Hull Wills', in R. B. Dobson (ed.), *The Church, Politics and Patronage in the Fifteenth Century* (Gloucester, 1984), 209–34.

HEERS, JACQUES, *Le Clan familial au Moyen Âge* (Paris, 1974).

HELMHOLZ, R. M., *Marriage Litigation in Medieval England* (Cambridge, 1974).

HEMBRY, PHYLLIS, *The Bishops of Bath and Wells, 1540–1640: Social and Economic Problems* (London, 1967).

HEMMEON, M. de W., *Burgage Tenure in Medieval England* (Cambridge, Mass., 1914).

HERLIHY, DAVID, *Medieval and Renaissance Pistoia: The Social History of an Italian Town, 1200–1430* (New Haven, Conn., 1967).

—— *Opera Muliebria: Women and Work in Medieval Europe* (New York, 1990).

—— and KLAPISCH-ZUBER, CHRISTIANE, *Les Toscans et leurs familles: Un Étude de catasto florentin de 1427* (Paris, 1978).

HILL, DAVID, 'Towns as Structures and Functioning Communities through Time: The Development of Central Places from 600–1066', in Della Hooke (ed.), *Anglo-Saxon Settlements* (Oxford, 1988), 197–212.

HILL, J. W. F., *Medieval Lincoln* (Cambridge, 1948).

HILTON, RODNEY, *A Medieval Society: The West Midlands at the End of the Thirteenth Century* (London, 1966).

—— *The English Peasantry in the Later Middle Ages* (Oxford, 1975).

—— 'Lords, Burgesses and Hucksters', *Past and Present* 97 (1982), 3–15.

—— 'Towns in Societies: Medieval England', *UHY* (1982), 7–13.

—— *Class Conflict and the Crisis of Feudalism* (London, 1985).

—— and ASTON, T. A. (eds.), *The English Rising of 1381* (Cambridge, 1984).

HOLDSWORTH, WILLIAM, *A History of English Law*, 16 vols. (London, 1952–66).

HOLLINGWORTH, T. H., *Historical Demography* (London, 1969).

HOLMES, GEORGE, 'The Emergence of an Urban Ideology at Florence c.1250–1450', *TRHS*, 5th ser., 23 (1973), 111–34.

HOLT, RICHARD, 'Whose Were the Profits of Corn Milling? An Aspect of the Changing Relationship between the Abbots of Glastonbury and their Servants, 1086–1350', *Past and Present* 116 (1987), 3–23.

—— *The Mills of Medieval England* (Oxford, 1988).

——and ROSSER, GERVASE, *The Medieval Town: A Reader in English Urban History, 1200–1540* (London, 1990).

HOOKE, DELLA, (ed.), *Anglo-Saxon Settlements* (Oxford, 1988).

HORROX, ROSEMARY, 'The Urban Gentry in the Fifteenth Century', in J. A. F. Thomson (ed.), *Towns and Townspeople in the Fifteenth Century* (Gloucester, 1983), 22–44.

HOSKINS, W. G., *Local History in England*, 2nd edn. (London, 1972).

HOULBROOKE, R., *Church Courts and the People during the English Reformation, 1520–70* (Oxford, 1979).

HOWELL, MARTHA C., 'Women, the Family Economy and the Structures of Market Production in Cities of Northern Europe during the Later Middle Ages', in Barbara Hanawalt (ed.), *Women and Work in Preindustrial Europe* (Bloomington, Ind., 1985), 198–222.

—— *Production and Patriarchy in Late Medieval Cities* (Chicago, 1986).

HUDSON, ANNE, *The Premature Reformation* (Oxford, 1988).

HULBERT, N. F., 'A Survey of Somerset Fairs', *SANHS* 82 (1936), 87–117.

JALLAND, PATRICIA, 'The "Revolution" in Northern Borough Representation in Mid-Fifteenth-Century England', *Northern History* 11 (1976), 27–51.

JAMES, MARGERY K., *Studies in the Medieval Wine Trade* (Oxford, 1971).

JAMES, M. K., 'Ritual Drama and the Social Body in the Later Medieval Town', *Past and Present* 98 (1983), 1–29.

JOLLY, KAREN LOUISE, 'Anglo-Saxon Charms in the Context of a Christian Worldview', *Journal of Medieval History* 11 (1985), 279–93.

JONES, DOUGLAS, *The Church in Chester 1300–1540*, Chetham Society, 3rd ser., 7 (Manchester, 1957).

JONES, G. R. J., 'Multiple Estates and Early Settlement', in P. H. Sawyer (ed), *Medieval Settlement* (London, 1976), 15–40.

JONES, P. J., 'Communes and Despots: The City State in Late Medieval Italy', *TRHS*, 5th ser., 15 (1965), 71–96.

JUSSERAND, J. J., *English Wayfaring Life in the Middle Ages* (London, 1961; orig. edn., 1889).

KAEUPER, RICHARD W., 'Two Early Lists of Literates in England, 1334, 1373', *English Historical Review* 99 (1984), 363–9.

KARRAS, RUTH M., 'The Regulation of Brothels in Later Medieval England', in Judith M. Bennett *et al.* (eds.), *Sisters and Workers in the Middle Ages* (Chicago, 1989), 100–34.

KEEN, M. H., *England in the Later Middle Ages* (London, 1973).

—— *English Society in the Later Middle Ages 1348–1500* (Harmondsworth, 1990).

KEENE, Derek, 'Sources for Medieval Urban History', *Archives* 11 (1974), 220–3.

—— *A Survey of Medieval Winchester*, 2 vols., (Oxford, 1985).

KERMODE, JENNIFER, 'Urban Decline? The Flight from Office in Late Medieval York,' *ECHR*, 2nd ser., 35 (1982), 179–98.

—— 'Obvious Observations on the Formation of Oligarchies in Late Medieval English Towns', in J. A. F. Thomson (ed.), *Towns and Townspeople in the Fifteenth Century* (Gloucester, 1988), 87–106.

KERSHAW, Ian, 'The Great Famine and Agrarian Crisis in England, 1315–22', in R. H. Hilton (ed.), *Peasants, Knights and Heretics* (Cambridge, 1976), 85–132.

KLAPISCH-ZUBER, CHRISTIANE, *Histoire des femmes en occident*, ii. *Le Moyen Âge* (Plon, 1990).

KNOWLES, DAVID, *The Religious Orders in England*, 3 vols. (Cambridge, 1948–59).

—— *The English Mystical Tradition* (London, 1961).

—— and HADCOCK, R. N., *Medieval Religious Houses* (London, 1971).

—— and OBOLENSKY, DIMITRI, *The Middle Ages* (New York, 1968).

KOWALESKI, MARYANNE, 'The Commercial Dominance of a Medieval Provincial Oligarchy: Exeter in the Late Fourteenth Century', *Mediaeval Studies* 46 (1984), 355–84.

—— 'Women's Work in a Market Town: Exeter in the Late Fourteenth Century', in Barbara Hanawalt (ed.), *Women and Work in Preindustrial Europe* (Bloomington, Ind., 1985), 145–64.

KRAUSE, J., 'The Medieval Household: Large or Small,' *ECHR*, 2nd ser., 9 (1957), 420–32.

LARNER, CHRISTINA, *Enemies of God: The Witch-Hunt in Scotland* (Baltimore, 1981).

LATHAM, R. E. (ed.), *The Revised Medieval Latin Wordlist* (London, 1965).

LECONTEUX, CLAUDE, 'Paganisme, christianisme et merveilleux', *Annales: Économies, Sociétés, Civilisations* 37 (1982), 700–16.

LEFF, GORDON, *Heresy in the Later Middle Ages*, 2 vols. (Manchester, 1967).

LE GOFF, JACQUES, 'L'apogée de la France urbaine mediévale', in id. (ed.), *Histoire de la France urbaine*, ii (Paris, 1980).

—— *Time, Work and Culture in the Middle Ages*, trans. Arthur Goldhammer (Chicago, 1980).

LE NEVE, JOHN, *Fasti Ecclesiae Anglicanae 1300–1541: Bath and Wells*, ed. B. Jones (London, 1964).

LENNARD, R., 'Early Manorial Juries', *English Historical Review* 77 (1962), 511–18.

LESNICK, DAVID R., *Preaching in Medieval Florence* (Athens, Ga., 1989).

LIPSON, E., *The History of the Woollens and Worsted Industries* (London, 1921).

—— *The Economic History of England: The Middle Ages*, 12th edn. (London, 1959).

LLOYD, T. H., *The Movement of Wool Prices in Medieval England*, (Economic History Review Supplement, 6; Cambridge, 1973).

—— *The English Wool Trade in the Middle Ages* (Cambridge, 1977).

LOBEL, M. D., 'A Detailed Account of the Rising in Bury St Edmunds in 1326–27 and the Subsequent Trial', *Proceedings of the Suffolk Institute of Archaeology* 21 (1932), 215–31.

LOGAN, F. DONALD, *Excommunication and the Secular Arm in Medieval England* (Toronto, 1968).

LUCAS, HENRY S., 'The Great European Famine of 1315, 1316 and 1317', in E. M. Carus Wilson (ed.), *Essays in Economic History*, ii (London, 1962).

MACFARLANE, ALAN, *The Origins of English Individualism* (Oxford, 1978).

MCFARLANE, K. B., *John Wycliffe and the Beginning of English Nonconformity* (London, 1952).

—— 'Parliament and Bastard Feudalism', in id., *England in the Fifteenth Century* (London, 1981), 1–21.

MACKENNEY, RICHARD, *Tradesmen and Traders: The World of the Guilds in Venice and Europe* c. 1250–1650 (London, 1987).

MCKISACK, MAY, *The Parliamentary Representation of the English Boroughs during the Middle Ages* (Oxford, 1932).

MCLURE, PETER, 'Patterns of Migration in the Late Middle Ages: The Evidence of English Place-Name Surnames', *ECHR*, 2nd ser., 32 (1975), 67–82.

MAITLAND, F. W., *Township and Borough* (Cambridge, 1898).

MAKOWER, F., *The Constitutional History and Constitution of the Church of England* (London, 1895).

MÂLE, ÉMILE, *The Gothic Image: Religious Art in France of the Thirteenth Century*, trans. Dora Nussey (New York, 1958: orig. Fr. edn., 1913).

MANNING, B. L., *The People's Faith in the Time of Wyclif* (Cambridge, 1919).

MASON, EMMA, 'The Role of the English Parishioner, 1100–1500', *JEH* 27 (1976), 17–29.

MERTES, KATE, *The English Noble Household, 1250–1600* (Oxford, 1988).

MICHAUD-FRÉJAVILLE, FRANÇOISE, 'Bons et loyaux services: Les Contrats d'apprentissage en Orléanais (1380–1480)', in *Les Entrées dans la vie: Initiations et apprentissages* (Nancy, 1982), 183–208.

MILLER, EDWARD, 'The Fortunes of the English Textile Trade during the Thirteenth Century', *ECHR*, 2nd ser., 18 (1965), 64–82.

MILLER, EDWARD,'Rulers of Thirteenth-Century Towns: The Cases of York and Newcastle upon Tyne', in P. R. Coss and S. D. Lloyd (eds.), *Thirteenth-Century England,* i. *Proceedings of the Newcastle upon Tyne Conference, 1985* (Woodbridge, 1986), 128–41.

MISRASKI, JACQUELINE, 'Criminalité et pauvreté en France à l'époque de la guerre de cent ans', in M. Mollat (ed.), *Études sur l'histoire de la pauvreté,* ii, (Paris, 1974), 535–46.

MOLLAT, M. (ed.), *Études sur l'histoire de la pauvreté,* ii (Paris, 1974).

—— *Les Pauvres au Moyen Âge* (Paris, 1978).

—— and WOLFF, PHILIPPE, *Ongles bleus, Jacques et Ciompi* (Paris, 1970).

MOORE, ELLEN WEDERMEYER, *The Fairs of Medieval England: An Introductory Study* (Toronto, 1988).

MORGAN, D. A. L., 'The Individual Style of the English Gentleman', in M. Jones (ed.), *Gentry and Lesser Nobility in Late Medieval Europe* (Gloucester, 1986), 15–35.

MUNRO, J. H., 'Wool Price Schedules and the Qualities of English Wools in the Later Middle Ages, *c.* 1270–1469,' *Textile History* 9 (1978), 118–69.

MURRAY, ALEXANDER, 'Religion among the Poor in Thirteenth-Century France: Humbert of Romans', *Traditio* 30 (1974), 285–324.

NICHOLAS, DAVID, *Town and Countryside: Social, Economic and Political Tensions in Fourteenth-Century Flanders* (Bruges, 1971).

—— *The Domestic Life of a Medieval Family* (Lincoln, 1985).

ORME, NICHOLAS, *English Schools in the Middle Ages* (London, 1973).

—— *Education in the West of England, 1066–1548* (Exeter, 1976).

OWEN, DOROTHY M., *Church and Society in Medieval Lincolnshire* (Lincoln, 1971).

OWST, G. R., *Preaching in Medieval England* (Cambridge, 1926).

Oxford English Dictionary, compact edn. (Oxford, 1971).

PALLISER, D. M., *Tudor York* (Oxford, 1979).

—— 'Urban Decay Revisited', in J. A. F. Thomson (ed.), *Towns and Townspeople in the Fifteenth Century* (Gloucester, 1983), 1–17.

PANTIN, W. A., *The English Church in the Fourteenth Century* (Cambridge, 1955).

—— 'Instructions for a Devout and Literate Layman', in J. G. Alexander and M. T. Gibson (eds.), *Medieval Learning and Literature* (Oxford, 1976), 398–422.

PARTNER, NANCY, 'Reading *The Book of Margery Kempe*', *Exemplaria,* 3 (1991), 29–66.

PENN, SIMON A. C. and DYER, CHRISTOPHER, 'Wages and Earnings in Later Medieval England: Evidence from the Enforcement of the Labour Laws', *ECHR,* 2nd ser., 43 (1990), 356–76.

PEVSNER, NIKOLAUS, *North Somerset and Bristol* (Harmondsworth, 1958).

PFAFF, RICHARD W., *New Liturgical Feasts in Later Medieval England* (Oxford, 1970).

PHELPS BROWN, E. H., and HOPKINS, SHEILA V., *A Perspective on Wages and Prices* (London, 1981).

PHYTHIAN-ADAMS, CHARLES, 'Ceremony and the Citizen: The Communal Year at Coventry, 1450–1500,' P. Clark and P. Slack (eds.), *Crisis and Order in English Towns, 1500–1700* (London, 1972), 59–80.

—— 'Urban Decay in Late Medieval England', in P. Abrams and E. A. Wrigley (eds.), *Towns in Societies* (Cambridge, 1978), 159–85.

—— *Desolation of a City: Coventry and the Urban Crisis of the Late Middle Ages* (Cambridge, 1979).

PLATT, COLIN, *Medieval Southampton* (London, 1973).

—— *The English Medieval Town* (London, 1976).

PLUCKNETT, F. T., 'Parliament, 1327–36', in E. B. Fryde and Edward Miller (eds.), *Historical Studies of the English Parliament*, i. *Origins to 1369* (Cambridge, 1970), 195–241.

POLLOCK, F. and MAITLAND, F. W., *The History of English Law before the Time of Edward I*, 2nd edn. (Cambridge, 1911).

POSTAN, M. M., 'Some Economic Evidence of Decline in Population in the Later Middle Ages', *ECHR*, 2nd ser., 2 (1950), 221–46.

—— 'Medieval Agrarian Society in its Prime: England', *Cambridge Economic History of Europe*, i, ed. M. M. Postan, 2nd edn. (Cambridge, 1966), 548–632.

—— *Essays on Medieval Agriculture and General Problems of the Medieval Economy* (Cambridge, 1973).

—— *Medieval Trade and Finance* (London, 1973).

—— *The Medieval Economy and Society* (Harmondsworth, 1975).

POUND, J. F., 'The Social and Trade Structure of Norwich, 1525–75', *Past and Present* 34 (1966), 49–69.

—— *Poverty and Vagrancy in Tudor England* (London, 1971).

—— 'The Validity of the Freemen's Lists: Some Norwich Evidence', *ECHR*, 2nd ser., 34 (1981), 48–59.

POUNDS, N. J. G., *An Historical Geography of Europe, 450 BC–1330 AD* (Cambridge, 1973).

POWELL, EDWARD, 'Arbitration and the Law in England in the Late Middle Ages', *TRHS*, 5th ser., (1984), 49–67.

—— 'The Restoration of Law and Order,' in G. L. Harriss (ed.), *Henry V: The Practice of Kingship* (Oxford, 1984).

POWER, EILEEN, 'The Wool Trade in the Fifteenth Century', in M. M. Postan and Eileen Power (eds.), *Studies in English Trade in the Fifteenth Century* (London, 1933), 39–90.

—— *The Medieval English Wool Trade* (London, 1941).

—— *Medieval Women*, ed. M. M. Postan (Cambridge, 1975).

PULLAN, BRIAN, *Rich and Poor in Renaissance Venice* (Oxford, 1971).

PUTNAM, B. H., *The Enforcement of the Statute of Labourers* (New York, 1908).

RABAN, SANDRA, *Mortmain Legislation and the English Church, 1279–1500* (Oxford, 1982).

RAFTIS, J. A., *Tenure and Mobility* (Toronto, 1964).

—— *A Small Town in Late Medieval England: Godmanchester, 1278–1400* (Toronto, 1982).

RAPP, FRANCIS, *L'Église et la vie réligieuse en occident à la fin du Moyen Âge* (Paris, 1971).

RAVENSDALE, JACK, 'Population Changes and the Transfer of Customary Land on a Cambridgeshire Manor in the Fourteenth Century', in Richard M. Smith (ed.), *Land, Kinship and Lifecycle* (Cambridge, 1984), 197–225.

REED, MICHAEL, 'Markets and Fairs in Medieval Buckinghamshire', *Records of Buckinghamshire* 20 (1978), 563–85.

REIN, MARTIN, 'Problems in the Definition and Measurement of Poverty', in Peter Townsend (ed.), *The Concept of Poverty* (London, 1970), 46–63.

REYERSON, KATHRYN L., 'Women in Business in Medieval Montpellier', in Barbara Hanawalt (ed.), *Women and Work in Preindustrial Europe* (Bloomington, Ind., 1985), 117–44.

REYNOLDS, SUSAN, 'The Rulers of London in the Twelfth Century', *History* 57 (1972), 337–57.

—— *An Introduction to the History of English Medieval Towns* (Oxford, 1977).

—— 'Decline and Decay in Late Medieval Towns', *UHY* (1980), 76–8.

—— *Kingdoms and Communities in Western Europe, 900–1300* (Oxford, 1984).

—— 'Medieval Urban History and the History of Political Thought', *UHY* (1986), 14–23.

RICCI, G., 'La Naissance du pauvre honteux: entre l'histoire des idées et l'histoire sociale', *Annales: Économies, Sociétés, Civilisations* 38 (1983), 158–77.

RIGBY, S. H., 'Urban Decline in the Later Middle Ages: Some Problems in Interpreting the Statistical Data,' *UHY* (1979), 46–59.

—— 'Urban Decline in the Later Middle Ages: The Reliability of the Non-Statistical Evidence', *UHY* (1984), 45–60.

—— ' "Sore Decay" and "Fair Dwellings": Boston and Urban Decline in the later Middle Ages', *Midland History* 10 (1985), 47–61.

—— 'Urban "Oligarchy" in Late Medieval England', in J. A. F. Thomson (ed.), *Towns and Townspeople in the Fifteenth Century* (Gloucester, 1988), 62–86.

RITCHIE, C. A., *The Ecclesiastical Courts of York* (Arbroath, 1956).

RODWELL, WARWICK, 'Wells: The Cathedral and the City', *Current Archaeology* 7 (1980), 38–44.

—— 'The Anglo-Saxon and Norman Churches at Wells', in L. S. Colchester (ed.), *Wells Cathedral: A History* (West Compton, 1982), 1–23.

ROGERS, ALAN, *The Making of Stamford* (Leicester, 1965).

—— 'Late Medieval Stamford: A Study of the Town Council,' in Alan Everitt (ed.), *Perspectives in English Urban History* (London, 1973), 16–38.

RÖRIG, FRITZ, *The Medieval Town*, trans. Don Bryant (London, 1967; orig. edn., 1932).

ROSENTHAL, JOEL, *The Purchase of Paradise* (London, 1972).

ROSKELL, J. S., *The Commons in the Parliament of 1422* (Manchester, 1954).

ROSSER, GERVASE, 'The Essence of Medieval Urban Communities', *TRHS*, 5th ser., 34 (1984), 91–112.

—— 'Communities of Parish and Guild in the Late Middle Ages', in S. J. Wright (ed.), *Parish, Church, and People* (London, 1988), 29–55.

—— *Medieval Westminster 1200–1540* (Oxford, 1989).

ROSSIAUD, JACQUES, 'Crises et consolidations, 1330–1530', in J. Le Goff (ed.), *Histoire de la France urbaine*, ii (Paris, 1980), 408–603.

ROUND, J. HORACE, *The King's Servants and Officers of State* (London, 1911).

RUBIN, MIRI, *Charity and Community in Medieval Cambridge* (Cambridge, 1987).

—— *Corpus Christi* (Cambridge, 1991).

RUSSELL, JOSIAH COX, *British Medieval Population* (Albuquerque, NM, 1948).

—— 'Population in Europe, 500–1500', in *The Fontana Economic History of the Middle Ages*, ed. Carlo M. Cipolla (London, 1972), 25–70.

—— 'The Clerical Population of Medieval England', *Traditio* 2 (1944), 177–212.

SAUL, NIGEL, *Knights and Esquires: The Gloucestershire Gentry in the Fourteenth Century* (Oxford, 1981).

SAWYER, P. H., *Anglo-Saxon Charters* (London, 1968).

SCARISBRICK, J. J., *The Reformation and the English People* (Oxford, 1984).

SCHOFIELD, R. S., 'The Geographical Distribution of Wealth in England, 1334–1649', *ECHR*, 2nd ser., 18 (1965), 482–510.

SCRASE, A. J., 'The Mills at Wells', *SDNQ* 31 (1982), 238–43.

—— 'Wells Inns', *SDNQ* 31 (1984), 378–95.

SCRASE, A. J., 'Development and Change in Burgage Plots: The Example of Wells', *Journal of Historical Geography* 15 (1989), 349–65.
—— 'Peter Moniers and his Lane', forthcoming.
SHREWSBURY, J. F. D., *A History of Bubonic Plague in the British Isles* (Cambridge, 1971).
SLACK, PAUL, 'The Reactions of the Poor to Poverty in England, *c.* 1500–1750', in Thomas Riis (ed.), *Aspects of Poverty in Early Modern Europe*, ii (Odense, 1986), 19–26.
SMITH, RICHARD M., 'Families and their Property in Rural England, 1250–1800', in R. M. Smith (ed.), *Land, Kinship and Life-Cycle* (Cambridge, 1984), 135–95.
—— ' "Modernization" and the Corporate Medieval Village Community in England: Some Sceptical Reflections', in Alan R. H. Baker and Derek Gregory (eds.), *Explorations in Historical Geography* (Cambridge, 1984), 141–79.
—— 'Demographic Developments in Rural England, 1300–48: A Survey', in Bruce M. S. Campbell (ed.), *Before the Black Death* (Manchester, 1991).
SOUTHERN, R. W., *Western Society and the Church in the Middle Ages* (Harmondsworth, 1970).
SPUFFORD, MARGARET, *The Great Reclothing of Rural England* (London, 1984).
STOREY, R. L., 'Gentlemen-Bureaucrats', in C. H. Clough (ed.), *Profession, Vocation and Culture in later Medieval England* (Liverpool, 1982), 90–129.
SWANSON, HEATHER, 'The Illusion of Economic Structure: Craft Guilds in Late Medieval English Towns', *Past and Present* 121 (1988), 29–48.
—— *Medieval Artisans* (Oxford, 1989).
TAIT, JAMES, *Medieval Manchester and the Beginnings of Lancashire* (Manchester, 1904).
—— *The Medieval English Borough* (Manchester, 1936).
TANNER, NORMAN P., *The Church in Late Medieval Norwich, 1370–1532* (Toronto, 1984).
TATTON-BROWN, TIM, 'The Anglo-Saxon Towns of Kent', in Della Hooke (ed.), *Anglo-Saxon Settlements* (Oxford, 1988), 213–32.
TAYLOR, MICHAEL, *Community, Anarchy, and Liberty* (Cambridge, 1982).
THOMAS, KEITH, 'Work and Leisure', *Past and Present* 29 (1964), 50–62.
THOMPSON, A. HAMILTON, 'A Corrody from Leicester Abbey, AD 1393–4: With Some Notes on Corrodies', *Transactions of the Leicestershire Archaeological Society* 14 (1924), 114–34.
—— *The English Clergy and their Organization in the Later Middle Ages* (Oxford, 1947).
THOMSON, J. A. F., *The Later Lollards, 1414–1520* (Oxford, 1965).

—— 'Piety and Charity in Late Medieval London', *JEH* 16 (1965), 178–95.

THOMSON, RODNEY M., *William of Malmesbury* (Woodbridge, 1987).

THRUPP, SYLVIA, 'The Grocers of London: A Study in Redistributive Trade', in M. M. Postan and Eileen Power (eds.), *Studies in English Trade in the Fifteenth Century* (London, 1933), 247–92.

—— *The Merchant Class of Medieval London* (Ann Arbor, Mich., 1948).

—— 'The Alien Population of England in 1440', *Speculum* 32 (1957), 262–73.

—— 'Gilds', in *Cambridge Economic History of Europe*, iii, ed. M. M. Postan, E. E. Rich, and E. Miller (Cambridge, 1963), 230–80.

—— 'Plague Effects in Medieval Europe', *Comparative Studies in Society and History* 8 (1965–6), 474–83.

—— 'Medieval Industry, 1000–1500', *Fontana Economic History of the Middle Ages*, ed. Carlo M. Cipolla (London, 1972), 221–73.

TIERNEY, BRIAN, 'The Decretists and the "Deserving Poor" ', *Comparative Studies in Society and History* 1 (1958–9), 360–73.

—— *Medieval Poor Law* (Berkeley, Calif., 1969).

TITOW, J. Z., 'Some Evidence of the Thirteenth-Century Population Increase', *ECHR*, 2nd ser., 14 (1961), 218–23.

—— *English Rural Society, 1200–1350* (London, 1969).

TITS-DIEUAIDE, J., 'L'Assistance aux pauvres à Louvain au xvᵉ siècle,' in *Hommage au Professeur Bonenfant* (Brussels, 1965), 421–39.

TÖNNIES, FERDINAND, *Community and Society*, trans. Charles P. Loomis, 2nd edn. (New Brunswick, NJ, 1988).

TRENHOLME, NORMAN M., *The English Monastic Borough* (Columbia, Miss., 1927).

ULLMANN, WALTER, *Medieval Political Thought* (Harmondsworth, 1975).

UNWIN, GEORGE, *The Gilds and Companies of London* (London, 1908).

VEALE, E. M., 'Craftsmen and the Economy of London in the Fourteenth Century', in A. E. J. Hollaender and W. Kellaway (eds.), *Studies in London History* (London, 1969), 133–51.

VERLINDEN, C., 'Markets and Fairs', in *Cambridge Economic History of Europe*, ii, ed. M. M. Postan, E. E. Rich, and E. Miller (Cambridge, 1965), 119–53.

Victoria History of the County of Leicester, iv, ed. R. A. McKinley (London, 1958).

Victoria History of the County of Somerset, i–ii, ed. William Page (London, 1906–11).

Victoria History of the County of Suffolk, ii, ed. William Page (London, 1907).

Victoria History of Wiltshire, vi, ed. Elizabeth Crittall (London, 1962).

Victoria History of the County of Worcester, iii, ed. J. W. Willis-Bund (London, 1913).

VODOLA, ELIZABETH, *Excommunication in the Middle Ages* (Berkeley, Calif., 1986).

'Vowells', *SDNQ* 18 (1926), 10.

WALES, TIM, 'Poverty, Poor Relief, and the Life-Cycle', in R. M. Smith (ed.), *Land, Kinship, and Life-Cycle* (Cambridge, 1984), 351–404.

WARREN, ANN K., *Anchorites and their Patrons in Medieval England* (Berkeley, Calif., 1985).

WEDGEWOOD, JOSIAH, *History of Parliament, 1439–1509: Biographies* (London, 1936).

WEISSMAN, R. F. E., *Ritual Brotherhood in Renaissance Florence, 1200–1600* (New York, 1982).

WELLDON FINN, R., and WHEATLEY, P., 'Somerset', in H. C. Darby and R. Welldon Finn (eds.), *A Domesday Geography of South-West England* (Cambridge, 1967),

WESTLAKE, H. F., *The Parish Gilds of Medieval England* (Oxford, 1919).

WILKINSON, B., *The Mediaeval Council of Exeter* (Manchester, 1931).

WOOD-LEGH, K. L., *Perpetual Chantries in Britain* (Cambridge, 1965).

WOODWARD, D. M., 'Sources for Urban History: The Freemen's Rolls', *Local Historian* 9 (1970), 89–95.

—— 'Wage Rates and Living Standards in Pre-Industrial England', *Past and Present* 91 (1981), 28–46.

WRIGLEY, E. A., *Population and History* (London, 1969).

Index